Court Procedure and Evidence Issues

ASPEN COLLEGE SERIES

Court Procedure and Evidence Issues

NEAL R. BEVANS, J.D.

Wolters Kluwer
Law & Business

Published by Wolters Kluwer Law & Business in New York.

Wolters Kluwer Law & Business serves customers worldwide with CCH, Aspen Publishers, and Kluwer Law International products. (www.wolterskluwerlb.com)

To contact Customer Service, e-mail customer.service@wolterskluwer.com, call 1-800-234-1660, fax 1-800-901-9075, or mail correspondence to:

Wolters Kluwer Law & Business
Attn: Order Department
PO Box 990
Frederick, MD 21705

Printed in the United States of America.

1 2 3 4 5 6 7 8 9 0

ISBN 978-0-7355-0765-4

Library of Congress Cataloging-in-Publication Data

Bevans, Neal R., 1961-
Court procedure and evidence issues / Neal R. Bevans.
p. cm. — (Aspen college series)
Includes index.
ISBN-13: 978-0-7355-0765-4
ISBN-10: 0-7355-0765-1
1. Courts — United States. 2. Justice, Administration of — United States. 3. Court rules.
I. Title.
KF8719.B48 2012
347.73′1 — dc23

2011032165

About Wolters Kluwer Law & Business

Wolters Kluwer Law & Business is a leading global provider of intelligent information and digital solutions for legal and business professionals in key specialty areas, and respected educational resources for professors and law students. Wolters Kluwer Law & Business connects legal and business professionals as well as those in the education market with timely, specialized authoritative content and information-enabled solutions to support success through productivity, accuracy and mobility.

Serving customers worldwide, Wolters Kluwer Law & Business products include those under the Aspen Publishers, CCH, Kluwer Law International, Loislaw, Best Case, ftwilliam.com and MediRegs family of products.

CCH products have been a trusted resource since 1913, and are highly regarded resources for legal, securities, antitrust and trade regulation, government contracting, banking, pension, payroll, employment and labor, and healthcare reimbursement and compliance professionals.

Aspen Publishers products provide essential information to attorneys, business professionals and law students. Written by preeminent authorities, the product line offers analytical and practical information in a range of specialty practice areas from securities law and intellectual property to mergers and acquisitions and pension/benefits. Aspen's trusted legal education resources provide professors and students with high-quality, up-to-date and effective resources for successful instruction and study in all areas of the law.

Kluwer Law International products provide the global business community with reliable international legal information in English. Legal practitioners, corporate counsel and business executives around the world rely on Kluwer Law journals, looseleafs, books, and electronic products for comprehensive information in many areas of international legal practice.

Loislaw is a comprehensive online legal research product providing legal content to law firm practitioners of various specializations. Loislaw provides attorneys with the ability to quickly and efficiently find the necessary legal information they need, when and where they need it, by facilitating access to primary law as well as state-specific law, records, forms and treatises.

Best Case Solutions is the leading bankruptcy software product to the bankruptcy industry. It provides software and workflow tools to flawlessly streamline petition preparation and the electronic filing process, while timely incorporating ever-changing court requirements.

ftwilliam.com offers employee benefits professionals the highest quality plan documents (retirement, welfare and non-qualified) and government forms (5500/PBGC, 1099 and IRS) software at highly competitive prices.

MediRegs products provide integrated health care compliance content and software solutions for professionals in healthcare, higher education and life sciences, including professionals in accounting, law and consulting.

Wolters Kluwer Law & Business, a division of Wolters Kluwer, is headquartered in New York. Wolters Kluwer is a market-leading global information services company focused on professionals.

For my sister, Lisa Burnett, who has always been there for me.

Summary of Contents

Contents

5 Beginning the Case

6 Discovery and Pretrial Motions

Preface

Court procedure and judicial process courses are offered in nearly every criminal justice program in the United States. Many of these courses combine aspects of court procedure along with an overview of evidentiary issues. However, the texts available for these courses generally take a theoretical approach rather than addressing practical concerns and procedures of the various phases of a criminal case. This text, written by an attorney with extensive trial and classroom experience, seeks to address that deficit. In *Court Procedure and Evidence Issues*, the author explores the details of the judicial process, explaining the various phases of a criminal prosecution in a clear and often entertaining style. The book provides a balance between theoretical discussions and practical, down-to-earth examples of law in action at every phase of a criminal proceeding. The text emphasizes the practical aspects of criminal procedure and evidentiary issues and provides real-world examples, while still discussing the theoretical and academic bases of trial procedures

FEATURES OF THE TEXTBOOK:

- Chapter objectives that are stated clearly and succinctly
- Terms and legal vocabulary set out in bold in the body of the text and defined immediately in the margin for the ease of student comprehension
- Figures and tables to illustrate crucial points, designed to capitalize on different learning styles among students
- Scenarios to help students develop their understanding of the material
- Excerpts from seminal or otherwise noteworthy appellate cases
- End-of-chapter questions, activities, and assignments to hone students' understanding
- Websites for further research and/or discussion

- "Profiling the Professional" features that include interview excerpts from professionals currently practicing in criminal justice and provide valuable insights into the real world of crime and criminal prosecution and defense

TEXTBOOK RESOURCES

The companion website for this text at http://www.aspenparalegaled.com/books/bevans_court/ includes additional resources for students and instructors, including:

- Study aids to help students master the key concepts for this course. Visit the site to access interactive StudyMate exercises such as flash cards, matching, fill-in-the-blank, and crosswords. These activities are also available for download to an iPod or other hand-held device.

- Instructor resources to accompany the text

- Links to helpful websites and updates

Blackboard and eCollege course materials are available to supplement this text. This online courseware is designed to streamline the teaching of the course, providing valuable resources from the book in an accessible electronic format.

Instructor resources to accompany this text include a comprehensive Instructor's Manual, Test Bank, and PowerPoint slides. All of these materials are available on a CD-ROM or for download from our companion website.

Acknowledgments

I would like to acknowledge the tremendous help, effort, and support that the following individuals provided in bringing this book to its final form: Jacqueline Landis, Betsy Kenny, David Herzig, Lisa Mazzonetto, and Lisa Burnett.

I would also like to thank the reviewers who contributed their time and insight to help shape this text:

Richard Becker, Lone Star College—Tomball
Scott Donaldson, Tarrant City College
Mary Eastep, University of Central Florida
Kimberly Hassell, University of Wisconsin—Milwaukee
Vincent Jones, Governors State University
Cathryn Lavery, Iona College
Elizabeth Maier, Norwich College
Emmanuel Onyeozili, University of Maryland—Eastern Shore
Sara Jane Phillips, University of Texas—Arlington
Judith Revels, University of North Florida

1

An Introduction to the Court System

Chapter Objectives

- Explain the basic differences between civil and criminal law
- Differentiate between the burden of proof in a civil case versus a criminal case
- Define and provide examples of the common law
- Explain the organization of both state and federal court systems
- Explain the concept of jurisdiction

I INTRODUCTION TO THE CRIMINAL JUSTICE SYSTEM

"The jury has reached a decision." These simple words can produce an unequaled level of tension and excitement in the courtroom. What will it be? Guilty or not guilty?

Criminal trials hold people's attention because, unlike what they see on television, this story is real. The names have not been changed to protect the innocent. The person charged with the crime—the **defendant**—is present in the courtroom, right where the jury can see him. The witnesses are real people, with all the prejudices and weaknesses of real people. These days, viewers watch reality shows to see the fascinating and bizarre aspects of other people's lives. In a trial, these lives are laid bare for all to see. That is what a trial is all about. In this book we will unfold the story of a criminal trial, beginning with the crime, and then examining the various aspects of the defendant's arrest, the procedural rights of the criminal defendant, the trial, and the appeal.

Defendant
The person charged with a crime.

However, before we can begin an in-depth examination of criminal law and procedure, we must first address a basic question: What is criminal law and how is it different from other types of law?

A. THE DIFFERENCES BETWEEN CIVIL AND CRIMINAL CASES

We all have some familiarity with criminal law. We know that some people are charged with crimes and that these individuals, if convicted, go to prison, pay fines, or both. But we also know that there are other forms of law. Broadly speaking, we can divide law into two categories: criminal law and civil law (see Figure 1-1). This book is about criminal law—specifically, the procedural steps involved in bringing a person charged with a crime to justice. However, it is also important, at least at this early stage, to draw a distinction between criminal law and other types of law. We will address civil law in this chapter only for the purposes of making that distinction.

Criminal law is a field of law that is as specialized in its own way as family law, personal injury law, or medical malpractice. The important difference is that criminal law involves the prosecution of individuals for violating the law. In criminal law, the state takes action against an individual and imprisons that person for breaking the law. This is the most important distinction between criminal and civil law, but there are other key distinctions.

Here is a brief summary of the important differences between civil and criminal law:

- Outcome of the case
- Burden of proof
- Parties who initiate and maintain the civil action
- Pleadings

1. OUTCOME OF THE CASE

Guilty
The verdict in a criminal case in which the jurors have determined that the defendant has committed a crime.

Liable
A finding that a party has a duty or obligation to the other party to pay damages or to carry out some other action.

One of the best ways to illustrate the important differences between civil law and criminal law is to focus on the end of the case, or the outcome. When a person is found **guilty** in a criminal case, that person faces imprisonment, fines, restitution, probation, or parole. That is not the situation in a civil case. At the conclusion of a civil case, a person may be found **liable**. A party who is found liable may be required to pay monetary damages to the opposing parties. However, no one who has lost a civil case will go to prison or face a term on probation or parole.

FIGURE 1-1

Civil Versus Criminal Case Types

Examples of Civil Cases	Examples of Criminal Cases
Divorce	Fraud
Alimony	Rape
Child support	Murder
Medical malpractice	Arson
Slander	Robbery
Negligence	

EXAMPLE

Mark was recently in a car accident. As he was driving through his neighborhood, one of his neighbors pulled out in front of him and Mark ran into the back of the neighbor's car. Is this a civil case or a criminal case or neither?

Answer: This is most likely a civil case. Unless there is some evidence that the neighbor acted intentionally, such as intending to ram his car into Mark's, chances are that this case, if it ever goes to trial, will be a civil case in which Mark will allege that his neighbor was being negligent and not keeping a proper lookout.

In a criminal trial, the government, whether it is the federal or state government, has strict rules that it must follow. Before a defendant can be found guilty, the state must present evidence that the defendant committed the crime. Witnesses will testify, evidence will be admitted, and the jury will be asked to determine a verdict. In a criminal trial, for example, the government is not permitted to call the defendant to the stand to ask him any questions or to make any negative inference from the defendant's failure to take the stand. But in civil cases, the evidence that can be presented against a defendant has less stringent rules. A defendant in a civil action can be called to the stand. Why the discrepancy? Under our criminal justice system, it is and should be more difficult to convict someone of a crime than to find a person liable in a civil action. One of the factors that make criminal cases more difficult to prove is the difference in the burdens of proof between civil and criminal cases.

Sidebar

Throughout this text, we will use the terms government and state interchangeably to refer to the body that brings and prosecutes criminal charges against a defendant. Later, we will address these issues in greater detail to show how the state is actually composed of several different agencies, including prosecutors, law enforcement, judges, and others.

a. The Verdicts

The verdict is the jury's determination of the facts of the case. In short, a verdict refers to who wins and who loses. As we have already mentioned, the verdicts in civil and criminal cases are markedly different. At the conclusion of a civil trial, the losing party is found liable to the other party. The verdicts in a criminal case are of a completely different order. At the conclusion of a criminal trial, a defendant may be found guilty, not guilty, guilty but mentally ill, or not guilty by reason of insanity.

i. Guilty

When a jury determines that the defendant has committed the crime, it votes guilty. This finding of guilt subjects the defendant to a possible prison sentence, probation, parole, and/or fines. The defendant may also be required to pay restitution to the victim during the course of his or her probation.

ii. Not Guilty

A jury's determination that the defendant is not guilty means that the criminal case against the defendant is over and she will be set free (assuming that there aren't any other cases pending). A not guilty verdict has specific constitutional implications. For example, a defendant who has been found not guilty cannot be retried for the same offense. Referred to as "double jeopardy," the Fifth Amendment to the U.S. Constitution specifically prohibits the government from trying a defendant again for the same offense for which she has been found not guilty (see Figure 1-2).

FIGURE 1-2

Amendment V, U.S. Constitution

"No person shall be held to answer for a capital, or otherwise infamous crime, unless on a presentment or indictment of a Grand Jury, except in cases arising in the land or naval forces, or in the Militia, when in actual service in time of War or public danger; **nor shall any person be subject for the same offense to be twice put in jeopardy of life or limb**; nor shall be compelled in any criminal case to be a witness against himself, nor be deprived of life, liberty, or property, without due process of law; nor shall private property be taken for public use, without just compensation." [Emphasis added.]

iii. Guilty but Mentally Ill

In some jurisdictions, jurors have an alternative to a finding of guilt. If the jurors believe that the defendant was mentally ill at the time of the offense, some states allow the jurors to find the defendant guilty but mentally ill. This is a different verdict from a determination that the defendant was insane at the time of the crime. As we will see, a finding of insanity absolves the defendant of any culpability for the crime, but a verdict of guilty but mentally ill does not. In this circumstance, a defendant who receives this verdict will still serve a prison sentence, but most states require that the defendant receive counseling or psychiatric services during his tenure with the prison system.

iv. Not Guilty by Reason of Insanity (NGRI)

In the United States, jurors have always had the option of finding a defendant not guilty by reason of insanity. This verdict is based on the jury's conclusion that the defendant was legally insane at the time that she committed the crime. American law does not punish those who are unable to understand the difference between right and wrong at the time that they commit a crime. However, as we will see later in this text, actually establishing that a defendant is legally insane is not as easy as it is portrayed on television.

Furthermore, statistics show that the NGRI defense is used in fewer than 1 percent of criminal cases, and only about 25 percent of those defenses are successful. You might remember the high-profile Andrea Yates case in which the insanity defense was used successfully. Yates drowned her five children in a bathtub but was acquitted of capital murder because she was found to be insane at the time of the crime. Such cases are quite rare, but because they garner a lot of attention, the public believes that the insanity defense is more common than it truly is.

EXAMPLE

Harry has been charged with aggravated assault. However, when he appears in court, he declares that he is Darth Vader and refuses to answer to any other name. The charges in the indictment show that he beat up several people with a "light saber" that was actually a hollow tube filled with rocks and painted with fluorescent paint. He claims that he attacked them because they were trying to steal his "force." Should Harry's attorney urge a plea of not guilty by reason of insanity?

Answer: Yes. Harry should at least receive a mental evaluation; if it can be shown that he actually believed that he was acting under the delusion that he was Darth Vader and did not know the difference between right and wrong, then he very well might be found not guilty by reason of insanity.

b. Verdicts in Civil Cases

In contrast to the verdicts in criminal cases, jurors in civil cases determine who is liable. A plaintiff who brings suit against a defendant will attempt to prove that the defendant is liable to the plaintiff, but a defendant may also bring proof that the plaintiff is actually liable to the defendant. In the end, a jury can as easily find the plaintiff liable to the defendant as it could the defendant liable to the plaintiff. In either event, the jury's finding of liability results in an assessment of **damages**.

Damages
A jury's assessment of the money that a liable party owes to the other party in a civil case.

In a civil trial, the jury can award monetary payments from one party to another. For instance, a jury can award compensatory damages—money payments from the defendant designed to compensate the plaintiffs for their losses. A civil jury can also award punitive damages against a defendant. Simply put, punitive damages are monetary assessments designed to punish the defendant and send a message to the community that such behavior will not be tolerated.

For example, several tobacco companies in recent years have been ordered to pay enormous punitive damages awards, sometimes in the tens of millions of dollars. The basis for the punitive damages is that the tobacco companies have maliciously defrauded the defendants and the public by not being honest about the dangers of smoking.

2. BURDEN OF PROOF IS DIFFERENT

The **burden of proof** is a phrase that refers to one side's obligation to prove the allegations against the other side. In most civil cases, that burden is **preponderance of the evidence**. This means that when a **plaintiff** brings suit against a defendant, the plaintiff must prove that her allegations are more likely true than not. Many commentators have compared this burden of proof to an old-fashioned scale, where putting more weight on one side makes the scale dip in one direction. Preponderance of the evidence is like that. A plaintiff must simply show that the evidence supports her claim against the defendant. The defendant will attempt to refute this proof, but if the jury does not credit the defendant's claim, then the scale will remain tilted in the plaintiff's favor and the plaintiff will win the civil suit.

Burden of proof
The amount of proof that a party must bring to sustain an action against another party. The burden of proof is different in civil and criminal cases.

Preponderance of the evidence
A showing by one side in a civil suit that its version of the facts is more likely to be true than not.

Plaintiff
The name for the party who brings a civil suit.

However, the situation changes dramatically when it comes to the state's burden of proof in a criminal trial. There, the standard of proof is **beyond a reasonable doubt**. This standard doesn't lend itself to such a clear example; however, if we are to continue with the scale metaphor, we'd have to say that at the beginning of the trial, the scales are loaded in the defendant's favor, and the prosecution must present enough proof to not only bring the scales back to even but to tip them in the state's favor. The result is that the standard that a prosecutor has to meet in order to convict someone is much higher than the standard a plaintiff in a civil suit is called upon to prove.

Beyond a reasonable doubt
The burden of proof in a criminal case; when one has a reasonable doubt, it is not mere conjecture but a doubt that would cause a prudent, rational person to hesitate before finding a defendant guilty of a crime.

Proof beyond a reasonable doubt has been defined in various ways for centuries, but as most jurors learn at the conclusion of a criminal trial, this burden simply means that the state must prove each and every element against the

Sidebar

It is improper to refer to the state as the plaintiff *in a criminal action. The state is always referred to as the* state *or the* government, *not as a plaintiff.*

defendant. If a juror still believes that the state has failed to do that, and the juror has a specific, reasonable point of contention with the state's case, the juror is not only encouraged but required to find the defendant not guilty. Proving that someone has committed a crime beyond a reasonable doubt is quite a high standard. The reason that the burden is so high is that in our country the accused is presumed innocent until proven guilty and is protected by other constitutional guarantees that we will discuss in greater detail later in this text.

If the outcome and the burdens of proof were not enough to distinguish civil cases from criminal cases, there is also the issue of who brings the actions in the first place. That takes us into the issue of the parties to civil and criminal cases.

EXAMPLE

At the end of Angela's trial for aggravated assault, the jurors believe that Angela actually committed the crime, but they are sure that the state has not proved it beyond a reasonable doubt. How should they vote?

Answer: They should vote not guilty because the state is required to prove a person guilty beyond a reasonable doubt. So, even if the jurors believe that a person is guilty, if the state has not proven the case to the appropriate standard, the jurors are required to return a not guilty verdict.

3. PARTIES WHO INITIATE AND MAINTAIN THE CIVIL ACTION

A criminal prosecution is brought by federal or state governments in the name of their citizens. A private individual brings a civil lawsuit. A crime is a violation of law and infringes on all of our rights when it occurs. Although there may be a specific victim, it is, in the final analysis, a wrong committed against all of society. A civil action, on the other hand, is generally a personal wrong between the parties involved and may have no greater implications for society as a whole.

At this point, we should address some important terminology that is used in many types of civil cases. As noted, the person who brings a civil suit is referred to as the *plaintiff* (or the *respondent*). The person who is being sued is the *defendant.* The terminology of plaintiff versus defendant is reserved for civil actions. In criminal cases, the parties are referred to as the *government* and the *defendant.* Unfortunately, the term *defendant* is used in both actions, and that sometimes causes confusion. A civil action is usually based on the private wrong suffered by an individual. The individual brings suit when he has suffered a financial, emotional, or physical loss. The right to bring a civil suit is not limited to natural persons only. Corporations and businesses may also sue in their own right. When cases from appellate courts are published, the first detail that you will see is the **style**, or caption, of the case. This is always given as the names of the parties involved. Civil cases are captioned *Plaintiff A v. Defendant B.* Because the government always brings criminal cases, the government is listed by name, not as a plaintiff. Criminal cases are captioned *Government (or State) v. Defendant.* When you examine the caption of the case, you can usually determine whether the case is civil or criminal. However, you should keep in mind that there are times when the government brings civil suits, so you should read

Style
(caption) The title or heading listing the parties to a case.

deeper into the case to determine if it is, in fact, a criminal case. Contrast the styles of civil versus criminal cases found in Figure 1-3.

FIGURE 1-3

Styles of Civil Versus Criminal Cases

Style of a Civil Case

STATE OF PLACID
COUNTY OF JOHNSTON
SUPERIOR COURT OF JOHNSTON COUNTY

Katie M. Burnett,	)	
	)	
Plaintiff,	)	
	)	
v.	)	COMPLAINT
	)	
	)	Civil Action File No.: _____
Amanda Strang,	)	
	)	
Defendant.	)	
	)	
____________________	)	

Style of a Criminal Case

STATE OF PLACID
COUNTY OF JOHNSTON
SUPERIOR COURT OF JOHNSTON COUNTY

INDICTMENT NO: ____________________

STATE	)
	)
	)
v.	)
	)
	)
John Doe,	)
	)
Defendant.	)
	)
____________________	)

4. THE PLEADINGS

Complaint
The document filed by the plaintiff and served on the defendant that sets out the plaintiff's factual allegations that show the defendant is responsible for the plaintiff's injuries.

Answer
The defendant's written response to the complaint, usually containing denials of the defendant's responsibility for the plaintiff's injuries.

Pleadings refer to the legal documents that state the nature of the claim against the parties. In a civil lawsuit, most states refer to the plaintiff's pleading as a **complaint** (also known as a petition). This document sets out the plaintiff's factual allegations against the defendant and requests the jury to award monetary damages to the plaintiff as a result of the defendant's actions. The defendant responds with an **answer**, also known as a reply. In the answer, the defendant denies the plaintiff's factual allegations and also denies any responsibility for the plaintiff injuries.

B. STATUTORY LAW, CASE LAW, AND COMMON LAW

Whenever we discuss criminal law and procedure, we must address the authority of the courts and others and where they get this power. We know that a police officer has the power to arrest people. We know that judges have the power to sentence convicted defendants, but what is the source of this authority? What are its limits? In criminal law, we have multiple sources of authority:

- U.S. Constitution
- Statutory law
- Judicial decisions
- Court rules
- Agency rules and regulations
- Common law

1. THE U.S. CONSTITUTION

The Constitution of the United States provides that the government has the power to maintain the welfare of its citizens and to pass laws that regulate behavior and punish those who break these laws. This so-called police power of the Constitution is the source of both federal and state criminal laws. However, there is no specific text in the U.S. Constitution that clearly states that Congress shall enact criminal laws. Most commentators agree that the power to make and enforce criminal laws is reserved to the states through the Tenth Amendment to the U.S. Constitution. In later chapters, we will address specific parts of the U.S. Constitution and show its impact on court procedures and the use of evidence. You will find the complete text of the U.S. Constitution in the Appendix.

a. State Constitutions

A state constitution functions in virtually the same manner as the U.S. Constitution. However, state constitutions govern state law and state citizens only, while the U.S. Constitution governs the entire nation. If this suggests a potential source of conflict, it often is. There are times when a crime comes under both state and federal jurisdiction. This means that either the federal or state government could

> **This Constitution, and the Laws of the United States which shall . . . be the supreme Law of the Land; and the Judges in every State shall be bound thereby, any Thing in the Constitution or Laws of any State to the Contrary notwithstanding.**

FIGURE 1-4

Article VI, U.S. Constitution

prosecute. In such a situation, a conflict often arises as to which government takes precedence. Fortunately, the framers of the U.S. Constitution anticipated such problems and included the **Supremacy Clause** in Article VI of the Constitution (see Figure 1-4). This constitutional provision dictates that when there is a conflict between federal and state law, federal law takes priority. In such a situation, the federal authorities would have the right to try the defendant first. They may decide to waive their priority and turn the defendant over to the state government. In addition to jurisdictional questions about federal and state law, there is an additional element to consider in many states: common law, which we will examine later in this chapter.

Supremacy Clause
The provision in Article VI of the U.S. Constitution that the U.S. Constitution, laws, and treaties take precedence over conflicting state constitutions or laws.

2. STATUTORY LAW

Once a bill has been enacted, it is referred to as a **statute.** Not all statutes involve criminal activity. There are many statutes created every year, on both the federal and state levels, that have nothing to do with criminal law. The statutes that deal with crime are usually grouped together in the state **code** for ease of reference. Most crimes are violations of state laws, not federal statutes. There are comparatively few federal crimes, but there are 50 states, and each state has its own criminal statutes.

Statute
A law that is voted on by the legislative branch of government and enacted by the executive branch.

Code
A collection of laws.

Statutes consist of legislative bills that are voted on by the legislative branch of government and enacted by the executive branch. On the federal level, the U.S. Congress is the legislative branch, and it votes on bills before sending them to the president (the executive branch) for signature. If the president signs the legislation, it becomes a binding law. On the state level, the legislature votes on bills and submits them to the governor for signature. In both instances, the laws that are created are referred to as statutes. But this is only one small part of the large body of what American legal scholars consider to be the law.

Because most criminal prosecutions occur on the state level, we will spend a great deal of time in this text discussing the implications of statutory law on court procedure and evidentiary rules. We will also be addressing U.S. statutory law, found in the U.S. Code.

a. Agency Rules, Regulations, and Ordinances

Once a statute has been created, a governmental agency may create an administrative rule or regulation to put the statute into effect. For instance, the Sixteenth Amendment gives the federal government the power to levy income taxes but provides no details on the process of actually carrying out tax collection (see Figure 1-5). Instead, the Treasury Department, acting through its Internal Revenue Service, creates administrative rules and regulations that govern who

FIGURE 1-5

Amendment XVI, U.S. Constitution

> **The Congress shall have power to lay and collect taxes on incomes, from whatever source derived, without apportionment among the several states, and without regard to any census or enumeration.**

should pay income taxes along with how and when. These rules and regulations carry the same force as a statute.

As we have seen, statutes are laws passed by a state or federal government. However, there is an entire class of laws passed by local governments, such as municipalities and towns, that regulate behavior at a local level. These are not referred to as statutes. Instead, they are called **ordinances**. An ordinance has limited application and a strict geographic limit, such as the town limits or the county boundary. Ordinances cannot conflict with statutes. If they do, the ordinance is ruled unconstitutional and the statute takes precedence.

Ordinance
A law passed by a local government, such as a town council or city government.

3. CASE LAW

In addition to statutory law, there is another, and equally important, source of law: case law. **Case law** is the huge body of published decisions by appellate courts. Laypersons often do not realize the significance of case law. When an appellate court reaches a decision in a case on appeal, the reasons for the decision are encapsulated in a written opinion. This opinion discusses not only the facts of the particular case on appeal, but also the law that applies to the facts. For legal professionals, case law can be one of the most important sources of legal authority in the United States. The importance of case law can be demonstrated by reviewing a decision by the U.S. Supreme Court.

Case law
The written decisions by appellate courts explaining the outcome of a case on appeal.

a. Case Law and the U.S. Supreme Court

Suppose that the U.S. Congress passes a bill stating that the punitive damages available to civil litigants are limited to a specific formula. The formula set out by the federal legislation is that punitive damages (those monetary payments made above and beyond the monetary damages intended to compensate the plaintiff for his injuries) must be limited to a formula of twice the amount of proven actual damages. The statute is clear and unambiguous. The most that an injured plaintiff could receive in any case (no matter how egregiously the defendant acted) is twice the plaintiff's actual damages. This means that if the plaintiff's proven damages are $1,000, the most that the plaintiff could receive is $2,000. However, if a litigant who falls under this statute appeals to the U.S. Supreme Court, that court is free to rule that the Congress overstepped its bounds by limiting awards in this way. The court's written opinion in that case would be vitally important case law for anyone else with a pending case involving punitive damages. That case law would be as important as any statute.

Another example of the importance of case law is the famous U.S. Supreme Court decision in *Miranda v. Arizona*. In that case, the court outlined specific rights that must be read to suspects after they have been arrested. Those rights have never been embodied in a federal or state statute, yet they remain important legal authority.

One might be tempted to think that the only important source of case law in the United States is the U.S. Supreme Court. However, case law comes from every level of the court system. As we will see later in this chapter, both state and federal courts generate case law—and do so at different levels, from trial courts to appellate courts to the U.S. Supreme Court.

4. COMMON LAW

To further complicate the issue, there is one more important source of law that has a huge impact in the area of criminal law in several states: the **common law.** The development of the common law in the United States has a very interesting history.

Common law
(1) Either all case law or the case law that is made by judges in the absence of relevant statutes. (2) The legal system that originated in England and is composed of case law and statutes.

After the American colonies declared independence from Great Britain and decided to form their own country, they were faced with several immediate issues, not the least of which was how they would govern themselves and how would they enforce the laws that were passed. At the time, there were no state-created laws, because there were no state legislatures to pass them. Instead of creating an entirely new body of law, the colonists adopted the system they were the most familiar with: English criminal and civil law. The problem with this method is that the two systems, although superficially similar, were based on diametrically opposed foundations: monarchy versus democracy. Under the English system, the judge is a representative of the monarchy. Our system was based on democratic principles, which included the core belief that there should be three separate branches of government, equal in power, each with some authority to oversee—but not to interfere in—the functions of the other branches.

The English system of common law was adopted by the early United States for the sake of expediency and also because after centuries of use, the common law had quite literally thousands of tried-and-true methods of dealing with legal issues. All of this, however, raises the question: What is common law?

The historical development of common law is a subject about which entire books have been written. Because this is not a book about the history of law but about criminal justice, we will examine only the important points of the development of common law. Consider a specific and universal problem that has plagued human beings for thousands of years: illiteracy. Although we take for granted that almost anyone we meet can read and write, in the past such skills were reserved for the rich and powerful. The vast majority of the populace in England and the early United States was illiterate. How then could a person know what the law on a particular subject was? This is the origin of common law, or the law of the common people. Fans of Old West movies are familiar with the concept of judges who "ride the circuit." Criminals would be held in jail until the judge rode into town to dispense justice for a few weeks before riding on to the next town. That concept did not originate in the Old West. It was created by the English.

As English judges went from village to hamlet, they were presented with legal issues and made decisions in cases. Over time, as identical legal issues were presented, judges began to create a uniform system of rules that would help them and future judges to reach fair decisions. As there was no written law to interpret, the judges would come up with guidelines of their own. Judges from various jurisdictions would come together in meetings and would discuss their decisions in their cases. Early on, judges saw the benefit of creating a uniform system of decisions. In order to show that the legal system was fair, judges agreed that each judge would be bound by decisions of other judges on specific issues. This is not a unique phenomenon. We all create our own little rules that we use to guide our own actions. If the forecast calls for rain, we take an umbrella. If our first child was allowed to stay up until 11 P.M. when he turned 16, then when the second child turns the same age, we follow the same rule. Common law is the body of decisions of judges that carries the same weight as law. You have probably heard numerous examples but never realized that they are actually common law rules and laws that were created by legislatures. We will discuss three such common law rules to see how common law has affected citizens for centuries.

a. Common Law Marriage

In Figure 1-6, you see three examples of common law. The first, common law marriage, is an ancient rule that is still followed in some states. Under common law, a man and a woman who live together and state to others that they are married are considered legally married for judicial purposes. There is no need for a ceremony and no waiting period before such a union is recognized as legal. To be considered married under this rule, a person need only live with a member of the opposite sex and profess the belief that they considered themselves to be married. The reason for common law marriage no doubt had a great deal to do with the fact that in centuries past, most people could not afford elaborate weddings, and some rule had to be created for the vast majority of couples who never had the time or the resources for an "official" wedding.

b. Year and a Day Rule

Although most states abolished common law marriage decades ago, the so-called "year and a day rule" has only recently come under attack. The year and a day rule is an old common law rule that applied in murder cases. Under this rule, if a person was attacked by a defendant and it took more than a year and a day for the victim to die, the defendant could not be prosecuted for murder. Although this rule seems ridiculous to our modern view, consider the times in which it was created. The state of medical care even 100 years ago was so atrocious that most people who

FIGURE 1-6

Examples of Common Law

- Common law marriage
- The year and a day rule
- Possession is nine-tenths of the law

entered a hospital never came out alive again. Given the reality of medical care, if a person took over a year to die from an attack, chances were that some other agent, such as infection, bad medical treatment, or some other contagion had probably killed him. The year and a day rule prevented a defendant from being charged with murder for the simple reason that if the victim had been severely injured in the initial attack, he would probably have died within a relatively short period of time. This rule has survived in some states into the new millennium, although most states have specifically repealed it and most appellate courts have abolished it.

c. Possession Is Nine-Tenths of the Law

We have probably all heard this famous maxim, usually yelled at us by a sibling or someone else who has taken something that belongs to us. In fact, it is surprising how many people have heard this expression without realizing that it is a common law rule. The origin of the rule is rather mundane. Suppose a case involves a farm animal that has wandered away from its owner and then been acquired by an adjoining farmer. Because the rule originated in times when most people could not read or write, the animal has no collar or other symbol identifying it as belonging to Farmer A. Farmer B now has possession of the animal, and Farmer A sues to have it returned. How does the judge rule? Neither farmer could produce any proof of who originally owned the animal, so the case involves the word of Farmer A against the word of Farmer B. The judge must decide who should be allowed to keep the animal. In such a situation, the judge could simply refer to the common law principle that "possession is nine-tenths of the law." In this context, the ruling would mean that whoever possessed a disputed item that no one could show ownership of would be allowed to keep it.

These three examples are only a tiny portion of the hundreds of common law rules that became embodied in English law and were later adopted by American jurists.

d. Common Law Today

It would be tempting to think that common law is simply a quaint relic of the past with no immediate relevancy for criminal justice professionals. However, such a conclusion would be wrong. Common law was originally adopted by the thirteen colonies that later became the first thirteen states. Many of those states took some or all common law principles, enacted them as legislation, and then revoked the original English common law so that two systems (legislative law and common law) would not exist side by side. However, several states never abolished common law, and it remains an active and vital part of day-to-day practice.

Some states abolished only part of the common law and kept other parts. What this means is that for people in common law states, it is possible to have two different kinds of criminal violations. In North Carolina, for example, a suspect can be charged with statutory burglary or common law burglary. In Virginia, a criminal defendant can be charged with statutory arson or common law arson. The only way to find out whether your state is a common law state is to research its criminal statutes and cases.

i. Statutory Crimes and Common Law Crimes

In states where common law coexists with statutory law, a defendant can be charged with either one. This can often cause a great deal of confusion, especially when a defendant reads a charging document, such as an indictment, that charges him with two crimes for a single action. One crime is a statutory offense and one is a common law offense. In all states that still have this system, the defendant can be sentenced on only one offense. We will discuss sentencing in greater detail in Chapter 10.

Given the fact that all of the states that originally followed common law have enacted statutory crimes, one might be tempted to wonder why all states have not abolished common law in favor of statutory crimes. In the states that still follow the common law, there are many proponents for keeping the system as it exists. For one thing, everyone inside the state is familiar and quite comfortable with the two systems. But comfort is not the only reason for continuing to follow the common law. There are still some important uses of the common law in modern legal practice.

ii. Common Law in Day-to-day Practice

Although most states have abolished common law in favor of statutory law, a surprising number have abolished only some aspects of common law while keeping others (such as abolishing all common law crimes but keeping common law marriage), while others have not abolished common law at all. In those states, there are powerful arguments for keeping common law, including sentencing and new legal issues.

When it comes to sentencing, a judge must follow the statutory guidelines for imposing the sentence. However, what happens when a legislature enacts a law but fails to provide a sentence? In that situation, a state that has abolished common law may find itself in a legal quandary that will require additional legislation. In common law states, however, a judge is permitted to use common law sentencing guidelines.

We have all heard that there is nothing new under the sun. Whether or not you believe that statement, there is no question that common law dates back for centuries. During that time, nearly every type of legal question that has arisen has been addressed by a judge at one time or another. A judge who is presented with a seemingly new question could peruse the old common law to see if a similar argument has ever been raised. In such a situation, the judge could benefit from hundreds of years of cases to help her decide the best course in a current case.

III FEDERAL PROSECUTIONS VERSUS STATE PROSECUTIONS

Just as there are states where statutory law and common law exist side by side, the entire United States exists under a dual system that might be confusing to someone from another country. In the United States, we have both a federal criminal justice system and individual state criminal justice systems. A person may be prosecuted by the federal government or the state government or, in limited circumstances, by both.

For instance, in the Jared Loughner case, in which Loughner was accused of murdering a federal judge and another federal employee, along with wounding U.S. Representative Gabrielle Giffords, the federal government charged and tried the defendant first. The state of Arizona, where the crimes took place, maintained the right to charge and try Loughner later, but the federal case took precedence.

The U.S. Constitution grants power to both the states and the federal government to create laws criminalizing certain behaviors. As you will see in later chapters, most prosecutions are actually violations of state statutes, not federal statutes. In creating our government, the writers of the U.S. Constitution designated certain powers to be held in the federal government and vested the remaining powers in the states. Among these powers was the power to create laws listing certain activities as illegal. Before we can discuss the interplay of the federal and state systems, we must first address the issue of jurisdiction.

Defense Attorney

"The differences between state court and federal court are numerous. The rules are completely different. Sentencing procedures are very different. The discovery rules are very different. Everything is different."

B.J. Bernstein, Defense Attorney

PROFILING THE PROFESSIONAL

A. FEDERAL JURISDICTION

When we use the term **jurisdiction**, we are referring to power or authority. If a court has jurisdiction, it can control the actions of the parties, negate charging documents, and sentence defendants who have been found guilty of crimes, to name just a few powers. In later chapters, we will specifically examine the role of federal prosecutors, including the attorney general, various U.S. attorneys, federal law enforcement officers, and the many others involved in investigating, charging, and prosecuting federal crimes. As we have already seen in this chapter, when there is a conflict between a federal law and a state law, the federal law takes precedence (see Figure 1-7). The same rule applies in federal and state prosecutions.

Jurisdiction
The persons about whom and the subject matters about which a court has the right and power to make decisions that are legally binding.

B. STATE JURISDICTION

Although it would seem to be a logical step to assume that all states follow the federal model when it comes to the court system in general or criminal

FIGURE 1-7

Federal Courts Handled 20% of the Nation's Felony Weapon Convictions in 2004

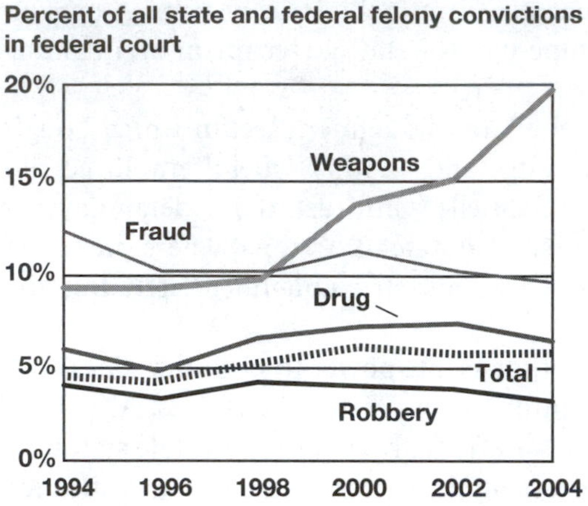

Source: Federal Justice Statistics, 2005, September 2008, NCJ 220383, Bureau of Justice Statistics, U.S. Department of Justice.

prosecution in particular, this assumption is incorrect. States have the power to enact their own laws, not only to criminalize behavior but also to include different procedural steps. Because most criminal prosecutions occur on the state level, we will spend a great deal of time discussing state-based procedural steps, but you should keep in mind that there is a great deal of variation among the states. All states must follow the minimum standards set out in the U.S. Constitution, but this does not prevent a state from adding more safeguards for a criminal defendant, and many do so. Throughout this text, we will address specific states and how they proceed with certain steps following the arrest of a suspect and continuing through to sentence and appeal. However, there is no way to address the differences among all the states, so we will limit our discussion to the most commonly found procedural steps and constitutional safeguards, while occasionally addressing the differences in particular states.

1. STATE PROSECUTIONS VERSUS FEDERAL PROSECUTIONS

In this text we focus a great deal of attention on prosecution at the state level for the simple reason that that is where most prosecutions occur. There are far more state-based prosecutions than there are federal prosecutions. After all, there is only one federal government, while there are fifty states (see Figure 1-8). However, this is not simply a matter of arithmetic. We tend to think of the federal government as monolithic and pervasive, but in comparison to any particular state's criminal code, the federal criminal code is relatively smaller. This stems not only from the fact that federal courts are courts of limited jurisdiction, as we will see in the next section, but also from the fact that it wasn't until the twentieth century that the federal criminal system was organized and fully integrated. States, on the other hand, have been prosecuting individuals since they were founded.

FIGURE 1-8

Felony Defendants Convicted in State and Federal Courts, 2004, 2000, and 1996

	2004	2000	1996	Average annual growth rate 1996–2004*
Total felony convictions	1,145,467	983,938	10,040,986	5.5%
Federal	5.8%	6.0%	4.1%	250.0
State	94.2	94.0	95.9	4.7
Total sentenced to incarceration	799,093	676,388	718,397	6.1%
Federal	7.1%	7.3%	4.8%	29.0
State	92.9	92.7	95.2	5.0
Mean incarceration sentance				
Federal	61mo.	58mo.	64mo.	
State	37mo.	36mo.	38mo.	

*Calculated using each annul count from 1996, 2000, and 2004.
Source: Federal Justice Statistics, 2005, September 2008, NCJ 220383, Bureau of Justice Statistics, U.S. Department of Justice.

FEDERAL VERSUS STATE COURT SYSTEMS

The organization of the federal and state court systems may, at first glance, seem extremely confusing. However, on closer examination, we will see that this is not so. The federal court system is often represented as a triangle, with the base consisting of trial courts, the middle of appellate courts, and the top portion of the U.S. Supreme Court. This same model works for state courts as well, although the names of the courts differ. The U.S. Supreme Court is the top court in the federal system; it interprets all questions regarding the U.S. Constitution and hears appeals in all federal criminal cases. Each state has its own supreme court, although it may not actually bear that name. In the next section, we will examine the structure of the American court system, beginning with the federal system and then addressing the structure of the state court systems.

A. THE LEVELS OF THE FEDERAL COURT SYSTEM

Whether on the federal or the state level, all court systems are designed as a hierarchy. At the top of the court system is a court that is often, but not always, referred to as the *Supreme Court.* This court is responsible for making final decisions on appeals in cases. It interprets both state and federal constitutions and applies these principles to individual cases on appeal. Below this court are a number of U.S. courts of appeal. These are intermediate appellate courts. There are thirteen circuit courts of appeal on the federal level. These circuits encompass several states and hear appeals from all district courts located in any of those states. At the bottom of the hierarchy are the federal trial courts, known as federal district courts. We will discuss these courts first and then show how a case moves from federal court to the appropriate federal district court of appeals and, finally, to the U.S. Supreme Court.

1. TRIAL COURTS: FEDERAL DISTRICT COURT

The federal court system has courts that encompass the entire United States and its territories. There are a total of 94 U.S. district courts in the United States. Federal district courts are the trial courts of the federal system, and it is in the federal court where civil and criminal cases are heard (see Figure 1-9). Defendants who are

FIGURE 1-9

Disposition and Case Proceeding Time of Defendants in Cases Concluded in U.S. District Court, 2005

		Percent convicted		Percent not convicted	
	Number of cases concluded	Guilty plea	Bench/ jury trial	Bench/ jury trial	Dismissed
All offenses	86,680	86.2%	3.9	0.7	9.3
Violent	3,304	81.5%	6.3	1.9	10.3
Property	14,669	84.1%	3.6	0.6	11.7
Drug	30,129	86.9%	4.2	0.5	8.3
Public order	11,024	75.1%	4.7	1.0	19.3
Weapon	9,853	84.0%	7.0	1.2	7.8
Immigration	17,701	95.5%	0.9	0.1	3.4
Southwest U.S. border district					
Yes	24,200	92.9%	1.6	0.3	5.2
No	62,480	83.5%	4.8	0.8	10.9
District size					
Small	4,989	82.1%	5.9	1.0	11.0
Medium	37,380	85.2%	3.7	0.6	10.5
Large	44,311	87.5%	3.8	0.7	8.1
Median time from filing to disposition	6.8 mo.	6.7 mo.	14.3 mo.	7.1 mo.	6.2 mo.

Source: Federal Justice Statistics, 2005, September 2008, NCJ 220383, Bureau of Justice Statistics, U.S. Department of Justice.

charged with federal crimes can receive a jury trial in federal district court. Every state has at least one federal court, with some states having several, placed at different locations around the state. The geographic distribution of federal district courts has more to do with population than size of a state, which explains why there are many more federal district courts in the northeast than in the west or northwest part of the country. The formal name of any individual federal court is the U.S. District Court for ________ Circuit. The blank represents the numeric designation of the circuit in which the court is located. There are twelve circuits located around the country. Look at Figure 1-10 for a map showing the various circuits in the United States.

Each federal district court has at least one presiding judge, referred to as a U.S. district judge. We will discuss federal judges in greater detail in Chapter 2. Federal district courts are courts of **limited jurisdiction**, meaning that they may hear only those cases in which they have been specifically granted jurisdictional power by statute or by the U.S. Constitution. Before a court will examine the merits of any case, the parties must first allege that they have met the court's limited jurisdiction threshold.

Sidebar

There are actually 89 federal district courts scattered among the fifty states. The remaining courts are found in territories or the District of Columbia.

Limited jurisdiction
The authority of a court to hear and consider only specifically enumerated matters.

2. APPELLATE COURTS: COURT OF APPEALS

We have seen that each federal district court is established inside one of twelve different federal circuits. (There is a thirteenth circuit, but it is reserved for special cases arising out of the DC circuit). When a case is heard on appeal from any district court, the case goes to the corresponding court of appeals for that district. The U.S. courts of appeal are the midlevel or intermediate courts between the trial courts (federal district court) and the U.S. Supreme Court. In criminal cases, when a defendant is found guilty in federal district court, she can appeal that conviction to the federal circuit court of appeals for that particular circuit. See Figure 1-11 for the locations of the various federal circuit courts of appeal for every circuit.

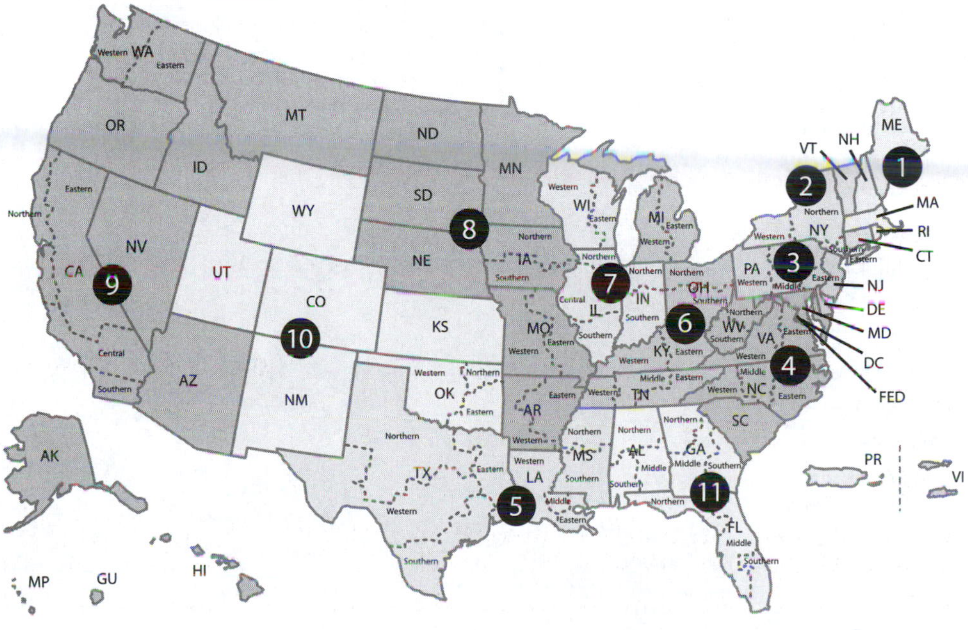

FIGURE 1-10

Federal Circuits of the United States

FIGURE 1-11

States Within Each Federal Circuit

Circuit	Court of Appeals Located in
DC Circuit	Washington, DC
First Circuit	Boston, MA
Maine	
Massachusetts	
New Hampshire	
Puerto Rico	
Rhode Island	
Second Circuit	New York, NY
Connecticut	
New York	
Vermont	
Third Circuit	Philadelphia, PA
Delaware	
New Jersey	
Pennsylvania	
U.S. Virgin Islands	
Fourth Circuit	Richmond, VA
Maryland	
North Carolina	
South Carolina	
Virginia	
West Virginia	
Fifth Circuit	New Orleans, LA
Louisiana	
Mississippi	
Texas	
Sixth Circuit	Cincinnati, OH
Kentucky	
Michigan	
Ohio	
Tennessee	
Seventh Circuit	Chicago, IL
Illinois	
Indiana	
Wisconsin	
Eighth Circuit	St. Louis, MO
Arkansas	
Iowa	
Minnesota	
Missouri	
Nebraska	
North Dakota	
South Dakota	

Circuit	Court of Appeals Located in
Ninth Circuit	San Francisco, CA
Alaska	
Arizona	
California	
Guam	
Hawaii	
Idaho	
Montana	
Nevada	
Northern Mariana Islands	
Oregon	
Washington	
Tenth Circuit	Denver, CO
Colorado	
Kansas	
New Mexico	
Oklahoma	
Utah	
Wyoming	
Eleventh Circuit	Atlanta, GA
Alabama	
Florida	
Georgia	
Federal Circuit	Washington, DC

FIGURE 1-11

(Continued)

A judge who sits on any of the U.S. circuit courts of appeals is nominated by the president and must be confirmed by the Senate before he can take the seat. As we will see in the next chapter, most federal judges and all federal circuit court of appeals judges are protected by the provisions of Article III of the U.S. Constitution. Although that designation brings with it many powers and duties, the most important for this discussion is that a judge who serves in the federal district court or the federal circuit court of appeals does so for life. These judges cannot be removed unless they are impeached. Impeachment almost always means that a judge has violated a criminal statute. Barring that drastic remedy, once a judge is appointed, she cannot be fired or demoted by a future president.

Sidebar

Judges who serve on the federal circuit courts of appeal earn an average of $180,000 per year.

In Chapter 11, we will discuss how and under what circumstances a federal circuit court of appeals might hear a criminal appeal. For the purposes of this chapter, we will merely say that these courts hear the appeals of the U.S. federal district courts located within their circuits and leave it at that.

FIGURE 1-12

The Current Members of the Supreme Court

Chief Justice of the United States John G. Roberts, Jr.

Associate Justices
Antonin Scalia
Anthony M. Kennedy
Clarence Thomas
Ruth Bader Ginsburg
Stephen Breyer
Samuel Alito, Jr.
Sonia Sotomayor
Elena Kagan

3. U.S. SUPREME COURT

The U.S. Supreme Court is the highest court in the federal system. It hears all appeals from the various federal circuit courts of appeal located around the country. As we will see in Chapter 11, the U.S. Supreme Court is not required to hear all appeals presented to it. The Court may pick and choose, in most situations, which cases it will hear and which cases it will not hear. See Figure 1-12.

Just as we saw with other federal judges, the members of the U.S. Supreme Court are protected under Article III and may serve for life. See Figure 1-13. When a position becomes vacant, through either death or retirement, the president has the authority to nominate a replacement who must then be approved by the Senate. The U.S. Supreme Court building is located in Washington, DC, directly across from the Capitol. The Court begins its session on the first Monday in October and continues through the first Monday of the following May. The Court is in recess from June through September.

The U.S. Supreme Court is a unique institution for many reasons. As we have already said, it sits atop the federal court hierarchy and is the final arbiter for all questions and interpretations of the U.S. Constitution. However, as we will see in the next section, the U.S. Supreme Court has another distinction. It is also the final authority on questions of state law and has the final say in all state appeals as well.

B. THE LEVELS OF THE STATE COURT SYSTEM

Now that we have examined the levels of the federal court system, we will turn our attention to the organization of the state court systems. One of the problems

FIGURE 1-13

Article III, §1, U.S. Constitution

The judicial Power of the United States, shall be vested in one supreme Court, and in such inferior Courts as the Congress may from time to time ordain and establish.

inherent in any examination of state court systems is the variation seen among the states. All states have trial courts, but they do not go by the same name or have the same powers as courts in other states. In some states, there are state courts that are empowered to hear **misdemeanor** cases, before juries of six people, while superior courts hear **felony** cases before juries of twelve individuals. In other states, there are no juries for misdemeanor cases and the defendant may appeal to the superior court for a new trial (and a jury) if he is convicted in state court. Because this is an introductory chapter, we will not examine all the possible variations among the states. Instead, we will simplify the discussion by referring to one trial court and discuss how a case proceeds there and how an appeal from that court would proceed. For our purposes, we will simply pretend that there is only a superior court.

Misdemeanor
A crime punishable by a maximum sentence of one year in prison.

Felony
A crime punishable by more than one year in prison.

1. TRIAL COURTS

In our simplified discussion of trial courts, the Superior Court is the court where criminal trials occur. Juries are empanelled in this courtroom, and defendants are brought to trial. You can see fictionalized versions of this process nearly every night on television. If a defendant is found not guilty, he is released and there is no appeal. If a defendant is found guilty, he will likely bring an appeal to the state court of appeals.

2. APPELLATE COURTS

Just as we saw with trial courts, each state has its own version of appellate courts. Most states follow the federal model of a trial court, an intermediate court of appeals and a state supreme court, but not all states use these names to refer to these courts. In most states, the intermediate appellate court is referred to as the state court of appeals. It resembles the federal system closely. Defendants who are found guilty in superior court bring their appeal to this court. (Unlike at the federal level, there is only one court of appeals per state.) If either party loses on appeal before the state court of appeals, they may be allowed to appeal to the state's highest court: the state supreme court.

3. STATE SUPREME COURT

At the top of the state hierarchy is a court that hears all appeals from the state court of appeals. This court is, technically, the final decision maker on state-based questions, but as we have already seen, litigants can, and often do, attempt to take their case to the highest court in the United States, the U.S. Supreme Court. However, the vast majority of criminal appeals are concluded in the state supreme courts and are never heard before the U.S. Supreme Court. (There are some important exceptions to that rule that we will address in Chapter 11.)

In the following case excerpt, pay particular attention to the concept of judicial notice. As you are reading, also consider why it is important to establish that the crime occurred at night. At the conclusion of this case excerpt, you will have some questions to answer that probe these topics.

CASE EXCERPT

STATE v. MCCORMICK

693 S.E.2d 195 (2010)

Hunter, Jr., Robert N., Judge.

Donald Lee McCormick ("defendant") appeals as a matter of right from a verdict finding him guilty of two counts of assault by pointing a gun, two counts of communicating threats, assault with a deadly weapon inflicting serious injury and first-degree burglary. After review, we hold that defendant's trial and judgment was free of error.

I. FACTUAL BACKGROUND

The Watauga County grand jury indicted defendant for two counts of assault by pointing a gun, two counts of communicating threats, assault with a deadly weapon inflicting serious injury and first-degree burglary. The language, as pertinent to this appeal, contained in the 1 January 2008 indictment for first-degree burglary, in violation of N.C. Gen.Stat. §14-51 (2009), provided the following:

> The jurors for the State upon their oath present that on or about the date of offense shown and in the county named above the defendant named above unlawfully, willfully and feloniously did during the nighttime break and enter the dwelling house of Lisa McCromick [sic] located at 407 Wards Branch Road, Sugar Grove, Watauga County. At the time of the breaking and entering the dwelling house was actually occupied by Timothy James Ward, Amy Dancy, and Matthew Minton. The defendant broke and entered with the intent to commit a felony therein, to wit: Assault with a Deadly Weapon Inflicting Serious Injury.

At trial, the State's evidence tended to show the following: Defendant and Lisa McCormick ("Ms. McCormick") were married in 2001, had a daughter in 2003, and separated in 2006. After the couple separated, Ms. McCormick and the couple's daughter moved to a house located on Ward's Branch Road in Watauga County, North Carolina. The events which transpired and subsequently led to defendant's arrest and indictment occurred at the Ward's Branch Road residence.

On 1 January 2008, during the daylight afternoon hours, Ms. McCormick's brother Timothy James Ward ("Tim"), Tim's girlfriend Amy Dancy ("Amy"), and Matthew Minton ("Matthew") arrived at Ms. McCormick's house on Ward's Branch Road. They began drinking, playing poker, and listening to music while waiting for Ms. McCormick to arrive at the home. Approximately one hour after their arrival, Tim answered the telephone and recognized defendant's voice, who asked to speak to Ms. McCormick. Tim told defendant that Ms. McCormick was not at home, but was expected to arrive shortly; the phone call ended. Approximately five minutes later, defendant called a second time and began cursing at Tim when he answered defendant's call, whereupon Tim hung up the phone. Defendant called a third time and left a voice message when no one answered. Two other messages were subsequently left on the machine which Tim found threatening. Tim called his brother, Dennis Presnell ("Dennis"), and requested that he come to Ms. McCormick's house to help calm down defendant should he arrive. Dennis testified that he received three calls from Tim, the first at approximately 5:30 P.M., the second around 6:00 P.M., and the third call at approximately 6:15 P.M. On the third call, Dennis testified that he heard defendant's voice and recognized Tim's voice crying.

Approximately fifteen to twenty minutes after the last message from defendant to Tim, defendant arrived at Ms. McCormick's home, kicked in the backdoor, and fired three shots with his .22 caliber revolver. Matthew fled outside the home. Amy locked herself in a bathroom. Tim initially ran to hide in the house, but after realizing his girlfriend Amy was locked in the bathroom, left his hiding place and approached the bathroom, at which point defendant hit Tim with the butt of the revolver, knocking him to the floor. Defendant continued to hit Tim about the face and head with the gun, stopping on several occasions to intermittently put the barrel of the weapon in Tim's mouth while threatening to shoot him.

Amy opened the bathroom door and saw defendant kicking and hitting Tim with the gun as he laid unconscious and bleeding. When Amy went to Tim's aid, defendant pulled her by her hair and threw her on the floor, while pointing the gun in her face and telling her, "Bitch, I will kill you."

Defendant dragged Tim into a nearby bedroom, whereupon Amy found a cell phone, called for emergency help, and fled to the back porch of the house. Tim regained consciousness and escaped out of the front door while defendant was momentarily distracted by the arrival of Tim's brother, Dennis, and Erin Street ("Erin"), Dennis's girlfriend. Tim collapsed into his brother's arms on the front porch as he was coming out of the front door. Dennis testified that he "believed it was like 8:30" and it was dark at the time he arrived at the home.

Defendant then emerged from the house, pulled out the revolver, pointed the barrel of the gun into Dennis's mouth, and asked Dennis if he wanted to die. Defendant threatened Erin also after she confronted defendant and slapped him. After this confrontation, Erin, Dennis, and Tim retreated to the driveway area. While they were retreating, a state trooper arrived and the trio took cover behind the highway patrol vehicle. Shortly thereafter, Deputy Edward Hodges and one other Watauga County Sheriff's Deputy arrived and arrested defendant. Lieutenant Green of the Watauga County Sheriff's Office testified that he was dispatched to the scene at approximately 7:07 P.M. and was the third officer to arrive at the scene.

Dr. Carol Olsen, the emergency medical physician who treated Tim, testified that his injuries included abrasions on his head, arms, and hip, damage to his teeth, a laceration to his right ear, a scalp laceration that was stapled, and a two-and-a-half-centimeter laceration through his lower lip that required stitches. Tim was confined to bed for two weeks and his injuries to his mouth and teeth required him to be fed by drinking from a straw.

At the close of the State's evidence, the State filed a motion with the court to take judicial notice of the time of sunset and civil twilight pursuant to Rule 201 of the North Carolina Rules of Evidence. The trial judge granted the State's motion and gave the jury the following instruction:

The court will take judicial notice of two facts. In this case you may but are not required to accept as conclusive any fact judicially noticed by the Court.

The facts judicially noticed in this case are as follows. First that on January 1st, 2008 in Boone, North Carolina the sun set at 5:23 in the afternoon. And second, on January 1st, 2008 in Boone, North Carolina the end of civil twilight was 5:51 in the afternoon.

Civil twilight is defined to begin in the morning and to end in the evening when the center of the sun is geometrically six degrees below the horizon. This is the limit at which twilight illumination is sufficient under good weather conditions for terrestrial objects to be clearly distinguished. In the evening after the end of civil twilight artificial illumination is normally required to carry on outdoor activities.

Again, the Court will take judicial notice of these two facts, and you may but are not required to accept them as conclusive on these two issues.

Defendant's evidence tended to show the following: As his first witness, defendant recalled Deputy Edward Hodges. Deputy Hodges testified that the records of the Watauga County Sheriff's emergency system indicated that a 911 call was received from Melvie Ann Dollars at 7:06 P.M. This was the call to which Deputy Hodges responded when he arrived at Ward's Branch Road.

Defendant testified that he and Ms. McCormick lived together at the Ward's Branch Road residence after their separation during a brief, but failed attempt at reconciliation. Defendant moved out of the residence in April of 2007. Defendant further testified regarding his army service, employment history, and prior convictions for drunk driving and assault with a deadly weapon.

Regarding the 1 January 2008 incident, defendant testified that he called his wife's residence to speak with his daughter. Tim answered the phone and cursed at defendant. In two subsequent phone calls, defendant testified that Tim told him that when his four-year-old daughter arrived at the house, he was going to have a "real good time with her." This conversation angered defendant. Defendant grabbed his gun and about ten minutes later arrived at 317 Ward's Branch Road, where he entered the house. Defendant testified that he did not intend to injure anyone when he entered the house, and that the gun accidentally fired when he came through the back door. Defendant describes the confrontations that took place in the house and admits to fighting with Tim and beating him.

On cross-examination, defendant admits that the answering machine showed the final call from defendant to the house to be at 6:36 P.M., and that it took defendant about 10 to 15 minutes to arrive thereafter. Defendant also admitted that it was getting dark when he arrived at the house. Furthermore, when the police arrived, defendant testified that he surrendered after being asked to do so.

At the close of all of the evidence, defendant renewed his motion to dismiss the charges, which was denied. After receiving instructions from the court, the jury found defendant guilty of two counts of assault by pointing a gun and communicating threats, assault with a deadly weapon inflicting serious injury, and first-degree burglary.

II. FIRST-DEGREE BURGLARY CONVICTION

Defendant's primary challenge in this appeal is to his conviction for first-degree burglary in violation of N.C. Gen.Stat. §14-51. Specifically, defendant contends that (1) the trial court should have granted his motion to dismiss this charge on the basis that there was a fatal variance between the indictment and the proof, and (2) the trial court lacked jurisdiction because the indictment did not allege that the breaking and entering was done "without consent" and that there was insufficient evidence of lack of consent. We disagree with both contentions.

First-degree burglary is defined as the unlawful breaking and entering of an occupied dwelling or sleeping apartment, at nighttime, with the intent to commit a felony therein. *State v. Hannah*, 149 N.C.App. 713, 719, 563 S.E.2d 1, 5 (2002). It is clear from comparing the elements of this common law crime, as described above from case law, and examining the indictment in this case that all of the legal elements of first-degree burglary were properly charged in the indictment.

III. JUDICIAL NOTICE

Defendant argues that taking judicial notice of the time of sunset in a burglary case, which requires that the acts be done at "nighttime," has the effect of impermissibly supplying an essential element of the offense, lowers the State's burden of proof, and amounts to an unfair weighing in by the Court. We disagree.

N.C. Gen.Stat. §8C-1, Rule 201, Judicial Notice of Adjudicative Facts, provides as follows:

(a) Scope of rule. This rule governs only judicial notice of adjudicative facts.

(b) Kinds of facts. A judicially noticed fact must be one not subject to reasonable dispute in that it is either (1) generally known within the territorial jurisdiction of the trial court or (2) capable of accurate and ready determination by resort to sources whose accuracy cannot reasonably be questioned.

(c) When discretionary. A court may take judicial notice, whether requested or not.

(d) When mandatory. A court shall take judicial notice if requested by a party and supplied with the necessary information.

(e) Opportunity to be heard. In a trial court, a party is entitled upon timely request to an opportunity to be heard as to the propriety of taking judicial notice and the tenor of the matter noticed. In the absence of prior notification, the request may be made after judicial notice has been taken.

(f) Time of taking notice. Judicial notice may be taken at any stage of the proceeding.

(g) Instructing jury. In a civil action or proceeding, the court shall instruct the jury to accept as conclusive any fact judicially noticed. In a criminal case, the court shall instruct the jury that it may, but is not required to, accept as conclusive any fact judicially noticed.

At the end of the State's case-in-chief, and before defendant began presentation of his defense, the State filed a written motion with the court to take judicial notice of the time of the sunset and the time of civil sunset as established by the Naval Observatory. The court, out of the presence of the jury, gave defendant the opportunity to be heard as to the propriety of taking judicial notice and the tenor of the matter noticed. Subsequently, the judge instructed the jury that it "may, but is not required to, accept as conclusive any fact judicially noticed."

Our Courts have taken judicial notice of days, weeks, and months of the calendar. Our Courts have also taken judicial notice of the time of sunrise and sunset on a particular date. Furthermore, our Courts have taken judicial notice of the phase of the moon and the time of its rising from the records of the U.S. Naval Observatory. The application of this rule of evidence in the present case is a routine application of this evidentiary principle, thus we hold that judicial notice was procedurally taken. The court committed no error in admitting the celestial timetable.

CONCLUSION

Based on the foregoing, we hold that there was no error in the trial of defendant, but remand this matter to the trial court for correction of clerical errors in the judgment sentencing defendant.

Judges Elmore and Jackson concur.

CASE QUESTIONS

1. According to this court, what is "judicial notice?"
2. Why is it important to establish that the burglary charge occurred "at night"?
3. Did the state proceed on a statutory charge of burglary or on a common law charge of burglary?
4. Was the trial court allowed to take notice that the burglary had occurred at night and had therefore established the elements of common law burglary?

CHAPTER SUMMARY

In this chapter, we have seen that criminal law is different from civil law in a wide variety of ways. In a civil case, for example, a plaintiff sues a defendant, usually for monetary damages. In a criminal case, on the other hand, the state or government brings charges against an individual and seeks to have that person convicted of a crime. At the conclusion of a civil case, the winner may be paid monetary damages by the loser. In a criminal case, if the defendant loses, she is convicted of a crime and may be sentenced to incarceration. Among the important differences between civil law and criminal law is the burden of proof. In a criminal case, the government must prove that the defendant is guilty beyond a reasonable doubt before the jury is permitted to find that the defendant is guilty.

There are several sources of law that criminalize behavior. The U.S. Constitution empowers state and federal governments to enact criminal statutes. However, criminal law is also governed by case law, which consists of the decisions of appellate courts that have been called upon to interpret federal and state laws and apply them in a particular situation. Common law is an ancient body of law, originally created in England, that provided a series of rules that helped judges decide cases fairly. Some states still follow the common law, while most have abolished it.

Prosecution of criminal defendants occurs on both the state and federal levels. Before anyone can be prosecuted in a U.S. federal district court, the prosecution must satisfy the threshold question of jurisdiction. This term refers to the power of the court to make rulings on both the subject matter and the individuals involved in a case. Federal courts are courts of limited jurisdiction, but the same is not true of state courts. The federal system is organized as a hierarchy, with the U.S. Supreme Court at the very top, 12 separate circuit courts of appeal, and 94 federal district courts scattered across the country. Appeals from federal district court go to the U.S. circuit court of appeals for that particular region. Appeals from the circuit courts go to the U.S. Supreme Court. State courts are often organized in a very similar manner, with trial courts at the bottom, an intermediate appellate court, often referred to as the state court of appeals, and a high court that often bears the name of the state supreme court. It is important to keep in mind that although the federal system is uniform throughout the country, there is a wide variation among the states in procedural matters and even in the names of the various courts.

KEY TERMS

Key terms are listed here in order of appearance in chapter.

- Defendant
- Guilty
- Liable
- Damages
- Burden of proof
- Preponderance of the evidence
- Plaintiff
- Beyond a reasonable doubt
- Style
- Complaint
- Answer
- Supremacy Clause
- Statute
- Code
- Ordinance
- Case law
- Common law
- Jurisdiction
- Limited jurisdiction
- Misdemeanor
- Felony

REVIEW QUESTIONS

1. What is a plaintiff?
2. List and explain at least four important differences between civil law and criminal law.
3. What are the verdicts in a civil case and how do they compare to the verdicts in a criminal case?
4. List and explain the four types of verdicts available in criminal cases.
5. What are damages?
6. What is the burden of proof in a civil case?
7. What is the burden of proof in a criminal case?
8. Explain how the style or caption of a criminal case differs from that of a civil case.
9. What is statutory law?
10. Explain case law.
11. What is the Supremacy Clause?
12. What is the difference between a statute and an ordinance?
13. Explain the impact that the U.S. Supreme Court has on case law.
14. What is common law?
15. Give some examples of common law rules.
16. What is the difference between a statutory crime and a common law crime?
17. Define jurisdiction.
18. List the three levels of the federal court system, beginning with the trial court and ending with the highest court.
19. How many federal circuits exist in the United States?
20. In which circuit is your state located?
21. How many justices serve on the U.S. Supreme Court?
22. Which article of the U.S. Constitution authorizes the creation of the U.S. Supreme Court?
23. What is the difference between a misdemeanor and felony?

WEB SURFING

Legal Information Institute: Criminal Law
http://topics.law.cornell.edu/wex/Criminal_law

Free Online Legal Dictionary
http://legal-dictionary.thefreedictionary.com/

Criminal Law Cases
http://www.ask.com/wiki/Criminal_law

EXERCISES

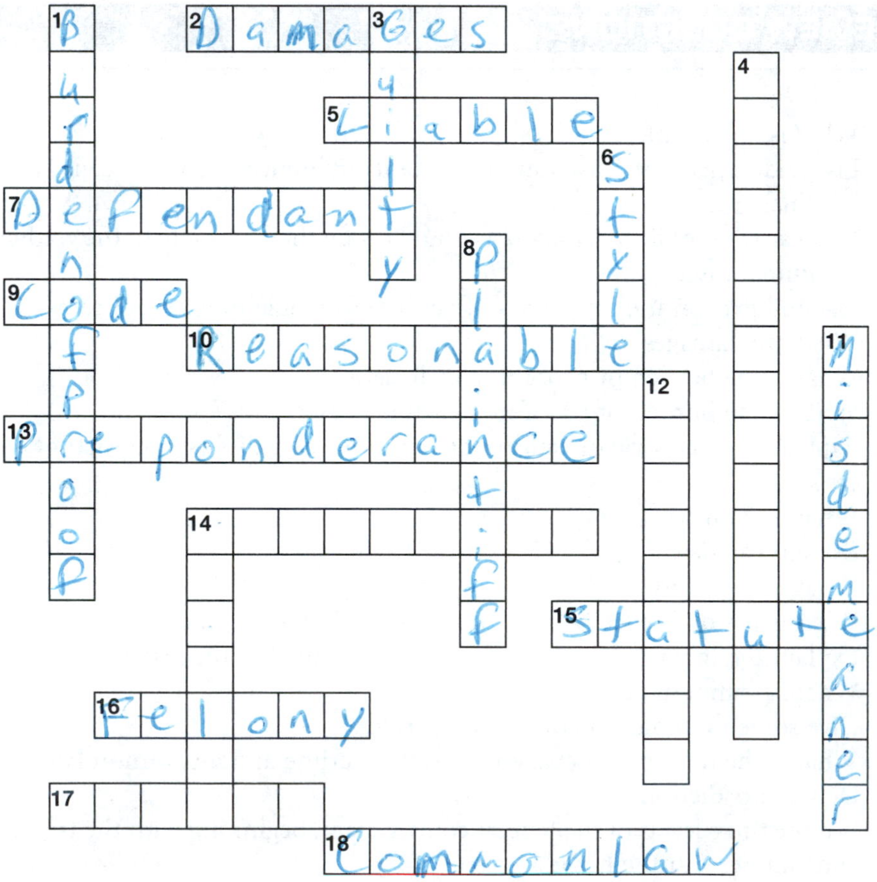

ACROSS

2. Jury's assessment of the money owed to other party in civil case

DOWN

1. Amount of proof that a party must bring to sustain action against another party

5. Duty or obligation to pay damages or fulfill other action to other party
7. The person charged with the crime
9. A collection of laws
10. Beyond a_____ doubt
13. _____ of the evidence
14. Petition
15. A law that is voted on by legislative branch and enacted by executive branch
16. A crime punishable by more than one year in prison
17. Reply
18. All case law or the case law made by judges in the absence of relevant statutes

3. Verdict where jurors determine defendant committed crime
4. Provision clarifying that federal laws take precedence over state laws
6. The title or heading listing the parties in the case
8. The party that brings a civil suit
11. A crime punishable by a maximum sentence of 12 months in prison
12. A law passed by local government
14. The written decisions by appellate courts explaining the outcome of a case on appeal

t	p	a	r	e	o	n	e	e	r	e	e	n	a	t	d	e	m	t	o	o	i	y	a	n	e
b	y	r	m	e	d	g	a	n	t	e	p	a	n	i	r	e	a	e	d	t	e	e	n	e	a
u	e	s	a	r	c	l	a	d	a	v	a	a	y	i	l	n	b	p	d	b	y	e	e	c	e
o	o	e	p	e	r	c	s	d	t	o	t	r	t	e	i	u	t	r	a	l	o	j	e	i	c
d	a	e	o	u	f	e	a	b	d	u	m	c	s	t	w	a	l	p	o	e	w	r	p	l	p
e	s	d	r	m	n	d	c	d	e	j	u	e	n	s	o	n	b	d	b	r	m	a	p	u	e
l	r	r	f	u	t	e	p	e	b	u	i	e	m	a	n	s	e	r	y	d	a	e	d	c	a
b	o	l	u	c	a	n	l	w	o	r	u	e	o	g	t	f	t	i	o	l	m	e	n	d	m
a	d	s	n	m	i	o	e	n	e	i	w	m	n	e	e	e	c	e	t	t	a	r	n	f	u
n	o	j	o	i	o	a	p	w	l	s	n	o	s	n	a	u	n	r	l	u	n	l	t	n	w
o	n	o	p	a	e	t	s	s	h	d	u	o	d	o	a	s	t	e	c	e	a	l	c	f	o
s	o	a	c	p	e	n	r	g	a	i	a	a	b	m	r	i	e	e	c	d	y	r	o	o	n
a	n	c	e	e	a	c	o	n	o	c	n	f	l	l	y	a	y	i	t	e	l	e	a	o	y
e	c	n	e	d	i	v	e	e	h	t	f	o	e	c	n	a	r	e	d	n	o	p	e	r	p
r	t	f	n	u	r	l	t	l	s	i	e	e	n	a	y	o	o	y	t	a	c	t	r	p	a
a	e	l	d	n	e	i	e	a	t	o	a	a	l	i	o	c	n	y	n	c	m	m	t	f	y
d	m	t	s	n	c	e	c	n	a	n	i	d	r	o	p	w	a	e	o	s	p	a	p	o	a
n	a	n	u	y	g	u	i	l	t	y	u	i	o	r	n	f	e	m	o	e	i	e	g	n	l
o	n	e	r	o	d	a	e	i	u	r	m	o	d	l	c	y	m	r	e	a	m	t	e	e	a
y	u	e	r	a	l	o	e	a	t	e	d	u	u	b	f	o	e	r	f	r	m	t	m	d	s
e	e	t	e	p	n	u	t	b	e	c	a	l	i	i	n	o	d	a	g	b	p	c	f	r	c
b	r	e	m	e	a	p	t	l	d	r	c	t	e	l	y	t	s	e	a	b	o	u	e	u	p
n	d	o	n	e	i	e	o	e	n	a	a	c	a	m	n	p	i	e	a	n	n	i	s	b	n
a	c	a	m	a	o	r	o	l	m	o	y	w	o	r	i	e	m	a	d	p	d	w	y	s	y
e	n	c	r	r	n	e	u	l	v	u	n	t	b	o	f	e	y	o	w	e	r	n	d	e	a
y	o	d	l	r	p	o	r	m	p	d	o	o	n	t	s	e	a	t	o	i	a	n	l	p	d

defendant	plaintiff	statute
guilty	beyond a reasonable doubt	code
liable	style	ordinance
damages	complaint	common law
burden of proof	answer	jurisdiction
preponderance of the evidence	supremacy clause	misdemeanor
		felony

QUESTIONS FOR ANALYSIS

1. Is the Supremacy Clause still relevant today? Should the clause be removed from the U.S. Constitution? Explain your answer.
2. Should the burden of proof in a criminal case be lowered to that of civil cases? Why or why not?
3. In the states that still follow the common law, should they be forced to abolish it? Explain your answer.

2

The Participants

Chapter Objectives

- **Explain the role that judges play in the criminal justice system**
- **Describe the importance of prosecutors in the American court system**
- **Define the objectives of probation and the role that probation officers play in achieving those objectives**
- **Explain the rights that victims of crime have in our system**
- **Define the important function that law enforcement officers have in the criminal justice system**

I JUDGES

We have all seen judges on television shows, whether they preside at fictitious criminal trials in shows like *Law & Order* or the more prosaic format of the civil cases battled out before *Judge Judy*. However, the vast majority of citizens are not familiar with the real functions of a judge. Most people do not know the extent of a judge's power, how a judge is selected for his post, or even what ethical rules a judge must follow.

We will begin our discussion on judges by focusing on their qualifications, discussing how they are selected, and then defining the important role that they play in criminal prosecutions. Later, we will see that there are many other individuals who may also be referred to as judges who not only lack the authority to hear a case but also lack some of the formal education that we associate with a traditional judge.

A. QUALIFICATIONS

Although we might be tempted to think that all judges have been, at least at one time, lawyers, that is not always the case. In the past, for example, many states had no requirement that a person who served as a judge must first have been an attorney. That requirement has changed. Many states now require that any person who becomes a judge must first be a member of the state bar.[1] However, there are also many jurisdictions where certain types of judicial positions do not require the judge to also be a lawyer. In many states, for example, magistrate judges can come from any profession and are simply required to complete training on judicial matters before engaging in their day-to-day duties. We will discuss magistrate judges later in this chapter and in much greater detail in Chapter 5, when we address the topic of arrest and search warrants.

EXAMPLE

In Susan's hometown, state law requires that anyone seeking the position of magistrate judge must be an attorney. Susan, who is not an attorney, believes that this law is unfair and a violation of her constitutional rights. She files suit against the county, alleging that her rights under the Equal Protection Clause of the U.S. Constitution have been infringed upon. Her argument is that the current rule gives a complete monopoly to attorneys for the position of magistrate and bars anyone else from applying for and being elected to the position. Will her suit be successful?

Answer: No. In the appellate courts that have dealt directly with this issue, all have found that there is no violation of the U.S. Constitution for a state to require additional standards of judges, including that they be members of the state bar.[2] Interestingly enough, a statute that required a judge to be not only a member of the bar but also a practicing attorney was considered to be a violation of the Constitution. The court in that case held that requiring members of the judicial branch to be experienced in the law was not the same as requiring that they actually be practicing law at the time that they are chosen or elected to become judges.[3]

In areas where a judge can serve as both a judge and an attorney, the usual procedure is to allow the judge to act as an attorney in civil matters, but not criminal cases. If a judge/attorney in this situation does take on a criminal case, she can be disbarred from the practice of law and also suspended from her judicial position.

B. ELECTED VERSUS APPOINTED

There are essentially two systems for selecting judges. In some jurisdictions, judges are elected, while in others they are appointed. When a judge runs for election it is very similar to any politician running for office. Judges run their campaigns, putting up posters and giving speeches, but they also have restrictions that other politicians do not. Most judicial elections are considered bipartisan. Judges usually do not announce their affiliation with either the Democratic or Republican Party.

---

[1] *Gamble v. White*, 566 So.2d 171 (La. Ct. App. 2d Cir. 1990), writ denied, 565 So.2d 923 (La. 1990).
[2] *Bullock v. State of Minn.*, 611 F.2d 258 (8th Cir. 1979); Torjesen v. Smith, 114 Ill. App.3d 147, 69 Ill. Dec. 813, 448 N.E.2d 273 (5th Dist. 1983).
[3] *LaFever v. Ware*, 211 Tenn. 393, 365 S.W.2d 44 (1963).

Instead, judges run on their record of efficiently moving cases through the court system, their tough stance on criminals, and their record on appeal.

Judicial appointments can come in two varieties. In some jurisdictions, the governor appoints a judge to fill a vacant position. This may also happen when an elected position is suddenly vacated because the occupant has died, been promoted to another office, or been sanctioned and removed. In jurisdictions that have the appointment system, there may also be a board that has a special mandate to interview and select candidates for judicial positions. This panel may make the final decision itself or make a recommendation to the governor, who then fills the position with the board's recommendation. The fastest way to find out which method your jurisdiction uses is to visit the state court website and see what it has to say about judicial selection.

C. ROLE IN THE PROCEEDINGS

It is one of the functions of a judge to preside at both civil and criminal trials. In our system, civil and criminal litigants use the same courthouse, the same clerk's office, and the same judges. In other countries, this is not the case. In those systems, civil and criminal cases are completely segregated. A judge may hear civil cases one week and criminal cases the next. A judge is responsible for the orderly function of the court system and has power to enforce that authority against any of the parties or attorneys involved in a specific case. Because we limit our discussions to criminal issues in this text, we will ignore the enormous and often complex duties that a judge may have in civil cases.

For the purpose of clarity, we will base our discussion on the duties, powers, and liabilities of a state judge who has countywide jurisdiction and is often referred to as a Superior Court judge. Superior Court is where major criminal cases are heard, and the judge who presides at these cases has the authority to control many aspects of the process, including instructing the jury, enforcing rulings against witnesses and attorneys, and, if the defendant is found guilty, imposing a sentence on him. It is important to keep in mind that the terminology we use here is not universal. There are many states that do not refer to this court as the Superior Court. Instead, the state might use terminology such as District Court, Court of Pleas, State Court, or some other designation. We will stick with Superior Court for the sake of clarity.

The Superior Court judge has many duties. The judge may hear bail requests, preside at probation revocation hearings, preside at hearings where motions are argued by both the state and the defense, and preside at a jury trial. During a jury trial, the judge instructs the jury what they must do. It is very common for a judge to instruct a jury, prior to hearing evidence in the case, that the jurors are not permitted to investigate the case on their own. They are not permitted to go to the crime scene, question witnesses on their own, or do their own research into the case. The jurors must base their verdict on the evidence that is presented during the trial.

At the conclusion of a jury trial, the judge issues instructions to the jury. These instructions guide the jury in their deliberations and also inform the jury about the law that applies in the case. In some states, instructions to the jury are given before closing arguments, while in other states they are given after closing arguments. Judges impose sentences in almost all criminal convictions. We will see, however, in a later chapter, that there are certain crimes for which the jury imposes sentence. Capital murder cases are the most common of these cases.

1. MAGISTRATES

Magistrates are usually referred to as judges as well. A magistrate is a court official with limited powers and duties. Magistrates may issue arrest and search warrants, preside at warrant application hearings, and even hear small claims in civil court. Magistrates play an important role in criminal law. A defendant appears before a magistrate at the **initial appearance** (Chapter 4). The initial appearance is known by different names in different states. For example, instead of using the phrase *initial appearance*, some states will use the term *presentment* or *arraignment*. During this hearing, magistrates inform defendants of their Miranda rights, confirm that the defendant is who the police claim she is, and give the defendant the right to contact an attorney. If the defendant cannot afford an attorney, the judge may appoint an attorney at this hearing.

Initial appearance
A court hearing held shortly after a defendant's arrest, during which the judge advises the defendant of her constitutional rights and appoints an attorney to represent the defendant if the defendant is unable to afford one.

PROFILING THE PROFESSIONAL

Initial (First) Appearance Hearing

"The first appearance hearing is similar to an arraignment in that it is the first opportunity for the defendant to be apprised with what he's actually charged with. If he doesn't have an understanding of that, he gets a copy of the charges against. He gets an opportunity to hear from the judge directly exactly what charges are preferred against him. Then we discuss whether or not he has a bond and what the bond amount is. One of the really key things that gets handled at the first appearance hearing is the question of the defendant's representation. Is it his intention to hire an attorney? Has he already hired an attorney? Are they going to be requesting an attorney to represent them? If it's that last request, then the magistrate must assess the defendant's financial situation to decide whether or not they are entitled to appointed counsel. The main piece of paper that you get from the defendant would be the financial affidavit where an inmate fills out information about their work, current work, work history, and whether or not they have any assets. Are they supporting other people besides themselves? Do they have other sources of income besides their employment? The judge makes assessment based on that information, which is communicated under oath whether or not they qualify for an appointed attorney. If they do, then the judge would make a decision about what attorney to represent that person for that particular case. The rest of what happens at the first appearance hearing is more about communication. They are not only apprised of their charges and their bond amount but also about their rights under the law, such as the right to remain silent, the right to ask for an attorney, the right to have a preliminary hearing."

Hon. George Hutchinson, Magistrate Judge

Magistrates are also responsible for issuing warrants. A police officer appears before a magistrate and presents evidence to establish that there is probable cause to believe that the defendant committed the crime alleged. We will discuss warrants in much greater detail in Chapter 4. The law requires that a magistrate must be neutral and detached. This means that the magistrate can have no vested interest in the outcome of the case, nor any prejudice or bias against the defendant. A magistrate is required to look at the case solely based on the facts and not on any feelings she may have toward the person suspected of the crime.

2. JUSTICE OF THE PEACE

Magistrates are often confused with a much older position: justice of the peace. Justices of the peace have existed for centuries and often served as multipurpose judges, especially when the legal system was less structured than it is today. A justice of the peace often presides at small claims court, is authorized to marry individuals at the courthouse, and may be permitted to issue arrest or search warrants. When it comes to justices of the peace, there is some confusion about whether they are actually judges. In some states, for example, a justice of the peace is not required to have any legal training or to be a member of the state bar. Proceedings before a justice of the peace may or may not be courts of record. The significance of a "court of record" is that a party may appeal from such a court, while such rights are not available when the hearing is not held in a court of record. Many states have abolished the position of justice of the peace or merged the duties of this position with those of magistrate. The office of justice of the peace came under close scrutiny in the 1960s, when several different U.S. Supreme Court decisions concluded that the justice of the peace system was unconstitutional when justices of the peace were paid by the number of cases that they heard or the number of search warrants that they issued. In either situation, justices of the peace had an inherent conflict of interest and could hardly be seen as impartial when they encouraged people to litigate or were paid for issuing search warrants and arrest warrants but were not paid if they refused to issue such warrants.

D. JUDICIAL ETHICS

The position of judge carries with it tremendous power and also a great deal of responsibility. Judges have been held in high esteem in our country since its founding (see Figure 2-1). Most judges strive to be fair, work hard at remaining unbiased (a very difficult thing to do), and devote themselves to what they believe is in the best interest of the community. They are well paid and enjoy great respect in the community. These perquisites often encourage attorneys to seek appointment or election as a judge.

Judges are bound by their own code of ethics. When a complaint is made against a judge, a special ethics panel convenes to investigate the judge's actions to determine if any breach of that ethical code has occurred. A judge is not allowed to have a financial or other personal interest in the outcome of any case that he

FIGURE 2-1

Judicial Positions

The term *judge* can apply to any of the following judicial positions:

- **The official who presides at hearings in the Superior Court, State Court, or District Court, where trials are conducted and jurors are empanelled**
- **The official who presides at small claims court**
- **The official who presides at traffic court**
- **The official who issues arrest and search warrants in Magistrate Court**
- **Justices of the peace**

hears and is therefore barred from taking the bench in any case where he would have a financial stake in the outcome. A judge is not permitted to speak with witnesses prior to the trial and seek their input about the guilt or innocence of the accused. Judges are prohibited from offering their own opinions about the defendant's guilt to the jury. Judges are required to be neutral in their rulings and may be disqualified for showing favoritism to one side in a case over the other. A judge has the power of contempt (discussed in a later chapter) to enforce her rulings and to maintain control of the courtroom. Contempt powers give the judge the right to put an unruly person in jail for a short period and/or fine him.

1. CIVIL IMMUNITY FOR JUDGES

Judges are exempt from civil and criminal liability for the decisions that they make in good faith in their position. This means that if a judge makes a ruling that a party does not like, the party is prevented from bringing suit against the judge to force the judge to change his mind. In some instances, a judge is even immune from arrest, but this right is limited only to pending judicial affairs. Judges have no greater immunity from civil suit than anyone else when they are not acting in their judicial capacity. Judges may be disciplined by a judicial ethics board if they engage in unethical practices or for "conduct unbecoming a member of the judiciary."[4]

EXAMPLE

Judge Smith is campaigning for reelection. Part of her campaign platform stresses the fact that she is closely allied with local police departments and police officers and that they work together to bring justice to the county. Is Judge Smith's election campaign platform conduct that is "unbecoming a member of the judicial branch"?

Answer: Yes. When a judge stresses in her campaign that she is an ally of the police, clearly giving the impression that she is not impartial when it comes to criminal matters, she is giving the impression that she will not be fair to defendants. Such a stance justifies sanctioning the judge.[5]

[4] *In re Kinsey*, 842 So.2d 77 (Fla. 2003), cert. denied, 540 U.S. 825, 124 S. Ct. 180, 157 L. Ed. 2d 47 (2003).
[5] *Id.*

2. RESTRICTIONS ON JUDGES

Along with the prestige and advantages of being a judge, there are some important limitations. Even where a statute does not prohibit a judge from practicing law, local rules and tradition may do so. When an attorney accepts the position of judge, he terminates any existing attorney-client relationships. Judges must be careful about clubs or associations to which they belong. For instance, a judge should not be a member of a board of directors of a local corporation, serve on banking committees, or engage in any business enterprise that could cause a potential conflict. Judges are also prevented from engaging in political activity, such as openly supporting one candidate for governor over another, one candidate for mayor over another, and so on. They cannot openly campaign for a candidate. If this seems like a restriction on a judge's First Amendment right of freedom of speech, courts have long decided that these limitations are important and have ruled against judges who have attempted to challenge them on constitutional grounds.[6] The ethical standard for a judge is that she must avoid even the appearance of impropriety. Even if there is nothing technically wrong with a certain business transaction, a judge would be well advised to avoid it simply because it may look wrong. Judges must serve the public interest, and that involves a certain amount of personal sacrifice.[7]

EXAMPLE

Judge Jones is planning on attending a foreclosure auction this Saturday for a piece of property that he would very much like to buy. The judge knows a lot about this property because the property owner sued the bank and Judge Jones was the presiding judge at the trial. It was his ruling, in favor of the bank, that allowed the foreclosure auction to take place. Should the judge bid at the foreclosure sale?

Answer: No. Although the matter of the foreclosure is legally concluded, it simply looks suspicious when the judge who ruled on the case is now bidding on the property. Having the judge who presided at the case be the successful bidder in the foreclosure auction certainly presents an appearance of impropriety, and that is enough to make it an ethical violation.

III PROSECUTOR

A prosecutor is the representative of the government. He must be a member of the state bar, meaning that the prosecutor is a fully licensed attorney. Like all lawyers, prosecutors attend three years of law school. A young attorney enters a prosecutor's office knowing full well that the pay will never be as high as for the attorneys in private practice earn. What attracts them? Why do so many seek such

[6] *Babineaux v. Judiciary Commission*, 341 So.2d 396 (La. 1976).
[7] *In re Allen*, 998 So.2d 557 (Fla. 2008).

employment? Primarily, they are drawn to it out of a sense of adventure, by a desire to become a trial attorney, by the prospect of gaining valuable experience that they can use in private practice, or by a genuine wish to serve their communities. They often put the lie to the statement that all attorneys want to get rich. No one ever gets rich working as a prosecutor. Some see the job simply as a stepping-stone to a much better-paying job at a private firm. They see their tenure as a prosecutor as a way of improving their trial skills and thus make themselves more marketable for a job in a private firm. Some see the life of a prosecutor as a step toward becoming a judge. Many prosecutors do what they do because they love it. They enjoy the excitement and thrill of trying cases and pitting themselves against other attorneys. They enjoy having to think on their feet and the mental gymnastics that any trial attorney must master.

Besides acting as the representative of the government in all prosecutions, prosecutors also act as legal advisors to the police. On the state and federal level, the prosecutor may spearhead a grand jury investigation or conduct preliminary hearings, both of which are discussed in detail in later chapters. Prosecutors usually draft the charging documents relied upon by the grand jury in their deliberations and present the evidence at trial to prove that a defendant is guilty.

Charging decision
The decision made by a prosecutor concerning the crimes that the defendant will be charged with.

One of the main functions of a prosecutor is to decide what crime to charge the defendant with. This **charging decision** can have profound implications for the person accused. For instance, if the prosecutor decides to charge the defendant with a felony, then she is facing a crime that is punishable by more than a year in custody. Some felonies carry maximum sentences of 10 or even 20 years, while others carry life sentences.

Charging decisions are not always as clear-cut as you might think. They require detailed investigation of the crime to make certain that the correct charges are filed and that a case can actually be made. For example, a recent hazing incident involving several high school basketball players in Hendricks County, Indiana, had locals sitting on the edges of their seats, awaiting multiple felony charges against the boys. The possible charges included battery, criminal confinement, and criminal deviate conduct. Much to everyone's surprise, the basketball players were ultimately charged only with misdemeanor battery and criminal recklessness. The prosecutor said that the reluctance of witnesses to come forward played a large role in his decision.

A prosecutor's charging decision is reflected in the documents filed by the prosecutor accusing the defendant of the crime. In the next section, we will explore the different types of charging documents that a prosecutor can rely upon.

Indictment
A charging document that charges a defendant with a felony.

Information
A charging document that charges a defendant with a misdemeanor

Charging documents refer to the actual papers that are filed with the clerk's office and that will later be served on the defendant and presented to the judge prior to the defendant's trial. The jury will review these documents during their deliberations and will usually write their verdict on these papers. On the federal level, there are two options: **indictment** or **information**. An indictment charges a defendant with a felony. An information, on the other hand, charges a defendant with a misdemeanor. An indictment must be presented to a grand jury, which must approve the charge before the prosecution can continue. There is no such requirement for an information. On the state level, most states use the same terminology, at least for felonies. States also file an indictment charging a defendant with a felony. When it comes to misdemeanors, there is greater variation among the states. Some states use the same terminology used on the federal level, filing an information to accuse someone of a misdemeanor. However, in many states, prosecutors file an **accusation**, which serves the same function as an information does on the federal level. In either the indictment or the accusation, the prosecutor must allege sufficient facts to put the defendant on notice of what crime she is charged with, including the facts of the crime, the date of the crime, and the location. The prosecutor must also be able to prove beyond a reasonable doubt the relevant facts in the charging documents.

Accusation
A charging document that charges a defendant with a misdemeanor—used only on the state level, not the federal level.

A. BECOMING A PROSECUTOR

Every state, as well as the federal court system, has the position of prosecuting attorney. However, not all states use the same terminology to refer to this individual. In many states, the prosecutor based at the county level is referred to as the *district attorney*. However, a prosecutor may also be referred to as a *county attorney*, *state's attorney*, *public prosecutor*, etc. (The position of county attorney is usually reserved for a separate office that advises county government and does not actually prosecute cases, but there are jurisdictions that refer to the prosecutor as the *county attorney*.) On the federal level, there are several different prosecution positions, including the U.S. attorney general, U.S. attorneys, and assistant U.S. attorneys, and many others. There are also many different law enforcement agencies interacting with all of these prosecution offices.

Because we already have police officers, one might wonder why we need prosecuting attorneys at all. The answer is very simple. Police are trained to investigate and arrest suspects, but they do not have the legal training necessary to ensure that a defendant's constitutional rights are protected while at the same time enforcing the laws of the state, arguing cases before a judge, handling appeals, and the myriad other activities that prosecutors engage in every day. Another basic question often arises when we talk about prosecutors. What branch of the government do prosecutors fall within? Although there may be an understandable tendency to think of them as agents of the judicial branch, they are not. Prosecutors operate independently of the judicial branch. They are entitled to decide which cases they are going to bring, how they will bring them, even whether or not to dismiss the case, and all without the intervention of the judicial branch. This makes prosecutors representatives of the executive branch.

In this section, we will first examine the position of federal prosecutors and then state-level prosecutors. We will see that on the state level, there are many variations. There are some states in which the office of prosecutor is statewide. There are also some jurisdictions in which the prosecutor is based in a municipality and has jurisdiction to hear cases only within the town limits. For the sake of clarity, when we come to state prosecutors, we will refer to them as district attorneys (or DAs, for short) keeping in mind that this terminology is by no means universal.

Officer of the court
A person, such as a prosecutor, judge, bailiff, defense attorney, or clerk, who has an ethical and legal obligation to promote justice, to tell the truth, and to help avoid perpetrating any fraud upon the court.

Prosecutors, whether on the federal or state level, are officers of the court. An **officer of the court** is a person who is required to show honesty and fair dealing to the judge and to the court system. An officer of the court is not permitted to lie or engage in illegal activity to further his case. They cannot knowingly commit fraud on the court or engage in deceit. Interestingly enough, defense attorneys are also officers of the court and have the same restrictions placed on them. This may run counter to the impression given by fictional TV attorneys who apparently have never heard the phrase "officer of the court."

1. CIVIL IMMUNITY FOR PROSECUTORS

Like judges, prosecutors are also immune from civil suit when they are acting within the scope of their responsibilities. Criminal defendants are prevented from suing prosecutors for the actions that they take in criminal cases, as long as these actions fall within the normal duties and responsibilities of the office. A prosecutor who violates ethical and legal rules is no longer protected by civil immunity. The principle behind civil immunity for prosecutors, like that of judges, is to ensure the efficiency of the court system. A prosecutor who faces the prospect of being sued for bringing a criminal action might be less inclined to do so, and that would have ramifications for society as a whole. However, just as we saw with judges, prosecutors who violate the law may be disbarred and disciplined by the state bar, including disbarment from the practice of law.

2. WHO CAN BECOME A PROSECUTOR?

Federal and state laws govern who may or may not be qualified to become a prosecutor. In general, anyone convicted of a felony cannot hold the office. All federal prosecutors and most state prosecutors must be members of a state bar. U.S. attorneys are required, in almost all cases, to live inside the circuit where they prosecute, and most district attorneys are bound by the same restriction.

B. ROLE IN THE PROCEEDINGS

Prosecutors do not represent victims of crimes. Instead, prosecutors represent the people. A prosecutor's client is the government. When it comes to criminal matters, prosecutors may offer counseling and other victim-related services, but in the end, they neither represent nor are controlled by victims. A prosecutor may make a decision to dismiss a case over the victim's objections. The opposite is also true. In domestic violence cases, for example, victims often wish to dismiss cases against their abusers. Many prosecutors refuse to do so. The case is not the victim's to dismiss; it is now in the province of the prosecutor who represents the interests of the government, not just the person who brought the initial charge.

Prosecutors also conduct trials against defendants. It is the prosecutor who gives an opening statement to the jury that outlines the facts of the prosecution's case, and it is a prosecutor who calls witnesses to the stand to prove beyond a reasonable doubt that the defendant is guilty of the crime charged. At the end of the trial, the prosecutor will give a closing argument to the jury, summarizing the case against the jury and asking the jury to find the defendant guilty on all counts.

There are many duties associated with prosecution. Prosecutors are responsible for bringing criminal charges, either based on the initial arrest by police officers or by special presentment of the grand jury. Prosecutors are not allowed to arrest individuals on their own. Instead, they must rely on the police to make arrests or on warrants issued by magistrates. Once a case reaches the prosecutor's office, the assistant assigned to the prosecution has nearly complete liberty in deciding what charges will be brought against the individual, even if these charges conflict with the original charge issued by a police officer. In addition to making a charging decision, the prosecutor also has the power to dismiss pending criminal charges. The prosecutor may dismiss a case over the objection of both the victims and the police officers involved. However, this is rare. Prosecution offices try to be sensitive to the needs of victims, and they must work closely with the police. Those relationships would be severely damaged by a prosecutor who continually dismisses cases.

When a prosecutor decides to dismiss a case, he or she will enter a **nolle prosequi**. This is a prosecutor's official declaration that she will not proceed with criminal charges against the defendant. The prosecutor's decision is independent of the judge's desires in the case. In a situation in which the judge wishes the prosecutor to proceed with the case and the prosecutor does not, the prosecutor's decision will stand. However, the rules are different once the trial has actually begun. Then, the case is fully within the judge's scope, and all rulings in the case are handled by the judge and not by the prosecutor.

Nolle prosequi
(Latin) Will not prosecute. An entry into the official record of the prosecutor's intention to dismiss a case and refuse to carry through with the prosecution of a particular individual in a pending case.

Prosecutors are also permitted to carry out additional investigations, above and beyond the initial investigation completed by the police. There is a common misconception about the relationship between police officers and prosecutors. Prosecutors are not the superiors or supervisors of police officers. Prosecutors do not have any direct say in how the police conduct their investigations and certainly have no power to hire police officers they like and fire those they do not like. The same holds true for police officers and their relationship to prosecutors. However, having said this, police and prosecutors tend to work very closely with one another and often build strong relationships. After conducting their own investigation, prosecutors may decide to bring additional charges against the defendant, as long as the evidence in the case supports these additional charges.

As we have already seen, prosecutors prepare the charging documents against the defendant. Once the decision to charge has been made, prosecutors are also responsible for scheduling court dates, often working in close collaboration with judges and the clerk's office to decide when a particular case will be heard. The clerk's office (or in some areas, the prosecutor's office) will prepare a list of the cases pending, referred to as a **calendar** or a **docket**.

Calendar/docket
A list of pending cases before a particular court.

1. JURISDICTIONAL LIMITS ON PROSECUTORS

Although we will discuss the important differences between federal and state prosecutors in a later section, it is important to note that all prosecutors have limitations on their powers. In most jurisdictions, the power of the district attorney falls within the county boundaries. The local district attorney has no power to bring criminal charges outside the county. However, as we have said, some states assign prosecutors on a statewide basis, and those prosecutors would have the power to bring a charge in any county. On the federal level, U.S. attorneys are assigned to specific circuits and are not authorized to initiate investigations or make decisions in cases pending in another circuit.

On the state level, the district attorney has the additional duty of being the legal advisor to the police. This is a limited duty. The district attorney is authorized to advise the police department on matters concerning valid searches and seizures, arrests, or other legal issues that arise in the course of a criminal prosecution. However, no one in the district attorney's office is authorized to offer legal advice to police officers on civil matters. A police officer who is being sued cannot rely on the legal services of the district attorney's office. Instead, that officer will have to hire a private attorney just as any other individual would.

C. PROSECUTORIAL ETHICS

A prosecutor's ethical duty is to seek justice, not convictions. In fact, most prosecutors, whether on the state or federal level, take an oath attesting to that principle. Prosecutors are not paid based on the number of people that they convict. They are paid to find and prosecute those who commit crimes and to try to bring justice in every case to which they are assigned.

In most states and on the federal level, prosecutors are prohibited from practicing law, such as handling civil cases or representing individuals charged with crimes. The reason is simple: There are simply too many possible conflicts of interest that can arise. Remember that we are again generalizing here. There are jurisdictions that do allow part-time prosecutors to practice civil law, just as there are jurisdictions that allow part-time judges to engage in the same practices. However, our discussion is focused on full-time state and federal prosecutors.

Prosecutors are bound by a strict code of ethics. They cannot, for example, prosecute a person they know is innocent simply to enhance their reputations. They cannot lie or trick a defendant into pleading guilty. In fact, during sentencing, as we will see in Chapter 10, a defendant is often questioned, on the record, about his understanding of the consequences of pleading guilty and must state that he is doing so voluntarily. Prosecutors can be sanctioned by the state bar if they engage in unethical practices, and they can also be charged with crimes for tampering with evidence or encouraging witnesses to commit perjury.

D. STATE AND FEDERAL PROSECUTORS

We have already seen that there are federal prosecutors who file charges based on federal law and prosecute these cases in federal courts scattered across the United States. There are also local prosecutors, often referred to as district attorneys. What is the relationship, if any, between these two offices? Who controls them? How are they organized? We will begin our discussion with the federal court system and the top law enforcement officer in the United States: the U.S. attorney general.

1. U.S. ATTORNEY GENERAL

The U.S. attorney general is the head of the Department of Justice and has authority over all of its employees and divisions. The attorney general has supervisory powers over the solicitor general and all U.S. attorneys. The attorney general is also a member of the president's cabinet and is actually in the line of succession should the president be assassinated or otherwise die in office, following seventh in line after the secretary of defense (see Figure 2-2).

The U.S. attorney general is authorized to give her advice about legal matters to the president; however, the attorney general is not burdened with the duty of advising Congress about legal matters.[8] The opinions of the U.S. attorney general are published annually and are available both online and in print volumes. The attorney general also has supervisory power over the FBI and other federal law enforcement agencies.

> **Sidebar**
>
> *If the person who was originally assigned as a U.S. attorney is replaced, the new individual serves out the balance of the original person's four-year period.*

Although it is the responsibility of the president to appoint U.S. attorneys, who must then be confirmed by the Senate, the U.S. attorney general may appoint an interim U.S. attorney when a vacancy in a particular office occurs. 28 U.S.C.A. §546(c). In some situations, the U.S. attorney general has the power to appoint an independent counsel or special prosecutor when allegations against high-ranking government officials have been raised. In recent years, independent counsels have been appointed to look into a wide variety of situations, from financial dealings to sex scandals. Undoubtedly the most widely known such investigation was Independent Counsel Kenneth Starr's inquiry into President Bill Clinton's relationships with Monica Lewinsky and Paula Jones, which led to Clinton's impeachment on charges of perjury and obstruction of justice.

The independent counsel reports not only to the attorney general but also to Congress. (The original designation of this position was *special prosecutor*, but it was changed to *independent counsel* by special legislation in 1983.)

FIGURE 2-2

Order of Succession After a Presidential Death

1. **Vice president**
2. **Speaker of the House**
3. **President pro tem of the Senate**
4. **Secretary of state**
5. **Secretary of the treasury**
6. **Secretary of defense**
7. **U.S. attorney general**

[8] *U.S. v. San Jacinto Tin Co.*, 125 U.S. 273, 8 S. Ct. 850, 31 L. Ed. 747 (1888).

2. U.S. ATTORNEYS

Sidebar

Individual citizens lack the power to prosecute federal crimes. However, they are free to report crimes to federal authorities, who may or may not initiate an investigation.[10]

U.S. attorneys are the prosecutors on the federal level. Unlike the attorney general, U.S. attorneys do not give legal advice to the president. Instead, they prosecute people who have committed federal crimes (see Figure 2-3). U.S. attorneys serve for four-year terms. They are appointed by the president and not only serve but reside in the district to which they have been assigned. Their appointment can be terminated for any reason. They serve at the pleasure of the president, and if the president decides that he no longer desires the services of a particular U.S. attorney, that person is fired.[9]

Several years ago, during the George W. Bush administration, there was controversy about the removal of several U.S. attorneys by the president. There were some allegations that these federal prosecutors were removed for political reasons. Whatever a person might say about that decision—and a great deal has been said—there is no question that the president has the power to remove U.S. attorneys anytime he wishes, without having to give a reason. Although there are 94 federal districts around the United States, there are only 93 U.S. attorneys, because one U.S. attorney handles both Guam and the North Mariana Islands.

U.S. attorneys and assistant U.S. attorneys are responsible for enforcing federal law by prosecuting individuals who have broken it (see Figure 2-4). Unlike state prosecutors, they may also bring and defend civil cases filed against the federal government. Like state prosecutors, federal prosecutors are barred from appearing as witnesses in a case in which they are also assigned as the lead prosecutor. This rule is frequently broken by fictional television and movie prosecutors.

Sidebar

Although all courts have found that it would be appropriate to disqualify a U.S. attorney from prosecuting a person that she once represented as a private client, there are few other grounds that would justify the disqualification of a U.S. attorney from acting as the prosecutor in a particular case.[11]

3. STATE ATTORNEYS GENERAL

State attorneys general are the chief law enforcement officers of the state, and they are the head of the state's legal department.[12] Attorneys general also advise their governors about legal matters and are authorized to issue legal opinions about the impact of a particular statute on state employees or state practices. In fact, the opinions of the state attorney general are often published annually and are available to the public. Of course, the opinion of the state attorney general is advisory only. The definitive ruling on a statute is always left to the court system

The relationship between state attorney general and state prosecutors is different from that found on the federal level between the U.S. attorney general and U.S. attorneys. On the federal level, the U.S. attorney general acts as the supervisor of all U.S. attorneys. This means that the U.S. attorney general has the power to recommend dismissal of U.S. attorneys and otherwise regulate their behavior. The same is not true of state-based attorneys general. On the

---

[9] 28 U.S.C.A. §541(c). Assistant U.S. attorneys can be removed by the attorney general. 28 U.S.C.A. §543(b)

[10] *Martinez v. Ensor*, 958 F. Supp. 515 (D. Colo. 1997); *People of State of N.Y. v. Muka*, 440 F. Supp. 33 (N.D. N.Y. 1977).

[11] *U.S. v. Caggiano*, 660 F.2d 184 (6th Cir. 1981).

[12] *State v. Hagerty*, 1998 ND 122, 580 N.W.2d 139 (N.D. 1998).

- **Prosecution of violations of federal criminal law**
- **Prosecution and defense of civil actions**
- **Actions for the collection of fines, penalties, and forfeitures for violation of the internal revenue laws**

FIGURE 2-3

The Duties of the U.S. Attorney

state level, the state attorney general is responsible for representing the state government in lawsuits and providing legal advice to the executive branch. The state attorney general has no authority over individual district attorneys within the state. The state attorney general, for example, is not permitted to fire a local district attorney. Instead, that duty falls to the voters, who may vote out the sitting DA. Obviously, a DA can be removed for committing crimes or for other unethical behaviors, but the state attorney general does not have sole discretion in those matters.

Sidebar

Most state attorneys general are elected positions, usually with four-year terms.

4. DISTRICT ATTORNEY

The district attorney, in most jurisdictions, is an elected position. The DA usually serves a four-year term and often hires assistants to handle the day-to-day business of being a prosecutor. It is rare, in large metropolitan areas, for the elected DA to try many cases. Instead, he is busy with budgets, committees, and the plethora of other duties of an elected official.

The real work of the district attorney's office is handled by the assistants. Assistant district attorneys are hired by the DA and serve at her pleasure, meaning that they can be fired at any time, for any legal reason. Assistant district attorneys attend preliminary hearings, negotiate bail with defense attorneys, and make charging decisions in cases in almost exactly the same way that a federal prosecutor might work. Assistant district attorneys file indictments for felonies and accusations (or

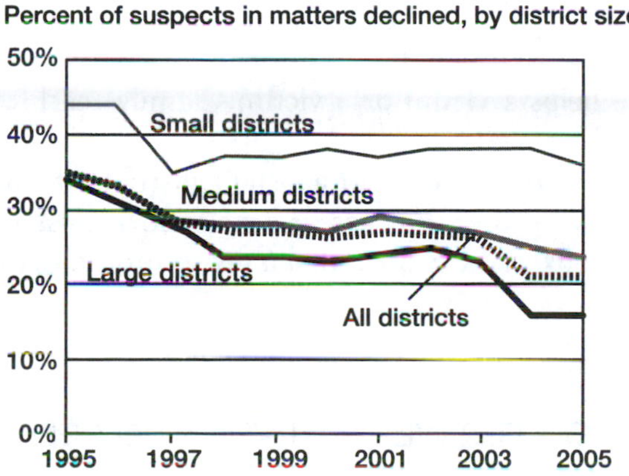

Source: Federal Justice Statistics, 2005, September 2008, NCJ 220383, Bureau of Justice Statistics, U.S. Department of Justice.

FIGURE 2-4

Percentage of Matters Declined by U.S. Attorneys

informations) against those accused of misdemeanors. In some states, prosecution is divided into two offices: solicitors and district attorneys. In those areas, the solicitor's office handles all misdemeanors, while the district attorney's office prosecutes all felonies. (This arrangement is usually seen in large metropolitan areas and not in rural areas, where the tax base could not afford two separate prosecution offices.) Assistant district attorneys offer plea bargains to defense attorneys, who then relay them to the defendant. We will talk in much greater detail about plea bargains in a later chapter, but a word about them here is also important. The essence of a plea bargain is that the state is making an offer to the defendant in exchange for something else. The offer is usually a reduced sentence, less than what the defendant might normally receive at the end of a jury trial. In exchange for that offer, the defendant agrees to plead guilty and waive her right to a jury trial and an appeal. Plea bargains are contracts and have almost all of the elements of a contract. Once made, they can be enforced by the defendant against the state. On the other hand, the contract is a bit lopsided. If a defendant decides, at the last minute, not to go through with the deal, then she is free to back out and have the jury trial after all. In that way, plea bargains are not like contracts.

Assistant district attorneys conduct jury trials and bench trials, argue motions, and carry out many other activities. Viewers of such TV shows as *Law & Order* might be surprised to learn that assistant district attorneys rarely go to crime scenes, and do not collect evidence or routinely attend autopsies. The simple reason is that they have far too many other duties of their own to complete, and they are not trained in evidence collection and do not have sufficient medical training to make viewing an autopsy anything more than a morbid experience.

The job of a prosecutor is stressful. In many places, attorneys who are fresh out of law school take jobs as assistant district attorneys, more for the experience that it gives them than for the pay. Assistant district attorneys are paid far less than their counterparts who work for large private law firms. Some attorneys work for the district attorney's office because they want the extensive trial experience that they can acquire, and then they plan to move on to much more lucrative positions in private practice. However, many assistant district attorneys remain at the job until they retire. They endure the low salaries, the stress, and the long hours because they have a strong commitment to their communities, and being a prosecutor is a very satisfying profession. An assistant district attorney can have a real sense of accomplishment when he helps a victim or a victim's family reach closure on a truly horrible chapter in their lives.

We will discuss the other duties of assistant district attorneys in Chapter 5, when we examine how a prosecution case is developed against a defendant, and in Chapter 7, when we look at the process that a prosecutor goes through to prepare for trial.

5. COORDINATION BETWEEN STATE AND FEDERAL AUTHORITIES

With all these federal and state prosecutors and their respective law enforcement agencies working toward the same goal–that is, catching criminals—one might expect a great deal of collaboration and cooperation between federal and state levels. However, the opposite is often true. Although there are occasional taskforces that combine local and federal law enforcement officials and prosecutors, it is far more common to find that the agencies do not cooperate with one another. The reasons for this are several. For one, federal law enforcement officials work on a much broader scale than local law enforcement. For another, there is a certain amount of jealousy among the various agencies. Federal officials rarely share information with local officials, and vice versa. After the terrible events of September 11, 2001, cooperation between the various agencies improved dramatically, but there is still a great deal of work to be done.

DEFENSE ATTORNEY

Criminal defense attorneys represent the people charged with criminal violations. They are the flip side of the coin from prosecutors (see Figure 2-5). They are often drawn to the life for the same reasons that prosecutors are drawn to it. Despite the fact that Hollywood often portrays them in a negative light, most defense attorneys are ethical, honest, and trustworthy people. They work very hard for clients who frequently do not appreciate them—and even more often do not pay them. They pit their meager resources against the investigative power of the state. They fulfill a crucial role in our legal system: safeguarding the rights of the accused. For their efforts, they are often castigated in the press and asked, "How can you defend those people?" Their answer is frequently that if they did not, who would?

An attorney is first and foremost an agent for the client. The attorney represents the client and works for the best interests of the client. Before we can discuss the details and responsibilities that arise from this relationship, we must address a basic issue: When is the attorney-client relationship established? Courts have weighed in on this issue for decades. The circumstances that determine when an attorney-client relationship is created are fairly simple:

- A person seeks legal advice from an attorney.
- The attorney is competent to give advice on the topic.
- The attorney gives legal advice.

FIGURE 2-5

Profiling Lawyers

- About 26 percent of lawyers are self-employed, either as partners in law firms or in solo practices.
- Formal requirements to become a lawyer usually include attaining a four-year college degree, completing three years of law school, and passing a written bar examination; however, some requirements may vary by state.
- Competition for admission to most law schools is intense.
- Competition for job opening should be keen because of the large number of students graduating from law school each year.

Source: Bureau of Labor Statistics, *Occupational Outlook Handbook*, 2010–11 Edition. Lawyers.

You will notice that there is nothing in the previous list about the payment of a retainer or any type of payment at all. The attorney-client relationship does not depend on whether the client actually pays the attorney money. The relationship is established when all three of the elements set out above are met.[13]

There is no requirement of a formal contract between the attorney and client to create a professional relationship. Obviously, a written contract is extremely helpful in figuring out the limitations of the attorney's authority, but attorneys take on clients every day in the United States without any written contract at all. In order for the courts to determine if an attorney-client relationship was created, they do not look for written contracts or the payment of fees. Instead, the courts look to the three steps outlined above and the surrounding circumstances. Did the client have a reasonable belief that the attorney represented her? If the answer to that question is yes, and the other three elements are met, a court will most likely determine that an attorney represents a client whether the attorney agrees to that ruling or not (see Figure 2-6).

In most cases, attorneys are acutely aware of having established an attorney-client relationship, but sometimes it is not so clear. In a California case, an attorney made a court appearance as a courtesy to the attorney of record even though he had never met the client. When the client sued the attorney of record, she also sued the attorney who made the court appearance. On appeal, the court determined that an attorney-client relationship could exist without benefit of the attorney having direct dealings with the client.[14]

Fiduciary
A relationship in which one person is obliged to act in a trustworthy and honest relationship to another person. The fiduciary has the responsibility to act in the best interests of the other.

When an attorney represents a client, the attorney becomes the client's **fiduciary**. A fiduciary responsibility requires the attorney to exercise good judgment, maintain confidentiality, and demonstrate that she is seeking the best interests of the client. An attorney is required to zealously represent the interests of the client. This is a high standard and means that the attorney must do everything legal and ethical to ensure a good result for the client. In criminal law, you might expect that the best interests of the client would be served by an acquittal. However, in this text we deal with the real world. Because most trials end with a verdict for the prosecution, it may be in the best interests of the client to work out a favorable plea negotiation and plead guilty rather than take the risk of going to trial.

A. ATTORNEY-CLIENT PRIVILEGE

One of the pillars of the attorney-client relationship is confidentiality. Communications between the client and the attorney are protected under the law. In fact, we refer to the discussions between the attorney and the client as *privileged.* A privileged communication is one that remains secret. The privilege protects the client and prevents an attorney from revealing communications that he had with the client. The privilege also prevents prosecutors and judges from compelling an attorney to reveal the communications that he had with the client. The privilege is

[13] *Stone v. Bank of Commerce,* 174 U.S. 412, 19 S. Ct. 747, 43 L. Ed. 1028 (1899).
[14] *Streit v. Covington & Crowe,* No. E023862 (Cal. App. July 20, 2000).

In May 2008, the median annual wages of all wage-and-salaried lawyers were $110,590. The middle half of the occupation earned between $74,980 and $163,320. Median annual wages in the industries employing the largest numbers of lawyers in May 2008 were:

Management of companies and enterprises	$145,770
Federal Executive Branch	126,080
Legal services	116,550
Local government	82,590
State government	78,540

Salaries of experienced attorneys vary widely according to the type, size, and location of their employer. Lawyers who own their own practices usually earn less than those who are partners in law firms. Lawyers starting their own practice may need to work part time in other occupations to supplement their income until their practice is well established. Median salaries of lawyers 9 months after graduation from law school in 2007 varied by type of work, as indicated in the following table.

Median salaries, 9 months after graduation

Employer	Salary
All graduates	$68,500
Private practice	108,500
Business	69,100
Government	50,000
Academic/judicial clerkships	48,000
SOURCE: National Association of Law Placement	

Most salaried lawyers are provided health and life insurance, and contributions are made to retirement plans on their behalf. Lawyers who practice independently are covered only if they arrange and pay for such benefits themselves.

Source: Bureau of Labor Statistics, Occupational Outlook Handbook, 2010-11 Edition. Lawyers.

FIGURE 2-6

Median Annual Wages of Lawyers, 2008

so powerful that even if the client reveals that she committed a crime, the attorney is forbidden to reveal that information to anyone. The idea behind the **attorney-client privilege** is simple. In order to encourage clients to give full information to their attorneys—and to ensure the best possible legal defense—clients must have the security of knowing that nothing they say to their lawyer can be revealed later. Similar privileges protect physicians and patients, psychiatrists and patients, and communications between a person and a member of the clergy.

Attorney-client privilege
A legal protection governing the communications, both oral and written, between an attorney and her client that prevents any legal process from forcing the attorney to reveal those communications.

A judge is not only prevented from asking an attorney to reveal confidential communications, but he is actually required to protect the communication as much as possible. The theory here is that by mandating that judges protect the attorney-client relationship, the judges will help safeguard the public's attitude about the legal profession and encourage clients to be as honest with their clients as possible.

There are some limitations on the attorney-client privilege. For instance, when the client communicates her desire to commit a future crime, the privilege no longer applies and the attorney is free to contact the police to prevent the crime from occurring. In some states, a client's admission that she has engaged in sexual contact with children may also be at odds with the attorney-client privilege. Some states make it a crime to fail to report any instance of child sexual contact, so an attorney may be placed in the uncomfortable position of either revealing a client communication and violating one of the basic tenets of the attorney's ethical code or violating the law and facing prosecution.

Sidebar

Even though the attorney-client relationship means that communications are privileged, most defense attorneys realize that their clients frequently do not tell them the truth.

EXAMPLE

Ms. Carlson represents a client who has told her that he intends to commit perjury when he takes the stand in his criminal case. As we have already seen, like judges and prosecutors, defense attorneys are officers of the court. As such, they are prohibited from engaging in any unlawful or unethical behavior. Carlson does not wish to violate her ethical code, but she must safeguard the communications she has had with her client. What should she do?

Answer: Carlson's only real option is to withdraw from the case. When the judge asks her why she wishes to withdraw, she will be unable to explain her request without violating the attorney-client privilege. Therefore, she cannot give a reason for her request to withdraw. If the judge refuses the request, Carlson is now in a very difficult position. She works for the client and therefore cannot prevent him from taking the stand if he wishes to do so. Carlson can advise her client about the dangers of committing perjury and may choose not to participate in questioning her client when he takes the stand.

IV DEFENDANT

Any discussion of the various individuals involved in the criminal justice system would be meaningless without addressing the pivotal position: the defendant. Without a suspect, there would be no need for police, prosecutors, judges, or probation officers. Throughout this text the role of the defendant will be discussed. The defendant enters the criminal justice arena protected by a wide variety of constitutional and other legal rights. There is also a long history in this country of judicial decisions guaranteeing and expanding those rights. However, no system is perfect. Our system was founded on the belief that in protecting the rights of a criminal defendant, the law protects us all. By ensuring that a person charged with a crime is provided with basic legal protections, no one could use the law to gain complete power over the citizenry, as has been done in many other countries.

As we explore the various safeguards established to protect a suspect, there will also be some attention to famous errors. The history of our country has been highlighted by both great legal battles and tremendous miscarriages of justice. Later, we will discuss the famous *Gideon* case, in which the U.S. Supreme Court ruled that a suspect charged with a felony must be provided with competent counsel. In other chapters, we will discuss the more infamous cases of the "Scottsboro boys" and others, which illustrate how a system can go wrong. Throughout our system, it is the defendant who keeps it going. The entire edifice would crumble overnight without a suspect to pursue. This causes an interdependence of police, criminal defense attorneys, prosecutors, and defendants. In the everyday world of prosecution, it is not unusual to see this relationship in action. Most people would be surprised at the often-cordial dealings between prosecutors, police, defense attorneys, and defendants. Essentially, this entire book is about the rights of defendants in criminal proceedings. We will introduce the concept of the criminal defendant here and then spend the entirety of the text addressing the rights that a criminal defendant has in the American criminal justice system. However, before we get into that level of detail, we must first address this basic question: Who is a defendant?

A **defendant** is a person who has been charged with a crime. A **suspect** is a person who has not been arrested but is a person who the police believe may have committed a crime. The distinction is very important; many constitutional rights do not trigger until a person becomes a defendant. A suspect, for example, may not have the right to counsel. A suspect certainly has no right to a trial by jury or the right to confront witnesses against him. The defendant, on the other hand, enjoys all of these rights and more. A person may become a defendant in a wide variety of ways. A person may be arrested by a police officer while that person is in the commission of a crime. A person may be arrested after an arrest warrant has been issued by a magistrate. A person may be arrested after the police collect statements from other witnesses who saw the suspect commit the crime. The suspect may be arrested when forensic evidence indicates that he was present at the crime scene.

Defendant
A person charged with a crime.

Suspect
A person who police believe may have committed a crime.

Once a person becomes a defendant in a criminal case, that person enjoys many constitutional protections. In later chapters, we will examine each of these constitutional protections in depth. The burden of proof on the government, whether it is a local district attorney or a federal U.S. attorney, is the same: The government must prove beyond a reasonable doubt that the defendant is guilty.

A. JUVENILE OFFENDERS

When it comes to juveniles, many of the rules that we understand for adult offenders are radically changed. Juveniles, for example, are not arrested. They are taken into custody. They are not tried and sentenced; they are "adjudicated." Juvenile court proceedings are not open to the public. There are no juries in juvenile trials. However, there are some instances in which juveniles may be tried as adults, even though they do not meet the age requirement. In Chapter 13, we will examine juvenile court procedures in depth.

States follow different rules when it comes to classifying juveniles. For example, some states may provide that everyone under the age of 18 is a juvenile offender. Other states may use the age of 17 or even 16. In the past, trying a juvenile as an adult was a rare occurrence. However, recent high-profile cases involving underage offenders committing brutal murders and rapes has encouraged state legislatures to decrease the age limit and allow offenders as young as 13 to be tried as adults. A recent Supreme Court case has held that juvenile offenders cannot be given the death sentence.[15]

V VICTIM

At some point, we may all be victims of a crime. It may be as simple as a minor theft or as terrible as a brutal killing of a family member. Once the crime has been committed and the police have arrived, most victims have no idea what will happen next. Too often, police and prosecutors fail to notify the victim of any further developments in the case. The victim is often left with many unanswered questions: Was there an arrest? Did the defendant plead guilty? Is there a chance that my stolen merchandise might be returned? Do I have the right to restitution for the damages that the defendant caused? Can I have some say in the sentencing phase?

Prosecutors and police have, in recent years, become much better at keeping the victim in the loop of the procedural steps involved in bringing a prosecution. Some states have even gone so far as to enact a so-called Victims' Bill of Rights that requires the prosecutor to notify every victim of the disposition of the case and to alert the victim to the fact that she may give a victim impact statement during the sentencing phase of the case.

A. VICTIM IMPACT STATEMENTS

Victim impact statement
A procedure that allows the victim of a crime to address the court and the defendant and explain the trauma that the defendant's actions have caused.

Most states allow victims to give statements during the sentencing phase of the trial. **Victim impact statements** are a common method for victims to explain to the judge what impact the crime has had on both the victim and the victim's family. In previous decades, victims had few or no rights when it came to criminal cases. After all, prosecutors do not represent victims; they represent the government. This often causes confusion when victims seek advice and counsel from prosecutors only to learn that there is very little that prosecutors can do for them. Prior to the enactment of victims' rights legislation, victims had no right to address the court during the defendant's sentencing and had no right to be informed about the plea bargain offered to the defendant, let alone to have any direct input on the prosecution of the case at all. Most states have addressed these problems by passing legislation that allows victims to give statements during sentencing hearings and also to be notified when particular court dates or other events in the case are scheduled.

1. MONETARY COMPENSATION AND RESTITUTION FOR VICTIMS

In recent decades, many states have enacted statutes that provide some monetary compensation to victims of violent crimes or crimes of theft. Of course, victims

[15] *Roper v. Simmons*, 543 U.S. 551 (2005).

have always had the right to bring a civil suit against the defendant, but that is often a hollow right. The victim might easily win a civil suit and would then be unable to collect anything from a defendant who is serving a lengthy prison sentence. States have passed legislation that allows for some form of payment to victims of crimes or, if the victim has died, to the victim's survivors.[16]

In addition to payment from a victim's compensation fund, federal and state laws allow judges to order defendants convicted of crimes to pay restitution to the victims. In situations in which the defendant may owe millions of dollars, it is questionable whether the victims will ever receive the full amount of their restitution. Victims also have the right to bring a civil suit against the defendant, but as we have already discussed, the chances of recovering any money from a person who is currently serving a lengthy prison sentence is virtually zero.

a. Victim-Witness Coordinators

Many prosecution offices also maintain an office referred to as a victim-witness coordinator. This person and his staff are charged with the mission of making the process of testifying as a victim or a witness during the trial as comfortable as possible. Victim-witness facilities often include private places where witnesses can sit and relax during breaks in the trial. Inside the victim-witness facility, which is usually located in the courthouse, witnesses and victims can make phone calls, check e-mail, and engage in other activities while they wait to be called to the stand to testify. Many victim-witness coordinators also offer on-site counseling services to victims or can at least direct them to those services in the community.

VI LAW ENFORCEMENT

Police serve the obviously important role of arresting suspects. They gather evidence, confer with witnesses, and initiate almost all criminal prosecutions. In a later chapter we will spend more time discussing the role of law enforcement in collecting evidence and testifying at trial. State and federal police officers are certified or licensed by the government with the power to make arrests. Most police officers earn minimal salaries. They work long shifts at odd hours. Their lives consist of long, boring hours punctuated every so often with heart-pounding excitement. A professional basketball player makes more in a week than the average police officer makes in a year. It is a tough profession that calls for a lot of physical and mental strength. The job takes a toll on police officers and explains why most are allowed to retire after 20 years of service.

[16] *Hartway v. State Board of Control*, 69 Cal. App.3d 502, 137 Cal. Rptr. 199 (1st Dist. 1976); *Wolf v. State*, 325 So.2d 342 (La. Ct. App. 4th Cir. 1975).

A. USE OF FORCE

Police officers are often placed in a situation in which they must use force to subdue a suspect or to arrest a person. In broad terms, we can divide the use of force into two categories: nondeadly force and deadly force. Nondeadly force is force that will not result in the death or serious injury of the person being arrested. Deadly force, on the other hand, is likely to result in the suspect's death. The question in these situations is how much force are police allowed to use? The Eighth Amendment to the U.S. Constitution prohibits cruel and unusual punishment, but it has nothing to say about police officers and the amount of force they may use during arrest. On the other hand (and despite common depictions on television and in movies), state law usually provides strict and explicit guidelines for when police may use force, especially deadly force. An officer may use deadly force only when presented with deadly force. Some states allow a police officer to use deadly force to prevent a felony, such as the murder or rape of another individual, but no state allows a police officer to use deadly force to prevent the commission of a misdemeanor. A police officer who kills a suspect will come under immediate investigation to determine whether the officer's use of deadly force was warranted. Moreover, with the prevalence of YouTube, no police officer wants to risk using excessive force only to have it go viral on the Internet.

The rules governing nondeadly force are fairly simple. The officer must use reasonable force—the type of force that a prudent and cautious person in the same situation would use—to subdue a suspect. Once the suspect is subdued, the police are not allowed to use additional force, such as punching the suspect in revenge for the suspect inflicting injuries on the officer.

1. USE OF POLICE DOGS

As we will see in Chapter 3, when we discuss the issuance of search warrants, no search warrant is required when police use specially trained police dogs to sniff the air around a suspect's car or person. If the police officer has a legal reason to be where she is at the time, and the police dog alerts on suspected narcotics, the officer may seize the narcotics. Obviously, police dogs cannot be used to intimidate suspects into giving statements or consent to search. Dogs can certainly not be used to inflict injuries on suspects, unless the dog and the officers are attempting to subdue a suspect. For many suspects, the cry, "Stop where you are or I'll send in the police dog!" is usually enough to cause them to reconsider fleeing from the police or taking violent action against them.

2. POLICE BRUTALITY AND CORRUPTION

Although there are periodic reports of police officers using excessive force and engaging in corrupt activities, the vast majority of police officers operate within the boundaries of their duties and are honest and hard-working individuals.

Police officers who engage in misconduct may face internal discipline as well as potential criminal prosecution. Police officers who obtain evidence illegally for use by the prosecution may be faced with the **exclusionary rule**, which prohibits the use of the evidence at trial. Finally, a police officer who routinely engages in misconduct may be fired from his position.

Exclusionary rule
A rule imposed by the U.S. Supreme Court that prohibits evidence seized illegally from being used in the prosecution of the defendant.

Most police departments engage in random drug tests for all of their police officers, putting the lie to the almost ubiquitous scene in television and movies where a police officer dips his or her finger into a bag of a suspected controlled substance and then tastes it. Only someone not familiar with police protocol or suicidally reckless would engage in such behavior. In the first case, if that bag of white, powdery substance is cocaine, there will be no taste—cocaine would simply numb the officer's tongue. Second, some of the cocaine would get into the officer's bloodstream through the tongue, possibly causing her to fail her next drug test. Third, the officer may have contaminated important evidence. Finally, and perhaps most importantly, if the white powdery substance is poison, the officer might die.

3. LIABILITY OF POLICE OFFICERS

If a police officer engages in excessive force against an individual, the person may bring a federal lawsuit against the officer and his department. The law authorizing this action is found in Title 42 of U.S. code, section 1983, often simply referred to as a "Section 1983" suit. However, the officer's liability may not end with a federal suit. State tort laws allow victims to bring suit for false arrest, battery, use of excessive force, wrongful death, and intentional infliction of emotional distress.

B. UNDERCOVER POLICE OFFICERS

There are many situations in which a police officer may go "undercover." The use of undercover officers has been standard practice in police departments for decades. Unlike what we see on television, undercover police officers are not permitted to engage in illegal conduct. They may pose as criminals, but they are not allowed to be criminals. Most undercover assignments are short term, some as short as a day. Long-term undercover operations are rare and usually reserved for federal prosecutions who not only have the budgets to maintain such an operation but also have interstate jurisdiction.

VIII PROBATION OFFICERS

Not all defendants who are convicted of crimes go to prison. In fact, many of them serve their criminal sentence on probation or parole. Here, we are again faced with the problem of terminology. Some states refer to probation, while other states refer to parole. Strictly speaking, these two terms are not interchangeable. Parole refers to the conditions placed on a person who has been recently released from prison. Probation, on the other hand, refers to a sentence that does not involve incarceration at all. However, for purposes of explaining what probation is, we will temporarily ignore parole and save that discussion for Chapter 12. A probation officer is charged with the duty of supervising an individual who has received a criminal sentence that does not involve incarceration. Probation officers work for the state and have cases assigned to them. Probation officers supervise defendants and make sure that they are gainfully employed, commit no further crimes, and do not engage in illegal drug use. They also enforce whatever conditions the judge has imposed in a particular case. One of the most important aspects of probation is the realization that it is a privilege, not a right.

When a defendant is sentenced to a term of probation, a probation officer monitors the defendant. The defendant is no longer referred as a defendant. Instead, she is a *probationer* or *parolee*. Probation officers are usually poorly paid and overworked. They are typically despised by the probationers who are serving their sentences. The probation officer ensures that the probationer obeys the terms of the sentence. If a defendant is sentenced to community service, for example, it is the probation officer who coordinates the probationer's service and keeps a record of compliance. Probation officers may bring a petition to revoke a defendant's probation when she commits a new crime or fails to abide by the terms of his probation. The hearing is referred to as a *probation revocation* hearing. If the judge agrees with the probation officer, the judge can order the defendant to serve out the remainder of the sentence in prison. If not, the judge may leave the probationer's current conditions in place.

There are many different types of probation. Some states employ a method referred to as *shock probation*. This program is very similar to the Scared Straight program that has been used in many states. Under shock probation, an offender is sent to prison for a brief period of time and then is released on probation. The theory is that once exposed to the harsh realities of prison life, the defendant will embrace the conditions of probation that allow him to live outside the prison environment. Another variation on probation is *intensive probation*. Intensive probation programs are used across the country. The theory underlying intensive probation is that if probationers are routinely required to submit to searches of their persons and their residences, given blood tests at random intervals, and even visited at their workplaces, they will be much more likely to follow the conditions of probation. In some states, intensive probation also means that the defendant is required to wear a monitoring device that tracks either the alcohol content in the defendant's bloodstream or where the defendant moves throughout the day. The monitoring device will report if the defendant leaves a specified area.

In order to ensure that a probationer is conforming to the conditions of probation, the probation officer may be required to visit her home, often at unannounced times, to see what the probationer is up to. A defendant in such a situation is not protected by the Fourth Amendment prohibition against searches without a warrant. In fact, routine searches of the defendant's person and premises may be conducted at the discretion of the probation officer. If the officer discovers any evidence of a crime, he can seek a probation revocation hearing. In many states, probation officers do not need probable cause before they search. The only requirement is reasonable suspicion and a condition imposed by a judge that the defendant can be searched.

VIII JURIES

Once a case has been called for trial and both the prosecution and the defense attorney have announced that they are ready for trial, the next step is to bring in citizens to serve as jurors. We will discuss jury selection in much greater detail in Chapter 9, but a brief word here is also necessary. After all, jury selection is the only time that most people ever have any contact with the criminal justice system.

Before we discuss the details of jury service, it is important to emphasize some of the terminology used during the jury selection process. People who are called for jury duty often report to the courthouse with no clear idea of what they should do. They follow signs to the jury room or office and then join others, summoned for the same day, who also have no idea of what will happen next.

In criminal cases, it is not accurate to say that a jury is selected. What really happens is that a large group of citizens is brought into the jury room as part of a **panel**, or **venire**. Instead of the prosecutor or defense attorney picking which of the panel members they would like to serve on the jury, they instead eliminate, or "strike," panel members until only 12 remain. Those 12 people are then called **jurors**. The process of carrying out jury selection is called **voir dire**.

Panel/venire
A group of people who have been called for jury duty; the final jury will be selected from this group.

Jurors
Those people who have been selected to sit on a jury; they will consider the evidence and reach a verdict in the case.

Voir dire
(French) To look, to speak. The process of questioning jurors about their potential biases in the case

During the voir dire process, the various members of the panel are questioned about their life experiences, their knowledge of the case and the parties, and any other relevant issues. The attorneys then evaluate these answers to decide which members of the panel should be removed or challenged.

When we discuss the trial of a case, we will see how the jury strike procedure works in the day-to-day practice of jury trials.

As you read the following case excerpt, try to determine what error the appellee alleges the court to have committed. Also, be mindful of the rules regarding victim impact statements. At the end of the excerpt, there will be some questions for you to answer.

CASE EXCERPT

PAIGE v. STATE

277 Ga.App. 687, 627 S.E.2d 370 (2006)

Paul Howard, Jr., District Attorney, Peggy Katz, Assistant District Attorney, for Appellee.
SMITH, Presiding Judge.

Following a jury trial, Anthony Paige appeals from his convictions of aggravated assault with intent to rape, aggravated battery, aggravated assault with a deadly weapon, and aggravated assault. Paige asserts the trial court erred by: allowing improper victim impact evidence during the sentencing hearing. We find no merit in any of Paige's enumerations of error, and we affirm the judgment.

Paige claims the trial court erred by allowing "improper and emotional victim impact evidence" during the sentencing hearing in violation of OCGA §17-10-1.2. The version of this Code section in effect at the time of Paige's trial in 2002 provided, in relevant part:

> (2) In all cases other than those in which the death penalty may be imposed, prior to fixing of the sentence as provided for in Code Section 17-10-1 or the imposing of life imprisonment as mandated by law, and before rendering the appropriate sentence, including any order of restitution, the court, within its discretion, may allow evidence from the victim, the family of the victim, or such other witness having personal knowledge of the impact of the crime on the victim, the family of the victim, or community. Such evidence shall be given in the presence of the defendant and shall be subject to cross-examination.
>
> (b) In presenting such evidence, the victim, the family of the victim, or such other witness having personal knowledge of the impact of the crime on the victim, the victim's family, or the community shall, if applicable:
>
> (4) Describe any change in the victim's personal welfare or familial relationships as a result of the offense; . . .
>
> (6) Include any other information related to the impact of the offense upon the victim, the victim's family, or the community that the court inquires of.

Paige contends that OCGA §17-10-1.2 precludes a victim from asking the court to impose the maximum sentence because she is afraid for her life. We disagree. "The introduction of oral victim impact testimony . . . is solely within the discretion of the trial court," and the trial court is vested with "unusually broad discretion in admitting such evidence. . . ." Additionally, "we presume that trial courts will follow the dictates of the statute in not admitting inflammatory or unduly prejudicial evidence."

We find no abuse of discretion here. OCGA §17-10-1.2 allows evidence of the impact of the crime upon the victim, and the victim gave a short and limited statement to the trial court.

Paige contends his counsel was ineffective for failing to move for a mistrial after the victim began crying on the witness stand, requiring a recess to be taken. The record shows that the victim completed her chronological description of her attack and attempted rape before the trial court ordered the jury out of the courtroom in order to allow the victim to compose herself. The victim apparently started crying "very hard" when she was asked to identify the clothing she was wearing at the time of her attack. She made no prejudicial comments and the trial court ordered the recess sua sponte. She remained composed when her testimony resumed and there were no further recesses.

In order to succeed on this ineffectiveness claim, Paige must show that if his counsel had moved for a mistrial, it would have been an abuse of discretion for the trial court to deny it. "Our standard of review for refusal to grant a mistrial is abuse of discretion. . . . [F]ailure to pursue a meritless motion cannot be evidence of ineffective assistance."

Many, if not most, trials by jury involve some degree of emotion by at least one party or the other. It would be unreasonable to expect that all emotions be completely frozen during a trial by jury when such effective bridle on emotions cannot be sustained elsewhere. Demonstrations and outbursts which occur during the course of a trial are matters within the trial court's discretion unless a new trial is necessary to insure a fair trial.

"Our reliance on the trial court's sound discretion is particularly appropriate when the objection is to the manner in which the witness testifies, since the trial court can see and hear the witness while we must rely on a cold record." In this case, the trial transcript shows only that the trial court ordered a recess during the victim's testimony; the only evidence that she was "crying very hard" comes from trial counsel agreeing to appellate counsel's question during the motion for new trial hearing. There is no evidence that she became hysterical or made any prejudicial comments, and trial counsel acknowledged that she was more composed after the recess. Based on this record, we cannot say that the trial court would have abused its discretion by denying a requested mistrial. We find no merit in this claim of ineffectiveness.

Judgment affirmed.

Ellington and Adams, J.J., concur.

CASE QUESTIONS

1 What error did Paige allege that the trial court committed?
2 What are the rules in this case about when and where a victim impact statement can be given?
3 Why did Paige allege that his trial counsel was ineffective with regard to the victim's emotional testimony?

CHAPTER SUMMARY

In this chapter, we have been introduced to the many different participants in the criminal justice system. Judges have the power to reach decisions in cases and to control the participants. They also play an important role in instructing the jury and sentencing a defendant when he is found guilty. Prosecutors are responsible for charging a defendant with a crime and then bringing the defendant to trial to prove beyond a reasonable doubt that he is guilty. There are prosecutors at both the federal and state levels. On the federal level, the U.S. attorney general is the top law enforcement official in the United States. The U.S. attorney general controls 93 U.S. attorneys, who are responsible for prosecuting federal crimes. There are also state and local prosecutors. Most states refer to their local prosecutors as district attorneys. District attorneys are empowered to investigate and charge defendants as well as to subpoena witnesses and conduct trials to prove beyond a reasonable doubt that a defendant is guilty of the crime charged. Representing the defendant is the defense attorney. Like the prosecutor, a defense attorney is a member of the state bar and has an ethical duty to zealously represent the interest of her client. Also like prosecutors, defense attorneys are officers of the court, which means that they cannot participate in any fraud or perjury or knowingly mislead the court.

Defendants are the individuals who are charged with crimes. If a defendant is found guilty at trial, or pleads guilty pursuant to a plea negotiation, then the defendant will be sentenced by the judge and may serve time in prison, probation, or some combination of both. During the sentencing phase, victims of crimes have the right to address the court and the defendant through victim impact statements that detail precisely how the defendant's actions have affected the victim and the victim's family. Many states have also passed legislation that requires prosecutors to keep victims informed about the progress of a criminal case, including whether or not the defendant has pled guilty to a plea bargain and when the case is scheduled for trial.

The criminal justice system could not exist without law enforcement officers to enforce the law. Law enforcement officers are certified by the state to make arrests and may use reasonable force to affect an arrest. Officers are not permitted to use deadly force unless they are presented with deadly force; if an officer uses unreasonable force or engages in police brutality, he can be sued under both federal and state laws and will probably also be fired.

After the defendant is released from prison, she will often serve a sentence on probation or parole. Probation officers are responsible for ensuring that defendants adhere to the rules of their sentence, including avoiding the use of illegal narcotics, possessing weapons, or associating with other known felons.

KEY TERMS

Key terms are listed here in order of appearance in chapter.

Initial appearance
Charging decision
Indictment
Information
Accusation
Officer of the court
Nolle prosequi
Calendar/docket
Fiduciary
Attorney-client privilege
Defendant
Suspect
Victim impact statements
Exclusionary rule
Panel/venire
Jurors
Voir dire

REVIEW QUESTIONS

1. What role do magistrates play in the issuance of search and arrest warrants?
2. Explain the phrase *charging decision* as it applies to prosecutors.
3. What is the difference between an indictment and an information?
4. What is an accusation?
5. Explain the methods that are used to select judges.
6. What is a justice of the peace?

7 Compare and contrast the position of U.S. attorney general and U.S. attorney.
8 What rules govern who may become a prosecutor?
9 What is a calendar or a docket?
10 Does the district attorney have the power to hire and fire police officers? Why or why not?
11 What does it mean when we say that the district attorney is the legal advisor to the police?
12 What rules must a convicted defendant follow while he is on probation?
13 Is it a violation of the Fourth Amendment for a probation officer to search a probationer's person?
14 Can a defense attorney allow her client to commit perjury? Explain your answer.
15 What powers does a Superior Court judge have?
16 What are the different duties of a Superior Court judge and a Magistrate Court judge?
17 What are the usual duties of a magistrate?

WEB SURFING

U.S. Attorney General
http://www.justice.gov/ag/

U.S. Attorneys
http://www.justice.gov/usao/

Cook County State's Attorney's Office
http://www.statesattorney.org/

New York District Attorney
http://manhattanda.org/

Miami-Dade Office of the State Attorney
http://www.miamisao.com/

EXERCISES

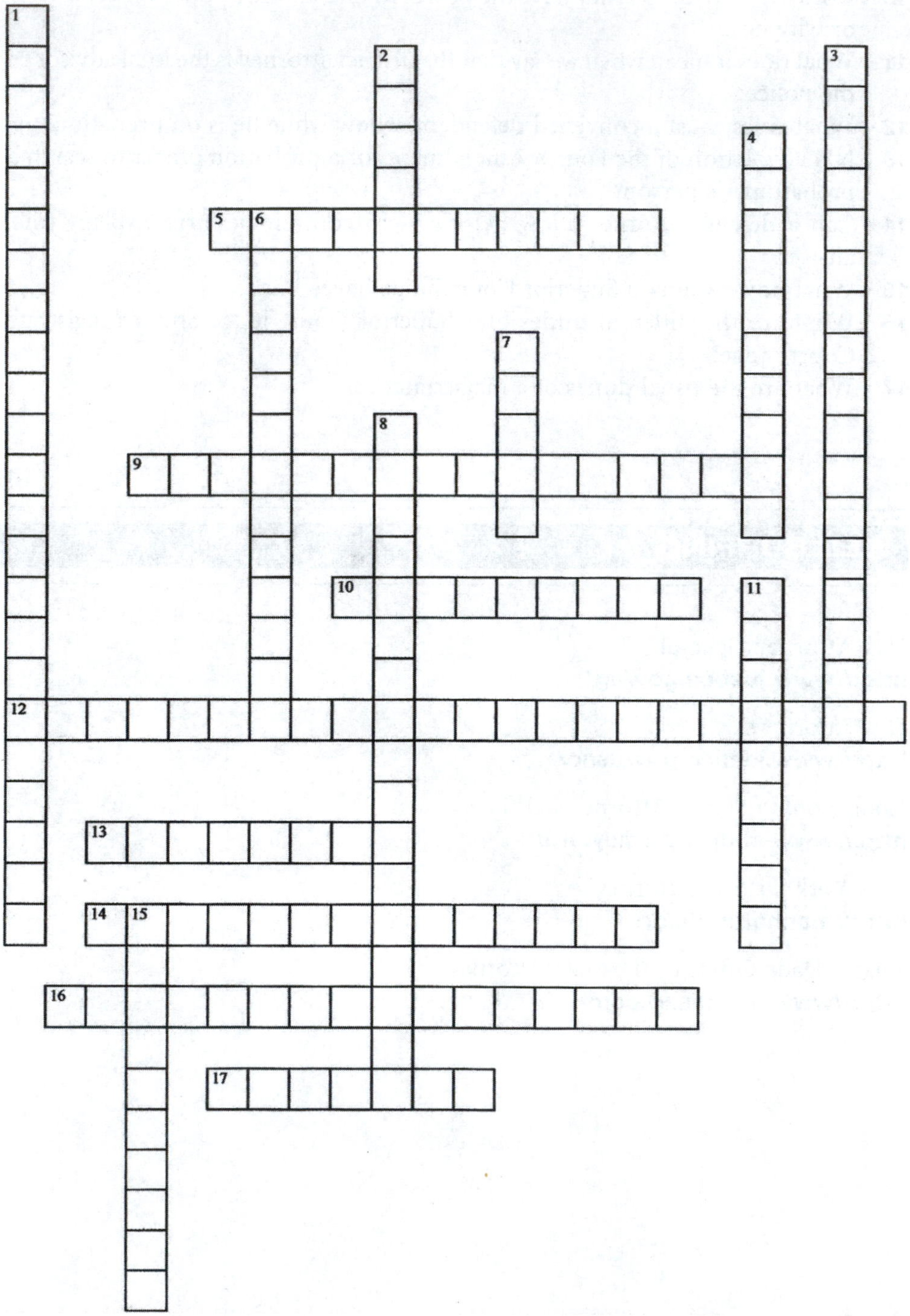

ACROSS

5. A charging document that charges a defendant with a misdemeanor
9. The decision made by a prosecutor concerning the crimes that the defendant will be charged with
10. A relationship in which one person is obliged to act in a trustworthy and honest relationship to another person
12. A procedure that allows the victim of a crime to address the court and the defendant and explain the trauma that the defendant's actions have caused.
13. The process of questioning jurors about their potential biases in the case
14. A list of pending cases before a particular court
16. A rule imposed by the U.S. Supreme Court that prohibits evidence seized illegally from being used in the prosecution of the defendant.
17. A person who police believe may have committed a crime

DOWN

1. A legal protection governing the communications between an attorney and his client that prevents any legal process from forcing the attorney to reveal those communications
2. Those people who have been selected to sit on a jury
3. A person, such as a prosecutor, judge, bailiff, or defense attorney who has an ethical and legal obligation to promote justice
4. A charging document that charges a defendant with a felony
6. An entry into the official record of the prosecutor's intention to dismiss a case
7. A group of people who have been called for jury duty; the final jury will be selected from this group
8. A court hearing held shortly after a defendant's arrest, where the judge advises the defendant of her rights
11. A person charged with a crime
15. A charging document that charges a defendant with a misdemeanor on the state level

d	v	d	i	o	o	p	l	a	f	a	r	l	e	e	a	e	s	i	u	c	f	t	c
n	e	s	n	v	f	i	g	r	c	l	e	s	f	t	t	l	t	v	-	c	r	c	i
s	d	o	u	/	o	a	u	f	n	p	g	y	e	t	t	s	o	d	y	o	l	a	n
n	t	g	r	r	e	o	o	q	a	r	n	c	f	i	o	i	c	r	e	i	e	t	n
t	s	n	a	y	f	e	t	i	e	t	i	c	u	t	r	c	m	t	v	u	e	o	c
s	i	p	e	f	i	i	r	a	n	s	n	o	a	d	n	s	e	t	r	s	s	c	u
k	f	i	m	m	o	n	d	e	o	o	o	o	i	n	e	m	n	o	t	n	c	r	e
e	/	r	o	p	e	g	m	u	i	o	l	r	e	u	y	n	a	g	m	f	n	t	g
n	e	c	/	f	x	t	u	t	c	-	e	g	p	t	-	e	f	p	n	s	c	a	i
e	d	a	e	o	c	h	a	r	g	i	n	g	d	e	c	i	s	i	o	n	l	i	c
l	m	l	o	i	l	s	c	t	t	e	a	i	s	c	l	l	f	r	o	u	o	a	c
p	a	e	d	j	u	r	o	r	s	u	p	r	e	d	i	l	i	n	s	r	a	i	e
i	s	n	m	c	s	m	t	i	r	t	i	l	y	t	e	t	o	n	s	a	t	c	a
u	i	d	c	o	i	d	c	f	e	n	c	o	e	e	n	n	r	n	m	h	t	m	t
l	d	a	c	o	o	u	o	t	g	r	e	a	e	r	t	a	e	d	a	i	l	e	i
n	t	r	r	e	n	s	p	t	a	h	f	f	p	m	p	d	d	a	y	n	i	k	a
m	c	/	o	r	a	i	l	r	n	o	i	t	a	m	r	o	f	n	i	i	n	i	f
m	t	d	f	o	r	l	g	l	i	n	c	g	s	n	i	o	d	s	e	x	c	a	o
f	i	o	p	e	y	q	v	e	a	e	t	t	t	i	v	m	d	c	i	f	t	r	t
s	e	c	n	a	r	a	e	p	p	a	l	a	i	t	i	n	i	d	i	e	e	i	o
f	s	k	o	t	u	t	m	s	c	y	o	e	n	v	l	s	t	t	e	d	r	d	e
i	i	e	a	u	l	p	u	c	e	c	g	a	e	e	e	i	i	d	c	s	x	v	r
n	i	t	u	l	e	s	e	s	r	e	t	t	h	r	g	m	a	l	l	i	i	m	r
c	l	i	a	t	r	u	o	c	e	h	t	f	o	r	e	c	i	f	f	o	v	a	e

initial appearance
charging decision
indictment
information
accusation
officer of the court
nolle prosequi
calendar/docket
fiduciary
attorney-client privilege
defendant
suspect
victim impact statements
exclusionary rule
panel
jurors
voir dire

QUESTIONS FOR ANALYSIS

Should the office of district attorney be abolished? Police officers have become more and more sophisticated in recent years. Shouldn't they also have the responsibility of prosecuting the cases that they have brought? After all, they are the most familiar with the facts in the case. Why shouldn't they also be allowed to prosecute the case?

3

Evidence

Chapter Objectives

- Discuss how evidence is used in criminal prosecutions
- Explain the difference between direct and circumstantial evidence
- Discuss the various kinds of evidence, such as physical, demonstrative, documentary, etc.
- Explain the significance of eyewitness testimony
- Discuss the constitutional limits on lineups and show-ups
- Explain the sanctions for improper lineups, show-ups, and other identification procedures
- Explain the importance of DNA, how it is used, and its significance
- Explain the exclusionary rule

I INTRODUCTION

On the federal level, the Federal Rules of Evidence (or FRE) govern what, how, and when evidence can be admitted at trial. The FRE can be found in the U.S. Code, but many private companies also publish them as a separate volume. The FRE govern the evidence used in both civil and criminal cases. The rules are very comprehensive and have served as a model for many states. As an example, see Figure 3-1 for the FRE's definition of "relevant evidence."

In Chapter 2's case excerpt, there was mention made of "judicial notice." The Federal Rules provide exact guidelines that control how and when a judge can take judicial notice of any fact. Consider Figure 3-2.

Each state has its own version of the rules of evidence. While some closely follow the federal rules, many do not. This makes evidence a tricky issue and very much a matter for the local rules.

The issues surrounding evidence can easily take up an entire textbook by themselves. In this chapter, we will discuss criminal evidence in general terms, how it is developed, how it is used, and ultimately what function it serves in the

FIGURE 3-1

Defining Relevant Evidence Under the Federal Rules

Rule 401. Definition of "Relevant Evidence"

"Relevant evidence" means evidence having any tendency to make the existence of any fact that is of consequence to the determination of the action more probable or less probable than it would be without the evidence.

jury's deliberations. In later chapters, we will focus on the use of this evidence in preliminary hearings, bond hearings, and the trial.

Evidence
All types of information (observations, recollections, documents, concrete objects, etc.) presented at a trial or other hearing. Statements made by judges and lawyers, however, are not considered evidence.

Evidence can first be divided into two broad categories: direct and circumstantial. Beyond that division, however, evidence can be further broken down into other subcategories, such as testimonial evidence, documentary evidence, and demonstrative evidence. We will begin with a review of the classifications of evidence and then proceed to a discussion of specific kinds of evidence and how this evidence is used in a criminal case. But first we must address the question of admissibility.

FIGURE 3-2

Judicial Notice

Rule 201. Judicial Notice of Adjudicative Facts

(a) Scope of rule.
This rule governs only judicial notice of adjudicative facts.

(b) Kinds of facts.
A judicially noticed fact must be one not subject to reasonable dispute in that it is either (1) generally known within the territorial jurisdiction of the trial court or (2) capable of accurate and ready determination by resort to sources whose accuracy cannot reasonably be questioned.

(c) When discretionary.
A court may take judicial notice, whether requested or not.

(d) When mandatory.
A court shall take judicial notice if requested by a party and supplied with the necessary information. . . .

(g) Instructing jury.
In a civil action or proceeding, the court shall instruct the jury to accept as conclusive any fact judicially noticed. In a criminal case, the court shall instruct the jury that it may, but is not required to, accept as conclusive any fact judicially noticed.

A. ADMISSIBILITY AND RELEVANCY

A judge rules on the admissibility of evidence during the trial. If a judge rules that certain evidence is **admissible**, this means that the jury will be allowed to hear it. When the evidence consists of physical objects such as the murder weapon or any other physical evidence, a ruling of admissibility means that the evidence will go into the jury room with the jurors when they deliberate at the end of the case. They will be permitted to handle the evidence and examine it for themselves. However, a judge might rule that particular evidence is inadmissible, meaning that the jury will not be permitted to hear it or see it. Evidence can be ruled inadmissible for a wide variety of reasons. The judge might decide that the evidence is not **relevant** to the issues in the case or that the evidence is too prejudicial and would result in an unfair trial if the jury were to know about it. For example, gruesome or obscene photos could be considered prejudicial if they might cause the jury to convict a defendant on the basis of emotion rather than facts. The most important initial questions about any evidence concern its relevancy to the issues in contention in the case and whether the evidence can be admitted to help prove or disprove those issues.

Admissible
Proper to be used in reaching a decision; describes evidence that should be "let in" or introduced in court, or evidence that the jury may use.

Relevant
Describes evidence that tends to prove or disprove some point in contention in the case.

EXAMPLE

Mr. Casey, the defendant's attorney, while cross-examining one of the state's witnesses, pulls a letter opener out of his coat pocket and declares to the jury, "This is the real murder weapon. I found it myself when I went to the crime scene." Will the jury be allowed to see and inspect the letter opener at this point?

Answer: Absolutely not. Casey has not followed any of the established rules for admission of evidence and has not even established any basics for proving what the letter opener is. Not only will the jury not be allowed to see the letter opener at this point, it's quite likely that Casey will be held in contempt for such an egregious breach of the rules of evidence.

B. CLASSIFYING EVIDENCE: DIRECT AND CIRCUMSTANTIAL

Evidence refers to anything that tends to prove or disprove any fact in a case. Evidence can be divided into two broad categories: direct and circumstantial. **Direct evidence** refers to any object or testimony that has an immediate connection with the facts in the case. Eyewitness testimony is direct evidence. When a person testifies that she saw the defendant commit the crime, this evidence goes to the very heart of the important issue in the case: the defendant's guilt. **Circumstantial evidence**, on the other hand, suggests conclusions and inferences but has no direct connection with the facts of the case. The classic example of circumstantial evidence is seeing footprints in the snow outside your window. Although you did not actually see a person make the footprints, you have circumstantial evidence that someone walked by your window. Later, you find a set of boots with snow still caked on them—that again is circumstantial evidence that whoever wore the boots made the footprints.

Direct evidence
Proof of a fact without the need for other facts leading up to it. For example, direct evidence that dodos are not extinct would be a live dodo.

Circumstantial evidence
Facts that indirectly prove a main fact in question.

In any trial there is often a mixture of both direct and circumstantial evidence. Of the two, circumstantial evidence is considered to be weaker than direct evidence. However, a conviction may be based on circumstantial evidence alone. Obviously, basing an entire prosecution on circumstantial evidence is not something the prosecution would prefer to do, but sometimes there is no choice. Circumstantial evidence may be the only type of evidence available (see testimonial evidence, below).

EXAMPLE

During a trial for murder, the prosecution asks a witness if he saw the defendant sneak into the back of the victim's home. The witness answers, "No. But I saw the defendant's truck pull up. It was night, but I saw someone get out. He went to the back door and went inside. I heard a shot. Then he came running out, got into his truck, and drove away. I walked over and found the defendant's lucky rabbit's foot. He never goes anywhere without it." Is this testimony direct or circumstantial?

Answer: It is partly both, but mostly circumstantial. The witness cannot testify with certainty that it was the defendant because he didn't get a good look at him, but the truck and the rabbit's foot are both suggestive of the fact that the defendant was there.

1. CLASSIFICATIONS OF DIRECT EVIDENCE

Direct evidence can be further broken down into subcategories. For instance, direct evidence can consist of physical evidence, documentary evidence, and testimonial evidence.

a. Physical Evidence

Physical evidence refers to objects and things. In a murder case, the victim's body is physical evidence, as is a murder weapon. It is important to distinguish between physical evidence, which can be any item, and bodily evidence, which is provided by the victim's body. Because the murder victim's body cannot be provided to the jury during the trial in the same way that a murder weapon could be, bodily evidence is presented through the testimony, photographs, x-rays, tissue and fingernail scrapings, and diagrams made during the autopsy of the body. Jurors must rely on this data about the body because they obviously cannot examine the body themselves. Since physical evidence is unique, foundation questions must be asked to determine the relevance and admissibility of the evidence at trial (see below).

b. Documentary Evidence

Documentary evidence
Evidence supported by writings and all other documents.

Document
Something with a message on it—for example, a contract, a map, a photograph, or a message on wood, etc.

Documentary evidence refers to writings. Contracts, letters, notes, agreements, etc. are all documentary evidence. The reason a distinction is drawn between **documents** and other forms of physical evidence is that a document can be copied, altered, or forged (often in such a way as to make it impossible to tell if it is the original). There are special rules about how and when documentary evidence can be admitted at trial.

c. Testimonial Evidence

The evidence given by the witnesses in the case is **testimonial evidence**. This **testimony** can involve directly observed facts (thus making it direct evidence), but it can also concern inferences and assumptions (making it also fall into the category of circumstantial evidence). When a witness testifies about the facts of the crime and how she personally observed them, this is direct testimony. However, in the same breath, a witness can also embark on circumstantial evidence. For instance, a witness could testify that the defendant left the room, and while he was gone she heard a loud noise. Later, she saw that a window was broken. This evidence would suggest that the defendant broke the window, but since the witness did not actually see the defendant break the window, it is circumstantial evidence.

Testimonial evidence
Oral evidence provided by a live witness who testifies during the trial.

Testimony
Evidence given by a witness under oath. Testimonial evidence is different from demonstrative evidence.

d. Demonstrative Evidence

Demonstrative evidence refers to any charts, diagrams, etc. used by the attorneys or witnesses to help illustrate or explain testimony. The parties normally prepare these exhibits, and since they are created for use in the trial to help the parties, they generally do not go back with the jury when the jury deliberates. Unlike physical and documentary evidence that was produced through the natural course of events, demonstrative evidence was created specifically to persuade the jury, and therefore most states do not permit it to go into the jury room for fear that the jury might give it more weight or credibility than the other forms of evidence.

Demonstrative evidence
Charts, diagrams or other displays designed to persuade the jury to a particular viewpoint.

Gathering Evidence in a Rape Case

"We explain to the victims that we need some information from them, so we understand exactly what happened. After we get a brief statement, we don't ask for complete, full details generally at that point, just to kind of confirm that the assault is actually what occurred. We explain to them that we need to get them examined. We make arrangements to take them over to the Sexual Assault Center or to have them taken. A lot of times people will call family or friends to be there with them, even before they call us. They sometimes prefer to ride with them. Our Sexual Assault Center has volunteers that come in to be there for a support system for the person. We'll go ahead and have them examined. After that, we do our more in-depth interview with them to get all the details of exactly what happened. If they know who the suspect is, then, generally, if there aren't any other witnesses to interview, we'll interview the suspect. If there are other witnesses or other information that needs to be followed up on, we'll do that prior to interviewing the suspect. That way we'll have all of the facts before we confront a person."

Detective Tina Pusbach, Sexual Assault Investigator

PROFILING THE PROFESSIONAL

e. Evidence Used to Identify the Defendant

Because identification of the defendant is such an important part of the case, courts have given close scrutiny to the various methods used by law enforcement to identify the defendant. There are very stringent rules about how such identifications are carried out. This is especially true in the area of lineups and show-ups.

Lineup
A group of persons, placed side by side in a line, shown to a witness of a crime to see if the witness will identify the person suspected of a committing the crime. A lineup should not be staged so that it is suggestive of one person.

A **lineup** is often depicted in television and movies. Several people, all roughly similar in appearance, are lined up in front of a two-way mirror. The victim of the crime is then asked to identify the perpetrator. Since the consequences of this lineup are so serious—because the person identified will be charged with a crime—the U.S. Supreme Court has placed numerous limitations on how lineups are conducted. For example, police are not permitted to "suggest" which member of the lineup the victim should identify. In addition, the lineup cannot be unduly suggestive. This means that law enforcement cannot place a suspect with dark hair in a lineup with five or six other individuals with blond hair, making one person stand out from the others. The height and general body appearance of all members of the lineup should be approximately equal. A lineup that suggests the identity of the perpetrator is a violation of a defendant's due process guarantees under the Constitution.[1] The penalty for a suggestive lineup is that the identification of the suspect will be inadmissible at trial.

i. The Importance of an Eyewitness Identification

Witnesses are often asked to identify the perpetrator from some form of lineup. These days, the most common form of lineup is a photographic lineup (discussed below). At the trial, the witness will again be asked to identify the perpetrator and to point him out to the jury. This has a profound psychological effect on the jury.

ii. Just How Accurate Is Eyewitness Testimony?

One area fraught with difficulty for the prosecution and one that should be closely scrutinized by the defense is the identification of the defendant by the victim or witnesses. Eyewitness testimony is notoriously unreliable, yet there is hardly a more dramatic moment in the trial than when the witness points to the defendant and says, "That's the man." Unfortunately, there are numerous studies showing that eyewitness testimony is generally unreliable. See the links at the end of this chapter that will take you to studies showing just how unreliable some forms of eyewitness testimony can be.

iii. Constitutional Limits on Lineups

One of the most important Supreme Court cases in the area of lineups is *U.S. v. Wade.*[2] Wade was placed in a lineup without his attorney's knowledge and identified as the suspect. Prior to the lineup, however, the witness saw Wade standing in the courtroom. The witness knew that Wade was the person charged with the offense before he identified him in the lineup. The Supreme Court held that the

[1] *Moore v. Illinois*, 434 U.S. 220, 98 S. Ct. 458, 54 L. Ed. 2d 424 (1977); *Foster v. California*, 394 U.S. 440, 89 S. Ct. 1127, 22 L. Ed. 2d 402 (1969).
[2] 388 U.S. 218 1967.

subsequent identification was unduly suggestive and thus that testimony about the identification should not have been allowed.

iv. Right to Counsel at a Lineup

The defendant's attorney should be present for any post-indictment lineups. The attorney has the right to observe how the witness responds and to hear anything that the witness says during the identification process. However, the attorney does not have a right to be present when the lineup occurs prior to a formal charge.

v. Participants in a Lineup

The people chosen to stand with the suspect at the lineup are selected on the basis of similarity to the suspect: same approximate age, race, build, hair and skin coloring, etc. The members of the lineup are allowed to pick where they will stand. Each position has a corresponding number so that no names will be used. Police are not permitted to draw the witness's attention to the suspect in any way, such as dressing him in different clothing or selecting people to serve in the lineup who do not resemble the defendant. The entire procedure in the pretrial lineup should be reliable. Without some indicia of reliability, the identification is useless.[3] Members of a lineup may also be asked to say certain words or phrases to aid the witness in voice recognition.

vi. Photographic Lineups

In many situations it is not practical to arrange a live lineup. In those situations, a police officer will go through the mug-shot books and arrange a photographic lineup to show to the eyewitness. Despite the fact that the lineup is photographic, the same rules apply. Those pictured should all look something like the suspect. The pictures are often taped to a file folder and numbered. As at a live lineup, no names are provided. The witness must pick out the suspect from the photographs. The defendant's attorney does not have the right to be present during a photographic lineup.[4]

Photographic lineups have several advantages over physical lineups. From a purely administrative viewpoint, it is far easier to obtain photographs of people who have a similar appearance than it is to locate five or six other people, on short notice, who have similar features. The disadvantage of a photo lineup is that the witness does not get to see the suspect in three dimensions. A flat photograph of a person is not always the best way to identify that person. Think about the photo on your driver's license, for example. However, photographic lineups do not have many of the legal problems that physical lineups have.

In either physical lineups or photographic lineups, there can be nothing especially suggestive about the defendant. An unduly suggestive lineup (one that sets the suspect off in some way from the others) may invalidate the entire identification process.

---

[3] *Manson v. Brathwaite*, 432 U.S. 98, 97 S. Ct. 2243, 53 L. Ed. 2d 140 (1977).
[4] *Milholland v. State*, 319 Ark. 604, 893 S.W.2d 327 (1995).

PROFILING THE PROFESSIONAL

Photographic Lineups

"It's always a good idea to review the photographic lineup to make sure that the police have put in pictures of people who actually do appear to be similar. A witness's identification may be inadmissible if the defendant was somehow singled out in the photographs. There should be no stray marks near the defendant's photograph. In physical lineups, law enforcement makes a videotape of the entire proceeding. This should also be reviewed. Was the defendant wearing something noticeably different from the other members of the live lineup?"

Prosecutor

vii. Single-Suspect Lineups

The U.S. Supreme Court has stated that one-person lineups are obviously impermissibly suggestive and should not be used.[5] The simple reasoning behind this is that when a witness is presented with only a single person to identify, he routinely identifies that person as the perpetrator. Such a procedure is rife with potential abuse and therefore unconstitutional.

viii. One-Person Show-Ups

Show-up
A pretrial identification procedure in which only one suspect and a witness are brought together.

If physical lineups are a potential legal minefield, one-person **show-ups** are even worse. Generally, a one-person show-up occurs when the police arrest a suspect and present her to the witness with the question "Is this the person?" The primary justification for the police using show-ups is the belief that the brief time lapse between the witness's observation of the suspect committing the crime and coming face-to-face with her can enhance accuracy of identification. Still, these situations could certainly fall into the category of unduly suggestive, and the identifications are often ruled inadmissible.

ix. Sanctions for an Improper Lineup

When the defendant's right to have his attorney present at a physical lineup has been violated or the lineup has been unduly suggestive, the punishment imposed on the state is that the testimony about the identification is ruled inadmissible.[6]

x. Self-Incrimination and Identification

The Fifth Amendment to the U.S. Constitution prohibits criminal defendants from being coerced into giving testimony against themselves. Is it a violation of the Fifth Amendment to have the defendant stand up in trial and show the jury the facial scar that the victim described as belonging to her attacker? According to the U.S.

[5] *Stovall v. Denno*, 388 U.S. 293, 87 S. Ct. 1967, 18 L. Ed. 2d 1199 (1967); disapproval on other grounds, *Griffith v. Kentucky*, 479 U.S. 314, 107 S. Ct. 708, 93 L. Ed. 2d 649 (1987).
[6] *Gilbert v California*, 388 US 263, 18 L Ed. 2d 1178, 87 S. Ct 1951.

Supreme Court, the answer is no. Physical traits, especially those that can be seen by ordinary observation, do not fall under the protection of the Fifth Amendment.[7] Making a defendant demonstrate a physical trait, such as a scar or tattoo, is not the same thing as compelling the defendant to admit to a crime.[8] However, there are some states that do not permit this kind of action because of the potential conflict it will cause with the defendant's constitutional rights.

EXAMPLE

During Karl's trial, the prosecutor asks the judge to order the defendant to stand up and display the unique, spiderweb tattoo that he has across his right cheek and neck. Both the victim and another witness identified him and described the tattoo in great detail. Will the judge grant the prosecutor's request?

Answer: Most likely, yes. Because it is a tattoo, it is similar to a scar or other feature, so the defendant will be required to show it to the jury.

C. OTHER EVIDENTIARY ISSUES

Although we have spent some time examining the issues surrounding the various methods used for eyewitness identification to implicate a suspect in a crime, there are many other forms of evidence that can achieve a similar result, some of which do not have as many possible avenues of abuse as eyewitness identification. One type of evidence that has become a staple of murder and rape prosecutions in recent decades is **DNA evidence**.

DNA evidence
Comparing body tissue samples (such as blood, skin, hair, or semen) to see if the genetic materials match. It is used to identify criminals by comparing their DNA with that found at a crime scene; it is also used to identify a child's parents.

1. DNA TESTING

In 1953, in work that would later earn them the Nobel Prize, James Watson and Francis Crick discovered the chemical and structural arrangement of deoxyribonucleic acid, or DNA.

DNA is composed of two strands of molecules arranged in the now famous double-helix configuration. The double helix is like a spiral staircase, in which the handrails are composed of sugars and phosphates and the steps are composed of matching pairs of four (and only four) chemical compounds. These bases are adenine, thymine, cytosine, and guanine. Normally abbreviated A, T, C, and G, these bases combine only in the following sequences: A–T and C–G. They are referred to as base pairs. The human genetic code, which contains all of the information required to develop a human being from a single cell, consists of three billion base pairs. It is the arrangement or sequence of the base pairs that is so important. Base pair arrangements determine the ultimate shape of the animal: cat, elephant, whale, or human being.

---

[7] *State v. Roy*, 220 La. 1017, 58 So.2d 323 (1952); *State v. Moore*, 308 S.C. 349, 417 S.E.2d 869 (1992).
[8] *Holt v. U.S.*, 218 U.S. 245, 31 S. Ct. 2, 54 L. Ed. 1021 (1910).

a. DNA As an Evidentiary Tool

The use of DNA as a forensic tool began in the mid-1980s. Researchers realized that since each person's DNA is different (with the exception of identical twins), there should be a way to harness this feature for identification purposes. Like fingerprints, DNA was seen as a method to link a suspect with a crime scene in a way that could either eliminate him or implicate him as a suspect with a relatively simple test.

Whether the DNA comes from a person's skin, hair, or body fluid, it will contain the identical DNA. This means that DNA forms the basis of the ultimate fingerprint: Every cell, no matter where it originates in a person's body, has exactly the same DNA. This principle underlies the use of DNA as a means of identifying a person. The known DNA of a person can be compared with an unknown sample—for instance, one found at a crime scene. If they match, it can be said quite conclusively that the suspect was at the scene.

DNA cannot show motive or bent of mind or planning. It can show, however, that the suspect was present or that he left incriminating evidence behind. In rape cases, sperm can be checked against the suspect's DNA type to determine whether the sperm is his.

Technicians can now obtain useful DNA from a wide variety of sources, including hair, saliva, blood, semen, tissue, and even badly decomposed bodies. Researchers have obtained DNA from corpses buried for decades, even centuries. DNA can be obtained from the bloodstained clothing of a victim or from any source where a person has left behind some cells from her body.

PROFILING THE PROFESSIONAL

"Touch" DNA

"We've started seeing cases where technicians can get "touch" DNA from some substances. For instance, I had a case where a man used a scarf to choke a woman. Her DNA was found in the center of the scarf, where it had been wrapped around her neck, but the defendant's DNA was found on the ends of the scarf, where he'd held it. That kind of evidence is devastating during a trial. He was found guilty."

Debra Sullivan, Prosecutor

The only people in the world who have the same DNA are identical twins. Even fraternal twins do not have the same DNA. Family members have DNA that is similar but clearly distinguishable.

b. DNA Databases

Many state and federal agencies have begun storing the results of DNA tests in computer databases. Similar to the creation of the FBI fingerprint database, the DNA database permits law enforcement to compare an unknown DNA sample with any of the known samples stored in the nationwide database. In the following case excerpt, see how DNA was used to convict the defendant and what advantages (and limitations) DNA provided in the case.

CASE EXCERPT

U.S. v. SHEA

159 F.3d 37 (N.H.1998)

I. BACKGROUND

At approximately 7:00 P.M. on Friday, August 4, 1995, Sheri Crawford, manager of the Londonderry, New Hampshire branch of the First New Hampshire Bank, and Tammy Lajoie, a bank teller, were closing up the bank when they heard the sound of breaking glass. The employees looked up to see two masked robbers wearing gloves and armed with revolvers. One of the robbers, who guarded Crawford, had a "forward, stretched-out neck" and held a shiny, silver revolver on Crawford throughout the robbery attempt. The other robber held a black revolver on Lajoie during the course of the robbery attempt. The men demanded all of the money in the bank but when they learned that Crawford and Lajoie were not able to open the bank's vault due to a timed locking device and that there was no money contained in the tellers' stations, they left the bank empty-handed.

The two men exited the bank through the same broken window through which they had entered. One of the robbers apparently cut himself on his way through the broken window, as bloodstains were discovered inside the bank and in a stolen minivan believed to have been used as a getaway vehicle. The police processed the evidence and transmitted it to the FBI DNA laboratory for analysis. After analysis, the FBI concluded that the defendant's genetic profile matched the genetic profile of some of the unknown evidentiary samples. The government introduced this DNA evidence at trial.

One week after the attempted Londonderry robbery, Shea was arrested for another robbery in Wakefield, Massachusetts. At the time of his arrest, Shea had in his possession a black, .357 caliber magnum revolver. The government sought to introduce the black revolver seized from Shea to prove that he was one of the men involved in the attempted robbery in Londonderry.

At trial, Sheri Crawford described the robber who held a gun on her during the course of the attempted robbery as "forward-walking" with a "forward, stretched-out" neck. She then identified a photograph of the defendant with the same "leaning forward with the head and the long neck." Crawford further testified that the robber with the "forward, stretched-out" neck held a shiny, silver revolver.

Tammy Lajoie testified that the second robber held a black revolver on her during the course of the attempted robbery. Lajoie described the gun as approximately four inches in length. When Lajoie was shown the government's exhibit, the black, .357 magnum revolver seized from the defendant, she testified that "it looked like the gun that was pointed at her" during the attempted robbery. Shea moved to exclude both the DNA evidence and the black revolver. After an extensive 5-day evidentiary hearing, the district court issued a detailed memorandum and order denying Shea's motion and admitting the DNA evidence. The district court also denied Shea's motion to exclude the black revolver. A jury convicted Shea of attempted armed bank robbery, use of a firearm during a crime of violence, and two counts of interstate transportation of stolen motor vehicles. He was acquitted on an additional count of being a felon in possession of a firearm. The district court sentenced Shea to 567 months of imprisonment. Shea appeals.

II. DISCUSSION

The additional evidence presented at trial consisted of: (1) DNA evidence establishing that the defendant's blood matched blood taken from a vertical blind at the bank and from three locations within the getaway vehicle; (2) the testimony of an FBI forensic scientist that the probability of a random DNA match was between 1 in 20,000 and 1 in 2,000,000; (3) Shea's statement to James Tracy, an associate of the defendant, that "If blood's enough to convict, I'm screwed."; (4) Sheri Crawford's physical description of one of the robbers which closely matched Shea's appearance and; (5) the testimony of a nursing assistant identifying a photograph of Shea as the man she treated for sutures on a number of hand lacerations several hours following the charged attempted robbery. Under such circumstances, it would be a waste of judicial resources to require a new trial where the result would almost certainly be the same. See *United States v. Rose*, 104 F.3d at 1414.

B. Admission of the DNA evidence

At trial, the government presented expert testimony comparing Shea's DNA with DNA extracted from several of the bloodstains discovered inside the Londonderry bank and in a stolen minivan believed to have been used as the getaway vehicle. The government's expert, a forensic scientist employed by the FBI, used a method of DNA analysis known as Polymerase Chain Reaction ("PCR"), in determining that Shea had the same DNA profile as the person who left the bloodstains at the crime scene and in the getaway vehicle.

Shea opposes the admission of the FBI's DNA evidence on the ground that the FBI's PCR method is unreliable science. In addition, Shea argues that evidence of a random match probability is barred by Rule 403 because the risk that the jury would be misled by the evidence substantially outweighs its probative value. (The Court disagreed, saying that DNA evidence is both reliable and admissible.)

III. CONCLUSION

For the foregoing reasons, the defendant's conviction is affirmed.

CASE QUESTIONS

1 Where did investigators obtain DNA evidence in this case?
2 How did the DNA lead investigators to the defendant?
3 Did the defendant make any statements that might also have incriminated him?
4 Was there any medical testimony showing that the defendant had a cut hand?
5 What type of DNA test was performed?

DNA results are checked both visually and by computer for accuracy. Using this method, DNA experts can often testify that the chances that a particular specimen came from someone other than the defendant are several billion to one.

Sidebar

An expert can test for DNA on a specimen smaller than the size of a pencil point.

2. FINGERPRINTING

Everyone is familiar with fingerprints. As early as 1605, scientists had noted that the patterns of grooves and whorls on different people's fingertips were as individual as their faces. It wasn't until the early 1900s, however, that law enforcement began using this fact as a means to identify perpetrators.

Crime Scene Tech

"When we go out, we get the victim to walk us through and we ask, 'Is there anything in here that is not yours?' Or we ask, 'Do you see anything unusual, like something that is out of place, something that was brought from one room to another and left?'"

Kathy Singleton, Crime Scene Evidence Technician

PROFILING THE PROFESSIONAL

Fingerprints can be left behind on a wide variety of surfaces, including human skin. Specially trained technicians search for fingerprints in likely places: doorknobs, tabletops, or any surface a person was likely to have touched.

The FBI maintains a nationwide database of fingerprints, which can now be computer matched in a short period of time.

Sidebar

Once a sample has been taken, it is treated with detergent to break down the cell membrane and get at the DNA on the chromosome. It is also treated with an enzyme to break out the DNA from the surrounding proteins. Once the DNA is separated, the solution is then suspended in a gel and an electric current is passed through it. Since different molecules of DNA have different weights, they move either faster or more slowly toward the electric current. When they finally settle out—usually after about an hour—they present a handy reference guide, showing bands at different places through the gel. Specimens from the same person will show exactly the same banding.

3. BLOOD TESTING

Blood tests are commonly performed in order to eliminate a suspect, rather than implicate one. The reason for this is simple. Blood testing—or typing—of the victim's or defendant's blood can usually tell the examiner only whether or not the blood is the same type as the unknown specimen found. It will not reveal if the unknown specimen of blood actually belongs to any particular person. As such, if the blood found is not the defendant's blood type, the only conclusion that can be reached is that the blood does not belong to him.

4. POLYGRAPH TESTING

Polygraph machines, or lie detectors, have been around in one form or another for decades. The basic principle behind any lie detector is that when a person tells a lie, it causes her physical stress. This stress can be measured in the form of increased heart rate, minute changes in the skin's resistance to electricity, and greater perspiration. However, because of their notorious unreliability, few courts have ever allowed them to be used as evidence. Occasionally, defense attorneys will attempt to use them to show that the defendant has been telling the truth, but in almost all cases, polygraph results remain inadmissible in criminal trials.

5. VOICE TESTING

A voice stress evaluation test is similar in some ways to a polygraph test. Although the application is different, the theory remains the same: When a person lies, this causes stress, and this stress can be measured. A person's voice is recorded and later examined by experts. Like polygraph tests, voice stress tests are normally inadmissible in a criminal trial.[9]

[9] *United States v. Traficant*, 566 F. Supp. 1046 (N.D. Ohio); *State v. Thompson*, 381 So.2d 823; *Smith v. State*, 355 A.2d 527.

D. USE OF EVIDENCE IN COURT PROCEEDINGS

So far, our discussion about evidence has consisted of defining it and examining how it is gathered. However, evidence serves a purpose. It is used during various criminal hearings to either prove or disprove some fact. In this section we will discuss how evidence is admitted during a hearing and then show the impact of various rules on the use and the evaluation of that evidence. In any criminal case, evidence must be properly admitted before it can be considered by either a judge or a jury. Proper admission requires the use of foundation questions.

1. FOUNDATION QUESTIONS

Admission of evidence
A decision by a judge to allow evidence to be used by the jury (or, in a trial with no jury, by the judge).

Foundation questions
Questions that must be asked of a witness to prove the relevance and reliability of different types of evidence.

One important aspect of evidence is the way that is used at the trial. Before the jury is permitted to inspect the evidence in the case, it must first be admitted into evidence. **Admission of evidence** refers to the process through which the attorney establishes the relevancy of the evidence and the judge then rules that the jury may view it. An attorney is not permitted to testify about the evidence. Instead, the attorney must ask a witness about the evidence. These questions are called **foundation questions**. Establishing how a piece of evidence is relevant is commonly referred to as *laying the foundation*. Different types of evidence require different kinds of questions.

2. CHAIN OF CUSTODY REQUIREMENTS

Chain of custody
The chronological list of those in continuous possession of a specific physical object. A person who presents evidence (such as a gun used in a crime) at a trial must account for its possession from time of receipt to time of trial in order for evidence to be admitted by the judge.

Whenever evidence is seized, it must be safeguarded. Police agencies have created evidence rooms, where this evidence is stored for later use at trial. Evidence requiring testing by the state crime lab or other agency must also be handled methodically. Before the evidence can be admitted at trial, the state must show that it has not been altered or tampered with in any way. This is called the **chain of custody** requirement. All the people who handle the evidence must take the stand and account for what they did with this evidence and where they took it. They must all testify that they did not tamper with the evidence. The "chain" is established by first having the crime scene technician testify to removing the evidence from the crime scene, then placing it into the evidence room. Then the person who removed it from the evidence area testifies, and so on until every person who has handled the evidence testifies.

The importance of the chain of custody is no better demonstrated than in the federal government's perjury case against baseball player Barry Bonds. The urine samples that tested positive for steroids were casually passed hand-to-hand by several people, or may have even gone through the mail, which left the door wide open for possible tampering. Even if no tampering took place, the break in the chain of custody was dramatic.

3. EVIDENCE ROOMS

The evidence room is a restricted area. The only people permitted into the area are the evidence room technicians. Police, prosecutors, and judges are all barred from entering the evidence room. When police deposit evidence there, they hand it over to technicians who are responsible for storing it. A break in the chain of custody could result in the evidence not being admitted at trial. If this evidence is crucial to the prosecution's case, the entire charge might fail.

PROFILING THE PROFESSIONAL

Clerk of Court

"The evidence room is for exhibits admitted into evidence during the trial of the case. If they are admitted into evidence, then we keep them. A lot of times there might be a weapon involved, a knife or gun, and it might be ordered to be turned over to the law enforcement agency to be destroyed or returned to its rightful owner. Any type of contraband, any type of drugs, pipes, marijuana pipes, that kind of stuff, is usually ordered destroyed or turned over to law enforcement for educational purposes. Sometimes we keep this evidence for a long time. Especially if the case is tried and then appealed to the North Carolina Court of Appeals, then a copy of everything has to be sent to Court of Appeals and so sometimes we have stuff a long time. Depending on the nature of the crime of the case, it just depends."

Mabel Lowman, Clerk of Court

E. THE EXCLUSIONARY RULE

As we saw in Chapter 2, the **exclusionary rule** is a rule created by the U.S. Supreme Court that dictates the punishment for failing to follow the correct procedures in obtaining evidence. Illegal or unconstitutional evidence cannot be used at trial. By providing such a sanction, the U.S. Supreme Court hoped to effectively force all law enforcement agencies to abide by constitutional provisions in seizing evidence. The exclusionary rule is the device used in numerous movie and television dramas as the "technicality" that allows an obviously guilty suspect to go free. However, since the court's ruling actually states that the police violated the Constitution in obtaining the evidence, to allow the evidence to be used in one case would invite police to circumvent the Constitution in future cases, too. A ruling that certain evidence was obtained unconstitutionally does not mean that the charges against the defendant are dropped. However, if all evidence against a defendant is ruled illegal, then for all practical purposes there is nothing that the prosecution can use that links the defendant to the crime.

Exclusionary rule
Illegally obtained evidence may not be used in a criminal trial.

Sidebar

It is extremely rare for all evidence against a defendant to be ruled unconstitutional. Even in cases in which some of the evidence was obtained illegally, the prosecution may still continue with the case. The government simply cannot use that evidence and will instead rely on other evidence that was obtained constitutionally.

1. "FRUIT OF THE POISONOUS TREE"

Occasionally, when evidence has been obtained in violation of the Constitution, this evidence will often lead to the discovery of additional evidence. What happens when other evidence is obtained, and obtained constitutionally, but is based on original evidence, which was obtained unconstitutionally? The courts have said that the exclusionary rule, to have any binding effect, must be applied to this new evidence as well. When new evidence is discovered only through unconstitutionally obtained evidence, this new evidence will be excluded at trial. This is the "**fruit of the poisonous tree" doctrine**. This doctrine holds that if the original evidence was tainted, any additional evidence obtained from it is also tainted and suffers the same penalty: exclusion at trial. Say, for example, that a key to a safe deposit box was found during an illegal search. The key itself (the poisonous tree) cannot be admitted into evidence during trial, nor can the contents of the safe deposit box (the fruit).

Fruit of the poisonous tree doctrine
The rule that evidence gathered as a result of evidence gained in an illegal search or questioning cannot be used against the person searched or questioned even if the later evidence was gathered lawfully.

a. Exceptions to the Exclusionary Rule

The exclusionary rule does have certain exceptions. Even though evidence may have been obtained unconstitutionally, there are provisions that allow it to be used at trial.

i. Inevitable Discovery

Under the inevitable discovery doctrine, evidence that would have been discovered under any circumstances can be admitted at trial; the fact that it was obtained unconstitutionally may not necessarily impact its admissibility.

ii. Good Faith

Evidence may be admitted when law enforcement was acting on a good faith belief that a warrant was legally sufficient, when in fact it was not.

iii. Independent Source

Under the independent source rule, the evidence, although obtained unconstitutionally, is admissible if it is also verified by an independent source that is not tainted by any unconstitutional problems.

F. HOW THE JUDGE AND JURY USE PHYSICAL EVIDENCE

When evidence has been admitted at trial, it means that the jury will be allowed to view the evidence in the jury room. If there is no jury, then the judge will consider the evidence and reach conclusions about the case based on that evidence. The murder weapon or the narcotics will go back with the jurors while they deliberate on the case. The jurors are instructed that they have the final say on how much or how little weight to give any particular piece of evidence. Although the jury is not directly informed of this fact, the jury is permitted to disregard evidence entirely and reach a conclusion contrary to what the evidence suggests. The final verdict is always based on the individual jurors' beliefs, not on the quantity or quality of the evidence.

CHAPTER SUMMARY

The use of evidence in criminal cases raises a host of interesting and sometimes complex legal issues. Simply identifying the defendant as the perpetrator of the crime can trigger several constitutional protections. Lineups and show-ups are fraught with potential problems. Any identification of the defendant that results from unfair or suggestive law enforcement practices could be invalidated, meaning that the jury will never hear that testimony. In addition to eyewitness testimony, which has often been shown to be unreliable, other technological advances have been developed that can link a defendant with a crime. DNA has received a great deal of attention in the past few years, not only because it can almost conclusively link evidence to a specific person but also for its ability to conclusively state that a certain specimen did *not* come from a suspect. Older technologies, such as fingerprints, also are useful evidentiary tools. However, no one piece of evidence can conclusively decide a defendant's fate. The jury must evaluate all evidence, including its weight and credibility.

KEY TERMS

Key terms are listed here in order of appearance in chapter.

Evidence
Admissible
Relevant
Direct evidence
Circumstantial evidence
Documentary evidence
Document
Testimonial evidence
Testimony
Demonstrative evidence
Lineup
Show-up
DNA evidence
Admission of evidence
Foundation questions
Chain of custody
Exclusionary rule
Fruit of the poisonous tree

REVIEW QUESTIONS

1. Explain the difference between direct and circumstantial evidence.
2. What limits has the U.S. Supreme Court placed on lineups and show-ups?
3. When does a defendant have the right to have an attorney present at a lineup?
4. Explain how a photographic lineup is created.
5. What are foundation questions?
6. Is it a constitutional violation to make a defendant stand before the jury and put on evidence linked to the crime, such as a bloody glove?
7. Explain how DNA evidence is used to identify a suspect.

8. What is the "chain of custody?"
9. What is a voice test?
10. Explain the process of admitting evidence.
11. Are polygraph tests admissible in court? Why or why not?
12. Just how reliable is eyewitness testimony?
13. What is a DNA database and why is it important?
14. What is the purpose of an evidence room?
15. Explain the exclusionary rule.
16. What is the "fruit of the poisonous tree" doctrine?

WEB SURFING

Federal Rules of Evidence
http://www.law.cornell.edu/rules/fre/overview.html

Texas Supreme Court
http://www.supreme.courts.state.tx.us/

Hawaii Supreme Court
http://www.courts.state.hi.us/courts/supreme/hawaii_supreme_court.html

Studies on Eyewitness Testimony
http://agora.stanford.edu/sjls/Issue%20One/fisher&tversky.htm
https://webfiles.uci.edu/eloftus/Morgan_SurvivalEyewitness_IJPL07.pdf

EXERCISES

ACROSS

8. The chronological presentation of witnesses who have handled a specific item of evidence to show that it has not been tampered with or changed in any way from the time that it was seized
10. Any charts, diagrams, or displays that were created by the parties to a case with the intention of using them to persuade the jury
11. Any information (including observations, memories, documents, physical objects, etc.) that is presented at trial or other hearing and offered to prove or disprove a fact in contention
13. A rule that requires that any evidence discovered as a consequence of unconstitutionally seized evidence must also be excluded at trial
14. Particular questions that are asked to establish the relevancy of particular types of evidence
15. A rule created by the U.S. Supreme Court that requires that evidence seized in violation of the Constitution cannot be used at trial
17. An article that contains a message, such as a photo, contract, etc.

DOWN

1. A judge's decision that he will allow the jury to view a particular piece of evidence
2. The standard that any offered evidence must meet at trial; something that tends to prove or disprove a point in contention
3. Oral evidence given by a witness under oath
4. Facts that suggest a conclusion about a fact in question in the case
5. Evidence that proves a fact
6. Evidence supported by writings and all other documents
7. A ruling by a judge that a specific item of evidence can be presented to the jury and can be used by them in reaching a verdict in the case
9. A method used by police to help the crime victim identify her attacker from a group of people placed side-by-side in a line
12. Deoxyribonucleic acid, a source of genetic material that is unique to each human being, except identical twins
16. Pretrial identification of the suspect where only the victim, the police, and the suspect are present

d	v	f	n	e	e	e	t	r	o	u	s	e	q	c	u	n	o	e	e	c	u	c	a	e	r	n	u	c	e	o
i	d	x	e	e	e	r	s	o	n	a	e	c	c	o	n	e	e	e	d	t	e	d	c	a	t	n	t	r	y	f
n	r	h	l	i	t	c	c	d	e	s	e	n	t	c	m	p	d	v	f	n	u	c	f	i	e	a	l	e	r	e
m	t	n	e	y	d	n	r	e	c	t	o	c	e	v	e	i	o	o	n	e	v	d	e	i	c	n	o	n	s	u
y	d	a	l	u	d	t	c	c	a	c	e	i	s	o	t	s	n	e	t	i	t	a	v	d	v	e	o	c	c	u
t	s	a	u	p	u	-	e	n	i	l	s	n	e	e	h	e	s	t	a	a	r	t	n	u	f	e	o	e	d	o
e	n	i	r	t	c	o	d	e	e	r	t	s	u	o	n	o	s	i	o	p	e	h	t	f	o	t	i	u	r	f
r	r	i	y	c	e	v	i	d	e	n	c	e	w	r	i	e	d	t	e	s	r	e	u	l	e	e	s	d	e	y
d	e	e	r	o	t	e	e	i	i	o	c	u	e	t	e	i	i	n	t	d	e	e	t	h	o	t	l	s	l	a
e	e	a	a	n	c	i	v	v	t	t	p	c	m	n	o	y	h	i	t	u	c	a	u	o	a	n	c	a	u	e
f	e	c	n	e	d	i	v	e	f	o	n	o	i	s	s	i	m	d	a	f	e	o	d	d	u	d	t	n	n	i
e	a	d	o	s	r	v	t	e	d	e	o	e	a	p	t	o	i	o	o	e	r	-	m	c	d	n	o	i	o	e
t	s	a	i	e	y	v	f	v	d	e	d	i	m	p	n	a	i	u	n	m	t	i	e	i	r	u	v	c	e	l
u	i	e	s	d	c	d	n	i	h	n	i	a	u	y	t	l	n	n	c	d	s	y	c	p	v	c	i	s	e	s
i	e	h	u	n	o	l	v	t	s	d	l	i	o	d	x	d	c	t	d	s	c	n	t	e	e	a	o	d	f	i
e	o	r	l	i	e	e	d	a	x	a	e	o	f	o	a	n	n	n	i	o	o	t	e	d	d	m	e	h	e	u
n	e	u	c	e	t	o	-	r	e	u	-	r	-	t	o	e	p	b	e	a	i	e	n	h	t	t	w	c	s	e
n	r	n	x	c	n	o	i	t	c	s	e	c	i	s	m	l	l	y	o	e	l	o	i	i	d	u	n	a	i	d
r	i	v	e	u	p	a	o	s	y	e	d	o	c	u	m	e	n	t	a	r	y	e	v	i	d	e	n	c	e	o
c	f	r	d	e	e	u	o	n	o	a	n	f	c	c	u	t	t	a	e	e	i	a	v	p	d	s	i	e	e	n
n	i	m	e	e	r	e	e	o	s	q	d	o	a	f	w	m	r	e	c	l	y	r	i	i	o	a	i	f	d	s
d	m	c	m	c	o	r	t	m	u	m	d	s	o	o	c	d	v	s	t	e	t	i	v	e	d	o	v	e	n	n
c	d	m	i	e	a	o	y	e	c	n	s	n	r	n	t	i	r	u	c	v	d	e	n	s	i	e	e	y	d	s
n	t	o	n	i	c	a	s	d	y	e	d	a	r	i	a	t	c	o	t	a	a	i	e	e	e	r	n	s	e	y
s	o	a	e	e	c	t	r	n	i	d	o	c	n	a	s	t	d	e	r	n	y	i	n	f	n	u	y	c	t	t
o	u	m	f	u	i	r	t	a	e	a	e	c	o	h	e	i	e	l	d	c	c	l	f	c	v	e	o	n	e	c
e	n	n	u	o	n	d	-	c	l	c	u	l	e	c	m	n	y	e	e	y	u	i	n	r	s	c	s	e	o	e
u	v	d	n	u	a	d	r	s	i	e	i	w	v	t	o	n	s	c	a	c	v	f	c	n	s	y	v	i	u	t
u	e	s	p	d	a	c	i	e	i	t	i	c	u	d	u	o	t	r	p	a	t	f	v	i	s	o	m	y	e	d
e	b	e	y	c	s	o	n	e	c	o	w	s	m	o	e	e	n	r	m	v	i	v	s	d	d	d	n	y	s	e
e	d	o	s	e	e	c	l	c	h	s	i	i	e	n	t	o	d	o	a	c	n	d	e	e	v	e	v	f	h	n

evidence
circumstantial evidence
relevancy
admissible
direct evidence
admission of evidence
foundation questions

chain of custody
document
documentary evidence
testimony
demonstrative evidence
line-up
show up

dna evidence
exclusionary rule
fruit of the poisonous
tree doctrine

QUESTIONS FOR ANALYSIS

1 If studies have shown that eyewitness testimony is generally unreliable, why do courts and prosecutors continue to rely on it so heavily?

2 If DNA is such an effective investigative tool, why shouldn't everyone in the U.S. be required to give a DNA sample, whether or not they have been convicted of a crime?

4

Court Procedure and Evidence

Chapter Objectives

- Define probable cause and how it applies to both arrest and search warrants
- Explain the legal definition of arrest
- Discuss the role of *Miranda* warnings in post-arrest statements
- Demonstrate your understanding of the initial appearance hearing
- Define the role of the preliminary hearing
- Explain the factors that are considered in issuing a bail bond

I PROBABLE CAUSE AND THE FOURTH AMENDMENT

The Fourth Amendment provides, "The right of the people to be secure in their persons . . . against unreasonable searches and seizures, shall not be violated." In our system, police officers are routinely faced with issues of whether they can use certain devices to help gather evidence. Consider the next scenario.

EXAMPLE

Officer Antonelli has a device that allows her to take a video of a home at night in order to see where the individuals are simply by their heat signatures. When she aims the device at the house, she can get a real-time image of the people inside and any other heat sources. When she aims the camera at the basement, she discovers a large heat source there. In her training, she has learned that suburban marijuana growers often use large banks of lights to help their marijuana grow, and these lights are often left on late into the evening to help the marijuana plants grow to a large size. Does Officer Antonellis have probable cause to arrest the individuals for growing pot?

Answer: No. As we are about to see in the next section, the Fourth Amendment requires probable cause before a person can be arrested or a home searched. Officer Antonellis surely believes that she has probable cause based on the heat signatures in the basement, but is that enough? We will examine this question in greater detail in the next few sections.

A. PROBABLE CAUSE

Probable cause
The reasonable belief that a crime has occurred or is about to occur.

The Fourth Amendment requires **probable cause** before an arrest can be made or a search warrant issued. What, exactly, is probable cause and how is it determined? The simple answer is that probable cause is a belief, based on observable facts, that someone has committed a crime.

The degree of proof needed to establish probable cause is not as high as the standard that will later be used to prove that the defendant is guilty of the crime. That standard is proof *beyond a reasonable doubt.* If police had to prove cause beyond a reasonable doubt, it is likely that they would be unable to make many arrests. But probable cause is a *reasonable belief* that a crime has occurred, not a definitive verdict that a person has committed a crime beyond a reasonable doubt.

How do courts define probable cause? First, the police officer must establish that he observed facts that led him to the belief that a crime was occurring, and that this belief existed at the moment of arrest. This is not a vague requirement. It is quite possible that the officer may take the stand at some point in the case and recount the exact circumstances surrounding the arrest. (Officers may be required to testify about probable cause at the preliminary hearing and again during a motion to suppress hearing. We will address motions to suppress in Chapter 6.)

The standard to prove probable cause is that the facts and circumstances, at the moment of the arrest, "warrant a man of reasonable caution in the belief that an offense had been committed."[1] Probable cause must be based on something more substantial than mere rumor or speculation.[2] This means that police officers must often independently verify facts related to them before they will have sufficient probable cause to make an arrest. Probable cause is a middle ground between mere suspicion that an action may be a criminal act and proof beyond a reasonable doubt. The admonitions of the Fourth Amendment were carefully drafted to prohibit police officers from simply arresting persons based on emotions, hunches, prejudices, or any other questionable practices. Instead, police officers must be able to articulate the precise elements that made them believe that a crime was occurring.

1. THE PREFERENCE FOR WARRANTS

Courts have a preference for warrants, for both arrests and searches. The reason is simple: When a warrant is issued, a magistrate or other judge has reviewed the facts

---

[1] *Carroll v. United States*, 267 U.S. 132, 45 S. Ct. 280, 69 LE 543 (1925).
[2] *Clark v. State*, 189 Ga. App 124, 375 S.E. 2d 230 (1988).

and made a determination that probable cause exists. This does not mean that an arrest or a search conducted without a warrant is automatically unconstitutional. What it does mean is that arrests—and especially searches—are given greater scrutiny when no warrant has been issued. Of the two, courts give officers greater latitude in making warrantless arrests than they do for warrantless searches. The reason for this is that a person is mobile and may flee. A person can also be extremely dangerous, and waiting around for a warrant to arrest could subject the officer and others to violence or even death. However, the same cannot be said of property. An apartment building is not going to flee, so there is nothing stopping the police from securing the premises, prohibiting anyone from entering, and seeking a warrant to search it. Although there are many instances in which the police may search without a warrant, the default approach is that the police must have a warrant before searching, unless they can clearly show that the search fell into a court-established exception.

a. Exceptions to the Warrant Requirement

Although this is not a text about proper search-and-seizure techniques, it is important to note that there are widely accepted exceptions to the preference for warrants to search and seize items. The most common of these exceptions are as follows:

- Contraband
- Consent
- Abandoned property
- Pat down
- Exigent circumstances

i. Contraband

Police do not need a warrant to seize **contraband**. An item is considered contraband when it is illegal to possess it. Examples of contraband include illegal narcotics, automatic weapons, and child pornography, to name a few. When police come across these items, wherever they happen to find them, they are authorized to seize them without first obtaining a search warrant to do so.

Contraband
Items that are illegal to possess, import, export, or sell.

ii. Consent

Police are not required to obtain a search warrant when the person who owns the item voluntarily gives police consent to search it. The key word here is *voluntary*. Police officers cannot threaten or coerce a person into giving consent. Instead, if the person freely and voluntarily allows the police to search an item, such as an automobile, then that person has waived the warrant requirement.

iii. Abandoned Property

There is no requirement for law enforcement to obtain a warrant to search and seize abandoned property. Garbage is a perfect example. If an item—for example, drug paraphernalia—has been thrown into a communal trash receptacle, or even into a private trash receptacle subsequently taken to the curb for collection, the person throwing it away has tossed away any constitutional objections to having the item seized. The U.S. Supreme Court has ruled that there is no reasonable expectation of privacy for discarded garbage.[3] Of course, there are limits to the rule on the police obtaining abandoned property. They cannot, for instance, trespass in order to get to a suspect's trash. In that case, they would have to wait until the trashcan has been placed on the curb for collection and is off the suspect's property.

iv. Pat-Down

There are times when police officers are authorized to pat down a suspect for weapons without a warrant. If, during the course of this pat-down, they discover evidence of a crime, they are allowed to seize it. The law about pat-downs and frisks can get more complicated than the simple statement provided above, but it is important to know that officers are authorized to pat down suspects when they encounter them and do not need a warrant to do so.

v. Exigent Circumstances

Exigent circumstance
An emergency situation that calls for swift action to avoid danger to people or property and allows law enforcement to bypass some constitutional rules.

Police are not required to obtain a search warrant if they can show that an emergency (exigent) circumstance exists. An **exigent circumstance** is some danger to property or people such that waiting to obtain a warrant might result in the loss of evidence or injury to a person. An example is a situation in which police officers hear two people having a violent fight inside their home. They do not have to wait for a warrant before entering and stopping one person from killing the other.

Now that we have explored the most common situations in which police can search without warrants, we will turn our attention to the various methods that probable cause can be communicated to a police officer, beyond her personal observations.

2. BASING PROBABLE CAUSE ON INFORMATION PROVIDED BY ANOTHER POLICE OFFICER

Courts have recognized that a police officer may arrest a suspect based solely on information provided by another police officer. The arresting officer is not required to conduct an independent investigation into the allegations before making the arrest. Instead, the officer may arrest based on the information relayed by another officer. When the second officer verifies the description of the individual involved, the second officer is authorized to arrest, even though the crime did not occur within that officer's presence. Because it did occur in the presence of the other officer, that is sufficient to establish probable cause.[4]

3. BASING PROBABLE CAUSE ON INFORMATION PROVIDED BY A CONFIDENTIAL INFORMANT

If an officer can arrest a suspect based on information relayed from another officer, then does the same rule apply to information provided by a confidential informant

---

[3] *California v. Greenwood*, 486 U.S. 35 (1988).
[4] *State v. Thompson*, 295 N.W.2d 8 (S.D. 1980).

(CI)? The answer is no. A CI must have an established track record with the officer. The officer must have evidence that the CI provided truthful, accurate, and detailed information in the past. In a specific instance, the officer may use the CI's knowledge, previous track record, and basis of the CI's knowledge in the current case to apply for an arrest or search warrant. But acting on such information to make an arrest or search without a warrant would raise constitutional issues and might even result in a ruling that the search was unlawful. An officer who receives information from a CI and then verifies the information independently may be permitted to make an arrest or a search without a warrant, but here the focus is on what the officer observed after first receiving the information from the CI.[5]

4. BASING PROBABLE CAUSE ON INFORMATION PROVIDED BY A CITIZEN OR WITNESS

When an officer receives information about a crime from a citizen or crime victim, as long as the information is specific and detailed about the person who committed the crime, the officer may arrest. However, as we will see in the next section, such information is not sufficient to justify a warrantless search. In that situation, the officer would use the victim's description, coupled with the officer's own observations, to apply for a warrant, unless the officer can show that the search fell within one of the clearly established exceptions to searches without a warrant.[6]

5. BASING PROBABLE CAUSE ON ANONYMOUS TIPS

Anonymous tips, by themselves, will not form the basis of probable cause to arrest or search. An anonymous tip has no indicia of reliability. The officer has nothing to go on when he receives an anonymous tip. There is nothing to point to, such as the trustworthy information relayed by a fellow police officer or the past record of a confidential informant or the officer's own observations. In such a case, an officer acting solely on an anonymous tip would run the risk of having the arrest or search ruled unconstitutional.[7]

6. BASING PROBABLE CAUSE ON SPECIALIZED TRAINING

Probable cause is not limited to what a citizen would know or understand about criminal activity. Police officers receive extensive training about crime and can use that training as the basis of probable cause in situations in which an ordinary person might have no inkling that a crime has occurred.

---

[5] *U.S. v. Traxler*, 477 F.3d 1243 (10th Cir. 2007).
[6] *People v. Wolff*, 182 Ill. App. 3d 583, 131 Ill. Dec. 235, 538 N.E.2d 610 (3d Dist. 1989).
[7] *Holloway v. Vargas*, 535 F. Supp. 2d 1219 (D. Kan. 2008).

EXAMPLE

Officer Tate is parked at the end of a street in a known drug area. There have been reports about drug activity in the area, especially at a particular gas station. Officer Tate can see the gas station from her vantage point. It is 2 A.M., and while she is watching, Joe drives up to the gas station, talks briefly to a man standing in front of the garage, hands the man something and is in turn handed something back, and then drives away. The entire transaction takes less than a minute. Officer Tate pulls over Joe's car and arrests him. Does she have sufficient probable cause?

Answer: Yes, she does. Although this transaction may not appear to involve a crime, the officer can take into account several factors not readily apparent to someone that does not have her training. For instance, the area is known for drug activity. There are the additional factors of the time of day, the furtive actions of the people involved, and the length of the transaction, which in her training and experience lead her to believe that a drug transaction has just occurred.[8]

Because of their training and experience, police officers might be alerted to a potential crime where a civilian would not. These factors, as we have seen in the previous scenario, can include elements such as location, time of day, and the interaction among suspects, but it can also be based on physical items that an untrained person might not readily identify as evidence of a crime.

EXAMPLE

Officer Javier pulls over a driver for running a red light. As the officer is talking with the driver, he notices a soda can that has been bent in the middle and has a hole in the crease. There are burn marks in the crease of the can. The officer arrests the driver for possession of drug paraphernalia. Does Officer Javier have sufficient probable cause?

Answer: Yes. Officers are trained to know that people who smoke crack cocaine often make homemade crack pipes. One of the devices they use is a soda can in which the crack is placed in the crease and lit with a lighter, and the smoke is inhaled through the top of the can.

B. STANDARDS FOR THE ISSUANCE OF AN ARREST WARRANT

When is an arrest valid? An arrest is constitutionally valid "if, at the moment the arrest is made, the facts and circumstances within the knowledge of the arresting officers and of which they had reasonably trustworthy information were sufficient to warrant a prudent man in believing that the accused had committed or was committing an offense."[9]

[8] *State v. Cook*, 161 P.3d 779 (Kan. Ct. App. 2007).
[9] *Beck v. Ohio*, 379 U.S. 89, 85 S. Ct. 223, 13 L. Ed. 2d 142 (1964).

1. ARREST WARRANTS

The importance of a valid arrest warrant is that, if an appellate court decides that the initial arrest warrant was insufficient under the Constitution, then everything that occurred following the arrest may be deemed unconstitutional as well. Evidence that was seized following an invalid arrest may not be used at trial. Statements that a defendant makes may also be excluded from being used at trial. An application for an arrest warrant, to be sufficient, must give the reviewing magistrate sufficient probable cause to believe that a crime has occurred. The magistrate cannot rely simply on the officer's opinion about the facts of the case. Instead, the officer must accurately identify the person who committed the crime, give details of the crime itself, and provide any supporting documentation, such as statements by witnesses to help establish probable cause. Once that presentation has been made, the magistrate—who is supposed to be neutral and detached from the proceedings—must evaluate whether probable cause exists based on the documentation that has been presented. Magistrates may not rely on the opinion or "word" of an officer with whom the magistrate has worked on prior occasions. Each case is evaluated on its own merits, and if sufficient probable cause is not found in the initial arrest warrant, the entire case may be invalidated.

Once issued, an arrest warrant must describe with particularity the person to be arrested. Magistrates are not allowed to issue blank warrants or warrants that

Issuing Warrants

PROFILING THE PROFESSIONAL

"We do use video technology to do both arrest and searches. We use the EWI system. That stands for electronic warrants interface and it is a system that allows a judge and a police officer located at two separate locations to communicate with each other via videoconference link. We can have a hearing concerning the issuance of an arrest or search for and communicate all the information we need necessary to accomplish that task and then also issue the warrant electronically and create both original and copy documents for the judge, the officer, and anybody else that might need it. We have terminals here at the jail and we have terminals out at the regular courthouse, and each of the police precincts and police headquarters and all of the municipal law enforcement agencies have terminals in their buildings. An officer can stop at any one of those locations, log in, and establish a video communication with the judge at the jail, and we now have magistrates here 24 hours a day, seven days a week so they can do this all day and all night if they want to. Through that video connection and that computer connection we can do everything that is necessary to issue an arrest warrant or search warrant without ever having to physically come to the jail to do so. We probably do 80 percent, or even more than that, using the EWI system."

Hon. George Hutchinson, Magistrate Judge

allow the police to pick up any individual at any time. Instead, the arrest warrant must adequately describe the persons to be arrested and the crime for which they are being arrested. You will notice that we did not indicate that the warrant must give the suspect's proper legal name. There are times when the police cannot identify a suspect by his proper name and must instead rely on other information, such as tattoos, street name, place of residence, or other identifying characteristics that separate the suspect from anyone else in the vicinity. Police may not learn the legal name of a suspect until after he has been placed into custody.

2. ARRESTS OUTSIDE THE OFFICER'S JURISDICTION

Fresh pursuit doctrine
A court-created doctrine that allows police officers to arrest suspects without warrants and to cross territorial boundaries while they are still pursuing the suspect.

Although the general rule is that police officers cannot arrest a person outside their territorial jurisdiction, there are exceptions. One such exception is the **fresh pursuit doctrine**. Under this ruling, if the police are pursuing a person who has committed a felony, they can chase that person across county or state lines and arrest him, even though they have no lawful authority to arrest in that jurisdiction. Of course, the fresh pursuit doctrine has its own limitations, including rulings on just how "fresh" the pursuit must be. It is obviously not a fresh pursuit if the officer arrests the suspect hours or even days after the pursuit has ended. In court rulings, fresh pursuit means just what it suggests: an ongoing, immediate pursuit that happens to cross some boundary. Without that showing of immediacy, officers would have no greater authority to arrest someone outside their jurisdiction than would a citizen (see Figure 4-1).

3. CITIZEN'S ARREST

Citizen's arrest
A legal doctrine that holds harmless a citizen who detains a person observed to have committed a crime. When a person makes a citizen's arrest, she is immune from civil suit for battery or false imprisonment of the person detained, provided the person detained actually committed a crime.

Perhaps the most important thing to remember about **citizen's arrest** is that it is not actually an arrest at all. Citizens are not empowered to arrest anyone. The phrase should, more correctly, be called *citizen's detention*. Under this doctrine, persons have the right to physically restrain a person who has committed a crime in their presence and hold this person for the police. A citizen's arrest is used most commonly in cases of shoplifting—a store manager or employee detains a person suspected of shoplifting until the police arrive. This doctrine has more importance in the area of civil law, where it protects the citizen from being sued for battery in restraining the individual and holding her until the police arrive to effectuate a real arrest.[10]

4. ARRESTING WITHOUT A WARRANT FOR MISDEMEANORS

When it comes to misdemeanors, the officer must see and observe the crime before the officer is permitted to arrest. The theory here is that because the crime is less serious, a victim or an officer can go before a magistrate and seek a warrant and thus establish probable cause through a neutral and detached third party rather

[10] *State v. Garcia*, 146 Wash. App. 821, 193 P.3d 181 (Div. 3 2008).

FIGURE 4-1

Suspects Arrested and Booked by U.S. Marshals

	2005	1995	Average annual growth rate 1995-2005*
Total	140,200	83,324	5.4%
Offense at arrest	100.0%	100.0%	
Violent	3.0%	4.7%	1.4%
Property	10.7	19.5	−0.8
Drug	23.8	28.6	3.4
Weapons	6.9	4.5	10.6
Immigration	27.3	12.7	14.6
Material witness	4.4	1.4	19.6
Public order	6.5	12.4	−1.3
Supervision violations	17.4	16.2	6.1
District of arrest	100.0%	100.0%	
Southwest U.S. border districts	39.6%	23.3%	11.6%
Arizona	9.8	3.9	17.1
California-Southern	3.3	7.3	−1.8
New Mexico	3.4	1.4	15.4
Texas-Southern	12.2	5.1	16.1
Texas-Western	10.9	5.7	13.4
Non-Southwest U.S. border Districts	60.4%	76.7%	2.9%

*Calculated using each fiscal yearly count from 1995 to 2005.
Source: *Federal Justice Statistics, 2005*, September 2008, NCJ 220383, Bureau of Justice Statistics, U.S. Department of Justice.

than rely on the hearsay statements of others.[11] (By contrast, a police officer may arrest someone for a felony that the officer did not witness and that did not occur in the officer's presence. In this case, there is greater danger to the public at large, and taking the suspect into custody might prevent injury to persons or property.)

a. What Constitutes the Officer's "Presence"?

An officer must be present to observe the factors that give rise to probable cause. However, this raises the question of what actually constitutes the officer's "presence." Obviously, if the officer is standing beside the offender when the crime

[11] *Lucien v. State*, 557 So.2d 918 (Fla. Dist. Ct. App. 4th Dist. 1990).

occurs, the officer is present. But real life often presents scenarios that are not as easily dispensed with. For example, suppose the officer observes the criminal behavior through binoculars. He is obviously not in close proximity to the suspect but has observed criminal activity. Is the officer "present"? According to the courts, the answer is yes.[12] Because the officer personally observed the activity, long-distance viewing can still constitute presence. However, the issues become murkier when the officer relies on senses other than seeing. Suppose that the officer hears what she believes to be a crime occurring. Does that, by itself, give the officer probable cause to arrest? The answer is probably no. The officer would need additional verification, such as entering the area and making additional observations. The same would be true for the officer's sense of smell. Consider the next scenario.

EXAMPLE

Officer Olivieri is on foot patrol downtown. There are many streets and allies, and as Olivieri passes an alley, she catches the familiar smell of burning marijuana. She enters the alley and arrests two people who are standing next to a trashcan. She does not recover any marijuana but later testifies that part of her training at the police academy included a demonstration of the smell of burning marijuana. Does Olivieri have sufficient probable cause for an arrest?

Answer: No. Although the sense of smell can lead the officer to an area, the officer must make additional observations before making an arrest. The sense of smell, by itself, is not sufficient to arrest under these circumstances.

C. STANDARDS FOR ISSUANCE OF A SEARCH WARRANT

Expectation of privacy
A two-part test created in *Katz v. U.S.*, where the court created a standard by which searches could be evaluated to see if they are in violation of the Fourth Amendment. The test is both subjective and objective. The party who is searched must have a subjective expectation of privacy in the area to be searched, and an objective, hypothetical third party must also believe that the area to be searched has a high degree of expectation of privacy.

We have already seen that police have greater latitude in making warrantless arrests than they do in conducting warrantless searches. The reason behind this is simple: Police can secure a location and obtain a warrant to search it, but they often do not have the same option when it comes to a human being. As with arrest warrants, before issuing a search warrant, a magistrate judge must review all of the applicable facts and make a determination that there is sufficient probable cause to believe that a crime has occurred. In making that determination, a magistrate must look at the surrounding circumstances. For instance, is a warrant to search even necessary? In order to answer that question, the judge must look at the issue of **expectation of privacy**. When the location to be searched enjoys a high degree of expectation of privacy, then police must obtain a warrant before conducting a search. However, if the expectation of privacy is very low, police may not be required to obtain a search warrant at all. What, then, is expectation of privacy?

[12] *Roynon v. Battin*, 55 Cal. App. 2d 861, 132 P.2d 266 (4th Dist. 1942).

If you look to the Constitution for the phrase *expectation of privacy* you will not find it. In fact, the Fourth Amendment is a marvel of brevity when it comes to establishing rights of individuals. It was left to the courts to explain what the Fourth Amendment signified and how it applied in particular cases. The courts, in their interpretation of the Fourth Amendment, created a test that must be satisfied before search warrants are issued. That test is expectation of privacy. It was originally developed as a concurring opinion in the case of *Katz v. U.S.*[13] In that opinion, Justice John M. Harlan II created a two-pronged test to determine whether a search was unconstitutional. One prong of the test was subjective and the other was objective. What Harlan said was that for the Fourth Amendment to have any significance, the person challenging the search must first have a subjective expectation of privacy in the item searched. The second part of the test was to evaluate the search from an objective, hypothetical third party's perspective. Would this hypothetical third party believe that the area searched would have a high expectation of privacy? If the answer to both of these questions is yes, then the police must obtain a search warrant.

Essentially, if a suspect has a high degree of expectation of privacy, then the police have a higher burden to meet before search warrants will be issued. A person has an expectation of privacy in personal papers, his residence, and any other private areas. People do not have a high expectation of privacy in the items that can be clearly seen in public. If we were to create a bar graph with the highest level of expectation of privacy on one end and the lowest expectation of privacy on the other end, most of us would agree that our homes should have the highest degree of expectation of privacy. This explains why there are very few instances in which courts will allow warrantless searches of a person's home. Before police may enter your home, a magistrate must issue a search warrant authorizing them to do so. On the other end of the spectrum, if you are sitting in the food court at a local mall and have a suspicious item on the table in front of you, you would be hard-pressed to say that you have a high degree of expectation of privacy in something that any passerby could look at. In such a situation, a court may not require that the police obtain a search warrant. Police and magistrates face these issues every day in trying to determine what areas have a high degree of expectation of privacy and then establishing sufficient probable cause for a magistrate to issue a warrant to search that area.

Thus, in order to evaluate the constitutional validity of a search, the court must go through a two-step process. The use of two views on the question of expectation of privacy avoids a practical problem: If the test were purely subjective, then suspects would claim that they had an expectation of privacy in anything to be searched, and the police would be hampered, if not completely unable to perform any searches. On the other hand, if the court were to use a purely objective approach, then it would not allow for the many unusual situations that people find themselves in. Consider the following scenario.

[13] 389 U.S. 347 (1967).

EXAMPLE

John is homeless. Several years ago, he began bringing various pieces of abandoned property, wood, and other discarded objects together to form a new home in the woods. What began as an assemblage of junk has now blossomed into a two-room tent/shanty that John calls home. A police officer was recently working his way through the woods and came across John's tent. He immediately searched it and found marijuana. John wishes to challenge the search. Does John have an expectation of privacy?

Answer: Yes. Viewed under both standards, subjective and objective, there may be some conflict here. John certainly has a subjective belief that his tent/shanty is his home, and he professes a high degree of expectation of privacy. Objectively, would a third person share this belief? In a close case, the courts will almost always side with the suspect. The most likely ruling is that the officer should have obtained a search warrant before searching. Because he had no probable cause, he would undoubtedly have been unable to receive one.

Just as we saw in the previous scenario, when courts address searches, they must consider all of the surrounding circumstances, including the suspect's expectation of privacy, the needs of law enforcement, and society's need for privacy. This is a delicate balancing act, requiring each case to be evaluated on its merits, without regard to bright-line tests. Courts take each case as it comes.

D. WHO CAN CHALLENGE A SEARCH?

Standing
A recognized legal right to bring suit or to challenge a legal decision.

The question of a legal challenge to a search involves the issue of **standing**. Broadly speaking, standing is the requirement that the person making the challenge must have some personal interest in the search. Mere ownership rights are not enough. This explains why a renter may have standing to challenge a search, but the landlord might not. A renter actually lives on the premises and has an obvious expectation of privacy, whereas the landlord, who does not live on the premises, may lack such an expectation. Similarly, when an entity finances the purchase of a car, it is the driver who can challenge a search of the car, not the financing company. Courts impose the requirement of standing to keep anyone from challenging any legal action against anyone. In order to bring suit, that individual's rights or property must be seized.

EXAMPLE

Ted is a squatter in an empty building. The structure has been condemned, and no one is allowed to live on the premises. Ted has no ownership interest in the property and does not lease the premises from anyone. One afternoon, a police officer hears Ted inside the building, enters, and searches Ted's belongings, finding an illegal narcotic. Does Ted have standing to challenge the search?

Answer: No. Ted does not own, lease, or control the premises, and he has no legal right to be there. Because of that, he has no legitimate expectation of privacy and cannot challenge the search.

Standing is a function of ownership or direct rights being placed in jeopardy. Without one or the other, a court may decide that a person has no standing to bring a challenge to the constitutionality of a search and dismiss the person's motion.

EXAMPLE

Bill is a passenger in a cab. A police officer stops the cab driver for speeding and an illegal lane change, and asks both Bill and the cab driver to get out. After talking with the cab driver, the police officer searches the driver's compartment and discovers a kilo of cocaine. The officer charges the cab driver with possession of cocaine. Does Bill have standing to challenge the search?

Answer: No. Passengers in cabs or other public transports do not have an expectation of privacy and cannot challenge the search based on standing. The driver, on the other hand, would have standing to challenge the search.

EXAMPLE

Alicia is a guest at a hotel. At 2 A.M., police storm into her room, search it, and find an automatic weapon. Does Alicia have standing to challenge the search?

Answer: Yes. Hotel guests have a reasonable expectation of privacy and therefore can challenge warrantless searches of their rooms. In this situation, the police should have obtained a warrant.

INTERROGATION AND *MIRANDA*

It is quite common for the police to interrogate a defendant following an arrest. If they do so, they must first read the defendant his *Miranda* rights. We have all seen this process carried out on television and in movies and can probably recite the *Miranda* warnings without much prompting. Specifically, police must inform the suspect that he has the right to remain silent, and if he gives up that right to remain silent, anything that he says can and will be used against him during the trial.

Although there are many instances in which the police interrogate a defendant after arrest, there are also a sizable number of instances in which the police do not question a suspect at all. For example, if a defendant is picked up on a parole violation, there is very little need to question the defendant. He has violated probationary terms, and it does not matter to the police why the defendant chose to violate them. Similarly, police rarely question a DUI suspect after arrest. There is very little information that the police could gain from the defendant in that situation, and because police must ascertain that a defendant is of sound mind and not under the influence of any drugs or medicine during an interrogation, interviewing an obviously intoxicated defendant would violate several of those rules.

A. ORAL AND WRITTEN STATEMENTS

When the police decide to question a suspect, they usually do so verbally. However, once the defendant has told her story, it is quite common for the police to reduce that statement to writing and have the defendant sign a statement to indicate that she is in complete agreement with the facts as they are presented in the statement.

B. *MIRANDA v. ARIZONA*

Once a defendant has been placed under arrest, a panoply of constitutional rights are triggered, including the right to have an attorney, the right to a trial by jury, the right to be presumed innocent, the right not to incriminate oneself, and the right to remain silent. In previous decades, federal and state police agencies were in agreement that these rights existed, but there was a great deal of confusion about how the suspect should be informed of these rights or even if the suspect should be advised at all. Police officers argued that they were in the worst position to advise the suspect of his rights. They are not lawyers and have no pretense to understanding the nuances of constitutional interpretation. Before the Supreme Court weighed in on this phase of the criminal prosecution, suspects might or might not be advised of their rights, and the person responsible for informing the suspect might be any of a number of individuals, from local magistrates to officers handing out printed documents to everyone placed under arrest, whether they could actually read the rights or not.

Miranda v. Arizona[14] was a highly controversial case when it was first decided, but it did put an end to speculation about when a suspect should be advised of her constitutional rights and who should do the advising. As anyone who watches TV or movie legal dramas knows, police officers are responsible for advising suspects, and they must be advised before they are interrogated.

1. HISTORY OF THE *MIRANDA* CASE

Ernesto Miranda was arrested for the kidnapping and rape of a young woman. After his arrest, he was interrogated by police officers for several hours and eventually confessed to the crime. The *Miranda* decision came about when Miranda's attorney appealed his conviction on the basis that his confession should not have been used in his trial because he had never been informed of his rights under the law. The U.S. Supreme Court consolidated Miranda's case with several others in which the same issue was raised and then reached its famous decision. Because Miranda's name was first on the Court's opinion, the ruling became known as the *Miranda decision*, and the requirements imposed by the Court on police became known as *Miranda warnings* (see Figure 4-2).

Under the ruling, the prosecution may not use any statement that was made by the defendant until the state has proven that the defendant knew all of her

[14] 384 U.S. 436, 86 S. Ct. 1602, 16 L. Ed. 2d 694 (1966).

When a police officer reads a suspect his "rights," the officer normally follows some variation of the following:

You have the right to remain silent. If you give up the right to remain silent, anything you say can and will be used against you at trial. If you cannot afford an attorney to represent you, you may qualify to have the state appoint an attorney for you. Do you understand these rights as I read them to you?

FIGURE 4-2

The *Miranda* Rights

constitutional rights, had the ability to invoke them, and then waived them and gave a statement to police. Among these rights, police must specifically tell a suspect that the Fifth Amendment provides the right to remain silent and not incriminate oneself, and if a person waives that right, any statement that she makes may be used against her during the trial to prove that she committed the crime. Before the prosecution can introduce the defendant's confession at trial, the prosecutor must call police witnesses to testify that they read the defendant her rights, that she appeared to understand them, that she was not coerced or promised anything to waive her rights, and that she gave her statement after waiving her constitutional rights.

Suspects must be warned of their *Miranda* rights even when they know their rights as well as the officers. For instance, if a person has been arrested many times before, he must still be informed of his *Miranda* rights. The rights must be read to suspects even when these suspects are legal professionals, such as attorneys or judges. Interestingly enough, a recent U.S. Supreme Court case has held that police do not have to use the same wording as every other state or federal agency. As long as each and every *Miranda* right is conveyed to the suspect, it does not matter that the police vary the phrasing.[15]

2. EXCEPTIONS TO *MIRANDA*

Miranda rights must be read to a suspect who is taken into custody or arrested only if he is going to be questioned. That is an important point to remember. An arrest is not unconstitutional if the police fail to read a suspect his or her *Miranda* rights. A suspect must be read the rights before being questioned, but there are circumstances, as noted previously, in which the police have no intention of questioning a defendant and therefore do not need to read the suspect *Miranda* warnings. There is also no requirement that the police must read a person the *Miranda* warnings before being arrested. *Miranda* applies only to postarrest questioning and interrogation. One might be tempted to think that the police would wish to question everyone that they arrest, but there are numerous circumstances when such questioning never occurs.

---

[15] *Florida v. Powell*, 130 S. Ct. 1195 (2010).

There are also other circumstances in which the *Miranda* rights warnings are not required:

- Background or routine police questioning
- Exigent circumstances
- Voluntary statements
- Traffic stops

a. Background or Routine Police Questioning

When police arrive at the scene of a crime, they will ask questions that we would all expect to hear. What happened? Who did it? Where is the person who did the crime? What is the relationship of the people present to one another, to the victim, and to the defendant? In these situations, the police are not required to preface their questions with the *Miranda* warnings. When they focus their attention on a specific suspect and begin to ask questions that could incriminate him, they have moved beyond background or routine questioning and *Miranda* rights would then apply. However, until that time, officers may question people at the scene without any need to Mirandize everyone they meet.

b. Exigent Circumstances

We have already encountered exigent circumstances previously in this chapter in our discussion of the exception to the search warrant requirement. U.S. Supreme Court decisions have also created an exigent circumstances exception that applies to *Miranda* warnings. An exigent circumstance is a situation that is inherently dangerous to police officers, to civilians, or to both. Police are allowed to ask questions that will help them prevent harm to others or prevent evidence from being destroyed without first having to read anyone the *Miranda* warnings. The most common example of an exigent circumstance question is when the police ask people at the scene where a weapon is so that they can secure it before it is used on anyone else. If the person who points out the location of the weapon also eventually ends up being the person charged with a crime, her statement about the location of the weapon will not be ruled inadmissible even though the suspect was not Mirandized, because the questions fall under the category of exigent circumstances.

c. Voluntary Statements

If a suspect voluntarily agrees to speak with police, *Miranda* does not apply. By volunteering, the suspect is waiving his or her constitutional rights—the very rights spelled out in the *Miranda* warnings. A suspect always has the right to waive the application of those rights to his case and freely discuss it with the police. However, law enforcement officers are not permitted to use subterfuge to trick the defendant into giving a "voluntary" statement. For instance, police cannot address one another within earshot of the suspect and say that the suspect is hiding behind his rights or that a "real man would own up to what he had done." Unfortunately, this rule is routinely and almost universally abused by television detectives.

i. When It Is Lawful to Use Trickery

We have just established that law enforcement cannot use trickery or deceit to make a suspect give up her constitutional rights. However, that prohibition does not extend to other areas. Police may lie to a defendant, so long as the lie is not designed to circumvent any constitutional protections. Law enforcement might lie to a suspect and tell her that a witness saw her commit the crime or that they have evidence tying her to the scene when they actually do not. Trickery and deception are not commonplace during most interrogations because of the difficulties involved in maintaining the deception. Lies often lead to other lies. If the defendant knows that she wore gloves during the crime and the detectives claim that they recovered her fingerprints from the scene, the defendant will realize that they are lying and may question just how much evidence they actually have that incriminates her. In cases where police use trickery, courts always examine the officers' actions very closely, and that is yet another reason police hesitate to wander into this legal minefield.

EXAMPLE

Theo is being questioned by the police for the murder of his wife. He has just invoked his right to remain silent and has requested an attorney. There is a tape recorder on the table between the officer and Theo, and when the battery on the unit suddenly dies, the officer leans over and tells Theo, "Just look me in the eye and tell me. Man to man. Off the record. You killed her, didn't you?"

Theo asks, "Off the record?"

The officer nods.

"Yes," Theo says. "I did it."

Will Theo's confession be admissible at trial?

Answer: No. An officer cannot use trickery to deceive a defendant into giving up a right. It is trickery to tell the suspect that a statement is "off the record" when it will be used against him.[16]

d. Traffic Stops

When police officers pull over automobile drivers for routine infractions, such as speeding or improper passing, this stop is not considered to be an arrest, and therefore *Miranda* warnings are not required.[17] However, *Miranda* warnings would apply if the police officer were to remove the driver from her automobile and place her under arrest or transport her back to police headquarters for questioning.[18]

---

[16] *Frazier v. Cupp*, 394 U.S. 731 (1969).
[17] *Pennsylvania v. Bruder*, 488 U.S. 292 (1990).
[18] *Berkemer v. McCarty*, 103 S. Ct. 3138 (1984).

3. REINITIATING QUESTIONING AND *MIRANDA* RIGHTS

A question often arises during the course of repeated interrogations of a suspect: How long are the *Miranda* rights "good" for? Put another way, is it sufficient to read the suspect her *Miranda* rights once and then never read them again? Do the rights eventually expire? When police officers initially question a suspect and read that suspect the *Miranda* warnings, must they be read every time that they question the suspect after that?

Police officers are not required to re-Mirandize a suspect each and every time that they question him. However, once the suspect has invoked his right to remain silent, the situation changes. In one case, *Edwards v. Arizona*,[19] a suspect (Edwards) was arrested on burglary and murder charges. During questioning, Edwards said that he wanted to consult with an attorney before making any further statements. The police officers stopped the interview and returned Edwards to his cell. At this point, the officers had acted in accordance with *Miranda*. However, the following day, two other police officers appeared at the jail and asked to see Edwards. He refused to speak with the officers but was told by a guard that he must. He was read his *Miranda* rights again, and during this interrogation made incriminating statements that were later used against him at trial. The U.S. Supreme Court held that the use of his statement violated his right to have an attorney present during his questioning. Edwards, according to the Court, had made an unequivocal request for an attorney. His questioning the next day did not waive that right, because a suspect must knowingly and intelligently relinquish his rights. The U.S. Supreme Court has placed the burden for showing compliance with its decisions squarely on the shoulders of the state. Therefore, the state must show that the defendant voluntarily waived his rights before the statement can be read to the jury. When police reinitiate questioning of a suspect, they may rely on the fact that they Mirandized the suspect the first time; however, if any appreciable period of time has passed between the first questioning and the second, police must read the suspect his *Miranda* rights again. Courts have been vague on just how long this appreciable period is. The safest course for a police officer to follow when there is any doubt about whether the first reading of *Miranda* rights was sufficient is to Mirandize the suspect again.

4. WHEN MUST THE POLICE STOP QUESTIONING A SUSPECT?

A criminal suspect has an absolute right to remain silent. When a defendant states that he has nothing to say, police are not permitted to force him to make incriminating statements. A statement obtained in a coercive way is not admissible at trial. When the suspect states that he does not wish to say anything until he speaks with his attorney, questioning must also stop at that point. Police officers are not allowed to try to talk the suspect out of his need for an attorney or to continue questioning him until his attorney arrives. A recent Supreme Court case has held,

[19] 451 U.S. 477 (1981).

however, that a defendant must tell the police that he intends to remain silent. The suspect cannot simply refuse to answer and have the police infer that he intends to remain silent.[20]

ARREST

We have discussed the elements of search and arrest warrants and even outlined various events that may give police officers probable cause to arrest, but we have not yet considered the question of what the legal definition of arrest is. What is the significance of being placed under arrest and what procedural steps happen after that event?

A. DEFINING ARREST

To **arrest** a person is to detain that person so that she is not free to leave. Although it is common for a person who is under arrest to be placed in handcuffs, it is not legally required in order for a person to be considered under arrest. An arrest can occur under a wide variety of situations. There is no requirement that the police must use the word "arrest" before a detention is considered to be an arrest. The problem with defining arrest is that there are so many interactions between police and suspects in so many varied locations and under such a wide variety of circumstances that simply defining arrest as taking someone into custody is not sufficient. The real issue with defining arrest has to do with constitutional rights. Before a person is legally considered under arrest, she does not have the right to a trial by jury, the right to have an attorney present during questioning, or many other rights. There is a natural tension between suspects and police when it comes to defining the precise moment when an arrest occurred. For the suspect, the sooner she is considered to be under arrest, the better. Similarly, a police officer may wish to put off the moment of arrest as long as possible in order to take advantage of the questions and tactics that would not be available to him once the suspect is considered to be under arrest. As a result, courts do not look to the subjective intent of either the suspect or the police officer in determining when an arrest occurred. Instead, courts look to the surrounding circumstances. A person is under arrest when a third party, viewing the facts and circumstances, would believe that the suspect was not free to leave.[21] This classification of not being free to leave, of being restrained and not being able to go about one's business, defines when a suspect is actually under arrest and when all of her constitutional rights are triggered.

Arrest
Restraint of a person by the police such that the person is not free to leave.

[20] *Berghuis v. Thompkins*, 130 S. Ct. 1499 (2010).
[21] *U.S. v. Hastamorir*, 881 F.2d 1551, 1556 (11th Cir. 1989); *United States v. Hammock*, 860 F.2d 390, 393 (11th Cir. 1988).

B. WHAT HAPPENS AFTER ARREST?

Once a person is placed under arrest, he is then transported to the local detention facility where the typical book-in procedures take place. The person will be fingerprinted, have all belongings taken away and stored for safekeeping, issued a jail uniform with sandals, and then assigned to a cell. However, there are numerous instances in which this procedure is not followed. For instance, suppose that a suspect has been arrested on a misdemeanor count. Many jail facilities post bond amounts for specific types of offenses. For example, a first-offense theft by shoplifting might carry a bond of $500. If the defendant can pay the bond, then he will be released after being fingerprinted. If the defendant cannot make bond, then he will be held at the local detention facility until the initial appearance.

IV INITIAL APPEARANCE

Initial appearance
A court proceeding held shortly after the suspect's arrest in which the suspect is apprised of specific constitutional rights.

In some jurisdictions, the **initial appearance** is also called the preliminary examination. Whatever its name, the hearing itself has a specific function. It ensures that the person who has been placed under arrest is made aware of her rights under the Constitution.

A. THE PURPOSE OF THE INITIAL APPEARANCE

At the initial appearance, the accused is usually informed of:

- The seriousness of the charge against her
- The consequences of the hearing and future hearings
- The right to the assistance of counsel

The initial appearance hearing is specifically designed to ensure that the defendant is aware of his constitutional rights as early in the legal process as possible. The person who informs the defendant of his rights is often a magistrate judge. This same judge may appoint an attorney to represent the defendant if the defendant cannot afford to hire his own.

1. INFORMING THE ACCUSED

At the initial appearance, the judge will advise the defendant of the charge against him. The judge will also inform the defendant that this is a preliminary charge and that additional charges may be brought against him. The defendant will be told whether he is charged with a felony or a misdemeanor and the maximum possible sentence (although not all jurisdictions follow this last procedure).

The judge will also confirm the defendant's identity, making sure that the person the police have charged and placed under arrest is the same person referred to in the arrest warrant. To that end, the judge may sometimes require fingerprint analysis to confirm that the person in custody is in fact the person whom the police believe him to be.

2. RIGHTS OF THE ACCUSED

Although some initial appearance hearings are conducted by other officials, for the sake of clarity we will continue to refer to the presiding official at the initial appearance hearing as a magistrate judge. This judge will read the defendant her constitutional rights. The rights sound very similar to the *Miranda* rights read to the defendant shortly after being placed under arrest, and that similarity is no accident. The *Miranda* decision, as well as subsequent Supreme Court decisions, requires that the defendant be made aware of the fact that she is presumed innocent, that she has the right to remain silent, that she has the right to a jury trial, and that she has the right to an attorney. If the defendant cannot afford an attorney, the magistrate at the initial appearance hearing may appoint one there or advise the clerk's office or other administrator that the defendant's case should be routed to the public defender's office or to the appointed attorney list, depending on the procedure followed in that jurisdiction.

3. RIGHT TO COUNSEL

The right to an attorney is one of the cornerstones of the American judicial system. As we will see later in this text, that right has not always been universally available to those who cannot afford one. When we discuss the famous *Gideon v. Wainwright* case, we will see that prior to the decision in that case, those who faced felony charges and could not afford to hire a lawyer had to conduct their own trials.

A defendant may hire an attorney at any point following the arrest. The defendant may even have contacted an attorney before the arrest warrant was served, assuming that the defendant was aware of the warrant. In any event, as soon as an attorney is hired for the defendant, the attorney's first bit of advice to the client is usually to say nothing to the police. Defense attorneys know that it is far more likely that the defendant, in trying to explain his actions, will only dig the hole deeper and end up making the state's case that much easier. Once the defendant has invoked his right to remain silent, the police cannot question him any further. If an attorney is either retained or appointed to represent the defendant, that attorney will normally handle the defendant's case from that point onward. The attorney will discuss the case with the prosecutor and attend the preliminary hearing and any other hearings, as well as conduct the jury trial, should it come to that. A defense attorney may enter the picture at any of several different steps in the postarrest process. The defendant, or a family member, may retain an attorney to represent the defendant.

One of the first duties of a defense attorney is to attempt to have the defendant released from jail on bond. Whether or not bond is granted in a

FIGURE 4-3

Time Between Arrest and Sentencing

	Median time (in days)	Following arrest, cumulative percent sentenced within—Most serious conviction offense			
		1 month	3 months	6 months	1 Year
All offenses	265	4%	14%	33%	67%
Violent offenses	295	2%	9%	26%	62%
Murder/ Nonnegligent manslaughter	505	1	3	8	31
Sexual assault[a]	348	1	5	19	54
Robbery	282	1	7	25	65
Aggravated assault	279	2	10	29	65
Other violent[b]	244	4	14	35	72
Property offenses	237	3%	15%	38%	70%
Burglary	234	3	15	39	71
Larceny	220	5	18	41	71
Fraud/Forgery[c]	261	2	12	33	66
Drug offenses	271	6%	15%	32%	66%
Possession	257	9	20	35	68
Trafficking	282	3	12	30	64
Weapon offenses	253	4%	15%	34%	69%
Other specified offenses[d]	253	3%	14%	34%	69

Note: Data on time to dispose of felonies were reported for 33% of convicted felons.
[a]includes rape.
[b]includes offenses such as negligent manslaughter and kidnapping.
[c]includes embezzlement.
[d]Comprises nonviolent offenses such as vandalism and receiving stolen properly

Source: *Felony Sentences in State Courts, 2006.* Statistical Tables. Bureau of Justice Statistics, U.S. Department of Justice. Revised 11/22/2010.

defendant's case can have profound implications. If the judge grants bond and the defendant is able to raise the amount, he will be allowed to leave the jail and return to work (subject to certain conditions). However, if the defendant is unable to afford bond, or in the rare case in which a judge refuses to allow bond, the defendant may remain in jail for weeks or months before his case is finally resolved (see Figure 4-3).

V BAIL/BOND—GETTING OUT OF JAIL

The terms *bail* and *bond* have been used in many different ways over the decades and so have become a bit confused. For simplicity, however, we will use the terms interchangeably. **Bail** is a defendant's assurance that she will return to court at a specific date and time. The initial phases of a criminal prosecution vary dramatically from state to state and on the federal level. Being released from jail prior to trial on bail is one of those areas in which there is considerable difference between jurisdictions. Bail is often set at the initial appearance hearing, but this issue comes up more often at the preliminary hearing stage, which we will discuss later in this chapter.

Bail/bond
Terms that are used interchangeably to refer to an amount posted by a defendant (or posted on the defendant's behalf) to ensure that the defendant will return for future court hearings.

Bail can be set by magistrate judges or trial judges. The appellate courts have determined time and again that the judge is in the best position to review all of the available facts and to know the case "on the ground" better than an appellate court. As such, appellate courts are generally very reluctant to overturn a judge's decision regarding the amount of bail or even whether bail should be set at all. In many jurisdictions, a judge has wide latitude in deciding on bail. Usually, there is no set monetary amount for each case; the nature of the charge will determine the monetary amount of bail. The arresting officer has no authority to set the amount of bail. A judge will often consider the officer's recommendation but is not bound to follow it.

Note that some bails do not involve money or property at all. A person released on bail might be released on bail with no conditions, or on supervised bail, where she must check in with a court clerk or other official periodically. A defendant may also receive conditional bail or conditional release; in such a case the defendant's release from jail contains specific provisions that, if broken, will land her back in jail. One of the most common requirements of conditional bail is that the accused stay away from the victim in the case.

A. THE PURPOSE OF BAIL

Bail is not intended to punish the defendant before the case has been concluded. It is not, as has sometimes been portrayed in various media, a means for the court to financially cripple the accused before the trial ever occurs. Rather, the concept of bail arises under the presumption in American law that a person is innocent until proven guilty and should, therefore, not be held in jail until trial unless there is some overriding reason for doing so. Thus, one purpose of bail is to release the accused from jail—and presumably free up some room for others who have been arrested. The ultimate purpose of bail, however, is to prevent or at least discourage people accused of crimes from fleeing the jurisdiction. Having to forfeit a large sum of money is enough to encourage most people to return for future court hearings. If a person posts her own bail amount, then it will be returned to her when the case is resolved.

PROFILING THE PROFESSIONAL

Bonds

"Some of the criteria in determining bond is whether or not the defendant will commit other crimes, will harass or intimidate witnesses or is a risk to flee the jurisdiction, is a risk of committing other felonies while out on custody. We were doing a preliminary hearing and the case was bound over. The attorney put his client on the stand to begin asking him questions relative to bond. The attorneys will typically ask them about their connections to the community, we'll ask them about their prior criminal history, if that's something that needs to be addressed, the attorney will typically ask those four questions. So, in this case the attorney put his client on the stand and asked, 'Sir, if you were released on bond, would you commit any other felonies?'

The client said no, that he would not.
'Would you be or do you think you are a threat to the community?'
The client answered no, of course not.
'In the event that you were released from custody, would you attempt to harass or intimidate witnesses?'
Client answered no, he would never do that.
'Finally, if you were released from custody, would you return to court when you were directed to do so?'
The defendant paused, sort of looked at the ceiling, searching around there for answer to the question, looked back down at his attorney and said, 'Well, I'd sure think about it.'
Needless to say, he did not get a bond granted."

Hon. George Hutchinson, Magistrate Judge

Yet another purpose of bail is to allow the defendant to help his attorney prepare their defense. That is considerably easier to do when the defendant is out in the community rather than held at the local jail. The defendant, while out on bail, can continue to work, which will help him pay for legal services, and the defendant can also help the attorney locate witnesses beneficial to the defense.

Several different factors weigh in to a bail decision. As we will see in this section, there are stages in the criminal process during which bail cannot be granted for certain offenses or bail may be completely denied. Although there are many situations in which the court might deny bail, those reasons must be based on factors independent of the person's supposed guilt. Instead, the court must take into account other factors before deciding on the issue of bail.

1. FACTORS THAT COURTS CONSIDER BEFORE SETTING BAIL

Judges are required to consider several factors before setting a bail amount. The U.S. Constitution, in the Eighth Amendment, prohibits the setting of "excessive" bail amounts but does not clarify in its text how the word *excessive* should be defined. Before determining a bond amount, a judge must consider several factors:

- Seriousness of the offense
- Defendant's ties to the community
- Defendant's likelihood of flight
- Overall protection of the community

a. Seriousness of the Offense

Although a defendant is presumed innocent, a court may consider the seriousness of the offense as one of the factors in deciding on a bond amount. There are certain offenses, such as rape and murder, for which the court may deny bail entirely. In such a situation, the danger to the community, or to specific individuals, may be such that it outweighs the defendant's need for freedom pending trial. As we will see later in this chapter, there are some offenses, such as murder, for which magistrate judges are not allowed to set the bond amount at all.[22] Instead, the trial judge has exclusive jurisdiction to set the bond, and the defendant must remain in custody until he is brought before the trial judge for a bond hearing.

b. Defendant's Ties to the Community

Another factor that a judge will consider before setting a bond is the defendant's ties to the community. If the defendant is a stranger or someone simply passing through the area on his way to some other locale, there is a greater likelihood that he will abscond from the jurisdiction when he is released. On the other hand, consider a defendant with strong ties to the community, such as family members who live in the area, children who attend school in the jurisdiction, or long-term employment in the area. All of these factors will weigh in the defendant's favor. If the defendant cannot show any of these ties to the area, the bond amount will undoubtedly be larger than for someone charged with the same offense who can boast of these connections to the community.

c. Defendant's Likelihood of Flight

Closely linked with the consideration of the defendant's ties to the community is the issue of whether the defendant is likely to flee the jurisdiction once released. A defendant who leaves the area and fails to return for court hearings will forfeit her bond, but that may not be a large consideration for some individuals. Suppose that the defendant is charged with possession with intent to distribute narcotics. The defendant has a large supply of ready cash, and even if the court requires a $1

[22] *State v. Dodson*, 556 S.W.2d 938 (Mo. Ct. App. 1977).

million bond, the defendant could post the money and then flee, forfeiting the money but avoiding justice. It is not always easy for the judge to divine whether a person is likely to flee the jurisdiction if released. The defendant's attorney will certainly argue that she will not, while the prosecutor may just as forcefully argue that she might. The judge must make up his own mind about this issue. If the defendant has fled while on bond before, this factor by itself may be enough for the judge to deny any bond in the case.

d. Overall Protection of the Community

A defendant is presumed innocent until proven guilty at trial, but a judge who is considering allowing a defendant out on bond must consider what the defendant might do to the witnesses and victims in the case if he is set free. The judge must weigh delicate factors here: the defendant's constitutional right not to have excessive bail imposed on him, the defendant's presumption of innocence, and the possible danger that the defendant poses to society in general or to certain individuals in specific. There have certainly been many cases in which a defendant who was released on bond killed the witness against him or otherwise caused bodily injury and property damage. Judges do not have crystal balls; they must rely on their own experiences and the law as they weigh this element in with the other factors that must be considered before setting a bond amount.

B. TYPES OF BAIL

As we have already seen, a judge is permitted to create different types of bail and set specific conditions that the defendant must abide by while out on bail. If these conditions are violated, the judge has the power to revoke bail and have the defendant returned to jail pending trial.

1. MONETARY BAIL

In its simplest incarnation, the judge sets a monetary amount as bail. If the defendant has that amount of money or can raise it, the defendant will post the money with the clerk and then be released from jail, usually with a notice for the next court date.

a. Bonding Companies

A bonding company is in the business of posting monetary bail bonds for people who cannot afford to pay their own bail. Usually, these companies will charge a 10 percent nonrefundable fee to the defendant for this service. Suppose that a judge has set bail for Mr. X at $20,000 and imposed two conditions: 1) that he maintain gainful employment and 2) that he have no contact with Ms. Y. A bonding company would charge Mr. X $2,000 to post bond for him and would probably also check up on him periodically to make sure that he is following the other terms of his bail. After all, if the defendant violates the terms and conditions of his bail, the bonding company would be forced to pay the court $20,000. The bonding company therefore has a stake in making sure that the defendant appears for court.

In some states, bonding companies have been eliminated. There have been, over the years, allegations of abusive tactics used by bonding companies and their "bounty hunters," and some states have addressed this issue by taking over the business of posting bond. In these states, the defendant posts 10 percent of the bond amount in cash with a court clerk. Later, this money may be applied toward payment of a fine or restitution. If the defendant is found not guilty, the money will be returned.

i. Bounty Hunters

In states that do allow the existence of bonding companies, these companies often employ individuals to hunt down and return defendants who have fled the jurisdiction. State law often gives a grace period to the bonding company to produce the individual who has not appeared for court. This grace period might be anywhere from three to ten days, depending on the circumstances. If the bonding company is able to locate the defendant and return him to the jail, then the bonding company will not be required to forfeit the defendant's bond. This creates a system in which the bonding company has a strong interest to keep tabs on its client, and also gives law enforcement another tool to help locate defendants who have absconded. This is where the so-called bounty hunter enters the picture. The bonding company may pay a flat fee to an individual to find the defendant and bring him back to the jurisdiction. In other cases, the bounty hunter may be paid on a percentage basis, such as 10 percent of the bonding company's fee. In our previous example involving Mr. X, the bond fee was $2,000 and the bounty hunter assigned to find Mr. X (should he abscond) would receive 10 percent of that amount ($200) for finding him and bringing him back.

The use of bounty hunters has been called into question by several instances in which bounty hunters have used excessive force to subdue defendants and return them. In one notable case, a bounty hunter crossed into Mexico, kidnapped a defendant, and returned him to the United States. The Mexican government charged the bounty hunter with kidnapping, causing no end of confusion for all parties concerned.

2. PROPERTY BONDS

In addition to setting monetary amounts as a condition of release, some judges may also turn to property bonds in lieu of cash. A property bond is the posting of an individual's title to his home or other land as a guarantee of the defendant's return. If the defendant flees the jurisdiction and does not return for court hearings, then the court has the unenviable task of seizing someone's home as forfeiture of the bond. In that case, the owners would be removed from their home and the house and land would become property of the local government.

3. RECOGNIZANCE BAIL

Recognizance bail
The person accused simply gives his word that he will return for a specific court date.

Recognizance bail is seen less and less, but was once quite common. When someone posts a recognizance bail, she is simply giving a promise to return and not posting any money to ensure that return. Basically, the person is giving her word. In the past, when communities were much smaller, such a process could work with reasonable efficiency. The person who posted an OR (own recognizance) bail would simply promise to return to court and then would be released. The person would be known in the community, and tracking her down would not involve much effort if the person failed to appear. Recognizance bail is used much less in bigger cities and even in smaller communities where the populace is a more mobile than it once was.

C. REVOKING BAIL

Once a defendant has been released on bail, a judge has full discretion to revoke bail and have the defendant returned to jail pending trial. A judge can base this decision on allegations that the defendant is attempting to tamper with witnesses or has posed some other danger to the community or even to prevent the defendant from harming himself.[23]

D. POSTCONVICTION BOND

Although we will discuss appellate issues in Chapter 11, it is important to note here that a defendant may qualify for a bond after being found guilty at trial. Here, the dynamics of the bail process change dramatically. Instead of guaranteeing the appearance of a person at a trial where he is presumed innocent, the person has now been found guilty and would obviously have far greater incentive to flee the jurisdiction. As a result, if a judge grants post-conviction bail at all, the amount is frequently much larger than what would have been set prior to trial. In many of these situations, courts routinely refuse to grant bail, reasoning that the defendant is at his greatest temptation to flee the jurisdiction before sentencing.[24]

VI PRELIMINARY HEARING

As we have seen, there are different types of hearings held after the defendant's arrest. One is the initial appearance, where the defendant is identified and advised of his rights. As hearings go, the initial appearance is not very dramatic; however,

[23] *Stiegele v. State*, 685 P.2d 1255 (Alaska Ct. App. 1984).
[24] *Griffith v. State*, 641 P.2d 228 (Alaska Ct. App. 1982).

that is not true of the next hearing the defendant faces: the **preliminary hearing**. The preliminary hearing (also known as a probable cause hearing) is held within days of the defendant's arrest. It is an adversarial hearing, meaning that witnesses will testify and that a prosecutor and judge will be present, as well as a defense attorney. The defendant also has the opportunity to testify at the preliminary hearing, although this rarely happens.

Preliminary hearing
A court proceeding that determines whether there is probable cause to believe that the defendant committed the crime with which he is charged.

A. THE PURPOSE OF THE PRELIMINARY HEARING

The preliminary hearing has one purpose: to establish that there is sufficient probable cause for the defendant's arrest and continued detention. At the preliminary hearing, the government, through the prosecutor, is required to present witness testimony to establish probable cause. Normally, a preliminary hearing is held before a magistrate judge. The judge has the responsibility of deciding whether the prosecution has met the burden of showing probable cause. The actual procedure for carrying out a preliminary hearing varies somewhat from jurisdiction to jurisdiction, but the basic elements are the same everywhere: The state must present evidence to prove probable cause for the defendant's arrest.

B. THE PROCEDURE AT THE PRELIMINARY HEARING

Since the purpose of a preliminary hearing is to establish probable cause that the defendant committed the crime with which he is charged, the state must present some evidence to meet its burden. This burden never shifts to the defendant to prove his innocence. The state meets its burden by calling witnesses, who are often police officers, but frequently civilian witnesses as well. These witnesses will testify about the facts surrounding the crime and the defendant's arrest. The prosecutor calls her witnesses first and then the defense attorney has the right to cross-examine the witnesses about their testimony. This cross-examination is supposed to be limited to the issue of probable cause, but many defense attorneys see this as a perfect opportunity to learn more about the case. They will often ask questions outside the scope of the hearing to learn these facts. There is no requirement to prove probable cause beyond a reasonable doubt. Instead, the state must establish probable cause by a preponderance of evidence.

We have already talked about preponderance of evidence in Chapter 1 when we discussed civil cases. This is one of the few times that this standard of proof is used in a criminal case. At a preliminary hearing, the state's burden is simply to show that it is more likely than not that the defendant committed the crime. The state does not have to prove beyond a reasonable doubt that the defendant committed the crime, because this hearing is not held before a jury. The defendant will not be sentenced at the conclusion of the hearing, and the defendant's rights will not be infringed upon. Because the burden of proof at a preliminary hearing is much lower than that required at trial, there are some practical issues that come up during preliminary hearings that do not appear during a trial. For one thing, the rules of evidence are much more liberal at a preliminary hearing.

1. RULES OF EVIDENCE

The rules of evidence at a preliminary hearing are more relaxed than those used at the trial. For instance, hearsay testimony, which is generally inadmissible at trial, can be used in a preliminary hearing. The reason that the rules of evidence are not as rigorous goes to the very heart of the preliminary hearing. The defendant will not be found guilty or sentenced at the conclusion of the preliminary hearing. The jury in the defendant's case will never be told about the result of the preliminary hearing. As such, the standard of proof is much lower. Prosecutors routinely win preliminary hearings, and it is rare for a judge to rule that there is insufficient probable cause, given such a low standard of proof.

2. THE DEFENDANT'S ROLE IN THE PRELIMINARY HEARING

A defendant sits with his counsel during the preliminary hearing, and they are allowed to confer with one another as the hearing proceeds. Many defense counsels will meet with their clients shortly before the hearing to explain what will happen, to discuss the merits of the case, and also to explain that the hearing will not result in the defendant going to prison or being found guilty.

Defendants are permitted to testify at a preliminary hearing, but they are normally counseled to remain silent. A defense attorney usually advises her client not to say anything, realizing that because establishing probable cause is an easy thing to do, the chances are extremely high that the court will rule against the defendant. In this atmosphere, it would be a waste of time to have the defendant take the stand, and it could also be disastrous when the prosecutor begins to cross-examine the defendant about specific points in the case.

Preliminary hearings are not difficult to present, and this explains why many new prosecutors are assigned to this duty. The hearing superficially resembles a trial, and inexperienced prosecutors can gain valuable insights into the adversarial process without the prospect of losing a major trial.

3. THE PRELIMINARY HEARING DOCKET

A preliminary hearing docket or calendar often contains dozens of cases scheduled for any particular day. The actual hearings are often hectic and seem chaotic to the unprepared. Dozens of witnesses may be milling around. Attorneys are often talking with clients or state's witnesses or the prosecutor. In some jurisdictions, no prosecutor is present and the judge conducts the hearing. There are often many police officers present, because they are the main staple for prosecutors conducting the preliminary hearing. Because hearsay testimony is also allowed during a preliminary hearing, a police officer might actually testify about events that she did not personally witness but that were relayed to her by another officer.

C. NEGOTIATIONS AT THE PRELIMINARY HEARING

Just because a case is on the docket for a preliminary hearing does not mean that there will be a hearing. There is a certain amount of give and take between prosecutors and defense attorneys, and the negotiations between them can become intense. What are they negotiating about? On the surface, there would appear to be very little that a prosecutor could offer a defendant or anything that the defendant would want. But appearances can be deceiving. For one thing, if a prosecutor has dozens of cases scheduled for that day, conducting every one of them might take the court into the wee hours of the following morning.

A defendant could waive the hearing—that is, admit that probable cause exists. Why would a defendant ever waive this hearing? The answer is quite simple: He or his attorney has negotiated with the prosecutor and gotten something in return for waiving the hearing. The prosecutor may ask the defendant (through the defendant's attorney—prosecutors cannot speak directly to defendants if defendants have attorneys) to waive the hearing and agree that probable cause exists in exchange for a lower bond recommendation by the prosecution. Generally, the judge follows the state's bond recommendation at the preliminary hearing. The magistrate judge knows that the case will shortly be transferred to another court where the prosecutor will have control over it, so there is little reason to oppose the prosecutor's bond recommendation. By negotiating such an outcome, the prosecutor avoids a hearing and shortens by one case what could be a very long day of preliminary hearings. Prosecutors and defense attorneys spend a great deal of time negotiating. They negotiate at preliminary hearings, bond hearings, and motion hearings, and they also negotiate plea bargains.

D. THE DECISION AT THE PRELIMINARY HEARING

There are only two decisions at a preliminary hearing: a finding that the state has established probable cause or that it has not. In the vast majority of cases, the magistrate will find that probable cause exists. The explanation for this lies somewhere between the high standard of investigation of the case by the police and the lower standard of proof for the prosecutor. If the judge reaches the conclusion that the state has established probable cause, then the judge issues an order often referred to as "binding," or transferring the case to another court. In some states, the case is transferred to Superior Court. In others, the court would be called a District or State Court. If the judge concludes that the government has failed to establish probable cause, the judge will dismiss the charges against the defendant. Assuming that there are no other charges pending against the defendant, he will be released.

PROFILING THE PROFESSIONAL

Preliminary Hearings

"I like them, but you get fewer and fewer. Almost all jurisdictions have a rule that if you make bond, you don't get one. There was a time when you would. Certain jurisdictions were giving them to you whether or not your client made bond. Now, only when they're in custody do you get them and you have to make that decision: Do I want a hearing or do I want a bond? So, I've had fewer of them than I'm used to. When you have them, they can be a good thing, when your client is charged with a serious crime, you're having trouble getting them a bond anyway, so why not have the hearing? In my practice I'm just not getting as many as I used to."

B.J. Bernstein, defense attorney

As you read the following case excerpt, pay particular attention to the charges against Stiegele as well as his argument concerning postconviction bail. These points will assist you in answering the questions that follow this excerpt.

CASE EXCERPT

STIEGELE v. STATE

685 P.2d 1255 (1984)

SINGLETON, **Judge.**

A jury found Steven Stiegele guilty of three counts of second-degree murder, an unclassified felony. AS 11.41.110. He is presently awaiting sentencing. After the verdict was returned, the trial court revoked Stiegele's bail and committed him to custody. See AS 12.30.040(b). Stiegele appeals the trial court's order denying him bail. AS 12.30.030(b); We affirm.

FACTS

Stiegele was driving a pickup truck with four passengers when the vehicle left the road and ran into the woods. Three of the passengers were killed. A blood-alcohol test, administered to Stiegele about two hours after the accident, showed an alcohol content of .13, which indicated a much higher content at the time of the accident. Prior to trial, Stiegele was released without monetary bail to the custody of his parents. He complied with all of the conditions of release including a requirement that he report three times a week for alcohol and drug use monitoring. The results of the monitoring were all satisfactory. Stiegele is a longtime resident of Alaska and has a steady employment history. He has no prior criminal record, and, except for the incident in question, he has a generally good driving record. He has never missed a court appearance.

After the verdict, Stiegele gave notice of an intent to appeal his conviction. There is nothing in the record to suggest that Judge Buckalew would not have released Stiegele on bail pending his sentencing and appeal, if it had not been for AS 12.30.040, which provides:

> Release after conviction. (a) A person who has been convicted of an offense and is awaiting sentence, or who has filed an appeal shall be treated in accordance with the provisions of AS 12.30.020 unless the court has reason to believe that no one or more conditions of release will reasonably assure the appearance of the person as required or prevent the person from posing a danger to other persons in the community. If that determination is made, the person may be remanded to custody. This section does not affect the right of a person appealing from a judgment of conviction from a district court to the superior court to be released on bail pending appeal under Rule 2(c) of the District Court Rules of Criminal Procedure.
>
> (b) Notwithstanding the provisions of (a) of this section, if a person has been convicted of an offense which is an unclassified felony or a class A felony, the person may not be released on bail either before sentencing or pending appeal.

Stiegele first argues that this statute denies him his constitutional rights to due process and equal protection. U.S. Const. amend. XIV; Alaska Const. art. I, §1; art. I, §3. He contends that the legislature has arbitrarily discriminated among those convicted of dangerous crimes by allowing bail for some while denying it to others. His due process argument is essentially the same: he argues that allowing bail to dangerous offenders convicted of class B offenses but denying it in his case is irrational.

The Alaska Supreme Court has interpreted our state equal protection and due process provisions more broadly than federal courts have construed the comparable federal provisions. Therefore, if a statute satisfies Alaska constitutional requirements, it will also satisfy federal law. In Griffith v. State, 641 P.2d 228 (Alaska App.1982), we noted that in order to withstand an equal protection challenge, a legislative classification need not be perfect. It "must be reasonable, not arbitrary, and must rest upon some ground of difference having a fair and substantial relation to the object of the legislation, so that all persons similarly circumstanced shall be treated alike." In Griffith, we recognized two reasons for a statute limiting bail pending sentencing and appeal: (1) assurance of continued appearance and amenability to the further orders of the court; and (2) protection of the community. 641 P.2d at 232. Applying our equal protection standard in light of these criteria, we find AS 12.30.040 constitutional. In effect, the legislature has denied bail to those convicted of the most serious crimes which carry the most serious penalties.

Stiegele disputes this conclusion, pointing out that some individuals convicted of class B offenses, particularly repeat offenders, might receive longer sentences than first offenders convicted of unclassified or class A felonies. He also points out that his drunk driving, which resulted in a second-degree murder conviction, might have been charged, through prosecutorial discretion, as criminally negligent homicide, a class C felony. See AS 11.41.130. Moreover, in Stiegele's view, the death of his victims was fortuitous. Consequently, he concludes that his conduct was no worse than the conduct of a drunk driver whose victims were only injured. See AS 11.41.210(2) (a person recklessly causing serious physical injury to another is guilty of assault in the second degree, a class B felony). But cf. AS 11.41.200 (a person who recklessly causes serious physical injury to another by means of a dangerous instrument or who intentionally performs an act that results in serious physical injury to another under circumstances manifesting extreme indifference to the value of human life, is guilty of assault in the first degree, a class A felony).

We believe that Stiegele has misinterpreted our decision in Griffith. In that case we compared classes of offenders and not individual members from different classes. We are satisfied that the average member of the class comprised of those convicted of unclassified felonies and class A felonies will serve a longer sentence and therefore present a greater risk of flight than the average offender convicted of a class B felony or a lesser offense. In addition, it would not have been unreasonable for the legislature to conclude that the average unclassified or class A offender is more dangerous than the average class B or C offender. Therefore, we find a legitimate basis for the legislative classification distinguishing unclassified and class A felonies from class B felonies. Consequently, AS 12.30.040 does not deny Stiegele his substantive due process or equal protection rights. As we pointed out in Griffith, "a careful limitation on bail to dangerous convicted persons is indeed rationally related to the legislative purposes of continued appearance and community protection." 641 P.2d at 234.

We need not determine whether AS 12.30.040(b) is procedural or substantive, however, because we are satisfied that it does not conflict with a supreme court rule. Consequently, Stiegele's situation differs from the situation addressed in Leege. Three rules address bail. Criminal Rule 41 addresses bail prior to conviction. It provides that a defendant in a criminal proceeding is entitled to bail pursuant to AS 12.30.010-.080. Criminal Rule 32(a) addresses bail after conviction, pending sentencing. It authorizes a trial court to commit a defendant to custody pending sentence or to continue or alter his bail as provided in Rule 41(a). Finally, Appellate Rule 206(a)(1) provides that "a sentence of imprisonment shall be stayed if an appeal is taken and the defendant is released pending appeal."

The order of the superior court denying bail is AFFIRMED.

CASE QUESTIONS

1. What were the charges against Stiegele?
2. Was the defendant required to post a monetary bond? Were there any conditions on his bond and, if so, did he comply with them?
3. What is Stiegele's argument concerning postconviction bail?
4. How did the court rule on Stiegele's argument?

CHAPTER SUMMARY

The Fourth Amendment requires probable cause before the issuance of arrest and search warrants. Probable cause is a reasonable belief that a crime has occurred. Probable cause to arrest can be based on a wide variety of sources, including information relayed by fellow police officers, information relayed by citizens, and the personal observations of the officer. When an arrest warrant is issued, it must describe with specificity the person to be arrested and the crime for which the person is charged. In order to issue a search warrant, a judge must first consider the level of expectation of privacy that the suspect has in the place to be searched. A person who wishes to challenge the results of a search must have standing to do so.

Following an arrest, suspects are frequently questioned by the police. Before such questioning can occur, the suspects must be read their *Miranda* rights. There are circumstances in which *Miranda* does not apply, including traffic stops, background or routine questions, exigent circumstances, and voluntary statements made by the suspect.

A person who is placed under arrest is not free to leave. Determining the point of arrest is important because specific constitutional rights are triggered at the moment of arrest. One of those rights is to have an initial appearance hearing. Initial appearance hearings are held in order to inform the defendant of the charges against him, to advise the defendant of his constitutional rights, and also to ensure that the police have arrested the correct person. Before, during, or after the initial appearance hearing, a defendant may be able to make bail and be released from jail pending further proceedings. Bail is not granted in all cases. Courts must consider several factors before setting a bail amount. In some states, bonding companies work with defendants by charging them a nonrefundable fee and posting the remainder of the bond for the defendant.

Within days of the defendant's arrest, a preliminary hearing will be held. The purpose of a preliminary hearing is to determine that there is sufficient probable cause to arrest and hold the defendant. The standard of proof at a preliminary hearing is preponderance of evidence, and the rules of evidence are relaxed so that hearsay and other evidence that would not be admissible at trial may be used during a preliminary hearing.

KEY TERMS

Key terms are listed here in order of appearance in chapter.

Probable cause
Contraband
Exigent circumstance
Fresh pursuit doctrine
Citizen's arrest
Expectation of privacy
Standing
Arrest
Initial appearance
Bail/bond
Recognizance bail
Preliminary hearing
Miranda Rights

REVIEW QUESTIONS

1 Which amendment governs probable cause for arrests and search warrants?
2 What is probable cause?

3 What standards must be met before a search warrant can be issued?
4 Are police required to give *Miranda* warnings in precise language in every state?
5 Can a police officer arrest someone outside her jurisdiction? Explain.
6 Is there such a thing as "citizen's arrest"? Explain.
7 Under what situations can a police officer arrest someone for a crime that was not committed in her presence?
8 What are the *Miranda* warnings?
9 List and explain at least three exceptions to the *Miranda* rule.
10 What is the purpose of an initial appearance hearing?
11 What are some of the factors that a court considers before deciding on a bail amount?
12 Is there a difference between regular bail and recognizance bail?
13 In states that allow them, how do bonding companies make money?
14 What is the purpose of a preliminary hearing?
15 Are the rules of evidence followed as strictly in a preliminary hearing as they are in a trial? Explain your answer.
16 What kinds of negotiations occur at a preliminary hearing?
17 Can police rely solely on the information provided by a confidential informant? Why or why not?
18 Can an anonymous tip provide the basis for probable cause without any other investigation by the police? Explain your answer.

WEB SURFING

Legal Definition of Preliminary Hearing
http://www.lectlaw.com/def2/p073.htm

Federal Rules of Criminal Procedures—Preliminary Hearing
http://www.law.cornell.edu/rules/frcrmp/Rule5_1.htm

Requirements for Posting Property Bonds
http://www.pawd.uscourts.gov/Documents/Forms/propbdrq.pdf

Federal Rules of Criminal Procedure—Initial Appearance
http://www.law.cornell.edu/rules/frcrmp/Rule5.htm

EXERCISES

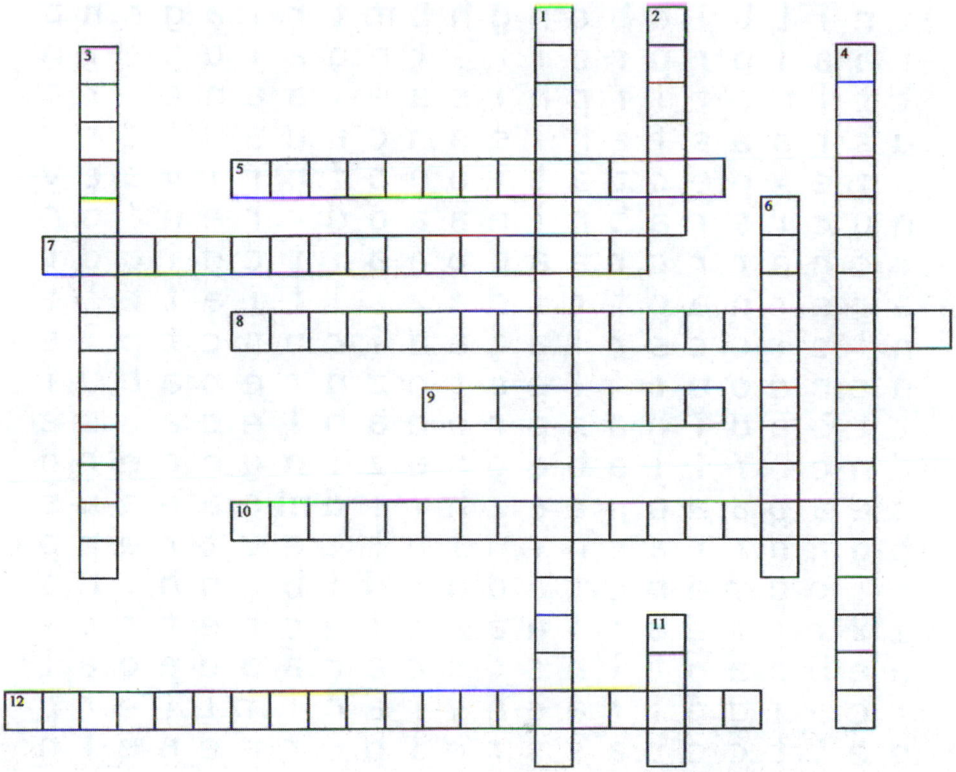

ACROSS

5. The reasonable belief that a crime has occurred or is about to occur
7. The person accused simply gives his word that he will return for a specific court date
8. An emergency situation that calls for swift action to avoid danger to people or property and allows law enforcement to bypass some Constitutional rules
9. A recognized legal right to bring suit or to challenge a legal decision
10. A court proceeding held shortly after the suspect's arrest in which he is apprised of specific constitutional rights
12. A court-created doctrine that allows police officers to arrest suspects without warrants and to cross territorial boundaries while they are still pursuing the suspect

DOWN

1. A standard by which searches can be evaluated to see if they are in violation of the fourth amendment
2. Restraint of a person by the police such that the person is not free to leave
3. A legal doctrine that holds harmless a citizen who detains a person observed to have committed a crime
4. A court proceeding that determines if there is probable cause to believe that the defendant committed the crime with which he is charged
6. Items that are illegal to possess, import, export, or sell
11. Terms that are used interchangeably to refer to an amount posted by a defendant (or posted on the defendant's behalf) to ensure that the defendant will return for future court hearings

```
r a o n t c r p g a g t z p d d a r c r d r
a e n n d i i z a i l a b n n z r n i o g r
a c s e a i p a b e e n a o / g e z g a e t
t n i t b i b b c n g h b m t r i a g s n b
r a a l n r p r o i r - t n g a i u a e i n
t t l d o t i r p n l s a e i a a n c c r s
u s r a a s f e n i e n n c a u a u ' d t r
a m e x p e c t a t i o n o f p r i v a c y
n u c r s r a b n i n a a o d c r e n ' o c
r c n o r r c r a a e p a a i t c d i o d r
a r e r n a p t r l d a z s i t i a t e t t
n i c i c t s r i a g a n i c n n c t p i e
n c n e o u r ' l p o t n z g r e p a b u i
t t b a d i g a n p r o b a b l e c a u s e
d n o b / l i a b e c n a z i n g o c e r o
a e a p a a o p z a z h / i d m e a e a u s
b g n n r t a c n r n i n t c e v t r e p p
c i c g m e b e t a d d t d i b z n b i h a
z x r r r e o r l n a a c i a c r e t r s i
a e h b a n t l h c c s c a c a p e p o e i
r c a i g n i r a e h y r a n i m i l e r p
e e t t c c t a s s r o l b c r n e n e f n
```

probable cause
contraband
exigent circumstance
fresh pursuit doctrine
citizen's arrest
expectation of privacy
standing
arrest
initial appearance
bail-bond
recognizance bail/bond
preliminary hearing

QUESTIONS FOR ANALYSIS

1 Why do courts have a preference for search warrants over searches without warrants? Explain your answer.

2 Explain the type of corroboration that a police officer must have in the following situations:
- Information provided by another police officer
- Information provided by a confidential informant
- Information provided by a citizen
- Information provided by an anonymous phone call

5

Beginning the Case

Chapter Objectives

- Discuss the function and purpose of the grand jury
- Explain how a subpoena from a grand jury would be quashed
- Define the purpose and function of an indictment
- Discuss the differences between state and federal grand jury and arraignment procedures
- Explain the importance of an arraignment in the process of a criminal case

I INTRODUCTION

In this chapter, we will examine the purpose and function of the grand jury and then proceed to the step that usually follows a grand jury indictment: arraignment. We will also examine the specifics of an indictment and how and under what circumstances a defendant might challenge either the grand jury proceedings or the actual indictment.

II GRAND JURY

According to the Fifth Amendment to the U.S. Constitution, "No person shall be held to answer for a capital, or otherwise infamous crime, unless on a presentment or indictment of a Grand Jury . . . ."

The U.S. Constitution requires a grand jury indictment for a person charged with a capital offense (one punishable by death) or "otherwise infamous crime." This phrase has come to mean any felony offense. However, the U.S. Supreme Court has never held that this provision of the Fifth Amendment applies to the states. In fact, some states do not use grand juries at all. However, since most states do, we will spend some time examining the functions and procedures of the grand jury.

Grand juries have been a feature of American and English law for centuries. The primary reason for the creation of a grand jury was to interpose a barrier between the government and the individual. As we will see, prosecutors must present their version of a criminal case to a grand jury and receive its permission to continue with the prosecution. Grand juries were traditionally seen as a way of allowing the community to protect innocent individuals from being persecuted by overzealous government officials and to prevent the government from using its power to bring criminal charges as a way to intimidate and silence those who disagreed with government policy.[1] Grand juries are features of criminal law only and have no place in civil cases. Similarly, grand juries are not required under the Uniform Military Code of Justice; they are also not required to accuse an individual of a misdemeanor in regular criminal courts. In states that have grand juries, they are governed entirely by statute and are often provided for in the state constitution. Most jurisdictions that have grand juries require them in any felony prosecution in which a person may be sentenced to more than one year in prison, or for capital murder when a person might receive a death sentence.

Grand juries do not reach verdicts. They find probable cause to continue the prosecution of a criminal case. A grand jury differs from a regular jury (sometimes called a petit jury) in several key ways. Grand juries:

- Have more than 12 members.
- Do not determine guilt or innocence.
- Do not recommend sentences.
- Meet regularly, often monthly, to consider numerous cases.

A. COMPOSITION OF THE GRAND JURY

A grand jury is selected in various ways in different jurisdictions. The most common method of selecting individual grand jurors is by using the same pool of jurors that would be used for a normal jury trial. Grand jurors:

- Must be members of the jurisdiction.
- Cannot have been convicted of a felony.
- Must be U.S. citizens.

A grand jury is made up of citizens of the county or federal district. They must be selected from a cross section of the community, including race, sex, occupation, etc.[2] Citizens cannot be excluded from a grand jury on the basis of their race, ethnic origin, or sex.[3] The usual number of jurors is between 12 and 23, again depending on the jurisdiction. Neither the federal system nor any state allows a grand jury to proceed with fewer than 12 members,[4] but many states allow a grand jury to

---

[1] *In re Grand Jury Appearance Request by Loigman*, 183 N.J. 133, 870 A.2d 249 (2005).
[2] *Campbell v. Louisiana*, 118 S. Ct. 1419 (1998).
[3] *Taylor v. Louisiana*, 95 S. Ct. 692 (1975); *Castaneda v. Partida*, 97 S. Ct. 1272 (1977).
[4] Fed. R. Crim. P. 6(f).

convene if some of its members are temporarily absent. Members are selected by the chief judge of the district.

When it comes to the actual composition of the grand jury, the members must represent a fair and impartial cross section of the jurisdiction, with the percentages of minorities reflected as closely as possible in the composition of the grand jury itself. There is no requirement that the exact percentages of race and ethnicity found in the jurisdiction must be represented in the composition of the grand jury. As long as no minority group is deliberately excluded, a defendant has no claim of improper grand jury composition if it turns out that a specific minority group was not represented on his particular grand jury. Beyond that, states vary considerably on who may serve as a grand juror. Most states specifically prohibit the victim from being a grand juror in her own case for obvious reasons. Many, but not all, states prohibit actively serving law enforcement officers from serving on a grand jury, and obviously the arresting officer is not permitted to act as a grand juror in his own case.[5]

Grand Juries

"Some states have it; some states don't. We have certain types of cases that we have to bring up before the grand jury. Felony cases, particularly if they are victim oriented, they have to go before the grand jury. My state has certain types of felonies that don't have to go before the grand jury, that would include theft by shoplifting, habitual violator, or some drug offenses. In those cases, we can draw an accusation and bypass the grand jury. The majority of the other cases must be presented to the grand jury."

Debra Sullivan, Assistant District Attorney

PROFILING THE PROFESSIONAL

1. CHALLENGING THE COMPOSITION OF THE GRAND JURY

A defendant may challenge the composition of the grand jury as not representing a fair cross section of the community, but unless the defendant can show a clear pattern of exclusion of individuals on the basis of ethnicity or race, the court is unlikely to rule that the composition was improper. In order to successfully challenge the composition of the grand jury, a defendant must show that there was some irregularity in the way that the grand jury was compiled, such as government officials deliberately ignoring statutory procedures or deliberately excluding individuals on the basis of race, religion, or ethnicity.

In an interesting Louisiana case, a white man indicted for and subsequently convicted of murder sought to quash his indictment on the grounds that the grand jury had not had a black person serve as foreperson for more than 16 years, even though 20 percent of the registered voters were black. The trial judge denied his

[5] *Stinski v. State*, 281 Ga. 783, 642 S.E.2d 1 (2007).

motion; he claimed that, as a white person, the defendant had no standing to complain about the lack of a black foreperson. The case worked its way to the Supreme Court, which held that "a white criminal defendant has the requisite standing to raise equal protection and due process objections to discrimination against black persons in the selection of grand jurors."[6]

B. PURPOSE OF THE GRAND JURY

The grand jury was devised to act as a buffer between the state and the defendant. Developed in England and later transplanted to the New World, the original concept of the grand jury has existed for more than 700 years. The grand jury is composed of citizens who sit in secret session and listen to evidence about specific cases. The essential function of the grand jury is to determine that there is probable cause to believe that a crime has occurred. Once they do, the grand jurors allow the prosecutor to continue with her case.[7] The grand jury authorizes continued prosecution by issuing an indictment. We will discuss the features of the indictment later in this chapter.

1. BURDEN OF PROOF BEFORE THE GRAND JURY

Unlike criminal trials, where prosecutors must prove beyond a reasonable doubt that a defendant is guilty of a crime, prosecutors have a much lower standard of proof for a grand jury. After all, the grand jury does not determine guilt or innocence; this, by itself, would justify a lower standard of proof.

Prima facie
(Latin) At first sight; a presumption that the facts as presented are true and establish a fact.

In order to justify an indictment, the government must present enough information for a **prima facie** case of guilt against a defendant. This means that the state must present a basic case to the grand jury showing that the defendant is the person who most likely committed the crime. Before the grand jury will permit the case to continue, it must be satisfied there is sufficient probable cause to believe that the defendant committed the crime. If the grand jury is satisfied, the words *True Bill* are written on the indictment. If the grand jury is not satisfied, the jurors write *No Bill* on the indictment and the prosecution ends. There is no appeal from the grand jury's decision.

> **Sidebar**
>
> ***The grand jury does not determine if the person charged is guilty or not guilty. It simply makes a determination that there is probable cause to believe that the defendant is guilty.***

The grand jury system has come under criticism over the years by groups claiming that it simply functions as a rubber stamp for the prosecutor. Critics claim that the prosecutor has too much control over the grand jury and can obtain indictments on anyone he chooses. However, others push back by pointing to frequent examples of grand juries refusing to indict cases brought before it. If the grand jury were a rubber stamp for the prosecution, then a vote of "no bill" would never occur. Whether the grand jury still functions as a bulwark between the individual and the vast power of the state or simply as a rubber stamp for the

[6] *Campbell v. Louisiana*, 523 U.S. 392 (1998).
[7] *State v. Hall*, 152 N.H. 374, 877 A.2d 222 (2005).

prosecutor probably depends on one's point of view. The truth is probably somewhere between these two opposing views.

The grand jury actually has several functions. The primary purpose of the grand jury is to determine if a crime has occurred. If the government can establish probable cause to believe that the defendant committed the crime presented, the grand jury has the power and duty to authorize further prosecution of the case.[8] As such, it is a key element of the criminal justice process. Witnesses appear before the grand jury and are asked questions to establish the basic merits of the case. In many states, an assistant DA is permitted to enter the grand jury room long enough to question the witness and establish the legal basis of the claim; in other states, the prosecutor is not permitted to be present at all, and law enforcement officers present the case. In all states, however, the grand jury votes in secret, with no one else present.

Beyond its strictly "bill or no bill" role, the grand jury is also empowered to conduct its own investigations into criminal allegations. The grand jury can investigate people or activities to determine if crimes have occurred. To this end, the grand jury can subpoena witnesses and documents and does not have to establish probable cause before doing so. As such, the grand jury has more latitude than police or prosecutors when investigating a case.

In its role as a supervisory body, the grand jury also oversees many local government offices and procedures. The grand jury is often called upon to make a written report about the condition of the buildings and other facilities found in the county.

But grand juries also have limitations on their power. They cannot for example, randomly subpoena witnesses to determine if some crime has occurred. The grand jury must be focused on a particular crime and does not function as an extension of the police department. The grand jury must confine its investigating and accusatory powers to investigating criminal cases. Grand juries do not involve themselves in civil cases.

> **Sidebar**
>
> *Grand juries serve different purposes in different jurisdictions. In some states, they investigate and accuse individuals of felonies. In some states they do not exist at all, while in others they may launch their own investigations.*

C. FEDERAL GRAND JURY VERSUS STATE GRAND JURY

Although grand juries are required under the federal system, that provision of the Fifth Amendment has never been made applicable to the states. As a result, many states do not follow the grand jury system at all, while others have different procedures that they use after installing a grand jury. In some states, for example, grand juries are responsible for investigating and reporting not only on crime, but also on county infrastructure and the jobs performed by public officials. We will ignore these duties in this chapter. Instead, we will focus on the grand jury as it is used both in the federal system and in many state systems: as a body that investigates and then accuses individuals of crimes.

---

[8] *State v. Kuznetsov*, 345 Or. 479, 199 P.3d 311 (2008).

In some states, certain felonies can bypass the grand jury. These relatively minor offenses, such as the driving offense of a habitual violator, may now be presented through an information or an accusation instead of an indictment. The states that have enacted these provisions have been primarily concerned with making more efficient use of the grand jury's time, especially in the face of growing caseloads.

The Federal Rules of Criminal Procedure authorize grand juries to serve a maximum of 18 months, although there are provisions that allow the grand jury to extend its time in rare instances.[9] However, an extension cannot be granted for more than six months.

Normally, grand juries on both the state and federal levels function without a judge being present. Once selected and sworn in, the grand jury carries out its day-to-day activities in the absence of any judicial review. In fact, the grand jury's decision to proceed with a prosecution is completely within its discretion and will not be overturned by a judge unless there is a clear showing of some impropriety.[10]

1. IMMUNITY IN THE FEDERAL GRAND JURY

Immunity
A grant to an individual that exempts him from being prosecuted based on the testimony that he gives.

There are times when federal grand juries wish to hear testimony from individuals who may also be facing charges themselves. Often, the only way to get such a witness to appear and testify before a grand jury is to grant the witness **immunity** from prosecution. When a person has been granted immunity, it means that the testimony given before the grand jury cannot be used as the basis to prosecute that person. In some states, the grand jury is empowered to grant immunity as a way of encouraging a witness to give evidence against others. In other states, it is the prosecutor who must petition the court for a grant of immunity for the witness. The granting of immunity in a particular case may be controversial. Once granted, the person who testifies cannot be prosecuted based on the testimony given before the grand jury, even if it turns out that the person who testified was the primary person behind the crime and may be exclusively responsible for the injuries to people and property that occurred. Because of this, grand juries must be careful about which witness will be offered immunity.

D. SUBPOENAS

Subpoena
A court order demanding that a person or item be produced to the court at a specific date and time.

A grand jury has the power to issue **subpoenas**. A subpoena is a court order requiring a person to appear and testify. Grand juries can issue subpoenas for people as well as for documents. Once issued and served on a person, the subpoena cannot be ignored. A person who fails to abide by a grand jury subpoena is subject to a finding of contempt of the grand jury and may be held in custody until she

---

[9] Fed. R. Crim. P. 6(g).
[10] *Cameron v. State*, 171 P.3d 1154 (Alaska 2007).

complies or until the grand jury's term ends, whichever comes first. This gives the grand jury great power, but this power is subject to some limitations. Suppose that the party objects to producing documents on the grounds that they contain trade secrets or communications between a person and his lawyer. In that case, it would not be left to the grand jury to decide whether the objection had merit. Instead, it would be up to a judge to decide. In such a situation, the party might file a motion to quash the grand jury's subpoena.

For example, an attorney for the New York State Independence Party moved to quash a grand jury subpoena in connection with an investigation into an alleged illegal transfer of campaign funds. The attorney argued that his appearance before the grand jury would constitute a violation of attorney-client privilege, and he would be forced to reveal secrets. For a number of reasons, most notable of which was that the evidence led directly to the attorney himself, the motion was denied.

1. QUASHING A SUBPOENA

A motion to **quash** a subpoena is filed with the court and describes the material that has been subject to subpoena and the reason that the party objects to producing those documents. As we will see later in this chapter, there are many reasons that the grand jury might not be allowed to see specific materials. In such a case, a judge would quash the subpoena and refuse to allow the grand jury to review the materials.

Quash
Do away with, annul, overthrow, cease.

E. GRAND JURY SECRECY

Grand juries carry out many of their duties in secret. Their discussions are not placed on any record, and often their identities remain secret until the indictment is unsealed or made public in the arraignment. This secrecy component of grand jury hearings allows the jurors to act more freely, knowing that none of their discussions will be reported. This secrecy extends to other areas as well. Some witnesses may be sworn not to reveal the substance of their testimony before a grand jury. However, many states do transcribe witness testimony before the grand jury but not the grand jurors' discussions as they decide whether to allow the case to continue.

The secrecy aspect of a grand jury's function extends to other areas. For example, there is no requirement that the grand jury must put a defendant on notice that she is being investigated. In fact, such notification might encourage a defendant to flee the jurisdiction before the grand jury has concluded its investigation.

Defendants have no right to appear before a grand jury, at least in most jurisdictions. In some, a defendant can request special permission to appear before the grand jurors and answer their questions. However, as we will see later in this chapter, most defendants who are subpoenaed to appear before the grand jury invoke their Fifth Amendment right to remain silent and avoid incriminating themselves.

PROFILING THE PROFESSIONAL

Grand Jury Secrecy

"The grand jury is a secretive body. Depending on the jurisdiction, they meet at different times. In some counties, they meet twice a week every month. Here's it's just once a month. You draft an indictment and you have witnesses presented to the grand jury. They testify under oath. A lot of times the investigator on the case testifies, but sometimes you have civilian witnesses come in and testify. You can use hearsay in grand jury proceedings. What's said in there is secret. What happens in there is their choice, their decision. The defendant is not part of the picture; he doesn't testify there. We bring the witness in, we swear them in, we read what the indictment says, and then we question the witness. Once they go through and cover the elements of the crime and the facts of the case, then we ask the grand jurors if they have any questions. If they have, they ask them. If they don't, we walk out and they vote whether or not to true bill it. If they true bill it, the case moves to the next level, arraignment in Superior Court. If they no bill it, then they don't think it's worth proceeding on that case. We have 16 to 23 people usually. You have to have a quorum of folks. Some people think that we should just get rid of the grand jury, that it's just a form of archaic procedure. From a prosecutor's standpoint, it's a way of letting the community have some say on the case. They might want to say, no, we're not going forward on that case and no bill it. It's an easy way of making someone else responsible for dismissing a case. I think we should have the guts to say whether a case is bad or not before we send it to the grand jury. Make the call up front. That's one of the hardest things to do in cases sometimes, bring the victims in and tell them that they we have to dismiss the case because we can't prove it."

Debra Sullivan, Assistant District Attorney

F. PROCEDURE BEFORE THE GRAND JURY

In some states, the prosecutor attends the grand jury meeting, questions the witnesses, and presents evidence. In other states, the grand jury conducts its own investigation and questioning. In either situation, grand jury members always have the right to ask questions of any witness.

Unlike other court proceedings, the rules of evidence do not apply to grand jury proceedings. This means that the grand jury can consider illegally obtained evidence and listen to hearsay evidence. However, the grand jury does have some limitations. It is not permitted to take unlimited "fishing expeditions" through people's lives and randomly subpoena documents in an effort to find evidence of some crime. The grand jury must focus on a specific investigation or risk having the indictment quashed.

1. PRESENTING A CASE TO THE GRAND JURY

A presentation before the grand jury is a lopsided affair. The grand jury hears only from the government, not from the defendant. The defendant has no right to testify before the grand jury or present any favorable evidence. This limitation has led to the most severe criticism of the grand jury system. Because the state is not obligated to present the defendant's version of the facts, it is highly likely that, having heard only the state's version of the events, the grand jury will decide that there is sufficient probable cause to continue the case. The defendant's attorney is not permitted to attend or make any statements to the grand jury. In addition, the state is not required to present a balanced account of the case. The U.S. Supreme Court has even held that the prosecution is under no obligation to present evidence that is favorable to the defendant during a grand jury hearing.[11] The actual presentation before the grand jury depends very much on state law. In some states, for example, the prosecutor will coordinate the hearing by calling witnesses, swearing them in, and asking them questions in the presence of the grand jurors. Once the prosecutor has completed the questioning process, she then turns the questioning over to the grand jurors themselves. If they have no questions, the state may call additional witnesses before retiring and requesting that the grand jury rule on the evidence as presented. However, there are states that do not allow prosecutors to go into the grand jury room. In that case, a police or district attorney investigator may present the case. In still other instances, the grand jurors themselves will coordinate which witnesses they wish to hear and in what order. Regardless of the particular procedures used, grand juries work very closely with the prosecution. Grand jurors, police officers, and prosecutors often develop friendly relationships with one another. After all, grand jurors may serve anywhere from 6 to 24 months and thus have a great deal of opportunity to get to know one another and the state representatives who appear in front of them regularly.

Some states specifically provide that the prosecutor is the grand jury's legal adviser. In those situations, the grand jurors will rely on the prosecutor's legal opinion about various matters. Prosecutors prepare the indictments that are presented to the grand jurors. It may also be left to the prosecutor to subpoena witnesses and documents requested by the grand jury. In some states, prosecutors play a central role in guiding the grand jury through its paces, directing the grand jury to particular crimes and individuals and sometimes forming a special grand jury to look into a particular crime or series of crimes. On the federal level, the attorney general and the assistant attorneys general appear before grand juries.

Although state law often invests the grand jury with the sole power to drive the investigation, it is not uncommon for a prosecutor to guide a grand jury in such a way that it would appear that the prosecutor is taking the lead. A grand jury is supposed to be independent of the prosecutor's office, but the reality is somewhat different. In order to maintain the separation between prosecution and grand jury, courts have held that a prosecutor must at least inform the grand jury that the

---

[11] *U.S. v. Williams*, 112 S. Ct. 1735 (1992).

defendant wishes to testify.[12] Prosecutors are barred from giving closing arguments before a grand jury to convince them to rule in a particular way.[13] (For an example of a case in which a prosecutor acted in an improper way before a grand jury, see this chapter's case excerpt.)

When there is a question about improprieties in the way that the grand jury conducted its investigation, the defendant has the burden of showing that the grand jury failed to act properly. This is one of the few instances in which the burden is on the defendant instead of on the state to prove wrongdoing.[14]

a. Testifying Before the Grand Jury

The grand jury can request anyone to appear before it to answer questions, but that does not always mean that the person will answer those questions. A witness does not lose his constitutionally guaranteed rights when he is subpoenaed to appear before the grand jury. Other provisions of law also protect the witness, including the guarantees of the Fifth Amendment and evidentiary privileges.

i. Pleading the "Fifth"

According to the Fifth Amendment, "[No person] shall be compelled in any criminal case to be a witness against himself . . . ."

The Fifth Amendment, which is the source of so many other rights for criminal defendants, also provides that persons cannot be compelled to give evidence against themselves. This protection follows defendants into the grand jury room as well. If a defendant or other person is subpoenaed before the grand jury, she does not have to admit to any criminal actions or give any testimony that might be incriminating. The defendant can invoke the Fifth Amendment and refuse to give any answers that might tend to implicate her in a crime. The grand jury is not authorized to override the witness's constitutional rights.

ii. Invoking a Privilege Before the Grand Jury

Privilege
A right to refuse to answer questions and to prevent disclosure of information communicated within a legally recognized confidential relationship.

Certain relationships are protected under law by **privilege**. A privilege is a legal right that protects a person from being compelled to testify about certain matters. Attorney-client discussions are privileged, which means that any discussion between a client and his attorney are protected from disclosure. A witness cannot be compelled to violate this privilege. For instance, if the defendant's attorney is subpoenaed by the grand jury and is asked about discussions the attorney had with the client, the attorney can invoke the attorney-client privilege and refuse to answer. Other examples of privileged communications include pastor-penitent, husband-wife, doctor-patient, psychiatrist-patient, etc. In each case, the professional who is asked to provide information about the other may invoke the privilege and refuse to answer any questions about that relationship.

---

[12] *Cameron v. State*, 171 P.3d 1154 (Alaska 2007).
[13] *State v. Penkaty*, 708 N.W.2d 185 (Minn. 2006).
[14] *State v. Francis*, 191 N.J. 571, 926 A.2d 305 (2007).

EXAMPLE

Mary is a reporter and has been subpoenaed to testify before the grand jury about a story she wrote last week in the town's newspaper. According to Mary's story, a city official has been taking bribes for several years and dismissing low-level crimes, such as driving under the influence and other misdemeanors in exchange for several thousand dollars per charge. Mary did not name her source for the story in the article. Now the grand jury has begun to investigate government corruption, and when Mary is seated before the grand jury, she is asked to identify her source for the article. She refuses to do so, stating that she has a constitutional right to protect her source. Is she right? Can the grand jury hold her in contempt for failing to answer the question?

Answer: Unlike evidentiary privileges that protect attorneys and clients, doctors and patients and others, there is no constitutional protection for newspaper reporters and their sources. The grand jury can demand that Mary answer the question and invoke its contempt powers to have Mary held in custody until she complies.[15]

In addition to the privileges that witnesses may invoke before the grand jury, individual grand jurors are protected by their own legally recognized privilege. In this case, the privilege does not have so much to do with testimony as it does from civil suit. As long as they are acting within the scope of their duties, they cannot be sued civilly for bringing an indictment against an individual.[16]

G. CONTEMPT POWERS OF THE GRAND JURY

If a witness fails to answer questions or present subpoenaed documents—and is not protected by the Constitution or by an evidentiary privilege—the grand jury can request that a Superior Court judge hold the witness in contempt. If the judge agrees, the witness can be held in custody until the witness decides to cooperate or until the grand jury's term ends, whichever comes first.

Instances in which a witness is held in custody for a long period of time do not happen often, but when they do, they tend to get a lot of press. In a case dating back to the mid-1990s, Susan McDougal, a partner with Bill and Hillary Clinton in the so-called Whitewater real estate venture, refused to answer three questions asked of her by the grand jury investigating the case. She claimed to be fearful of being accused of perjury because her story differed greatly from that of other witnesses. As a result of her failure to cooperate, she was sentenced to—and served—18 months in custody, the maximum sentence for civil contempt.

1. TRUE BILL VERSUS NO BILL

True bill
A grand jury's determination that there is sufficient probable cause to continue the prosecution against the accused.

When the grand jury decides that there is sufficient probable cause to believe that a crime has occurred, they will vote **true bill**. This means that the case can continue,

[15] *Branzburg v. Hayes*, 92 S. Ct. 2646 (1972).
[16] *Gore v. State*, 22 Ala. App. 136, 114 So. 791 (1927).

No bill
A grand jury's determination that there is insufficient probable cause to continue the prosecution against the accused.

and the foreperson of the grand jury signs the indictment indicating this fact. If the grand jury does not believe that sufficient probable cause has been established, the grand jury can vote **no bill**. Such a vote effectively ends the case against the defendant.

EXAMPLE

During the grand jury proceedings, the grand jurors decide to vote "no bill" on a particular case. The prosecutor disagrees with this finding. Can he order the grand jury to reconsider the case and insist they return a true bill?

Answer: No. The grand jury's findings are not only secret, but also final. A prosecutor cannot force a grand jury to do anything.

2. AFTER THE GRAND JURY'S DECISION

Once the grand jury has made its decision in the case, its function ceases. The case is assigned to a court for further adjudication. Members of the grand jury are prohibited from launching their own investigations or hiring private detectives to seek out additional evidence and information.[17] Furthermore, the grand jury cannot be used to gather additional evidence against an individual after it has made its decision to true bill an indictment.

Once the grand jury has true billed an indictment, the case will then be ready for arraignment, and the grand jury's role has ended. However, this does not mean that preparation ends for either the government or the defendant. In fact, the real work for the attorneys is just beginning. For one thing, the prosecutor must ensure that the indictment that is presented to the grand jury is legally sufficient; once a true bill is returned, the defense attorney will scrutinize the indictment closely for any irregularities.

III INDICTMENTS

We first addressed the topic of indictments in Chapter 2. In that chapter, we saw that an indictment is the charging document that is used to accuse a defendant of a felony. However, we will now explore indictments in much greater detail, including how and when they are drafted, what makes a legally sufficient indictment, and when and under what circumstances a defendant can challenge the wording of the indictment.

A. PURPOSE OF THE INDICTMENT

The purpose of an indictment is to advise the defendant of the charges against her. But the indictment does more than simply list charges. An indictment, in order to

[17] *William J. Burns International Detective Agency v. Doyle*, 46 Nev. 91, 208 P. 427, 26 A.L.R. 600 (1922).

be legally sufficient, must put a defendant on notice of the nature of the charges, including specific facts, such as dates, places, and individuals involved in the crime. An indictment must give the defendant enough specific facts so that she can refute the charge. As such, if an indictment does not list specific facts, it can be challenged for insufficiency. Courts review indictments in a commonsense manner. This is not an area in which a minor typo will result in a dismissal. Instead, the courts will find an indictment to be insufficient only if the defendant cannot understand what she is charged with and cannot present a valid defense to it.

B. DRAFTING THE INDICTMENT

Although the grand jury decides if there is sufficient probable cause to continue the case against the defendant and does so through the indictment, the grand jurors are not responsible for drafting the actual document. Instead, that duty falls to the prosecutor. The prosecution office staff prepares the indictment after conferring with the attorneys and often after additional consultation with the police before deciding which charge to bring against the defendant and what details of the crime to allege in the document itself. As we saw in Chapter 2, there are times when a prosecutor cannot present a case to a grand jury at all and might instead proceed with an information (also known as an accusation on the state level). Such cases include minor offenses, such as misdemeanors and some low-level felony cases.

In drafting the indictment, prosecutors must be careful to meet all statutory obligations. They must allege sufficient facts to put the defendant on notice of the charges against him and also to properly allege the specific statute that the defendant has violated.

C. CHALLENGING INDICTMENTS

If a defendant believes that the indictment is not legally sufficient, he may challenge the indictment and move to have it quashed. In addition to filing a motion to quash, the defendant might also file for a bill of particulars, seeking additional information about the case.

Challenging an Indictment

PROFILING THE PROFESSIONAL

"I still like to challenge an indictment (called a demurrer) when it's needed, like when there is a defect in the indictment. I do it in more complicated cases, like RICO, and longer indictments, that's a source for trying to knock things out of the case. My success rate varies. It's a small number. Everybody pretty much has a computer program that helps them draft indictments. Sometimes it's the small things that they leave out. Every now and then it's still there. I think the errors are created a lot by volume."

B.J. Bernstein, Defense Attorney

1. QUASHING AN INDICTMENT

As we have already seen, a subpoena issued by the grand jury can be quashed if a party objects and a judge rules that the information requested violates some evidentiary privilege. But the defense team may also move to quash the entire indictment once it has been returned by the grand jury.

When the grand jury acts in an improper way to bring a true bill, a court may quash or dismiss the indictment. A defendant will often file such a motion when he believes or even suspects that such unconstitutional action has occurred. An indictment may also be quashed when it fails to allege the crime with which the defendant has been charged or has some other legal deficiency.

2. BILL OF PARTICULARS

Bill of particulars
A motion filed by the defendant that requests additional information about the crime listed in a charging document.

In addition to a motion to dismiss the indictment, a defendant is allowed to file a **bill of particulars** concerning the indictment charging her. A bill of particulars is a motion, filed with the trial judge, that alleges that the state has not provided the defendant with sufficient information to prepare a defense and asks the judge to order the state to provide these additional details to the defendant. If the judge grants the order, the state must file a written response to the defendant and the court alleging the specific acts that the defendant committed, including dates and times (if known), names of victims and witnesses, and any other information that the state may have concerning the case. It is interesting to note that there is no similar motion that the state may bring against the defendant. A prosecutor cannot, for example, file a bill of particulars against a defendant, asking for specifics of the defense. Instead, the prosecutor must wait until the actual trial before many of the details of the defense become clear. (There are some exceptions to this rule, including the defenses of alibi and insanity, both of which we will address in Chapter 8.)

IV ARRAIGNMENT

Arraignment
A court hearing at which the defendant is informed of the charge against him and given the opportunity to enter a plea of guilty or not guilty.

When a grand jury returns a true bill, the next procedural step for the accused is the **arraignment**. In some jurisdictions, initial appearances and arraignments are held at the same time (usually when a person is charged with a misdemeanor), but for our purposes, we will continue our discussion for the procedures followed in felony cases.

The arraignment may occur days, weeks, or even months before the defendant's trial. In some jurisdictions, a defendant can be arraigned the day of the trial, but most follow a pattern that sets the arraignment several weeks before the next scheduled trial date. This period of time allows the prosecution and defense to comply with the discovery statutes. We will address discovery and pretrial motions in much greater detail in Chapter 6.

A. PURPOSE OF THE ARRAIGNMENT

An arraignment is a court hearing at which the defendant is brought before a judge and officially informed of the charges pending against him. This hearing might seem redundant—after all, the defendant has already been arrested, so why does he need to be informed of the charges? The simple answer is that the prosecutor may have amended those charges during the prosecutor's charging decision. The arraignment is the point during the case when the defendant receives the final word about the charges pending. The defendant is given a copy of the charges against him, which may consist of the indictment (for felonies) or an accusation (for state-level misdemeanors). The judge will also use the arraignment as an additional opportunity to inform the defendant of his rights and to inquire whether or not the defendant has an attorney. If the defendant cannot afford an attorney, the judge may appoint one at this stage. In many jurisdictions, the judge also informs the defendant of the maximum sentence possible for each of the charges pending against him.

The defendant also has the opportunity of entering a plea at an arraignment. If the defendant pleads not guilty, he will be scheduled to return at a later time for a trial. If the defendant chooses to plead guilty, the judge may impose sentence that day or defer sentencing for a later date.

B. FILING MOTIONS AT AN ARRAIGNMENT

In the past, the arraignment procedure had greater significance than it has today. For instance, it was common for defendants to request *formal arraignment*. A formal arraignment consists of either the judge or the prosecutor reading the entire indictment, out loud, before the defendant and the others present in the courtroom. The defendant would then have the opportunity of challenging the sufficiency of the indictment. However, modern practice has tended away from formal arraignment to a more informal procedure where the defense counsel expressly waives formal arraignment, requests a copy of the indictment and discovery, and reserves the right to file additional motions, including those challenging the sufficiency of the indictment for a later time. The defendant may also reserve the right to file additional motions after going through the indictment and whatever discovery the state may have served on him at the arraignment. We will discuss discovery in much greater detail in Chapter 7.

C. WAIVING ARRAIGNMENT

A defendant is always free to waive both formal and informal arraignment through her counsel or by filing a written notice waiving arraignment and filing motions about specific issues in the case.[18] As noted, formal arraignment refers to the prosecutor or the judge actually reading the indictment aloud in court. This practice dates back for centuries and was probably instituted in a time when most people could not read. These days, it is very common for a defense attorney to announce that the defendant waives formal arraignment

---

[18] *Shivers v. State*, 188 Ga. App. 21, 372 S.E.2d 2 (1988).

(or the full reading of the indictment) and agree to proceed with an informal arraignment.

D. FAILURE TO APPEAR FOR ARRAIGNMENT

In the past, a defendant was always required to be physically present for an arraignment, but some jurisdictions have softened this requirement, either by allowing an attorney to appear on behalf of the defendant or by conducting arraignments through closed-circuit television.[19] Defendants may not actually be in the courtroom during a video arraignment. Instead, they may be several miles away at the local jail, and they "appear" in court by stepping before a camera and answering the judge's questions.

Bench warrant
A court order directing law enforcement to arrest a specific individual and to hold him until a specific court date.

If a defendant fails to appear for an arraignment at all, the judge is authorized to issue a **bench warrant** for the defendant's arrest. A bench warrant permits any law enforcement officer to arrest the defendant and place him in custody pending a new court date. The defendant's bond is revoked, and if a bonding company posted bail for the defendant, the bond amount is forfeited to the state. Many states allow a grace period after arraignment for a bonding company to locate and surrender the defendant to the authorities without forfeiting the entire bond amount. Although the amount of time varies, 72 hours is common. During that time, if the bonding company can locate the defendant, they can save themselves the entire bond amount, giving them a strong interest in locating the defendant. It is for this process that the so-called bounty hunters enter the picture, as we discussed in Chapter 4.

EXAMPLE

Ted has been indicted and has been given a court date to appear for his arraignment. He hires an attorney to represent him. On the appointed court date, Ted's attorney appears and says that he represents Ted, but that he isn't sure where Ted is at the precise moment. Ted does not show up for court that day. Will the fact that he hired an attorney be enough to keep from having a bench warrant issued for his arrest?

Answer: No. It was Ted's (not his attorney's) obligation to appear for court. The court will issue a bench warrant to have Ted arrested.

The following case excerpt presents an excellent example of a defendant seeking to have his conviction overturned on the basis of prosecutorial misconduct before the grand jury. As you are reading the excerpt, note the various arguments the defendant makes, and consider whether they have merit in light of the facts of the case.

---

[19] *State v. Phillips*, 74 Ohio St. 3d 72, 1995-Ohio-171, 656 N.E.2d 643 (1995).

CASE EXCERPT

STATE v. PENKATY

708 N.W.2d 185, 190-208 (Minn., 2006)

District court did not err when it denied defendant's motion to dismiss an indictment based on allegations of prosecutorial misconduct, which alleged errors including presenting inadmissible evidence to the grand jury, failing to instruct the grand jury on affirmative defenses, failing to excuse from the grand jury a police officer who knew most of the witnesses, infringing on the independence of the grand jury, and informing the grand jury that the defendant declined to testify.

John M. Stuart, Office of the State Public Defender, Sara L. Martin, Assistant State Public Defender, Minneapolis, for appellant.
Mike Hatch, Minnesota State Attorney General, John B. Galus, Assistant Attorney General, St. Paul, LaMar Piper, Watonwan County Attorney, St. James, for respondent.
Heard, considered, and decided by the court en banc.

OPINION

Anderson, Paul H., Justice.

A Watonwan County jury found appellant Paul Penkaty, Sr. guilty of first-degree premeditated murder for the March 8, 2003 death of Christopher Knight. The district court convicted Penkaty of first-degree murder and sentenced him to life in prison. Penkaty appeals his conviction, arguing that (1) the court erred when it denied his motion to dismiss the grand jury indictment based on alleged prosecutorial misconduct. We reverse.

At the time of his death, Christopher Knight lived in Truman, Minnesota with his fiancée, Kimberly Penkaty, their three-month-old daughter, and Kimberly's three- and four-year-old sons from previous relationships. The house where Knight and Kimberly lived was owned by Kimberly's parents, appellant Paul Penkaty, Sr. (Penkaty) and his wife Beverly. Penkaty and Beverly lived seven miles away in Lewisville.

On March 8, 2003, Penkaty and Ben Davis spent the afternoon together. Before becoming involved with Knight, Kimberly had a six-year relationship with Davis. Davis was the father of one of Kimberly's sons, and her other son also knew Davis as his father. Penkaty and Davis remained friends after Davis's relationship with Kimberly had ended approximately two years earlier. Penkaty was also friends with Knight, but the two men had not spoken for at least a month before Knight's death because of a dispute over $100 that Knight had loaned Penkaty to buy a Christmas present.

On March 8, Penkaty picked Davis up in Fairmont around noon, and the two men drove to Winnebago to check out a car Davis was planning to buy from a friend. After looking at the car, they stopped at a nearby liquor store, where they purchased a 12-pack of beer. Penkaty and Davis began drinking the beer on the way to their next stop, Blue Earth, where Penkaty picked up two Great Dane puppies that a friend had asked him to nurse back to health. The two men drank the rest of the 12-pack in Blue Earth and as they drove back to Lewisville. Davis testified that he drank about half of the beers.

Meanwhile, Tonya Rhoda, a friend of Kimberly and her mother, called and offered to pick up Kimberly and the children and take them to the Penkaty home. Knight objected to the trip. Knight could not accompany Kimberly because he was under pretrial house arrest for burglary charges and could not leave the house except for emergencies. As a condition of his house arrest, Knight wore a GPS ankle bracelet to monitor his location. Kimberly's parents had paid for the GPS monitor so that Knight could be released from jail. As Kimberly was leaving around 4:00 P.M., Knight yelled that if she left, she could not come back. Kimberly left anyway.

Back at the Penkaty home in Lewisville, Penkaty and Davis were in Penkaty's car, which was parked in the driveway, when Kimberly, Rhoda, and the children arrived. Around 5:00 P.M., Michael Whitehead dropped by for a visit, and a six-year-old Penkaty grandson also came to the Penkaty home sometime in the early evening. From approximately 5:00 until 6:30 P.M., the children played with the Great Dane puppies while the adults socialized, listened to music, and drank beer in the living room. Beverly, who was not drinking, testified that Penkaty drank four or five beers. Rhoda testified that she drank between four and seven beers, and that Penkaty was keeping pace with her. Penkaty testified that he nursed one beer over the course of the evening. Kimberly could not recall whether she or her father had been drinking, but remembered opening some beers upon her arrival. Davis testified that he had three or four beers at the Penkaty home. Penkaty, Davis, and Rhoda also shared at least one bowl of marijuana.

Between 5:00 and 6:30 P.M., Knight telephoned Kimberly between three to eight times, telling her he wanted her to come home. As a result of Knight's repeated calls, Penkaty connected the computer to the internet so that when Knight called, he would receive a busy signal. Shortly after 6:30 P.M., Knight contacted the GPS monitoring agency and falsely reported that there was a medical emergency involving his daughter. At 6:44 P.M., Knight left his home in Truman and drove the seven miles to the Penkaty home in Lewisville, arriving at 6:52 P.M. Some witnesses said Knight knocked on the front door, and others said he pounded on the door. At the time Knight arrived, Penkaty and Whitehead were playing a videogame in the living room.

Beverly answered the door, after which Kimberly stepped outside to speak with Knight. It was a cold evening, but Kimberly neither took a jacket with her nor invited Knight into the house. Back inside the house, Beverly told Davis that he should remain in the bedroom until Knight left because Knight would be upset to see Davis at the house during Kimberly's visit. Beverly then went outside to check on Kimberly.

Knight told Kimberly that he wanted her to leave with him. Accounts of Knight's demeanor during this exchange vary. Kimberly testified that Knight was "not really yelling, but upset and saying it with authority that he wanted it to be done." Whitehead said Knight was shouting. Rhoda said Knight was "barking orders at Kim." Beverly described Knight's demeanor as both a "funny, strange calm" and "agitated." After talking with Knight, Kimberly agreed to leave with him, but then went into the house. Once inside, Kimberly attempted to lock the door to keep Knight outside, but Knight forced open the door and stepped into the living room, pushing Kimberly with the door in the process.

When Knight entered the room, Penkaty looked up from the videogame and ordered Knight to leave. There was conflicting testimony about how many times Penkaty told Knight to leave, and whether Beverly also told Knight to leave. Davis testified that at this point, "drinking beer" caused him to emerge from hiding and say something to Knight. It is unclear whether Davis told Knight to leave the house, or provoked him, or both. Several witnesses said Knight charged Davis upon seeing him. Davis, who was two inches shorter and 60 pounds lighter than Knight, testified that Knight motioned to him that they should "take it outside." Davis also testified that when Knight turned to leave, Davis tried to tackle Knight, and that Knight apparently heard Davis coming, turned around, and punched Davis in the face, splitting his lip.

Regardless of who started the Knight/Davis altercation, all witnesses agreed that Knight threw the first punch, and the two men wrestled in the living room. Kimberly and Rhoda gathered up the children and took them to a bedroom. Penkaty testified that he dialed 911 and then handed the telephone to Beverly. Beverly's testimony conflicted with Penkaty's on this point. She testified that she called 911 herself, but not until later. Knight and Davis continued to fight, knocking over a lamp and a recliner. Davis testified that Whitehead-who was standing by the front door-restrained Knight, and Davis then took this opportunity to punch Knight. Davis and Whitehead then pushed Knight out onto the front deck.

Witnesses disagreed about the seriousness of the fight, and Beverly, Kimberly, and Rhoda denied seeing any of the fight once it left the interior of the house. Kimberly testified that Knight did kick Davis in the head, that Davis did not stand a chance in the fight, and that Knight was "beating the sh** out of Ben." Penkaty testified that Knight pounded Davis, stomped him in the head, and dangled Davis by the collar in preparation for hitting him again. But Davis and Whitehead testified that Davis was neither kicked nor stomped, and Whitehead also testified that Davis and Knight were both upright during the struggle outside.

At some point during the fight, Penkaty went to the kitchen, picked up two large knives, and headed for the front door, holding the knives in front of his body with the blades pointed upward. Testimony conflicted as to whether Penkaty paused in the living room, but it is undisputed that Kimberly and Beverly grabbed Penkaty's shirt and tried to stop him from going outside. Penkaty testified that he said to his wife and daughter, "He's killing him! ***! Why won't you let me help him?" and then Penkaty's shirt ripped and he kept going. No one else testified that Penkaty said anything on his way out the door, but several people heard Kimberly yell, "Not in front of the kids!"

Whitehead, still in the front doorway, also tried to stop Penkaty, but was unsuccessful in this effort. Whitehead suffered a cut on his knuckle in the process. Kimberly and Whitehead testified that they tried to stop Penkaty because they feared for Penkaty's safety if he got involved in the fight. Beverly stated that as Penkaty left the house, she called 911 to report the fight while Kimberly sat on the couch and put her head down. Beverly also said that she took the phone into the bathroom so she could hear the 911 operator above the commotion.

The exact details of what happened next are unsettled. Davis originally told investigators that after he pushed Knight out the front door, Knight hit him so hard that he fell down and lost consciousness. When Davis came to, he observed that Knight was stumbling off the deck, having been stabbed. At trial, Davis first testified that as he and Knight were fighting on the front deck, Knight gave him "a very good blow" that caused him to see stars and stumble. Upon righting himself, Davis saw Penkaty pulling a big knife out of Knight's side. Davis later testified that as he and Knight were fighting on the front deck, Knight hit him, and then Davis saw Penkaty approach Knight, jab him with the knife, and pull it back out.

After being stabbed, Knight apparently stumbled off the deck, walked into the yard, turned around, and collapsed on his way back to the house. Penkaty went back into the house, where Beverly was talking to a 911 operator. On the 911 tape, Penkaty's voice can be heard in the background telling Beverly that Knight was dead. Penkaty testified that he opened the front door, told Beverly he had stabbed Knight, and asked her to call for an ambulance. Penkaty then dropped the knives in the kitchen sink and when he did so, he noticed that one of the knives was broken and the blade was missing.

Penkaty put on a new shirt and spoke briefly with Whitehead, who was leaving the house. Penkaty then went back outside, where Davis was trying to help Knight into the house. Penkaty and Davis dragged Knight into the living room, where Penkaty, Rhoda, and Kimberly performed CPR and applied pressure to the stab wound. At some point after the stabbing but before the police arrived, Penkaty took the telephone from Beverly and said to the 911 operator, "This man is dying. I need an ambulance here now. This man is dying. He is dying here. He is not going to make it." The call was disconnected after the operator asked Penkaty for the second time who had stabbed the victim.

At 7:07 P.M., approximately eight minutes after Beverly placed the 911 telephone call, the police arrived and met Beverly outside the home. An ambulance pulled up at approximately the same time. At 7:08 P.M., four police officers entered the home to secure it for the paramedics. An officer who entered through the front door asked Penkaty, Kimberly, and Rhoda where the suspect was. After the officer repeated the question, Penkaty responded, "I was the one who stabbed him." The officer then escorted Penkaty away from Knight and into the kitchen. On the way to the kitchen, Penkaty said, "I stabbed him, I stabbed him. He, he should have left me alone." When Penkaty and the officer entered the kitchen, a second officer directed the first officer's attention to a knife in the sink. Penkaty then volunteered, "That's the knife I stabbed him with."

Knight was transported by ambulance to the Madelia Hospital. The police arrested Penkaty and took him to the Watonwan County Law Enforcement Center. On the way, Penkaty asked if Knight was dead, apologized for stabbing him, and said, "Oh, God, I wished he had left me alone." Penkaty did not mention to the police that he had stabbed Knight because he was defending himself or someone else. Meanwhile, medical staff at the hospital attempted for 14 minutes to revive Knight before pronouncing him dead on arrival. An autopsy revealed nine knife wounds on Knight's body-one fatal stab wound, as well as six scratches, and two minor stab wounds, including a defensive wound on his wrist. Knight's death resulted from a knife entering the upper left quadrant of his abdomen and piercing the right ventricle of his heart.

A grand jury subsequently indicted Penkaty for first-degree premeditated murder in violation of Minn.Stat. §609.185(1) (2004). Penkaty moved to dismiss the indictment, claiming prosecutorial misconduct in the grand jury proceedings. The district court denied the motion, finding that although the state committed several errors during the grand jury proceedings, sufficient admissible evidence supported the indictment. Penkaty then filed a petition for discretionary review of the order denying his motion to dismiss. The court of appeals denied Penkaty's motion, concluding that (1) presentation of inadmissible evidence does not require dismissal of an indictment if there is sufficient admissible evidence to support the indictment, (2) the state had no clear duty to present possible defenses to the grand jury, and (3) no extraordinary circumstances warranted pretrial discretionary review. Penkaty filed a petition for pretrial review by our court, but then moved to dismiss the petition.

The jury trial began April 5, 2004. At trial, Penkaty admitted to stabbing Knight. His primary defense theory was defense of others-that he acted to prevent Knight from killing Davis. Penkaty testified that he had grabbed the knives merely to scare Knight, but while he was pushing Knight to get him to leave, Knight turned around and charged him. Penkaty testified that after Knight charged him, he looked down and realized that Knight had been stabbed.

After deliberating for nine and one-half hours, the jury found Penkaty guilty of first-degree premeditated murder. The district court ordered a presentence investigation. The court denied Penkaty's motion for a new trial, convicted Penkaty of first-degree premeditated murder, and sentenced him to life in prison.

I.

We first address Penkaty's assertion that the district court erred when it denied his motion to dismiss the grand jury indictment due to alleged prosecutorial misconduct during the grand jury proceedings. We have stated that a presumption of regularity attaches to a grand jury indictment, and it is a rare case where an indictment is invalidated. *State v. Greenleaf*, 591 N.W.2d 488, 498 (Minn.1999). But an indictment should be dismissed if the state knowingly engaged in misconduct that substantially influenced the grand jury's decision to indict and if we have grave doubts that the decision to indict was free of any influence of the misconduct. Id.

Before we address Penkaty's specific allegations of prosecutorial misconduct, a brief history of the function of a grand jury is instructive. The grand jury has existed for many centuries under English law, where it was originally both an accusing tribunal and a venue for trial. Historically, with limited exceptions, no English subject could be tried for a felony absent prior action by the grand jury. In effect, the grand jury "stood as a barrier against royal persecution."

Our grand jury system was correspondingly adopted based on "the theory not only of bringing wrongdoers to justice, but also of providing to one accused protection against unfounded and unreal accusations, whether these had their origin in governmental sources or were founded upon private passion or enmity." The United States Supreme Court has held that "the most valuable function of the grand jury was not only to examine into the commission of crimes, but to stand between the prosecutor and the accused, and to determine whether the charge was founded upon credible testimony or was dictated by malice or personal ill will."

We have repeatedly stated that a "prosecutor is a minister of justice whose obligation is to guard the rights of the accused as well as to enforce the rights of the public." The duty of a prosecutor is to see that justice is done on behalf of both the victim and the defendant. Therefore, a prosecutor does not "represent" the victim. A prosecutor represents the public interest and the sovereign and his goal is to see that justice is done. This places a special burden on prosecutors because they should prosecute with "earnestness and vigor," but must "refrain from improper methods calculated to produce a wrongful conviction." If a prosecutor abdicates his role as a minister of justice, the grand jury cannot serve its function of standing as a buffer between the state and the accused. We have stated that:

As a result of the prosecutor's unique relationship with the grand jury, opportunities for influence and manipulation of the process are omnipresent. In State v. Grose, the court of appeals noted that "the prosecutor is the person who draws up the indictment, calls and examines the witnesses, advises the grand jury about the law, and is in constant attendance during its proceedings." Prosecutors, therefore, must exercise extreme caution to ensure that the grand jury retains its independent role in our legal system.

Penkaty alleges that numerous errors occurred during the grand jury proceedings. He first asserts that the state engaged in misconduct when it examined three witnesses before acting to have grand juror 19, a St. James police officer, excused from the grand jury. Officers from the St. James Police Department-as well as other neighboring agencies-assisted the Watonwan County Sheriff's Department in responding to the 911 telephone call from the Penkaty home. Although grand juror 19 was not on duty at the time Knight was killed, he heard about the events from his fellow officers. Furthermore, when grand juror 19's work shift began at 9:00 P.M. on the date of Knight's death, one of his responsibilities was to attempt to locate the coroner. Grand juror 19 also indicated that he had "seen Penkaty in the jail," that he knew all of the police officers scheduled to testify before the grand jury, and that he also knew Whitehead "through my work." Despite the state's awareness of these facts, it failed to take any action to have grand juror 19 excused and began calling witnesses.

After the first grand jury witness testified, grand juror 19 asked the witness, who was a police officer, to repeat his answer to an earlier question about a statement Penkaty had made after he was arrested and informed of his Miranda rights. The second witness was one of grand juror 19's colleagues at the St. James Police Department. This officer testified about transporting Penkaty to the Watonwan County jail after Penkaty's arrest. After a third officer testified, the state requested that the district court excuse grand juror 19 from the grand jury. The court complied with the request, informing grand juror 19 that the rationale provided by the state was that he was "a police officer in St. James and, knew all of the parties involved that were investigating the crime, and may tend to believe their side of the story more than anyone else's because he was in the brotherhood." The state added that grand juror 19's "small tangential duty" related to the investigation also contributed to its decision.

The state argues that the record supports the district court's finding "that the impartiality of the grand jury was not compromised by the presence of grand juror 19" because grand juror 19 assured the court that he could be fair and impartial, and the other grand jurors had no opportunity to deliberate or discuss the case before grand juror 19 was excused. The record reflects that five other grand jurors also knew one or more of the police officers who testified, one grand juror had been Davis's Sunday School teacher, and two other grand jurors reported having had limited contact with Penkaty.

No other grand jurors were excused due to concerns about impartiality. While we acknowledge that grand juror 19 was not the only grand juror with previous contacts with witnesses or Penkaty, we conclude that there is a significant difference between a grand juror who knew one or more witnesses due to living in the same small community and grand juror 19. Grand juror 19 was a police officer who knew nearly all of the witnesses, many of whom were fellow police officers, and was already familiar with some witnesses' versions of the facts before commencement of grand jury proceedings. Therefore, we conclude that to preserve the integrity of the grand jury proceedings, the state should have acted to have grand juror 19 excused before it presented any evidence to the grand jury.

Penkaty also argues that the state committed misconduct by failing to instruct the grand jury on affirmative defenses, infringing on the independence of the grand jury, and giving an argumentative closing statement. Penkaty cites no legal authority for his proposition that the state has a duty to instruct the grand jury on affirmative defenses, and we decline to adopt this view. The absence of justification is not an element of first-degree premeditated murder.

Although the state need not instruct the grand jury on affirmative defenses, it does not follow that the state is free to summarily discount the possibility of justification as a defense. Furthermore, the state is to refrain from presenting an argumentative closing statement. In its closing statement to the grand jury, the state argued:

> Was he protecting someone? Not really. This wasn't a situation where Mr. Penkaty had to defend Mr. Davis by inflicting an immortal [sic] wound. That wasn't really a, a life-threatening situation. Mr. Davis didn't have any serious injuries. He, he didn't get a tooth knocked out. He didn't-he-nobody was jumping up and down on him. His life wasn't in danger. But Mr. Penkaty comes roaring out of there and goes to work with his knives. Penkaty was defending no one. And the force he used was clearly and dramatically all out of proportion to, to any risk. Mr. Penkaty was simply tired of dealing with Chris Knight.

The district court found that the state's closing statement "bordered on being argumentative," and this finding is supported by the record. But we have stated that dismissal of an indictment is not required when the state's closing statement to the grand jury was made "in a somewhat argumentative manner," so long as the state "repeatedly reminded the grand jurors of their independence." Here, despite the state's strong closing statement, both the state and the court instructed the grand jury on at least eight separate occasions regarding the grand jury's proper role and independence. While we do not condone the state's action in making a closing argument that "bordered on being argumentative," we conclude that the court did not err when it denied Penkaty's motion to dismiss the indictment because of the state's closing statement.

We next consider Penkaty's allegation that the state infringed on the independence of the grand jury. After the closing statement and in response to a grand juror's question about Knight, the state asserted, "the bottom line probably is, from our point of view, legally is that he certainly wasn't attacking Mr. Penkaty. We don't believe there's anything in the evidence that would justify taking his life, that's the bottom line." After considering this statement along with the state's closing argument, the district court found that the state acted improperly when it "essentially told the grand jury that there was no legal justification for the death of Mr. Knight." We agree with the district court's assessment. "Prosecutors . . . must exercise extreme caution to ensure that the grand jury retains its independent role in our legal system."

Penkaty also contends that the state committed misconduct when it informed the grand jury that Penkaty declined to testify. A grand juror asked the state what explanation Penkaty gave for arming himself with a knife when Knight was already outside the home. The Watonwan Assistant County Attorney responded, "Penkaty declined to speak with us." At this point, the county attorney quickly added, "he has exercised his right not to discuss that." The assistant county attorney then continued, "as you will hear from the instructions, whether or not he testified before you, that's his Constitutional Right, that is not anything you can hold against him in any way." A second grand juror then asked the state if Penkaty had made a decision not to testify, or if defendants generally did not participate in grand jury investigations. The assistant county attorney replied that

Penkaty was aware of the proceedings and declined to appear, but reiterated that this was Penkaty's right and was not a basis for the grand jury's decision to indict.

A defendant's right against self-incrimination extends to grand jury proceedings. Based on this right, we note that the assistant county attorney could have chosen his words more carefully when responding to the first grand juror's question. Further, if the state had been more careful in answering this first question, the second question may not have arisen. But given that the second question had to be answered, the issue of Penkaty's decision not to testify before the grand jury was unavoidable. The only option for the state in its response was to be as neutral as possible and emphasize that Penkaty was exercising his constitutional right. Even if the state's initial response to the grand jurors' questions was inartful, we are satisfied that the state ultimately fulfilled this obligation to vindicate Penkaty's constitutional right against self-incrimination.

Penkaty also argues that the state committed misconduct when it elicited testimony that Penkaty exercised his Miranda rights when speaking with investigators. Evidence that a defendant exercised his rights to remain silent or to have an attorney present for questioning is generally inadmissible at trial. Two police officers testified about statements Penkaty made after he was advised of his Miranda rights and invoked his right to counsel. The investigators' testimony that Penkaty requested counsel was revealed in the context of the investigator relating statements Penkaty made after the Miranda warning-not to show that Penkaty exercised his right to end questioning until his attorney was present. But to the extent that requesting counsel gives rise to an inference of culpability, providing this information was inappropriate.

Penkaty also argues that the state committed misconduct when it elicited inadmissible testimony during the grand jury proceedings about Penkaty's character. Penkaty contends that the state elicited information about Penkaty's prior contacts with the police to demonstrate that he had criminal tendencies. Evidence of prior bad acts by a defendant is not admissible to show a general propensity for criminal activity. Here, the state asked two police officers if they were sufficiently familiar with Paul and Beverly Penkaty that they could identify the Penkatys visually or by voice. The officers indicated that they were. Later, a grand juror asked one of the officers how he became familiar with the Penkatys. The officer responded by listing several incidents for which he had been dispatched to the Penkaty home or had otherwise encountered the Penkatys, including domestic disputes, disputes with neighbors, barking dog complaints, traffic stops, and the arrest of Knight at the Penkaty home. The district court concluded that the officer's response would have been admissible at trial to lay foundation for the officer's identification of Penkaty's voice. Even if this conclusion was erroneous, presentation of inadmissible evidence to the grand jury is not grounds for dismissal of the indictment if there is "sufficient admissible evidence to establish probable cause."

Finally, Penkaty argues that the cumulative effect of the state's misconduct during the grand jury process was unfairly prejudicial and therefore the district court erred in denying his motion to dismiss the indictment. "Cumulative error exists when the 'cumulative effect of the errors and indiscretions, none of which alone might have been enough to tip the scales, operate to the defendant's prejudice by producing a biased jury.'" Failing to take action to excuse a local police officer with specific knowledge of the investigation until after several witnesses testified, summarily discounting the possibility that Penkaty may have acted in self-defense, and giving a closing statement that bordered on being argumentative do not comport with the state's proper role in grand jury proceedings.

We find many aspects of the state's conduct to be troubling and it is for this reason we discussed them in detail. As we have previously noted, the state has special responsibilities as a minister of justice and has a unique relationship with the grand jury. Nevertheless, we agree with the district court that the state's errors and lapses in judgment are insufficient to overturn Penkaty's indictment for first-degree premeditated murder when sufficient admissible evidence was presented to substantiate probable cause and the grand jury was repeatedly reminded of its independence. We conclude that there was sufficient admissible evidence to substantiate probable cause, and that the grand jury was repeatedly reminded of its independence. Accordingly, we hold that the court did not err when it denied Penkaty's motion to dismiss the indictment.

Reversed [on other grounds raised by the defendant in his appeal] and remanded for a new trial.

CASE QUESTIONS

1. According to the court, was it improper to have a police officer sit on this grand jury?
2. Did the prosecutor commit the irregularity of arguing the case before the grand jury?
3. Is the prosecutor obligated to present the defendant's possible defenses during a grand jury hearing?
4. Did the prosecutor commit misconduct when he allowed the grand jury to hear that the defendant had invoked his right to remain silent?

CHAPTER SUMMARY

In this chapter we have examined the purpose, function, and composition of the grand jury. Made up of individuals numbering anywhere between 12 and 23, the grand jury holds hearings in felony cases to determine if there is sufficient probable cause to continue the case against the defendant. If the grand jury finds that there is probable cause, then it votes true bill on an indictment, and the case against the defendant proceeds to the arraignment phase. If the grand jury votes no bill on the indictment, then the case is effectively dismissed against the defendant.

Indictments have certain legal requirements. They must inform the defendant of the nature of the crimes with which he has been charged, and the indictment must provide facts to support that charge.

The indictment is officially delivered to the defendant at the arraignment. During the arraignment, the prosecution will give the defendant and his attorney a copy of the indictment. These days, formal arraignment is very rare. It is far more common to have informal arraignment and for the defendant to reserve the right to file any additional motions, including a motion to quash or dismiss the indictment.

KEY TERMS

Key terms are listed here in order of appearance in chapter.

Prima facie	Privilege	Arraignment
Immunity	True bill	Bench warrant
Subpoena	No bill	
Quash	Bill of particulars	

REVIEW QUESTIONS

1. Are some individuals barred from serving as grand jurors? Give some examples.
2. What is the normal length of service for a federal grand jury?
3. Do all states use grand juries? Why or why not?
4. What is the purpose of an arraignment?
5. What are the rules about the composition of the grand jury on either the state or federal level?
6. Which amendment to the U.S. Constitution authorizes the use of grand juries?
7. What is the purpose of a grand jury?
8. Explain how and under what circumstances a grand jury might grant immunity to a witness.
9. What is an indictment?
10. If an indictment is legally insufficient, what might a court do to it?
11. What is the purpose of an arraignment?
12. Can a defendant enter a plea during an arraignment?
13. What is the difference between formal and informal arraignment?
14. What does it mean when a defendant waives arraignment?
15. What will happen if a defendant pleads not guilty at the arraignment?
16. What is the consequence to the defendant if he fails to appear for an arraignment?

WEB SURFING

Merriam-Webster—Indictment
http://www.merriam-webster.com/dictionary/indictment

West's Encyclopedia of American—Indictment
http://www.answers.com/topic/indictment

Quiz Law—Arraignments
http://www.quizlaw.com/criminal_law/what_is_an_arraignment.php

EXERCISES

ACROSS

2. Do away with, annul, overthrow, cease
5. A presumption that the facts as presented are true and establish a fact

DOWN

1. A court order demanding that a person or item be produced to the court at a specific date and time
3. A right to refuse to answer questions and to prevent disclosure of information communicated within a legally recognized confidential relationship.
4. A grant to an individual that exempts him from being prosecuted based on the testimony that he gives

f	c	s	p	l	r	s	i	e	s
e	n	p	h	u	i	i	g	g	u
g	v	t	p	s	f	m	i	u	b
e	i	c	a	f	a	m	i	r	p
l	o	i	b	m	u	u	s	o	o
i	e	b	p	i	a	n	q	b	e
v	g	n	f	t	n	i	b	r	n
i	i	c	y	a	f	t	a	o	a
r	u	e	n	r	r	y	u	f	u
p	r	e	e	r	a	r	i	r	a

prima facie	subpoena	privilege
immunity	quash	

QUESTIONS FOR ANALYSIS

1 Is there really a need for grand juries anymore? Wouldn't it make more sense to simply allow the prosecution to charge everyone with an information or accusation and proceed that way? What do you think?

2 Should states allow police officers or convicted felons to serve on grand juries? Wouldn't both have unique perspectives on the process that would greatly help the grand jury with its duties?

6

Discovery and Pretrial Motions

Chapter Objectives

- Explain the purpose of discovery
- Describe the motions that a defendant typically files before trial
- Compare and contrast discovery methods in civil and criminal cases
- Describe the types of discovery that are normally produced by the state for the defendant
- Explain the significance of the *Brady* decision
- Describe types of information that are normally not discoverable
- Explain the kinds of motions that a prosecutor might bring against a defendant prior to trial

I DISCOVERY

Discovery refers to the process by which both sides in a civil or criminal case exchange information. In civil cases, the rules of discovery are quite liberal and the parties exchange a great deal of information. Both the plaintiff and defendant know the identities of each side's witnesses, what documents will be relied upon, what evidence will be presented, and even what each witness will say. This extensive exchange of information is not mirrored in criminal cases. Traditionally, very little discovery was allowed in criminal cases. Trials were conducted, and are to some extent to this day, by surprise and ambush. Where a civil litigant will know virtually every aspect of the case before the trial ever starts, a criminal prosecutor may not know who the defense is going to call as a witness or even what the defense to the crime may be until the defense attorney gives her opening statement.

Discovery
The exchange of information between sides in both civil and criminal lawsuits.

The "trial by surprise" aspect of criminal cases has been modified in recent years with some changes in discovery rules that force the prosecutor to give the

> **Sidebar**
>
> *Under the traditional criminal law system, where pretrial discovery procedures common to civil cases were not permitted in criminal trials, both the prosecutor and the defense attorney often began a trial with no clear idea of what the other side's witnesses would say. No doubt it made for an exciting trial, but it was not the most efficient use of court time. In many states, this traditional approach to discovery still exists.*

> **Sidebar**
>
> *Under traditional rules of discovery, the state had to produce certain items for the defendant, but there was no requirement on the defendant to produce anything. The result of this limited discovery was that a prosecutor often began a trial with no clear idea of what the defense would be, who the defense witnesses would be, what they would say, or what evidence the defense would seek to admit. The information that the state provided to the defense attorney was little better. The defense attorney would know the names of the state's witnesses but would not what these witnesses would say.*

defendant far more information than was ever required in the past. But these changes in discovery rules also now put some burden on the defense to produce information for the prosecutor. In the past, except in rare circumstances, this was unheard of. In this chapter, we will discuss both the traditional role of discovery in criminal cases and the more recent changes in discovery laws, including what burdens are placed on the defendant.

But the rules of discovery are different in criminal cases for other reasons. Even though there was very little statutory guidance about what a prosecutor should produce for the defense, there were at least two guiding principles that compelled prosecutors to act, even in the absence of statutes mandating certain actions. These two principles are a prosecutor's ethics and U.S. Supreme Court cases.

A prosecutor is not merely an advocate for a client. Prosecutors have moral and ethical duties to seek justice, not simply rack up convictions. Some courts have stated that a prosecutor has a moral, if not a legal, obligation to produce evidence for the defendant prior to trial to allow the defendant to present an adequate defense. This often places the prosecutor in the position of having to decide how much evidence to give to the defense to make sure that the prosecutor has met his obligation. It is the prosecutor's duty to ensure that full discovery, at least to the extent required by statute, is met. Courts have held, time and again, that the prosecutor's duty is to seek justice, not to guarantee convictions. Faced with this dilemma, most prosecutors choose to err on the side of caution and allow the defendant to see as much evidence as possible without jeopardizing the safety of witnesses. That way, there can be no allegation that the prosecution has suppressed or withheld pertinent evidence or witness statements. The prosecutor has both legal and ethical obligations to ensure a fair trial and cannot pick and choose among the evidence that he or she will provide to the defendant in order to make sure that the prosecutor secures a guilty verdict.[1] Balanced against that ethical and legal responsibility is the concept that there is no general right to discovery in criminal cases at all.[2] There is considerable variation among states about how much information the defendant should be provided with prior to trial. As we will see later in this chapter, some Supreme Court cases have preempted state law and require the state to produce certain types of information whether they are required by state law or not. The *Brady* case is a perfect example, and we will address that case in depth later in this chapter.

---

[1] *U.S. v. Consolidated Laundries Corp.*, 291 F.2d 563 (2d Cir. 1961); *State v. Spano*, 69 N.J. 231, 353 A.2d 97 (1976); *State v. Reiman*, 284 N.W.2d 860 (S.D. 1979).
[2] *Weatherford v. Bursey*, 429 U.S. 545, 97 S. Ct. 837, 51 L. Ed. 2d 30 (1977).

PROFILING THE PROFESSIONAL

Discovery

"Defendants have the right to ask for what we plan to use at trial. We give them that information, so they're not surprised. In my state, we have reciprocal discovery. They have to provide me with their discovery, as well. We include in our discovery a list of witnesses, certified copies of convictions if I'm going to use them to aggravate sentencing, similar transactions, prior difficulties between the parties, police reports, written statements, in my cases I have 911 calls, so I provide them with the actual recordings or the report that was generated about it. My theory about discovery is that I'm not going to hold things back; I don't want to play games with them. I don't want the defense playing games with me, either. If they've got stuff, I'd like to see it."

Debra Sullivan, Assistant District Attorney

A. DISCOVERY THAT IS NORMALLY PROVIDED BY THE PROSECUTION

Despite the fact that there is no general right of discovery in criminal cases, most states have enacted statutes that require a minimum amount of discovery to be produced by the state. Significantly, most states impose little or no obligation on the criminal defendant to produce any discovery for the state. Among the items that are most commonly provided to a defendant prior to trial are as follows:

- Witness list
- Scientific reports
- Defendant's statements
- Physical evidence

Sidebar

The prosecutor should always err on the side of giving the defense too much information, rather than too little.[3]

1. WITNESS LIST

State and federal prosecutors are required to give the defendant a list of the witnesses that the government intends to call during the trial. This list consists not only of the names of each witness but also their addresses and phone numbers (if known). Some states have even tried to expand this requirement by requiring the prosecution to produce the Social Security numbers of each of the state's witnesses. Those provisions have been challenged and ruled unconstitutional in many states. In any event, many a witness is troubled by the fact that the defendant will know her complete name, address, and telephone number. This would seem to be a sure

[3] *State v. Reiman*, 284 N.W.2d 860 (S.D. 1979).

ticket to attempts by the defendant to harass or intimidate witnesses, especially since the defendant knows exactly where to find each witness. Although witnesses have been harassed and even murdered prior to trial, in most cases the defendant does not contact the witnesses or try to intimidate them. Their attorneys will surely attempt to speak with them, but they are not compelled to speak with the attorney prior to trial and can refuse to do so if they wish.

2. SCIENTIFIC REPORTS

All states require the prosecution to give the defendant copies of any and all scientific reports prepared by prosecution witnesses. These scientific reports must be produced at least ten days prior to trial in most jurisdictions. This ten-day rule allows the defense to hire its own experts to review the tests and also to request permission to conduct tests on physical evidence. In an era in which shows like *CSI* dominate nightly TV rosters, it is surprising to note that in many cases there are no scientific reports to turn over at all. In many cases, there are no scientific tests even conducted. Crime scene technicians may be unable to lift fingerprints from various objects, and there is often no other evidence to test. In that situation, there are no scientific reports to pass along to the defendant. However, it must also be said that in high-profile cases, usually murder cases, law enforcement often pull out every tool in their arsenal, and they conduct DNA tests, carpet fiber analysis, blood-spatter pattern analysis, and fingerprint testing, to name just a few. All of these test results must be copied and made available to the defendant. Furthermore, if the defendant has received a mental evaluation, a copy of the report of this evaluation will also be provided.

3. DEFENDANT'S STATEMENTS

If the police have questioned the defendant, then the written statement they made of that interrogation must be provided to the defense. One might wonder, since the defendant was present when he made his statement, why he would need a copy of it. The answer is that it is really for the defendant's attorney. One of the defense attorney's obligations is to review police actions to make sure that the defendant was not coerced or threatened into giving a confession. If a video or audio recording of the interrogation was made, then the defense gets a copy of that, too. The rule about providing defendant's statements to the defense team also applies to statements by codefendants. It is important to note that the prosecution may not be able to admit the statement of codefendant A in the trial of codefendant B.[4]

Significantly, we have not mentioned the discovery of witness statements. As we will see later in this chapter when we discuss modern changes to discovery rules, witness statements have not always been made available to defendants.

---

[4] *Bruton v. United States*, 391 U.S. 123 (1968).

4. PHYSICAL EVIDENCE

In addition to receiving copies of scientific reports and the defendant's statements, the defense also has the right to see and inspect the state's evidence prior to trial. This includes weapons, documents, photographs, even scenes of the crime, depending on the nature of the case. If the state attempts to bar the defense from visiting a scene or viewing evidence, the defendant can file a motion requesting that the court give the defense team permission to do so (Figure 6-1).

FIGURE 6-1

Defendant's Motion for Discovery

NOW COMES the defendant in the above criminal action and files this MOTION FOR DISCOVERY AND INSPECTION OF PHYSICAL EVIDENCE. Pursuant to the State of Grace's Rules of Criminal Discovery, 4-102, defendant prays for discovery and inspection of the following items:

I.

1. The Defendant moves the Court to order and require the District Attorney to produce and permit by the Defendant or Defendant's counsel the inspection of and the copying and/or photographing of the following:

- Any and all documents, papers, books, accounts, letters, photographs, objects, digital recordings in any format or other tangible things not protected by a recognized legal privilege, which constitute, contain or could be construed as evidence relevant and material to any matter involved in the above-styled criminal action and which are in the possession, custody or control of the State or any of its agencies, including police departments and civilian witnesses acting on behalf of the State;
- Any written or oral statements of the Defendant;
- The defendant's criminal record consisting of any criminal conviction in this or any other state, territory or other recognized jurisdiction of the United States.
- Criminal records of each and every of the State's witnesses;
- Personnel records and internal memoranda relating to disciplinary actions taken by the lead police officers and/or detectives in this case.
- Any evidence that could be construed under *Brady v. Maryland* as exculpatory or mitigating for the defendant's benefit

WHEREFORE, the Defendant respectfully prays and submits that this Court grant this the Defendant's Motion for Discovery and Inspection.

Respectfully submitted,

____

(Attorney's Name, Address, State Bar Number)
ATTORNEY FOR DEFENDANT JOHN DOE

B. DEPOSITIONS IN CRIMINAL CASES

Depose
Give sworn testimony out of court.

To **depose** a witness is to ask him questions, under oath, before a court reporter, well in advance of trial. The deposition is then printed out as a transcript. In civil cases, depositions are common for all witnesses who may testify. However, this rule has not traditionally been applicable in criminal cases. One reason is that the Sixth Amendment gives a criminal defendant the right to confront any witnesses against him, so a witness in a criminal case must always appear in person to testify. A party in a civil case does not have this limitation. If a witness becomes unavailable in a civil case, the party may simply present the witness's deposition instead of the witness himself. This is generally not permissible in criminal cases. The witness must appear, take the stand, and testify. Witnesses often do not understand this distinction, especially if they have some familiarity with civil trials. They will often complain of missed time from work or other inconvenience in having to testify at trial and wonder why a deposition transcript or an affidavit is not being used instead. The other reason that depositions are not routinely used in criminal cases has more to do with tradition and custom. There are states that take depositions in criminal cases, but the vast majority have a tradition of not doing so. Instead, the attorneys wait until the witness is on the stand and then use the witness's prior written statement to impeach her.

As we will see, the rule and tradition about depositions in criminal cases is slowly changing, partly from changes to discovery rules and partly because of their usefulness to criminal defendants. A witness who has given an oral deposition that has been transcribed is far less prone to vary her testimony than a witness who gave a written statement at the time of the crime. New discovery rules allow both the government and the defense to use depositions, but only in limited circumstances.

C. ORGANIZING DISCOVERY

Sometimes the material provided by the state through discovery can be quite extensive. Organizing this material can be a daunting task but one that is particularly important for the defense team. Witness names and addresses should be noted. Incriminating statements by the defendant should be tagged for later review. Any possibly exculpatory information should be culled out. Potential defense witnesses should also be noted. State crime lab reports contain a wealth of information, if read closely.

D. DISCOVERY IN MISDEMEANOR CASES

In criminal cases, there is a general rule: The more serious the offense, the more material the government generates. In misdemeanor cases, such as shoplifting or driving under the influence of alcohol, the discovery materials could easily consist of just a few sheets of paper. In a capital murder case, on the other hand, the amount of witness statements, crime lab reports, and other items could easily fill several boxes.

E. VARIATION IN DISCOVERY RULES AROUND THE UNITED STATES

Although many states have modified their criminal discovery rules in recent years (see the next section), this is certainly not true in all states. In states that have not changed their discovery rules, a defendant must request discovery before he will receive most items from the prosecution. In such states, if the defendant fails to file discovery motions, then the prosecution is under no obligation to give him anything, except for *Brady* material, which we will discuss later in this chapter.

F. RECENT CHANGES IN DISCOVERY LAWS

Many states have recognized the discrepancy between civil and criminal discovery and have made changes in their criminal discovery statutes. For instance, many states have amended their rules about what information a prosecutor must serve on a defendant. These statutes were amended to protect defendants from the consequences of unfair surprise at trial and to assist them in locating evidence that they could offer in their defense.

These new discovery statutes are designed to encourage voluntary disclosures of information like the information exchange that takes place in civil cases every day. These statutes also give the court the power to compel either side to disclose relevant facts to the other side. The judge may order such disclosure prior to trial. Many of these new changes require the state to turn over far greater portions of its prosecution and police files to the defendant than was ever required before. This means that the state is now compelled to give the defendant copies of witness statements, police reports, and many other items traditionally withheld by the state.

Among the changes to the discovery rules is the requirement that the defense provide some information to the state. Traditionally, discovery in criminal cases was almost exclusively one-way. In some very limited circumstances, discussed below, a criminal defendant might have to provide some minimal information to the state, but in most situations, the criminal defendant was not compelled to provide any discovery whatsoever. That rule changed under the new discovery statutes.

A criminal defendant does not have to produce the same amount of material, nor to such an extent, as the state, but requiring the defendant to produce any information at all is a novelty in criminal law. Under the new discovery rules, a defendant must produce specifics about alibis or other legal defenses, as well as a list of defense witnesses and their addresses and telephone numbers (if known). This is still much less discovery than the state must provide to the defendant.

G. INFORMATION THAT IS NORMALLY NOT DISCOVERABLE BY THE DEFENDANT

The defendant is not allowed to use the discovery process as a "fishing expedition"—that is, as a means to go through all of the prosecution's files, hoping to find something useful. The defendant can request specific items or any exculpatory information (see the discussion of *Brady* material below), but is not permitted to submit a general request for "all information."

1. WORK PRODUCT

Work product
The prosecuting attorney's mental notes and strategy ideas about the case.

The prosecuting attorney's mental notes and strategy ideas about the case are not discoverable; they are referred to as **work product**. As a general rule, work product is not discoverable, either in criminal or civil cases. This is based on the premise that mental notes, ideas, and impressions form the very core of the service provided by an attorney, and requiring the disclosure of such information would severely limit the attorney's effectiveness. The exception to this rule, however, comes when these notes focus on witness testimony that may be exculpatory to the defendant, as we will see in *Brady* below.

2. CRIMINAL RECORDS OF WITNESSES

The issue of the criminal records of the state's witnesses has been controversial for years. Under the traditional approach, the prosecution was not obligated to provide their witnesses' criminal history, and the defense attorney was left to her own investigation to obtain this information. In many states that is still the case, while in others the state is required to produce for the defense any criminal records of its intended witnesses. Even in the states that require the state to hand over any criminal records of its witnesses, there is no uniformity about how much is provided. For instance, in some states the defense must be given a copy of the witness's criminal history, showing any convictions but not necessarily any arrests. In other states, all arrests and convictions must be produced.

a. Why the State Might Reveal a Witness's Criminal History

Even in states where there is no requirement to produce a witness's criminal history, many prosecutors do so anyway. First of all, this information may be required under *Brady*. If the main witnesses for the state all have criminal records, this could potentially assist the defense and might even be considered exculpatory information. However, even in situations in which it is clear that there is no *Brady* question, a prosecutor might still produce a witness's criminal history, absent any statutory requirement to do so. The reason is simple: A prosecutor is supposed to work for justice, not for convictions, and revealing this information to the defendant will help the defendant prepare his case. However, there is a more hard-nosed reason to produce this information. The prosecutor will probably mention during opening statements that the main witness is a convicted felon, so there is no point concealing this fact from the defense. Why would a prosecutor make such a statement early in the trial? Prosecutors reason that it is better that the jury hear that evidence from them rather than from the defense. It is always better to reveal awkward or damaging information yourself than to have the other side do so for you. Suppose, for instance, the defendant is on trial for theft, and the state's main witness has a criminal record for theft, too. Even if a court might rule that it is not a violation of *Brady* to turn that information over to the defense, the prosecutor would be better off doing so anyway.

The criminal record of a witness can be problematic for juries, which is why prosecutors and defense attorneys try to explain or defuse such records early in the trial. Sometimes it works, sometimes not. During the trial of a Manhattan crane operator, whose crane collapsed in 2008 and killed seven people, it came to light that a key defense witness had been fired from his job at the city Buildings Department for viewing porn on his work computer. After losing his job, he subsequently pleaded guilty to forgery for copying and using his parking pass from the department. The witness testified that the Buildings Department findings in the crane collapse were incorrect and that the incident was not the result of the crane operator's error. The prosecution tried to undermine his testimony, pointing out that he had reason to retaliate against the Buildings Department. In this case, the witness's criminal record did not seem to matter to the jury. The crane operator had been charged with 20 criminal counts, including manslaughter and criminally negligent homicide, and he was found not guilty on all counts.

It is common for the main witness in a criminal case to be a codefendant. This person has often negotiated a deal with the state for a recommendation of a lesser sentence in return for taking the stand against the defendant. In such cases, the defense has the right to know the details of any deal the defendant has made with the state. The defense will often file a motion requesting such information. The *Brady* decision might also require the handing over of any such information. But whether or not any Supreme Court cases require it, most prosecutors not only let the defense know about the state witnesses' prior convictions, they will let the jury know, too. In fact, somewhere in opening statements, the prosecutor will tell the jury that the main witness against the defendant is a convicted felon. Not only that, but also this witness is testifying because he's worked out a deal with the state so that he will get a lighter recommendation on sentencing in exchange for his testimony.

Why would the state volunteer this information to the jury right at the beginning of the trial? The primary reason is because the jury is going to learn it eventually anyway. The defense attorney is going to hammer this point home at every opportunity. Why not steal his thunder and tell the jury about it first? Revealing this information to the jury in opening statements shows that the state is being forthcoming, and it also gives the prosecutor an opportunity to shape the context of the testimony.

A prosecutor may even tell the jury that the state's main witness is not a nice person. He is, in fact, a convicted felon who is now ratting out his former friend. That may not make the witness a very likable person, but it does not make his testimony any less believable. Hearing it right from the start of the case prevents the defense from making a dramatic disclosure later on in the trial when the defense attorney can present the disclosure in a very negative light.

H. OPEN-FILE POLICY

Many prosecutors maintain an open-file policy, under which a defense attorney may review the entire state's file and copy anything useful or helpful. This policy short-circuits any claims that the defense has not been provided with all statutorily required information, since the state is essentially giving the defense everything that the state has. Open-file policies are not mandated by law but are set up by individual district attorneys. Some prosecutors favor these policies, while some do not. The fact that one district attorney's office operates under an open-file policy cannot be used to force a district attorney in another county or state to open up his files.[5]

III PROSECUTION MOTIONS

Motion
A request that a judge make a ruling or take some other action.

A **motion** is a request filed with a judge requesting that some action be taken. Before we discuss the wide array of motions that a defendant may raise in a case, we will first address the relatively few motions that a prosecutor may file against the defendant. As we will see later in this chapter, the defense routinely files a motion to suppress evidence in the case, but defense attorneys are not the only party that is permitted to file motions. The state may also bring motions against the defendant. The prosecutor, however, has much greater limitations on the types of motions that she can file. The only motions that a prosecutor can bring are the following:

- Similar transactions
- Aggravation of sentence
- Motion to join

A. SIMILAR TRANSACTIONS

Similar transactions
A motion filed by the prosecution that shows a defendant's state of mind or criminal intent by giving the jury in the current case evidence of a defendant's similar crime in a previous case.

Although the state generally does not file many motions before trial, there are a few that a prosecutor may consider. One such motion is referred to as **similar transactions**. In many states the prosecution is allowed to bring a similar transactions motion so that the jury can hear evidence of the defendant's prior crimes. Although the defendant's prior criminal record is normally inadmissible at trial, similar transaction laws do allow a limited use of such prior convictions. In a situation in which the current charge against the defendant is very similar to a previous conviction, the state is permitted to present evidence of the prior conviction to show a common method, plan, or scheme by the defendant to carry out certain kinds of crimes. "If the defendant is proven to be the perpetrator of another . . . crime and the facts of that crime are sufficiently similar or connected to the facts of the crime charged, the separate crime will be admissible to prove identity, motive, plan, scheme, bent of mind, or course of conduct.[6]

However, before the state is allowed to present any such evidence to the jury, the court must rule on the evidence. A similar transactions hearing must be held in

[5] *State v. Moore*, 335 N.C. 567, 440 S.E.2d 797, cert. denied, 513 U.S. 898, 115 S. Ct. 253, 130 L. Ed. 2d 174 (1994).
[6] *Hatcher v. State*, 224 Ga. App. 747, 752(3), 482 S.E.2d 443 (1997).

which the witnesses from the prior conviction testify and the state builds a case showing how the prior conviction has many of the same features as the current charge. If the judge rules that there is sufficient similarity between the two offenses to establish the defendant's common motive, plan, or conduct, then the evidence of the prior conviction can be used in the current case. The judge must give a limiting instruction to the jury, telling them that this evidence is being admitted for the limited purpose of showing the defendant's common approach to similar crimes. Under this limitation, a prosecutor can only admit evidence of crimes substantially similar to the current charge. A similar transactions motion does not allow the prosecutor to put the defendant's entire criminal record into evidence.

In a Georgia case, a 46-year-old middle school teacher was accused of aggravated child molestation for having a sexual relationship with a 13-year-old student. The judge in the case ruled that the state could present similar transactions evidence during the trial because the defendant had prior sexual contact with three other young men ranging in age from 18 to 21. The judge agreed with the prosecutor's contention that "[i]t goes to her lustful disposition for younger boys."

Using Similar Transactions as a Negotiating Ploy

PROFILING THE PROFESSIONAL

"When a defense attorney learns that I'm going to file a similar transactions, it puts even greater pressure on the defendant to plead guilty. The defense figures that if the jury hears about other charges, they'll make the obvious connection that this guy has done this thing before and that he's done it here, too. When you file a similar transactions motion, you are bringing up the heat on the defense. It also gives the defense attorney something to tell his client. 'Hey, they're going to bring in your priors. Your goose is cooked. You'd better plead out.'"

Keith Miles, Assistant District Attorney

B. AGGRAVATION OF SENTENCE

In addition to filing a motion for similar transactions, a prosecutor may also file a motion in *aggravation of sentence*. The prosecutor may file this motion prior to the trial or may wait and file it after the defendant has been found guilty. A motion in aggravation of sentence is a document that shows that the defendant has a lengthy criminal record or has a history of violence or of harming others. In addition to filing the written motion, the prosecutor will also provide certified copies of the defendant's prior convictions. The judge may or may not take the convictions into account when sentencing the defendant. Generally, when a defendant has a lengthy criminal record, he will receive a longer sentence on conviction than someone who has no prior record. One way of ensuring that the court is aware of the defendant's criminal record is for the prosecution to file a motion in aggravation of sentence.

FIGURE 6-2

Rule 13. Joint Trial of Separate Cases

> The court may order that separate cases be tried together as though brought in a single indictment or information if all offenses and all defendants could have been joined in a single indictment or information.[7]

C. MOTION TO JOIN

Motion to join
A prosecution motion that requests two or more codefendants to be tried at the same time.

State and federal rules allow a prosecutor to move the court to combine several cases into a single prosecution under specific circumstances. If there is one crime or a series of crimes committed by the same individuals, it may make more sense both in terms of time and economy to try all of the individuals at the same time, rather than try them one by one. In situations in which the government has separately indicted individuals for the same crime, a prosecutor can file a **motion to join** the defendants together and have them tried in one trial (Figure 6-2). Of course, the defense will often fight this motion, reasoning that if a jury sees a group of people charged, it will be harder for any single defendant to stand out as an innocent party.

DEFENSE MOTIONS

Defendants may raise a wide variety of motions before trial. These motions may involve evidentiary issues, but can also involve many other issues. Some defense attorneys will file dozens of motions before trial and insist that each motion be argued.

A. *Brady* Motion

***Brady* material**
Information available to the prosecutor that is favorable to the defendant, because it mitigates either his guilt or his sentence. This material must be provided to the defense prior to trial.

Regardless of whether a particular state has changed its discovery rules in criminal cases, the U.S. Supreme Court has mandated that certain kinds of information must be turned over to the defendant prior to trial in all criminal prosecutions. Such information has come to be known as ***Brady* material**.

In the *Brady v. Maryland*[8] decision, the Court ruled that when the state has evidence or information tending to show that the defendant is not guilty of the crime (exculpatory information), the state must produce such evidence for the defendant, whether or not the defendant has requested it. The Supreme Court reasoned that since the role of the prosecutor was not simply to convict a defendant but to seek justice, it was only proper that the state turn over such evidence to the defense in order for the defendant to have a fair trial.

[7] Rule 13. F.R.C.P

[8] *Brady v. Maryland*, 373 U.S. 83, 83 S. Ct. 1194, 10 L. Ed. 2d 215 (1963).

The *Brady* decision has been expanded over the years to include not only exculpatory information but also any evidence or information that might mitigate the defendant's guilt. *Brady*'s effect has been far-reaching. Most prosecutors now serve on the defendant a "*Brady* notice," detailing any evidence that has come to light during the state's investigation that might mitigate the charges against the defendant.

EXAMPLE

During the preparation of the defendant's case, his attorney comes across a note that the armed robbery with which the defendant has been charged was actually videotaped and saved on a DVD. The DVD clearly shows the defendant committing the armed robbery. When the defense attorney requests a copy of the DVD, he is informed that the DVD has been lost. There are some still photographs taken from the original DVD, but the rest of the evidence has been lost. The defense attorney challenges the prosecution by alleging that it has violated the principles of discovery in general and *Brady* in particular by failing to produce this evidence. Is this a violation of *Brady*?

Answer: No. *Brady* was designed to force the state to produce any evidence that might tend to exculpate or mitigate the defendant's guilt. The DVD, in contrast, would have actually further incriminated the defendant. There is no *Brady* violation.[9]

The key principle in *Brady* was enunciated as follows: "[T]he suppression by the prosecution of evidence favorable to an accused upon request violates due process where the evidence is material either to guilt or to punishment, irrespective of the good faith or bad faith of the prosecution."[10] This evidence must be revealed to the defendant even if the defendant does not request it.[11]

A particularly egregious example of a *Brady* violation is from a Dallas, Texas, case in which a man was convicted of sexual assault in the mid-1990s and sentenced to life in prison. Eventually it came to light that the victim had told the prosecutor the day before the trial began that the defendant did not assault her. The prosecutor placed a note to that effect in the file but did not disclose the information to the defense until more than 10 years later. The defendant was released from prison, and the DA's office chose not to retry him.

Sidebar

When a judge conducts an in camera hearing, she may do it in private or require the presence of both the prosecution and defense. The actual procedure involved in carrying out the hearing is left to the judge's discretion.[12]

1. *IN CAMERA* INSPECTIONS BY JUDGES

When a judge receives a request by a defense attorney under *Brady*, the judge must conduct an ***in camera*** inspection of the state's file. An *in camera* inspection is carried out by the judge in his chambers. The state provides the judge with its entire file, and the judge goes through all of the witness statements, police reports, and other material, looking for anything that might be construed under the *Brady* decision to be **exculpatory**. If the judge does find some material, he provides it

In camera
(Latin) In chambers; refers to a review of a file by a judge carried out in his private office.

Exculpatory
Refers to evidence that tends to provide an excuse or a justification for the defendant's actions or that shows that the defendant did not commit the crime charged.

---

[9] *U.S. v. Drake*, 543 F.3d 1080 (9th Cir. 2008).
[10] *Brady*, 373 U.S. at 87.
[11] *State v. Hunt*, 615 N.W.2d 294, 296-302 (Minn., 2000).
[12] *Com. v. Dias*, 451 Mass. 463, 886 N.E.2d 713 (2008).

to the defense. In this manner, the defense can be assured that an impartial party has reviewed the state's file, and the defense attorney does not have to take the prosecutor's word that all exculpatory information has been provided. The judge must make appropriate findings of fact, detailing that he has reviewed the state's file and found nothing that might be exculpatory to the defense that has not been already provided to the defendant.

EXAMPLE

During an *in camera* review of the prosecution file, the judge finds evidence that the defendant had some mental issues, and has been seeing a psychiatrist. The defendant is charged with stalking and aggravated assault on a woman that he was dating. Is this evidence that should be turned over to the defense?

Answer: Absolutely. Although it may not be exculpatory, it may have some impact on his sentence if he is found guilty, so the state should provide it to the defense.

B. MOTION TO SUPPRESS

Motion to suppress
A motion that requests that a court not allow the jury to hear specific information, such as the defendant's confession or other statements, based on improprieties in obtaining the information.

A **motion to suppress** requests the judge to rule that certain evidence be inadmissible at trial. The most common reason for this request is that the evidence was seized in violation of the defendant's constitutional rights. If evidence has been seized illegally, the judge is authorized to rule the evidence inadmissible and therefore unusable at trial. This is the famous exclusionary rule, first enunciated in the early 1900s and expanded by later U.S. Supreme Court decisions. Under the exclusionary rule, if law enforcement violate constitutional principles in obtaining evidence, their punishment is that they cannot use it at trial.

Defendants often file motions to suppress evidence even when there is no clear constitutional violation. Many defense attorneys believe that there is nothing to lose by filing such a motion. If the judge denies the motion, the defendant is in no worse a position than he was previously. If the judge grants the motion, a crucial piece of evidence will be excluded from the trial. However, if the judge rules against the government on a motion to suppress, the government is permitted to appeal that decision.

EXAMPLE

Clayton was driving late one night and was pulled over by Officer Green. Clayton asked why he was pulled over, and the officer told him that he had a broken taillight. However, when Clayton got out of the car and looked at his taillights, they were working perfectly. Clayton was eventually arrested and charged with possession of marijuana that the officer found on Clayton's passenger seat. Should he file a motion to suppress? If he does, what chance does he have that it might be granted?

Answer: Clayton has nothing to lose by filing a motion to suppress, and, as we have already seen, many defendants do so. In this case, however, Clayton may have solid constitutional grounds to challenge the original stop and thus may be successful on his motion to suppress the marijuana evidence.

A motion to suppress can be focused on any of a number of issues raised in the case, from the defendant's confession to the photographic lineup used to identify the defendant as the person responsible for the crime. Defense attorneys routinely file motions to suppress the following:

- Physical evidence
- Defendant's statement
- Photographic lineup
- Warrantless searches
- Searches with warrants
- Wiretaps

C. OTHER MOTIONS

In addition to typical discovery motions and motions to suppress, there are a wide variety of other motions that a defense attorney may bring. These are limited only by the creativity of the defense attorney. However, the judge always has the final say on whether the motions will be granted. Some of the typical motions filed by defense attorneys include to the following:

- Motion to sever offenses
- Motion to change venue
- Speedy trial demand
- Motion for continuance
- Motion in limine
- Motion to "reveal the deal"
- Motion to reveal the identity of confidential informants

1. MOTION TO SEVER

In some cases, the defendant may request a motion to **sever** offenses or parties. This is exactly the opposite of the state's motion to join. In a motion for joinder, the state requests that a series of crimes or multiple defendants be tried together. A motion for severance asks the court to try different counts of an indictment as separate trials or different codefendants in separate trials. A defense attorney requests severance when he believes that being tried together with several other defendants will unduly prejudice the case and prevent the defendant from receiving a fair trial. In a similar fashion, a motion to sever offenses requests a separate trial for offenses that may be unrelated in time or action from each other. The jury might not separate out the proof of one offense from the other but might instead be likely to assume that the defendant is guilty simply by the sheer number of offenses against him.

Sever
Separate or cut off into constituent parts.

2. MOTION TO CHANGE VENUE

A defendant who wants to move the location of the trial will request a change of venue. Generally, a defendant must show that his chances of receiving a fair trial in the original area have been diminished or completely negated, usually by intensive pretrial publicity. Defendants will often present evidence of newspaper or other media reports that have focused on the case in a negative way. Since the potential jurors for the trial will be drawn from the same area, a motion for change of venue alleges that the jury pool for this case has been influenced before they ever heard any testimony. If the judge grants a change of venue motion, it usually means that the trial will be moved to some other jurisdiction. The jury will be selected from the new area, but the prosecutor, judge, and defense attorney remain the same.

3. SPEEDY TRIAL DEMAND

The Sixth Amendment to the U.S. Constitution provides that "the accused shall enjoy the right to a speedy and public trial. . . ."

The right of an accused to a speedy trial has a long history. Originally mentioned in the Magna Carta in the year 1215, the defendant's right to a speedy trial was considered to be an important, if often ignored, right. The right to a speedy trial was embodied in the Virginia Declaration of Rights of 1776, then incorporated into the U.S. Constitution and eventually into all state constitutions. In *Klopfer v. North Carolina*,[13] the Supreme Court declared that the right to a speedy trial was as important as any other right guaranteed in the Sixth Amendment, calling it "one of the most basic rights preserved by our Constitution."

All states have laws that are commonly referred to as "speedy trial statutes." These statutes allow a defendant to serve on the state a demand that the defendant be tried in this or the next **term of court**.

Term of court
The period of time slated for court hearings; it can be as short as a week or as long as a year.

a. Dismissing a Case for Failure to Receive a Speedy Trial

If the defendant serves a speedy trial demand and is not tried in the specified time, then the charges against the defendant must be dismissed and the defendant released from confinement. Serving a "speedy" on a prosecutor often has a galvanizing effect on the state. Since a prosecutor knows that if the defendant is not tried, he must be released, the practical effect of serving a speedy trial demand is usually that the defendant's case is moved up to the number one trial in the next trial week. Even when the defendant is already in prison serving a sentence on an unrelated offense, he is still entitled to receive a speedy trial on another charge.[14]

b. How Speedy Must a "Speedy Trial" Be?

While this right is considered one of the fundamental rights guaranteed in the Constitution, defining what exactly constitutes a "speedy" trial has been difficult to quantify.

---

[13] 386 U.S. 213, 87 S. Ct. 988, 18 L. Ed. 2d 1 (1967).
[14] *Smith v. Hooey*, 393 U.S. 374, 89 S. Ct. 575, 21 L. Ed. 2d 607 (1969).

The Supreme Court has held that a delay of eight years between indictment and trial is too long;[15] five years may also be too long.[16] The problem is that each case must be considered on its own facts. The Supreme Court has been reluctant to state a maximum period that will always mean a violation of the Sixth Amendment. Despite the Court's reluctance to name a specific period of time in which a defendant must always be tried, the Court has been specific about the sanction imposed for failing to try a defendant. Where the defendant's right to a speedy trial has been violated, only one sanction is allowed: dismissal of the state's case. This drastic remedy was authorized in *Strunk v. United States.*[17]

In the O. J. Simpson case, for example, Simpson expressly requested a speedy trial, forcing prosecutors to work around the clock to build their case. The murders of Nicole Brown Simpson and Ronald Goldman took place in June 1994; Simpson was indicted a week later, and the court began seating the jury in October of that same year. Yet in other high-profile cases, years will sometimes lapse between the defendant being charged and the actual trial. In the case of Caylee Anthony, a Florida toddler who went missing in June 2008 and whose mother was indicted for her murder a few months later, the trial did not begin until 2011. The delay may have proved beneficial for the defendant who was acquitted on July 5, 2011. Numerous factors were responsible for the delay, including requests by the defense team to give them more time to prepare their case and to compile expert witness reports as ordered by the judge.

c. When the Defendant May Not Want a Speedy Trial After All

Although each state has a statute authorizing the filing of a speedy trial demand to enforce the Sixth Amendment guarantee, a speedy trial may actually work against the defendant. Often, a delay in bringing the case to trial will help the defendant. Memories fade over time. Evidence may be lost. In fact, taking a case to trial sooner rather than later may be helpful to the defendant only when the prosecution is not prepared. Otherwise, a quick trial may actually work against the defendant. The defense team should evaluate these potential difficulties before filing a statutory speedy trial demand.

d. When Is the Right to a Speedy Trial Triggered?

A question often arises in the context of speedy-trial demands: When is the right triggered? Put another way, at what point during the proceedings does the prosecution pass the point of no return, where the state fails to prosecute the defendant and the provisions of the speedy trial demand will necessitate dismissing the case? Courts have wrestled with that question for many years and have finally settled it at a specific point during the case. The right to receive a speedy trial is triggered when

---

[15] *Doggett v. United States,* 5 U.S. 647, 112 S. Ct. 2686, 120 L. Ed. 2d 520 (1992).
[16] *Barker v. Wingo,* 407 U.S. 514, 92 S. Ct. 2182, 33 L. Ed. 2d 101 (1972).
[17] 412 U.S. 434 (1973).

an indictment has been lodged against the defendant.[18] The right to a speedy trial also attaches when a defendant has been *accused*—that is, when he is charged with a misdemeanor. Of course, this assumes that the defendant has not filed for a motion for continuance (discussed below). If the defendant files such a motion, he waives the right to a speedy trial. After all, the defendant is requesting a trial to be held immediately and then, by his own request, wishes to put the trial off.

4. MOTION FOR CONTINUANCE

Motion for continuance
A request by one party to postpone a trial or other hearing for a future date.

A **motion for continuance** can be made by either side in a criminal case. When the party moves for a continuance, it is requesting that the case be taken off the current calendar and rescheduled for a later date. There are many reasons that a party might request a continuance. The party might not be prepared for the trial, a key witness might not be available, or some other factor weighs heavily against trying the case now and waiting to try it at a later date. A judge must approve the motion for a continuance, but if the opposing side does not object to the continuance, more often than not the judge will grant it.

5. MOTION IN LIMINE

Motion in limine
(Latin) Motion at the beginning; a motion by one party that requests specific judicial rulings at the outset of the trial.

In addition to motions to suppress, a defendant will also file numerous motions in limine. A **motion in limine** requests a ruling on the use of a particular piece of evidence, or a limitation on the kind of testimony that a witness may give on the stand. For instance, if a defense attorney has reason to believe that a particular state's witness will refer to the defendant's criminal history during her testimony, the defense attorney may file a motion in limine requesting the judge to order the witness to make no such references. Since a defendant's prior criminal record is normally not admissible at trial, such a motion will usually be granted. The defense may also file a motion in limine to restrict the use of other kinds of evidence or testimony. Each such motion will be argued by the attorneys and may involve the testimony of a witness at a motion hearing prior to trial. These motion hearings are often days or even weeks before the actual trial. Some motions may also be argued shortly before the trial begins. Still other motions may be raised during the course of the trial.

6. MOTION TO "REVEAL THE DEAL" (*GIGLIO*)

When a defense attorney suspects that a prosecution witness has been offered a deal for his testimony at trial, she can file a motion requesting the details of the arrangement. When a defense attorney requests information about any arrangements between the prosecution and a witness, it is commonly referred to as a motion to "reveal the deal" or a *Giglio* motion (from the case where it was first created).[19] This is a motion asking that the state be ordered to reveal any deal entered into with

---

[18] *Unites States v. Marion*, 404 U.S. 307 (1971).
[19] *Giglio v. United States*, 405 U.S. 150 (1972).

any witness in which the state has offered immunity or some other benefit in exchange for testimony. It is fairly common for a state's witness to be granted some form of immunity or the promise of a light recommendation on sentencing in exchange for the witness's testimony against another codefendant. Defense attorneys rightly assume that such a promise could have an effect on the witness's performance on the stand. Although a prosecutor would probably feel that any such promise would have to be revealed to the defense attorney because of the *Brady* decision (see above), a defense attorney might decide to cover her bases by filing a motion anyway.

7. MOTION TO REVEAL THE IDENTITY OF CONFIDENTIAL INFORMANTS

Defense attorneys may file a motion to reveal the identity of a confidential informant (CI) who was involved in the case. Generally, police and prosecutors protect their CIs, because to release their names to the defendant might put the CI in danger of being killed. Discovery rules allow a prosecutor to conceal the identity of a CI, but this right is not absolute. The court is allowed to weigh the right of the government to protect its confidential informants from retribution against the right of the defendant to receive a fair trial. If a judge decides that the only way to make sure that the defendant receives a fair and proper trial is to release the name of the confidential informant to the defense, then the judge is authorized to do so.[20] This is another example in which the judge would review the state's file *in camera* before making a decision on whether to reveal the CI's name.

At the conclusion of the following case excerpt, you'll find several questions pertaining to the state's primary witness in the case. As you're reading, pay close attention to this witness's actions, the prosecutor's actions, and the defendant's appeal, particularly as they relate to the *Brady* decision.

CASE EXCERPT

STATE v. HUNT

615 N.W.2d 294, 296-302 (Minn., 2000)

SYLLABUS BY THE COURT

1. Appellant is entitled to a new trial where the state failed to disclose the results of a psychological examination that found the state's key witness incompetent to stand trial.

John M. Stuart, State Public Defender, Sharon E. Jacks, Asst. State Public Defender, Lawrence Hammerling, Deputy State Public Defender, Minneapolis, for appellant.
Michael Hatch, Atty. Gen., St. Paul, Charles E. MacLean, Winona County Atty., Steve L. Schleicher, Asst. Winona County Atty., Winona, for respondent.
Heard, considered, and decided by the court en banc.

[20] *Drouin v. State*, 222 Md. 271, 160 A.2d 85 (1960).

OPINION

LANCASTER, Justice.

Appellant Raymond Buster Hunt (Hunt) was convicted in Winona County District Court of four counts of controlled substance crimes. Because the prosecution did not disclose to defense counsel until after the jury returned its guilty verdicts that a psychologist who examined the state's primary witness pursuant to Minn. R.Crim. P. 20.01 had determined that the witness was incompetent to stand trial, we reverse appellant's conviction and remand for a new trial.

The primary witness against Hunt at trial was Jonathan Schalow. Schalow was a government informant who met Hunt in jail in December of 1997. On or about December 22, at the direction of another inmate, Schalow approached law enforcement officials and offered to purchase cocaine from Hunt. Schalow then reported to authorities that Hunt had told him earlier in the day that Hunt could "reach out from in here" (jail) to sell Schalow crack cocaine upon Schalow's release. Law enforcement officials arranged for Schalow's release that same day. Once released, Schalow telephoned a juvenile who Hunt had said could supply Schalow with drugs. Schalow purchased several grams of crack cocaine from the juvenile, but police officers decided not to arrest the juvenile at the time for fear it would end their investigation of Hunt.

On January 1, 1998, Schalow was again arrested and jailed. Schalow immediately contacted the police and offered to make another purchase of cocaine from Hunt, who had since been released from jail. Police officers recorded Schalow's telephone conversation with Hunt, who promised that even if he did not have the drugs by the prearranged time, he would still meet Schalow to arrange a later delivery time. At the appointed hour and place, police officers observed a man who appeared to be looking for someone. They approached the man and identified him as Hunt.

According to the officer's testimony, Hunt stated that he was on his way to an area motel to meet a friend named "John" whose last name he did not know, and denied being there to sell drugs. Hunt did not have any contraband on him when the police officers arrested him. However, Hunt was carrying a piece of paper with Schalow's telephone number written below the word "Crank," Schalow's nickname. Subsequently, during two interviews, Hunt variously admitted and denied that his was the voice in the taped calls speaking to Schalow. Hunt was charged with one count of controlled substance crime in the first degree, one count of controlled substance crime in the fourth degree, and two counts of conspiracy to commit controlled substance crime in the first degree.

Schalow remained in jail after he set up the second controlled drug purchase. In March 1998 he attempted suicide. Shortly thereafter the prosecutor in Hunt's case decided to depose Schalow for fear he would not survive to testify. Defense counsel was present at the deposition.

In advance of his own and Hunt's trial, Schalow moved for an examination pursuant to Minn. R.Crim. P. 20.01 to determine if he was competent to stand trial. By an order dated July 9, 1998, the court in Schalow's case granted that motion. Schalow was examined by a psychologist on July 15, 1998.

Hunt's trial began on Monday, August 3, 1998. The state does not dispute the characterization of Schalow as its key witness at trial. At Hunt's trial, Schalow testified to his jailhouse discussion with Hunt about buying drugs; that Hunt said he could set a deal up from inside the jail; that Schalow bought drugs from Hunt's alleged co-conspirator while Hunt remained in jail; and that Schalow was again arrested and jailed and then set up a second deal with Hunt to secure his own release from jail. On cross-examination, Hunt attempted to establish that Schalow violated his agreement with law enforcement to act as a confidential informant, and threatened not to testify, or if he did testify to lie on the stand. No mention was made of Schalow's July 15 competency examination during Hunt's trial.

On Wednesday, August 5, 1999, the day before final arguments and the commencement of jury deliberations in Hunt's trial, the prosecutor's office received the psychologist's report from Schalow's Rule 20.01 examination, in which the psychologist concluded that Schalow was not competent*298 to stand trial. The prosecutor in Hunt's case apparently did not focus his attention on the report that week.

The jury returned guilty verdicts on all four counts on the afternoon of Thursday, August 6. By the following Monday, the prosecutor had digested the contents and appreciated the significance of the psychologist's report from Schalow's Rule 20.01 evaluation. At that point the prosecutor informed Hunt's counsel that she should bring a discovery motion to obtain the results in order to preserve the record for appeal.

Hunt then moved to compel discovery, to dismiss, for judgment of acquittal, and for a new trial. Meanwhile, the court in Schalow's case ordered an adverse competency evaluation. The court in Hunt's case observed that nothing "raised a red flag" during Schalow's testimony in Hunt's case with respect to Schalow's competency. Nonetheless, the court withheld ruling on Hunt's motions until the adverse Rule 20.01 examination of Schalow was completed.

After this second competency evaluation, conducted in September 1998, the examining psychologist reported his conclusion that Schalow was competent to assist in his own defense. At the same time the court received that information, it also received an affidavit signed by Schalow stating that he had deliberately tricked the first examiner into thinking that Schalow was incompetent. He did this, he said, because he was going to be returned to custody in Wisconsin where authorities insisted on incarcerating him alongside prisoners against whom he had testified, and he feared for his safety.

We first decide this question: When the state receives information that a psychologist conducting an examination pursuant to Minn. R.Crim. P. 20.01 has determined that the state's key witness is incompetent to stand trial, must that information be disclosed to the defense? We hold that it must.

The state's obligations in discovery derive from the Minnesota Rules of Criminal Procedure and also from the constitutional guarantees of due process. The rules require the prosecuting attorney to allow the defense access to "all matters . . . which relate to the case" and specifically require disclosure of any material in the possession or control of members of the prosecution staff.

The constitutional guarantees of due process also require disclosure. "The suppression by the prosecution of evidence favorable to an accused upon request violates due process where the evidence is material either to guilt or to punishment, irrespective of the good faith or bad faith of the prosecution." *Brady v. Maryland*, 373 U.S. 83, 87, 83 S.Ct. 1194, 10 L.Ed.2d 215 (1963). Since Brady, the Court has expanded the disclosure obligation to include impeaching information. See *United States v. Bagley*, 473 U.S. 667, 676, 105 S.Ct. 3375, 87 L.Ed.2d 481 (1985). The duty to disclose such evidence exists even where there has been no request by the accused, see *United States v. Agurs*, 427 U.S. 97, 107, 96 S.Ct. 2392, 49 L.Ed.2d 342 (1976), and the remedy for a Brady violation is a new trial, see *Giglio v. United States,* 405 U.S. 150, 154, 92 S.Ct. 763, 31 L.Ed.2d 104 (1972). Hunt argues here that the state was required to inform the defense of the results of Schalow's competency evaluation and that the failure to do so warrants a new trial.

Brady disclosure applies only to material evidence. See *Brady,* 373 U.S. at 87, 83 S.Ct. 1194. Evidence is material "if there is a reasonable probability that, had the evidence been disclosed to the defense, the result of the proceeding would have been different." *Bagley,* 473 U.S. at 682, 105 S.Ct. 3375. Recently the Court described the "three components of a true Brady violation: The evidence at issue must be favorable to the accused, either because it is exculpatory, or because it is impeaching; that evidence must have been suppressed by the State, either willfully or inadvertently; and prejudice must have ensued."

We conduct a similar, but not identical, inquiry under the Minnesota Constitution. We have at times followed a harmless error analysis for undisclosed evidence, not granting a new trial where the evidence could not in any reasonable likelihood have affected the judgment of the jury. See *State v. Poganski,* 257 N.W.2d 578, 579-80 (Minn.1977); see also *State v. Clobes,* 422 N.W.2d 252, 255 (Minn.1988). We consider, then, whether evidence that Schalow was found incompetent to stand trial could have affected the judgment of the jury.

The state correctly notes that the standard for competency to stand trial at which the Rule 20.01 evaluation is aimed is a different standard than the standard for witness competency. If a witness understands the obligation of an oath and is capable of correctly relating the facts to which the testimony relates, the witness is competent. In contrast, if the defendant "(1) lacks sufficient ability to consult with a reasonable degree of rational understanding with defense counsel; or (2) is mentally ill or mentally deficient so as to be incapable of understanding the proceedings or participating in the defense," the defendant is incompetent to stand trial. Minn. R.Crim. P. 20.01, subd. 1.

Notwithstanding the differences between witness competency and competency to stand trial, the fact that a witness has been determined to be incompetent to stand trial by an examining psychologist should seriously concern the prosecution about that individual's fitness to testify as a witness. A court's finding of incompetency under Rule 20.01 reflects a determination that the subject lacks the capacity to understand criminal proceedings or is mentally ill or deficient. The determination of a mentally ill person's competency to testify is usually made only after the court's preliminary examination of the witness. This procedural safeguard reflects our concern with the integrity of the presentation of evidence at trial. Only where the trial court is satisfied that the witness, despite a mental illness, understands the obligation of the oath and can relate the facts to which the testimony relates will the court allow the witness to testify. While we are concerned here with a psychologist's conclusion (rather than a court finding) that Schalow was incompetent to stand trial, the prosecution still had access to clearly impeaching evidence, and was thus obligated under Brady to disclose.

Nonetheless, the state maintains that the prejudice requirement of Brady is not met in this case. The state argues that Hunt cannot establish that he was prejudiced by not knowing that one of the state's witness had been determined by a psychologist to be incompetent to stand trial, when that witness was ultimately found by the court to be competent.

With the benefit of hindsight, there were events that happened after the undisclosed examination results came to the prosecutor's office that decreased the significance of the nondisclosure (the second examination and a court finding of competence). There were also events that increased the significance of the nondisclosure (Schalow's affidavit showing that he had lied to manipulate his psychological examination). We cannot say what might have occurred on a reopened cross-examination of Schalow if he had been questioned about the examination. However, at a minimum, we are convinced that had Schalow's competency report come to the attention of the trial court, the presiding judge would have been compelled to independently ascertain Schalow's competency as a witness. Had Schalow been deemed competent to testify, this new information would likely have given defense counsel new grounds for cross-examination regarding his mental stability and perhaps his ability to mislead.

Nondisclosure of evidence that is merely impeaching may not typically result in the kind of prejudice necessary to warrant a new trial. For example, where testimony of the witness sought to be impeached by nondisclosed evidence "was not the only damning evidence against defendant," we have determined that the likelihood of prejudice is decreased. In this case, however, the state concedes that its case rested largely on the testimony of Schalow. Hunt's cross-examination of Schalow exposed his threat to lie on the stand, but did not impugn his ability to accurately and honestly relate facts the way that the competency evaluation results would have. Where the nondisclosed evidence could have significantly impeached the state's key witness, regardless of subsequent developments with that evidence, we conclude that the defendant has suffered prejudice from the nondisclosure.

While we are satisfied that the prosecution acted in good faith, Schalow's examination should have been disclosed to the defense. Given his critical importance to the state, we cannot say that this evidence could not in any reasonable likelihood have affected the judgment of the jury. See Poganski, 257 N.W.2d at 579-80. Accordingly, Hunt is entitled to a new trial.

Concluding that the state violated the discovery rules by failing to timely disclose the results of a competency evaluation of its key witness, and that this nondisclosure prejudiced Hunt, we reverse Hunt's convictions and remand for a new trial.

Reversed and remanded.

CASE QUESTIONS

1 How did the state's primary witness factor into this case?
2 Were there any difficulties with Schalow following the first narcotics transaction?
3 What were the charges against the defendant in this case?
4 What were the results of the psychiatric evaluation of Schalow?
5 What action did the prosecutor take upon discovering a psychiatric evaluation of Schalow, and what effect did this have on the appeal?

CHAPTER SUMMARY

In this chapter we have seen that discovery is the process parties in a criminal case use to exchange information. Traditionally, there was very little discovery involved in a criminal case. In the past, a defendant would receive a copy of the list of witnesses against him, reports of any scientific tests, and a copy of the indictment. Unlike civil cases, where discovery is comprehensive, it is extremely limited in criminal cases.

Recent changes in discovery rules across the United States have somewhat changed the traditional approach. These days, prosecutors have a greater obligation to turn over more information to the defendant, while the defendant now has some obligation to deliver information to the state. No matter what a particular state's rules about discovery are, there are some U.S. Supreme Court cases that take precedence over state rules. The most famous of these is the *Brady* decision, which requires prosecutors to hand over to the defense any information that might be exculpatory in nature or show a bias or prejudice on the part of the witness, including any information that could be used to impeach one of the state's witnesses.

Defense attorneys routinely file pretrial motions seeking information from the state on a wide variety of topics. Defense attorneys may request information about any deals that the state has offered witnesses in order to convince them to testify against the defendant, as well as information about the crime itself and requests to examine the physical evidence by their own experts. It is extremely common for the defense to file a motion to suppress a critical piece of evidence ruled inadmissible and thus perhaps necessitating dismissal of the entire case.

Prosecutors are also allowed to file pretrial motions and events, such as similar transactions motions. These motions allow the state to present evidence that the defendant has committed similar crimes in the past, showing that the defendant had a similar pattern and methods, or cases that show views or her state of mind in the present case. Prosecutors may also file additional information in aggravation of the defendant's sentence, seeking to have the defendant's sentence enhanced because of negative information about the defendant, such as numerous prior convictions. In addition to these motions, a prosecutor may also file a motion to join. A joinder motion requests the court to combine disparate cases into one trial or even to combine several codefendants into a single trial in order to use court time more efficiently. The prosecution's motion for joinder will undoubtedly be opposed by a defendant's motion to sever. In such a motion, the defense request that they are be separate trials for different offenses or that each codefendant be tried separately, knowing that when there are several defendants on trial or numerous charges against a particular individual, the jury is far more likely to find a verdict of guilty. The Supreme Court's *Brady* decision requires the prosecution, no matter what the state law on the topic may be, to produce any information to the defendant that might tend to show that the defendant did not commit the crime or that may mitigate or lessen the defendant's sentence should he be found guilty after trial.

KEY TERMS

Key terms are listed here in order of appearance in chapter.

Discovery
Depose
Work product
Motion
Similar transactions
Motion to join
Brady material
In camera
Exculpatory
Motion to suppress
Sever
Term of court
Motion for continuance
Motion in limine

REVIEW QUESTIONS

1 How does discovery in criminal cases compare with discovery in civil cases?
2 Who bears the burden of producing evidence for the defendant, the prosecutor or the police officer? Explain your answer
3 Under the traditional rules of discovery, what items would a defendant typically receive from the state?
4 Is it common to use depositions in criminal cases? Why or why not?
5 Do the rules of discovery vary from state to state? If so, how?
6 Some states have made changes to their discovery rules in recent years. What are these changes?
7 Under the new rules of discovery, does the defendant have an obligation to produce any evidence for the prosecution? If so, what?
8 What is work product?
9 Is it common practice for the prosecution to provide the defendant with the criminal histories of its main witnesses?
10 Under what circumstances might a prosecutor tell a jury about one of its witness's criminal history, even if it is not required to be revealed under discovery laws?
11 What is an open-file policy?
12 What is a similar transactions motion?
13 Explain a motion to join.
14 What is the *Brady* case, and why is it important?
15 What is an *in camera* inspection, and who carries it out?
16 What is a motion to suppress?
17 What is a motion to sever?
18 Under what circumstances might a defendant file a motion to change venue?
19 What is a speedy trial demand?
20 What effect does a filing for a motion of continuance have on a speedy trial demand?
21 What is a motion to reveal the deal?

WEB SURFING

American Bar Association Rules on Criminal Discovery
http://www.americanbar.org/publications/criminal_justice_section_archive/crimjust_standards_discovery_tocold.html

U.S. Department of Justice Discovery Rules for Prosecutors
http://www.justice.gov/dag/discovery-guidance.html

EXERCISES

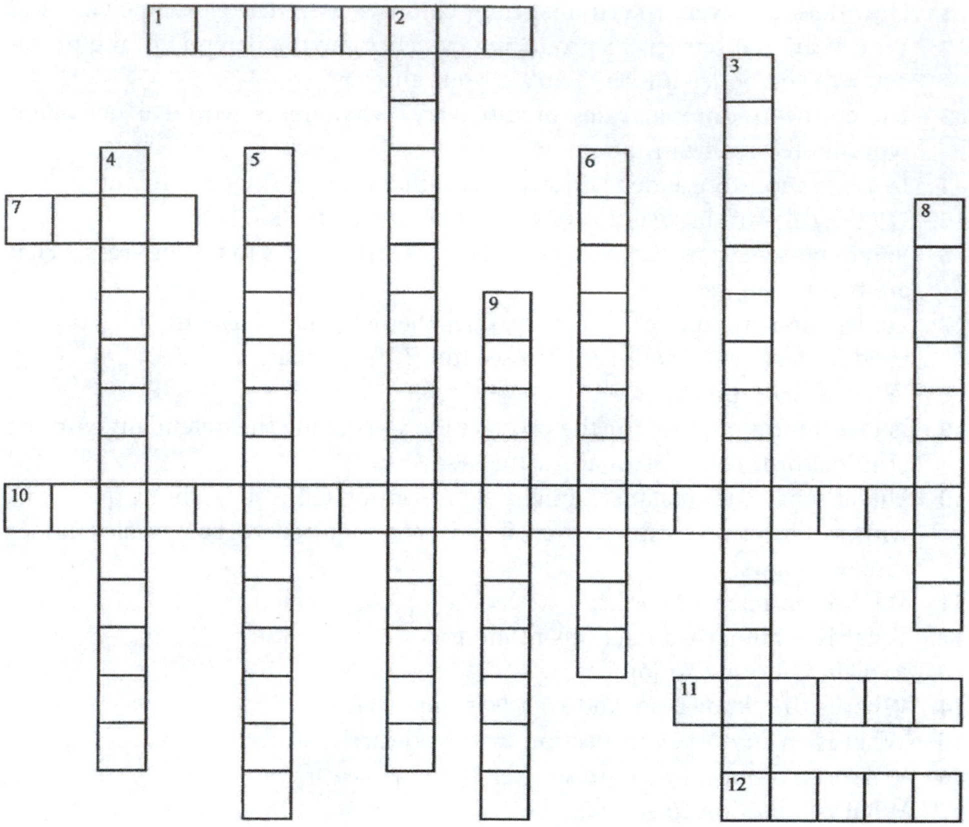

ACROSS

1. A review of a file by a judge carried out in his private chambers
7. The principle that a lawyer need not show the other side in a case any things gathered for the case unless the other side can convince the judge that it would be unjust for the thing to remain hidden
10. A request by one party to postpone a trial or other hearing for a future date
11. Give sworn testimony out of court
12. Separate or cut off into constituent parts

DOWN

2. The rule that states that evidence that has been obtained in violation of the Constitution cannot be used against the defendant at trial
3. A motion that requests a court not allow the jury to hear specific information
4. Information available to the prosecutor that is favorable to the defendant
5. A motion that requests specific judicial rulings at the outset of the trial
6. Evidence that tends to provide an excuse for the defendant's actions or that shows that the defendant did not commit the crime charged
8. The exchange of information between sides in both civil and criminal lawsuits
9. The period of time slated for court hearings

b	o	l	e	r	o	o	c	e	e	p	c	e	i	o	c	m	i	o	l
r	s	c	x	s	c	a	e	l	c	s	i	e	o	s	n	y	i	i	x
d	f	e	b	m	o	t	i	o	n	t	o	s	u	p	p	r	e	s	s
a	l	t	x	c	v	i	e	t	a	r	t	b	o	u	v	o	v	d	l
c	i	d	t	c	e	l	c	e	u	e	l	r	m	c	c	t	p	s	n
e	c	m	i	m	l	t	t	o	n	o	o	a	n	i	s	a	m	e	a
t	n	a	s	s	e	u	m	e	i	y	i	d	o	t	e	p	e	e	r
e	e	e	a	d	c	e	s	p	t	e	a	y	r	p	v	l	n	m	n
o	u	m	o	t	i	o	n	i	n	l	i	m	i	n	e	u	t	s	y
a	t	i	u	r	r	a	v	r	o	n	r	a	r	r	r	c	i	r	n
e	r	s	m	i	n	u	t	e	c	n	r	t	i	n	a	x	o	u	i
i	n	i	e	d	v	m	o	a	r	c	a	e	s	o	p	e	d	o	p
o	i	m	c	a	n	r	m	c	o	y	c	r	a	e	t	o	r	l	a
u	i	c	a	m	s	e	t	e	f	n	a	i	y	p	p	e	s	d	u
e	a	n	n	s	r	o	i	m	n	o	o	a	t	r	e	n	o	r	m
i	m	l	n	a	o	n	i	i	o	r	m	l	n	i	u	l	t	s	m
r	o	t	s	c	r	p	e	s	i	s	l	r	i	y	o	l	o	a	t
o	s	e	s	e	u	o	l	u	t	r	a	d	e	c	a	a	e	i	m
n	o	m	a	a	p	c	n	l	o	r	l	s	p	t	o	e	m	e	d
o	n	m	u	c	o	v	a	d	m	i	l	o	n	e	l	n	n	n	n

discovery
depose
brady material
in camera
exculpatory
motion to suppress
exclusionary rule
sever
term of court
motion for continuance
motion in limine

QUESTIONS FOR ANALYSIS

1 Should the discovery rules for criminal and civil cases be identical? Why or why not?

2 Under the new discovery rules, do defendants receive too much information? Are there concerns for the safety of witnesses?

3 Should prosecutors at all levels, state and federal, be required to turn their entire files over to the defense? Wouldn't this ensure that the defendant has all possible information to help prepare him for trial?

7

Preparing for the Trial: The Prosecution

Chapter Objectives

- Explain how a prosecutor reviews a trial docket for cases that are likely to go to trial
- Discuss why and how plea bargains are used in the criminal justice system
- Define the state's burden of proof in a criminal case
- Explain the difference between an inference and a presumption
- Describe the importance of the "elements" of an offense to both the prosecution and the defense

I. EVALUATING THE CASE FOR THE PROSECUTION

So far, our discussions about court procedures have focused on specific procedural events, such as arrest, initial appearance, and arraignment, to name a few. We have also examined the process that a prosecutor follows in deciding what charges to bring against a defendant. As we saw when we discussed the charging decision, a prosecutor must review both the facts and the law applicable to a case and then decide which charges best fit. However, once the indictment has been drafted and presented to the grand jury, the prosecutor no longer has control over what the charges against the defendant are. Instead, the prosecutor must focus on how to prove the allegations against the defendant. In order to do so, the prosecutor must now prepare the case for possible trial. In this chapter, we will examine how prosecutors go through the process of preparing a case for trial, by describing first the practicalities of trial dockets and then how prosecutors meet the legal burden of proving beyond a reasonable doubt that a defendant is guilty.

A. COURT DOCKETS

From an entirely practical level, prosecutors face several difficulties when they examine their trial dockets. In some large cities, prosecutors may have trials scheduled one or two weeks out of every four. That does not give a prosecutor much time to prepare for a case. But there are other practical difficulties. For instance, how does a prosecutor know which case to prepare?

Consider the fact that a prosecutor or a team of prosecutors may have from 20 to 100 cases on the next trial docket. With only one or two weeks to try these cases, it is physically impossible to try them all in the time allotted. In fact, if the prosecution team can try three cases in one week, that would be quite an achievement. Although not all crimes take a long time to try, there are many that can last several weeks, just for a single trial. Knowing this, the prosecutor must look over the docket of pending cases and try to decide which cases will go to trial and which cases will probably enter guilty pleas before the jury is brought in.

1. PLEA BARGAINS

Plea bargain
A prosecutor's recommendation for a somewhat lighter sentence than a defendant might normally receive in exchange for the defendant's plea of guilty to the offense charged.

There are ways that a prosecutor can move the docket more effectively. For one thing, the prosecutor will undoubtedly contact most of the attorneys who represent clients on the next trial docket and discuss their cases. The prosecutor may make an offer for a **plea bargain**. A plea bargain is essentially a contract between the prosecution and the defense in which the prosecutor agrees to recommend a lower sentence than she might ordinarily recommend in exchange for the defendant entering a plea of guilty. The entire criminal justice system functions on plea bargains. Using our previous example of a trial docket with 100 cases pending and only one week to try them, if the prosecutor does not work out negotiated guilty pleas in the vast majority of these cases, then the prosecutor faces a docket next month with 100 new cases added to the cases carried over from the previous month. In just a few months the docket would become so cumbersome that it would virtually grind to a halt.

Appellate courts have held that a plea bargain is a contract between the prosecutor and the defendant in which each gives up something in exchange for some benefit. The defendant gives up his right to a jury trial in exchange for a recommendation of a lower sentence. The prosecutor gives up her right to try the defendant and ask for the maximum sentence should the defendant be convicted in exchange for the defendant's guilty plea (and removing one more case from the pending court docket). Because a plea bargain is recognized as a bargain, once made, a prosecutor cannot back out of the agreement. However, this is where the analogy to contract law ends. Although a prosecutor cannot back out of a plea bargain agreement, a defendant can. If, at the last moment, the defendant changes his mind, then he can still have a jury trial. During the trial, the jury will never hear that the defendant was on the verge of pleading guilty before changing his mind. Any statements that the defendant or the defense attorney makes during the course of negotiating a plea bargain are inadmissible during the trial.

You will notice that there is some important wording in a plea bargain. A prosecutor offers to *recommend* a sentence. A prosecutor cannot guarantee that a defendant will receive a specific sentence. That duty falls entirely within the province of the judge. In many circumstances, a judge will accept the plea bargain worked out between the defense and the government, but the judge is free to refuse to impose the recommended sentence. If this occurs, then the defendant is free to change his plea from guilty to not guilty and have a jury trial after all. A defendant cannot be forced into pleading guilty. In fact, during the presentation of the defendant's guilty plea, the court will ask the defendant if entering a guilty plea is the defendant's decision, given freely and voluntarily. If the defendant says that it is not, then the court will refuse to accept the plea and will schedule the case for trial.

It is obvious why a prosecutor would want to move as many cases through plea bargains as possible, but what is the incentive for the defense? A defendant might reason that taking the case to a jury could result in a not guilty verdict and the defendant would be set free. Here again, reality presents a radically different picture than what is often seen on nightly TV shows about trials and attorneys. Most jury trials end with guilty verdicts. This runs counter to popular conception, but it is true. In the vast majority of jury trials, the prosecutor wins. A defense attorney must explain this devastating fact to a client as they discuss the plea bargain. Faced with the reality that the prosecution may win the case against the defendant, it might make a great deal more sense for the defendant to take the prosecutor's offer of a reduced sentence and/or fine. The other incentive for the defendant is the knowledge that the prosecutor will undoubtedly ask for the maximum sentence to be imposed after the defendant is guilty. Prosecutors justify this request because of the costs in time, energy, and budget to try the defendant (see Figure 7-1). This may sound like the prosecutor is punishing the defendant for taking the case to trial, and there are no doubt many defendants who sincerely believe this, but a prosecutor has a different set of concerns. If a defendant takes a case to trial and receives a sentence that is the same as he would have received in a plea bargain, then

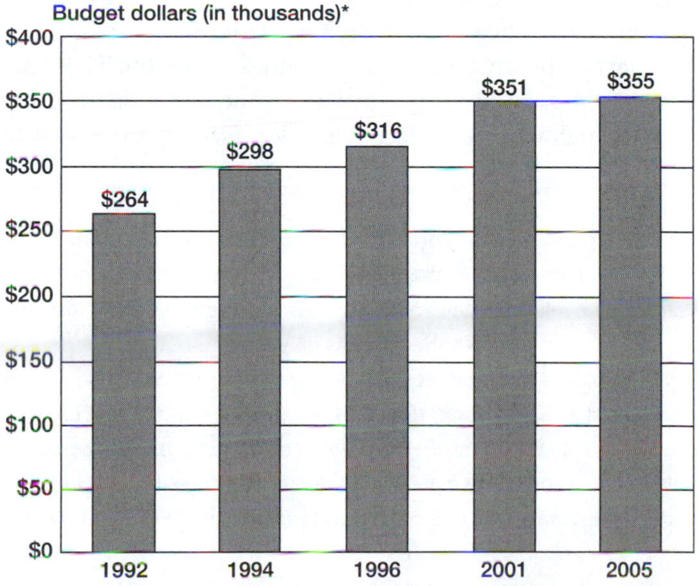

*Estimated budget information presented constant 2005 dollars.
Source: Prosecutors in State Courts, 2005. National Survey of Prosecutors. Bureau of Justice Statistics, U.S. Department of Justice, July 2006.

FIGURE 7-1

Median Annual Budget for State Prosecutors' Offices, 1992–2005

defendants would have no incentive to enter pleas of guilty. They would simply take their chances with a jury trial, and prosecutors, police, and judges would be faced with a massive backlog of cases waiting to be adjudicated. On the other hand, if the prosecutor asks for (and receives) the maximum possible sentence against a defendant after a guilty verdict, then the message is made clear to all other defendants on the docket: Take your chances on a jury and you will get the maximum sentence if you are found guilty.

To illustrate the power of the plea bargain, consider the restrictive handgun laws in Washington, DC. Although citizens are allowed to register and keep handguns in their homes, they are not allowed to carry them in public. Tourists who visit the capital city may not know that carrying handguns is illegal. While visiting the Capitol building, museums, and other attractions, they voluntarily surrender their handguns before going through metal detectors, believing they are doing nothing wrong. Police officers then confiscate the weapon and arrest the tourist. If the tourist agrees to accept a plea bargain, prosecutors will not seek a jail term. However, if the tourist insists on a jury trial, prosecutors advise that additional charges will be filed, specifically, possession of illegal ammunition—one count for each bullet in the gun. Not surprisingly, nearly all of the accused tourists accept the plea bargain.

a. Critics of the Plea Bargain System

Some critics of plea bargaining point out that the pressures brought to bear on a defendant, even one who is innocent, clearly point toward entering a plea of guilty and taking the "deal" instead of risking a jury trial. These critics claim that the current plea bargain system forces a defendant to choose between two unattractive alternatives: pleading guilty to a crime you did not commit or being found guilty and receiving a harsh sentence. Of course, this criticism is predicated on the idea that many defendants who are charged with crimes are guilty. There are also those who claim that plea bargaining has political overtones, with prosecutors seeking to keep their statistics high when they face reelection (see Figure 7-2). Wherever one

FIGURE 7-2

Term of Office, Length of Service, and Salary of Chief Prosecutors

In 2005, 85% of chief prosecutors reported they had been elected or appointed to a 4-year term. The median length of service was 8 years in 2005 (table 3). About a quarter of the chief prosecutors (28%) were relatively new to the job having served 4 years or less in 2005. The longest tenure among surveyed respondents was 35 years.

In 2005 half of all offices reported the chief prosecutor earned $85,000 per year or more, a 33% increase in median salary since 1996 ($64,000). Nearly 4 in 10 chief prosecutors (37%) had a salary of $100,000 or more. The amount of annual salary varied by size of jurisdiction served and whether the chief served full- or part-time. In 2005 the median salary for full-time large offices was $149,000 compared to a median of $42,000 for part-time offices.

Source: Prosecutors in State Courts, 2005. National Survey of Prosecutors. Bureau of Justice Statistics, U.S. Department of Justice, July 2006.

may come down on that issue, the statistics show a clear pattern: Most people charged with criminal offenses enter guilty pleas. We will address the mechanics of entering a guilty plea in Chapter 10.

B. PRIORITIZING THE CASES ON THE TRIAL DOCKET

Once a prosecutor has contacted the defense attorneys with cases pending on the upcoming trial docket, the prosecutor will have a better idea of which cases will enter pleas and which ones will go to trial. Of course, there are no guarantees. A defendant who has announced that he is ready for trial might enter a guilty plea at the last minute, and a defendant who has stated a preference for a plea bargain might reject it the last minute and demand a jury trial. Needless to say, this adds a certain amount of pressure on a prosecutor. Not all attorneys can handle the anxiety that comes from not knowing which cases will actually go to trial. These attorneys often leave the field of prosecution and enter other areas of legal practice. Other attorneys thrive in this environment of uncertainty.

When a prosecutor has worked within the system for several years, she can often make an educated guess about which cases will demand a jury trial and which will plead out (see Figure 7-3). To add a bit more certainty, a prosecutor may make a plea bargain offer to the defendant that contains a deadline. If the defendant does not agree to the plea bargain within five days of the beginning of the trial session, then the prosecutor will revoke the offer; if the defendant wishes to plead guilty then, he must rely on the mercy of the judge. Knowing this, many judges often give harsher sentences to defendants who plead guilty at the last possible moment than

FIGURE 7-3

2005 Profile of Prosecutors

- Half of prosecutors' offices nationwide employed nine or fewer people, and had a budget of $355,000 or less.
- State court prosecutors' offices (2,344) employed over 78,000 attorneys, investigators, and support staff nationwide, a 27% increase from 1992 and a 9% increase from 1996.
- A quarter of prosecutors' offices participated on a state or local homeland security task force, with a third having staff that attended homeland security training.
- 60% of prosecutors' litigated a variety of felony or misdemeanor crimes related to computer and electronic commerce fraud, a 20% increase compared to 2001.
- 70% of prosecutors' prosecuted at least one case involving the transmission of child pornography, an increase of 40% compared to 2001.
- Approximately 70% of prosecutors' nationwide litigated an identity theft case, an increase of 50% since 2001.
- A quarter of prosecutors' offices reported that their district maintains an offender DNA database.
- About 24% of prosecutors' offices assigned prosecutors to handle community-related activities.

Source: Bureau of Justice Statistics; Courts, Online Summary, Prosecutors, 2011.

to those who have announced their intent to plead guilty earlier in the process. Judges have similar pressures on them as do prosecutors. A judge has no desire to have his criminal trial docket clogged with cases. The judge, after all, has pending civil cases, and if these dockets are not cleared, then all of these cases will continue to mount up, and citizens might accurately criticize a judge for not doing his job.

If it seems that the discussion so far has excluded the considerations of the defense attorney, that omission is deliberate. We will discuss the different pressures brought to bear on defense attorneys in the next chapter, when we examine the process that the defense goes through to prepare its case for trial.

There are certain instances in which a prosecutor has no doubt that a certain case will go trial. If the defendant is facing a possible death sentence, then the chances of the defendant entering a plea of guilty is remote. A defendant will almost certainly take his chances on a trial, if for no other reason than that the prosecutor has no reduced sentence that he can offer in a plea bargain. In certain cases, the minimum sentence is also the maximum sentence. A defendant charged with capital murder will, if found guilty, at least serve a sentence of life. If the jury decides that a death sentence is warranted, then the defendant will face possible execution. In such a situation, even a remote chance at an acquittal is better than anything that the state could offer as a recommended sentence.

Other types of cases also fall into this dilemma. In the past 10 to 20 years, many states have enacted so-called "three strikes and you're out" laws. These statutes require a life sentence when a defendant is convicted on a third felony. Because this sentence is mandatory, the prosecutor cannot recommend a lower sentence on a plea bargain, and the defendant will take the case to a jury in the hopes that the jury will find him not guilty. There are even some states that have passed more stringent laws, often referred to as "one strike and you're out." In these states, if the defendant has a prior felony conviction on his record and then is charged with a specific type of felony (usually narcotics or violent crime), then the defendant faces an automatic life sentence. The prosecutor cannot offer to reduce the sentence, because it is required by law. There is no possible plea bargain, so the case will go to trial.

So far, the prosecutor has evaluated her docket to see which cases are likely to go to trial. With that process out of the way, the prosecutor will then proceed to preparing the cases for trial. In the next section, we will examine the burdens of proof, presumptions, and inferences that a prosecutor must contend with in order to prove that a defendant is guilty of the crime charged.

BURDENS OF PROOF, PRESUMPTIONS, AND INFERENCES

Burden of proof
The obligation on one party to produce sufficient evidence and testimony to establish facts that meet the elements of the crime charged.

In addition to the logistical concerns of plea bargains and trying to predict which cases will go to trial, a prosecutor has additional burdens. Throughout the pretrial motions and the trial itself, the prosecution has the **burden of proof**. This burden rests with the prosecution as a consequence of our decision as a society that the state must always prove that the defendant committed the crime—the burden is not on the defendant to prove his innocence. In practical terms, it means that the prosecutor must present evidence and testimony to establish each and every material allegation against the defendant and do so beyond a reasonable doubt.

A. BURDEN OF PROOF

In our system, the prosecutor bears the burden of proof in a criminal case. Simply put, the prosecutor must prove the case against the defendant beyond a reasonable doubt. This burden of proof rests with the prosecutor throughout the trial and never shifts to the defendant to prove his innocence. As we will see in the next chapter, when we discuss how defense attorneys prepare for their cases, the one factor that they do not have to worry about is proving that their clients are not guilty beyond a reasonable doubt. They do, however, have the obligation to present evidence about specific defenses.

We have raised two concepts here that bear further explanation: the burden of proof and the definition of reasonable doubt. When we use the phrase *burden of proof*, we are discussing the prosecutor's responsibility to prove each and every element of the crime. Failure to do so means that the case against the defendant will be dismissed. If the case somehow survives being dismissed on a motion for directed verdict, the jury is also informed that the prosecutor has the burden of proving to their satisfaction that the defendant committed all of the facts alleged in the indictment or accusation. So, the burden of proving that the defendant committed the crime rests solely with the prosecutor. The way that the prosecutor meets that burden is by presenting testimony from witnesses and introducing evidence to support the claims made in the charging document. But the burden of proof carries another subsidiary requirement that is rarely discussed but is equally important. A prosecutor has not only the burden of proof but also the **burden of persuasion**. The prosecutor must persuade the jury that the evidence presented does meet all of the legal requirements, and when the trial is concluded, the jury is persuaded that the defendant did commit the crime.

Burden of persuasion
The obligation on the party who has the burden of proof to not only establish facts but to convince the jury or judge that the facts are true and beyond dispute.

When it comes to defining proof beyond a reasonable doubt, courts have wrestled with the concept for centuries. Reasonable doubt has been interpreted and quoted thousands of times. In civil cases, defining the standard of proof is relatively simple. Most plaintiffs must simply prove their case to a preponderance of the evidence. Put another way, civil plaintiffs must prove that their version of the facts is more than likely true. But proving a criminal case beyond a reasonable doubt is not as easy to define. Trying to quantify exactly what reasonable doubt is may be easier if we approach it from what it is not. Reasonable doubt is not proof beyond all doubt. It is not proof beyond a shadow of a doubt. If the state were required to prove a case beyond all doubt, or beyond a shadow of a doubt, very few criminals would ever be convicted. What we can say with confidence is that proof beyond a reasonable doubt is a much higher standard to meet than the preponderance of the evidence.

At the conclusion of the trial, the judge will instruct the jury as to the meaning of proof beyond a reasonable doubt. The jurors will be told that the state is not required to prove the case beyond all doubt or beyond a shadow of a doubt.

Instead, the state must prove each allegation to the point where the jurors' minds are settled and to the point where they have no serious questions about the facts in the case. Reasonable doubt means a doubt based on a common sense reason, not some capricious or ill-advised opinion. If, at the end of the trial, a juror is still unsettled in his mind, or has qualms about the proof, this is a reasonable doubt. The judge's instruction to the jury leaves little question about what should happen if a juror has a reasonable doubt. In any situation in which a reasonable doubt exists, the juror must vote to acquit the defendant. It's difficult to illustrate reasonable doubt in lay terms, but some prosecutors use the analogy of a jigsaw puzzle. Imagine a puzzle of a kitten, and the puzzle has a piece of the background missing and perhaps a piece of the kitten's fur missing as well. The overall picture is still clear, however, and anyone looking at the completed puzzle would know beyond a reasonable doubt that the picture is indeed that of a kitten.

Some courts define reasonable doubt in practical terms. They say that a juror in a criminal case should be as convinced of the facts of the case as they would be if they were making an "important life decision." Here, reasonable doubt is phrased in terms of the amount of certainty that a person would need before deciding a serious and important affair in their personal lives. Not all states follow this formulation of reasonable doubt, but many find it an easier definition to follow than some of the more esoteric definitions of reasonable doubt that can often cause more confusion than they resolve.[1] If the jurors, at the conclusion of the trial, do not have that level of certainty, then their obligation is to vote not guilty, even if they believe that the defendant committed the crime but the state failed to prove it beyond a reasonable doubt. In this way, the burden of proof and the burden of persuasion are intertwined. The prosecutor may have presented sufficient facts to meet the threshold of proof but has failed to convince the jury that the facts are true and that, ultimately, the defendant is guilty as charged. This is how a prosecutor can meet the burden of proof but fail to establish the burden of persuasion.

> **Sidebar**
>
> *If, at the conclusion of a trial, a juror does not believe that the state has proven that the defendant was the person who committed the crime, then the state has failed to prove an essential element of the case, and the juror has a reasonable doubt. However, using the same example, if the juror is not sure that the brand of gun used in the killing is actually manufactured in the United States, that would not be grounds for reasonable doubt.*

1. THE BURDEN OF PROOF IS ALWAYS ON THE STATE

In a criminal trial, the burden of proof is always on the state to prove the defendant guilty beyond a reasonable doubt. This burden never shifts to the defendant. For instance, at the conclusion of the state's case, the burden does not shift to the defendant to prove his innocence. If a defendant presents a defense, such as an alibi or insanity, it continues to be the state's obligation to disprove the defense. The burden in a criminal case never rests on the defendant to prove that he is not guilty. In cases in which the defense is insanity, for instance, the state must present rebuttal evidence establishing that the defendant was legally sane at the time of the crime. However, as we will see in the next chapter, a defendant may have a burden of persuasion when it comes to presenting a defense. Like the prosecutor, once a defense is presented, the defense attorney bears the burden of persuading the jury that the defense is apt and should be taken into account.

[1] *Lord v. State*, 107 Nev. 28, 806 P.2d 548 (1991).

Jurors are instructed that even if they suspect that the defendant is guilty, but the state has failed to prove the case against the defendant, they have no choice but to reach a verdict of not guilty. This principle underlies every phase of a criminal trial. This is not to say, however, that the jury is prevented from making commonsense conclusions about the evidence produced at a trial. If, for instance, a witness takes the stand and identifies the defendant as the perpetrator of the crime, the jury is allowed to infer that the witness is telling the truth.

B. INFERENCES AND PRESUMPTIONS

As a prosecutor continues to prepare for an upcoming jury trial, there are other considerations that a prosecutor must take into account. Besides the fact that the burden of proof is always on the prosecutor, carrying with it the burden of persuasion to convince the jurors that the prosecution's version of the facts is true beyond a reasonable doubt, the prosecution must also contend with presumptions and inferences that protect the defendant and that also serve to shield the defendant unless and until the state proves that the defendant is guilty (see Figure 7-4 for examples). The most famous and most consistently applied presumption is the presumption of innocence.

1. PRESUMPTION OF INNOCENCE

When we use a word like **presumption** we are referring to a legal principle that requires jurors to hold a certain belief. In criminal cases, defendants are presumed innocent until proven guilty. The practical effect of this is that if the state presents only a mediocre case and does not persuade the jury, they must find the defendant not guilty. The presumption of innocence accompanies the defendant through every stage of a criminal proceeding and disappears only when the jurors are convinced of the defendant's guilt. At that point, we say that the presumption has been overcome.

Presumption
A conclusion of fact that is based on the existence of another fact. Example: The defendant is charged with a crime; the jury must presume that he is innocent.

- Presumption of a defendant's sanity
- Presumption that a state statute is constitutional
- Presumption of the defendant's competency to stand trial
- Presumption that a search warrant is valid
- Presumption that the indictment is legal and valid and based on sufficient evidence
- Presumption that a conviction is based on proof beyond a reasonable doubt
- Presumption that the defendant's counsel gave effective assistance to the defendant during the trial

FIGURE 7-4

Examples of Other Presumptions in Criminal Law

EXAMPLE

Julie has been summoned for jury duty. When she is called into a courtroom along with many other potential jurors, the judge advises them that the defendant is presumed to be innocent until proven guilty and that the jurors must hold this belief throughout the trial and may abandon it only when they believe that the defendant's guilt has been proven beyond a reasonable doubt. The judge then asks Julie, "Do you have any opinion about the defendant at this point?"

Julie answers, "No. I don't know if he's innocent or guilty."

The judge responds, "You are dismissed. Your duty is to answer that he is not guilty until proven otherwise. Does anyone else not understand this definition?"

Is the judge allowed to take such an action?

Answer: Yes. Although most judges would probably not take such drastic action, the judge's question and subsequent action are correct: A juror must presume that the defendant is innocent, and any juror who cannot or will not accept that presumption can be removed from the jury panel.

Sidebar

A presumption is a conclusion that a judge or jury must make in certain situations.

2. INFERENCES

Inference
A fact that is probably true or a fact that a jury can reasonably believe is true.

An **inference** is an assumption that *may* be made from the facts. If it snows during the night and you glance out your window and see footprints in the snow, you can infer that a person walked by your house. Similarly, juries are allowed to make simple deductions from evidence presented. When they do, they are making inferences.

An inference is a factual conclusion that the jury is allowed to make from the facts as they are presented. Inferences can also be deductions, such as the fact that someone walked across your snow-covered lawn, in the example given above. Juries are often told that they may infer that witnesses are telling the truth unless some party shows evidence to the contrary. Unlike presumptions, there is no such thing as a mandatory inference. Inferences are always permissive, and the jury is free to infer or not infer as it sees fit (see Figure 7-5). Jurors do not have the same latitude when it comes to presumptions. As we saw in the earlier scenario, jurors must abide by the presumption of innocence. During the trial, the jurors are told that they can make inferences based on the facts presented. But they are also told that they are never to presume that the defendant is guilty until the state proves it.

FIGURE 7-5

Sample Jury Charge on Inferences

> You may infer, if you wish to do so, that the acts of persons of sound mind and discretion are the product of his will, and you may infer, if you wish to do so, that a person of sound mind and discretion intends the natural and probable consequences of his acts. Whether you make any such inference or inferences in this case is a matter solely within the discretion of the jury.

C. ELEMENTS OF THE OFFENSE

So far, we have seen that a criminal defendant enters a trial protected by various presumptions. We've also seen that the state must prove that the defendant is guilty beyond a reasonable doubt. However, during that discussion, we made reference to a word that now bears further explanation. We have seen that the prosecution bears the burden of proving beyond a reasonable doubt that the defendant is guilty of each and every **element** of the offense charged. However, we have not yet defined what an element is.

Element
A necessary and component part of the crime.

When prosecutors prepare a case for trial, they review all of the necessary elements of the offense charged and make sure that they have sufficient evidence to prove each and every one of them. An element refers to a material factual allegation against a defendant that, when taken together with other material allegations, constitutes a crime. Let's consider the elements of the charge of murder in the first degree shown in Figure 7-6.

Let us suppose that a defendant has been charged with murder in the first degree. In preparing the case against him, the prosecutor reviews the indictment and carefully plots out each element of the offense. Then, the prosecutor reviews the evidence against the defendant and compares that with the elements of the offense. Put another way, the prosecutor must match witness testimony and evidence to each and every element. The law on the proof of the elements of criminal offenses is very simple: Failure to prove even one element will result in a dismissal of the entire case. Suppose the prosecutor has evidence to support the first three allegations of murder in the first degree but has no evidence as to premeditation. The prosecutor must either reinvestigate the case to find some evidence to support the allegation of premeditation or give some serious thought to dismissing the indictment and charging the defendant with a different crime, such as murder in the second degree, which does not contain this element.

Prosecutors are not allowed to offer an opinion to the jury or to state a fact for the record in a courtroom. Instead, a prosecutor must prove her case through evidence and witness testimony. A prosecutor cannot vouch for the evidence or take the stand and swear that she has established all of the elements of the offense. What a prosecutor must do is make sure that she has sufficient evidence and witness testimony to support every element on the charge. See Figure 7-7 for an example of how a prosecutor might chart out proof of a criminal case.

Sidebar

"In reviewing the sufficiency of the evidence to support a criminal conviction we apply a two-part test. First, we construe the evidence in the light most favorable to sustaining the verdict. Second, we determine whether upon the facts so construed and the inferences reasonably drawn therefrom the [jury] reasonably could have concluded that the cumulative force of the evidence established guilt beyond a reasonable doubt. . . . We note that the [jury] must find every element proven beyond a reasonable doubt in order to find the defendant guilty of the charged offense. . . ."[2]

- The unlawful killing
- of a human being by another
- done with malice
- and premeditation.

FIGURE 7-6

Elements of Murder in the First Degree

[2] *State v. Pauling*, 102 Conn. App. 556, 563, 925 A.2d 1200, cert. denied, 284 Conn. 924, 933 A.2d 727 (2007).

FIGURE 7-7

Proving the Elements of First-Degree Murder

Element	Evidence	Witness
The unlawful killing	No self-defense or other justifiable reason for the victim's death	Witness John Doe will testify that the defendant vowed to kill the victim and was present when the defendant shot the victim.
Of a human being by another	Medical testimony; photographs of victim's body prior to autopsy; chart showing the path of the bullet through the victim's body	Medical examiner will testify that the victim was alive at the time that he was shot and that he died as a consequence of the bullet wound.
Done with malice	Handgun	Detective Joe Green recovered a handgun at the scene after several witnesses showed him where it was located. Firearms expert will testify that the bullet recovered from the victim's body matches the handgun recovered. Witness Mary Jones will testify that the defendant stated that he hated the victim and that today was "his last day on earth."
And premeditation	Defendant's confession; defendant's statements to others; defendant seen at victim's residence waiting for victim for over an hour	Detective Joe Green will testify that he read the defendant his *Miranda* rights and questioned the defendant, and that the defendant confessed to killing victim.

How does a prosecutor know what the elements of a crime are? During the charging decision, which we discussed in the previous chapter, the prosecutor would have referred to a state statute that sets out the specific elements of each and every crime. Hopefully, the prosecutor relied on the statute before drafting the indictment or the accusation, and now the prosecutor will return to the statute, once again, to make sure that she has sufficient evidence to prove the case against the defendant. Although the prosecutor will often refer to the charging document, such as the indictment, in order to establish the elements of the offense, the real source of the elements for a crime lies in the statute that makes the behavior criminal in the first place. As we saw in the previous chapter, the prosecutor must review the statute before drafting an indictment or an accusation in order to make sure that each material element of the offense as it is laid out in the statute is also reflected in the charging document. While preparing the case for trial, the prosecutor will again return to the statute to make sure that the charging document is sufficient as drafted and also to ensure that all of the elements of the offense are actually listed.

D. VENUE

In addition to these stated elements of an offense, a prosecutor must also prove one element that is not listed in the criminal statute. That element is **venue**. In this context, venue refers to the location of the crime. A prosecutor must prove that the crime occurred within the jurisdiction where the case is being heard. If the prosecutor fails to prove that the murder occurred inside the jurisdiction, then the case against the defendant will be dismissed. Juries, police, prosecutors, and judges all have geographic limits on their power, and they are not permitted to prosecute someone who has committed a crime outside the venue.

Venue
The geographic area, often based on a county's boundaries, where a court may hear an action. In criminal cases, venue refers to the location where the crime occurred.

PROFILING THE PROFESSIONAL

The Importance of Venue

"They don't talk about venue a lot in law school. You wouldn't believe how embarrassing it is to work through an entire case and then to lose it because you failed to prove that it happened in your county. That's how important venue is. I lost my very first jury trial because I failed to ask even one witness, 'Did the crime occur in this county?' I was mortified, and about the only good thing I can say about it is that the case involved a pretty minor offense. Ever since then, I make it a habit of asking every single witness who testifies, 'Did the crime happen in this county?' "

Assistant District Attorney

PREPARING FOR TRIAL

Once the prosecutor has considered issues such as the presumption of evidence and how to overcome it by proving the elements of the offenses against the defendant, the next consideration is witness testimony and evidence. Witnesses will be called to testify about various aspects of the case. Some will be eyewitnesses to the crime, while others will be law enforcement officers who were involved in investigating or apprehending the defendant. Still others may testify about technical aspects of the case, including expert witnesses who may testify about all sorts of scientific analyses, from DNA analysis to bullet trajectory to carpet fiber analysis, to name only a few. The prosecutor will prepare for the trial by first learning the facts of the case as thoroughly as possible. Then, once the facts have been mastered, the prosecutor will meet with and prepare various witnesses to testify.

Preparing a witness for trial is very different from interrogating a witness during an investigation. Prosecutors are not trained to interrogate witnesses and rarely even view an interrogation, let alone participate in one. Even if a prosecutor were inclined to go to the police department and sit in on an interrogation, there would be little that she could contribute, and if the defendant made any type of incriminatory statement, then the prosecutor would be a witness to it. As we have already seen in previous chapters, an attorney cannot be both a witness and an advocate in the same trial.

A. THE DIFFERENCE BETWEEN "COACHING" AND PREPARING A WITNESS

Attorneys routinely interview witnesses, first to get additional information to draft a charging document and then to prepare the witness for trial. Here we must make a clear distinction between preparing a witness and "coaching" a witness. When a prosecutor prepares a witness for trial, the prosecutor goes over the witness's prior statements, and explains that the witness will be sworn in and then questioned under oath by the prosecutor. During the direct examination phase, the prosecutor will ask a series of questions designed to establish the elements of the offense and also to give the jury a clear picture of the crime. In preparing a witness for testifying, the prosecutor is not allowed to tell the witness what he must say. Instructing a witness to answer a question in a specific way is known as **coaching**. It is unethical and may also be illegal, especially if the prosecutor instructs the witness to lie.

Coaching
Telling a witness how she should answer specific questions without strict regard for the actual truth of the statement.

To avoid any appearance that the prosecution has coached a witness, the prosecutor will go through the questions that she intends to ask and will then ask the witness how the witness will respond. If the prosecutor does not like the witness's response to a particular question, the prosecutor can either rephrase the question, not ask it on the stand, or take the most common approach: Deal with the answer, whether the prosecutor likes it or not. The one thing that a prosecutor cannot do is to suggest to the witness that he change testimony to help improve the case against the defendant.

The line between preparing a witness and coaching a witness is sometimes fuzzy, occasionally being referred to as the difference between dawn and sunrise. A clear case of witness coaching, however, took place during the sentencing hearing of Zacarias Moussaoui, the so-called twentieth hijacker in the 9/11 attacks. A lawyer from the Transportation Security Administration allegedly coached seven aviation security witnesses. Under Rule 615 of the Federal Rules of Evidence, specifically, the Exclusion of Witnesses rule, judges are allowed to prevent witnesses from hearing the testimony of other witness. The aviation security witnesses were barred from the courtroom prior to their own scheduled testimony. However, the TSA lawyer not only violated the rule by advising the witnesses about certain elements of previous testimony but also left an e-mail trail of her breach. As a result, the judge banned the witnesses from testifying, nearly dismantling the case entirely. The jury ultimately decided against the death penalty for Moussaoui, and no one will ever know if the decision would have gone the other way had the aviation security witnesses been allowed to testify.

PROFILING THE PROFESSIONAL

Preparing for Trial (Prosecution)

"I approach it as three steps in preparation. My first step is the actual calendar call. I look at all of the cases. I might have from 12 to 18 cases on the calendar. I go through it and make sure that I have contact with most of the attorneys on those cases. I like to see what's going on. My cases are victim-oriented, so I try to have contact with all of the victims as well. I tell them what's going on and get a sense of where we need to go sentencing-wise if we're trying to work something out or not. I also like to let them know when and where they should be if they want to speak during sentencing. That's my prep for the calendar. In the midst of all of that, you start getting a feel for which cases may be trial cases. So, the next step is to talk to investigators and police and say that we may need to get these people lined up for a trial. I have a deal with the investigators: They call the police officers and I'll have the victim-witness people call the civilian witnesses. I've usually already talked to them, so they get a sense that this case might be going the trial route and we might want to set up additional meetings. I start to prepare them. It might mean bringing them in on the weekend or after work so that they can see the courtroom. That's part of the process that we go through in preparing for the case. The third part is trial mode. At that point, we go into high gear about what needs to happen. With children, I try to see them at their home, on their turf, and then have them come here. We review statements with witnesses. We watch videos that they may have made when they made their statements. I talk about the questions that I'll be asking and the questions that defense will probably ask."

Debra Sullivan, Assistant District Attorney

Interviewing witnesses and preparing them for trial is a skill that only comes with practice. If the witness is a police officer or an expert, such as a crime scene technician or a forensic expert, the prosecutor will only require minimal time preparing the witness. In fact, the prosecutor may simply go over the officer's police report or the expert's written opinion, confirm some details, and leave it at that. These witnesses have all testified many times before, and they know the pitfalls of testifying. However, a prosecutor must work more intensively with non-law-enforcement witnesses because many of them may have never even been inside the courthouse, let alone testified in a major criminal trial. Many of them will be nervous, or even hostile.

Sidebar

The best advice for any witness is to tell the truth, warts and all.

The job of a prosecutor is to explain the process of the trial to the witness and/or victim, take them through the various phases of the trial, and then go over their testimony with them so that they will know what to expect. In addition to telling the witness what questions the prosecution will have, the prosecutor will also try to give the witness some idea of the questions that he can expect from the defense. This is where the prosecutor's intimate knowledge of the system can pay real dividends. Not only can a prosecutor anticipate normal defense questions on cross-examination, but the prosecutor can also tell the witness what to expect from a particular defense attorney. It is quite common for prosecutors to have tried cases with the defense attorney before, and the prosecutor can share this previous experience with the witness. Is the defense attorney forceful or laid back in his approach? Does the defense attorney routinely attack witnesses on cross-examination or take a mild approach? The witness will always want to know if someone will be screaming or shouting at them, and the prosecutor can put their mind at ease that those types of tactics are rarely permitted in the real world.

1. PREPARING A SENSITIVE OR VULNERABLE WITNESS TO TESTIFY

If the prosecutor is preparing an especially sensitive or vulnerable witness, such as a child or a rape victim, then the prosecutor may wish to take extra steps to reassure the witness. The prosecutor may introduce the witness to the victim-witness coordinator, if the county is large enough to support such an office. The victim-witness coordinator will ensure that the witness arrives at the right courtroom on time and will also take the witness back to the district attorney's office after being questioned. The prosecutor, when dealing with a sensitive witness, may take the witness to the courtroom days before the actual trial, just so that the witness can see the layout. The prosecutor will have the witness sit in the witness stand, get used to speaking into a microphone, show the witness where the prosecutor and jury will be sitting and, if necessary, reassure the witness that there will be security personnel present to stop the defendant from attempting to harm him. This procedure often helps to alleviate some of the stress associated with testifying in particularly difficult cases, such as child molestation or rape cases.

2. SUBPOENAING WITNESSES

As the prosecutor prepares for trial, she must ensure that all of the witnesses necessary to prove the case have been subpoenaed. Prosecutors on the state and federal level routinely subpoena police officers and expert witnesses along with civilian witnesses. They do this to make sure that the witnesses have a legal incentive to appear for trial. Although a police officer might testify without the need for a subpoena, most prosecutors subpoena everyone involved. If the witness fails to appear for court, then the prosecutor can ask the judge for a bench warrant to have the witness arrested and brought to trial. Usually, the threat of such an action is enough to bring even the most recalcitrant witness to her senses.

3. INVESTIGATING THE STATE'S WITNESSES

As we saw in the previous chapter, the prosecutor does not always know who the defense witnesses are, but if they are known, then it would make sense for the prosecutor to investigate them before commencing the trial. The traditional method available to prosecutors is to run criminal histories on all of the known defense witnesses. However, many states now require the prosecution to run criminal histories on its own witnesses and turn any results over to the defense. But a prosecutor might do additional research on her own witnesses, just to avoid any nasty surprises at trial.

These days, there is a plethora of sources available to anyone who wants to learn more about a particular individual. Many people have their own websites, and these sites tell a reader a great deal about the person. Even more people have pages on social networking sites such as Facebook. A quick visit to each of the state's witness's sites can be instructional. The prosecutor knows that the defense attorney will undoubtedly try to dig up any negative information about a state's witness, so it is far better that the jury should hear about it from the prosecution first.

In addition to social networking sites, a prosecutor can now search civil records online and discover if any of the state's (or defense) witnesses have been involved in civil lawsuits. Perhaps the parties know each other because of a suit or have been involved with one another before because of a civil action. This is information that would be handy to know.

4. EVALUATING A WITNESS'S CREDIBILITY

Once a prosecutor has met with all of the witnesses who will be appearing for the government, the prosecutor must make a determination about the credibility of each witness. If an important and critical witness is not credible, then the prosecutor will need additional evidence to help bolster the witness's testimony. If, on the other hand, the witness is very credible, then the prosecutor may not need as much additional evidence to support the witness's statement. Evaluating a person for credibility involves many factors, including a general feel for the person. Does he seem believable? Does he have disagreeable character traits? Is he arrogant or self-important? Does he look as though he is not telling the truth? Should this witness be used at all if there is some other option?

a. Using Confidential Informants or Codefendants as Witnesses

One of most disagreeable types of witness is the confidential informant or a codefendant who has worked out a deal with the government in exchange for testifying. Confidential informants, unless they are undercover police officers, usually do not make appealing witnesses. They are often criminals themselves and have made an agreement for a reduced sentence in exchange for testifying against the defendant. It is easy for a defense attorney to paint the picture of a desperate person willing to say anything, incriminate anyone, just to save his own neck. The situation is even worse when the state's main witness is a codefendant. This person has even more incentive to lie and incriminate someone else. In cases in which the state is forced to use confidential informants or codefendants as witnesses, the prosecutor will often explain to the jury during opening statements that although the witness may not be very appealing, that doesn't change the fact that the witness is telling the truth.

B. EXHIBITS

Although we discussed evidence in depth in Chapter 3, a word about it here is also necessary. In Chapter 3, we examined the different types of evidence, including testimonial, documentary, physical, and demonstrative, among others. Instead of repeating what these types of evidence are, we must address a different question: How does a prosecutor use these various types of evidence to meet her burden of proof at the trial?

In order to prove the case, the prosecutor must present witnesses to testify about what occurred in the case. A witness may provide background on the relationship between the victim and the defendant or explain the details of the scene. The prosecutor may use a witness like this to give the jury a mental picture of the crime scene. The prosecutor will also inevitably call witnesses to identify the defendant as the person who committed the crime (assuming that there are eyewitnesses). The prosecutor will also call law enforcement officers to testify about the details involved in arresting the defendant and whether the defendant gave a statement to the police. As we have already seen, the admission of the defendant's statement has undoubtedly been challenged in a motion to suppress. Assuming that the state won that motion, a police officer will testify about the questions he asked the defendant and the answers that the defendant provided. The one thing that a jury will never hear is that the defendant invoked his right to remain silent and requested an attorney. Constitutional law prohibits the jury from hearing this evidence, under the assumption that if the jury did hear it, they might believe that the defendant was guilty because he chose to remain silent or because he requested to have an attorney during his questioning. Rather than risk having the jurors making a negative inference from the defendant's exercise of his constitutional rights, the prosecutor will not ask and the police officer will not testify that the defendant invoked these rights.

Besides civilian witnesses and law enforcement officers, a prosecutor may call other witnesses, including experts. An expert witness may be needed to explain complex or scientific principles to the jury that link the defendant to the crime.

C. EXPERT WITNESSES

There are occasionally situations in a jury trial in which the evidence required involves issues beyond the normal and regular experience of the average juror.

In this situation, either the prosecutor or the defendant can present expert-witness testimony. An expert is defined as a person whose knowledge, training, or experience would help the jury or judge understand a complex issue. Experts, once qualified, may give opinions about evidence in the trial and can even answer hypothetical questions posed by the parties.

EXAMPLE

A prosecutor is trying a case in which an elderly woman was shot in the side of the head at close range. A major issue in the case is the identification of the shooter. Crime scene technicians tested the defendant's shirt, found the day after the murder, and recovered high-velocity blood spatter from the right sleeve and shoulder. High-velocity blood spatter results from the concussive force of the bullet's impact with the skull and the gases that propel the bullet out of the barrel. Some of these gases force tiny particles of blood away from the wound and back toward the defendant, usually landing on the defendant's outstretched arm that is holding the gun. The prosecutor cannot explain high-velocity blood spatter to the jury herself, because she cannot testify. The police officers who investigated the case do not have the training, education, or experience to explain high-velocity blood spatter, but there is an expert on the subject at the state crime lab. Will the prosecutor use this expert to explain how high-velocity blood spatter works?

Answer: Yes. Because this is a topic that falls outside the education and training of the average person, the only way that the prosecutor is going to get this information before the jury is by using an expert.

Although an expert can testify about the likelihood of a particular event occurring, obviously the expert cannot testify that the specific defendant committed the act. That ultimate conclusion is left to the jury. Instead, the expert can explain how and when such an occurrence might happen and the scientific or technical knowledge that would assist the jury in making the determination of what occurred.

1. QUALIFYING AN EXPERT WITNESS

Under Rule 702 of the Federal Rules of Evidence, many different types of individuals can be qualified as experts. As long as a person has specialized knowledge, knowledge that is not available to the average juror, he may be qualified as an expert. The most common way of qualifying a person as an expert is to show that by their training, education, and experience, they have accumulated knowledge and expertise that would assist the jury in determining the facts of the case. When the party presents an expert, they must first go through the expert's training, education, and background and then tender the person to the court as an expert. This background questioning is referred to as *qualifying* the witness and serves as a basis for the expert's opinion. The opposing side has the right to challenge the person's status as an expert but only by showing that a person has not acquired specialized knowledge, training, or education. Given the broad wording of Rule 702, it is not very difficult to qualify a person as an expert. The United States

Supreme Court has weighed in on the issue of qualifying experts in the case of *Daubert v. Merrell Dow Pharmaceuticals, Inc.*[3] Under the decision in *Daubert*, the expert, when testifying about scientific knowledge, must base it on five factors:

1 testing of the theory or the technique
2 peer review and publication
3 the scientific technique's known or potential rate of error
4 existence and maintenance of standards controlling the technique's operation
5 the "general acceptance" of the theory in scientific circles

This test is used when either the prosecution or the defense presents a scientific test that has any bearing on the guilt or innocence of the defendant.

D. NONTESTIMONIAL EVIDENCE

In addition to witness testimony, the prosecutor will usually offer physical evidence during the trial to prove one or more essential elements of the crime (see Figure 7-8). Physical evidence covers such a wide swath of items that it is almost impossible to list them all. Essentially, physical evidence is some relevant item that tends to prove or disprove an element of the crime. Under this category could be items as diverse as a murder weapon or a videotape showing the defendant at the scene.

Depending on the nature of the crime charged, the prosecution may also present documentary evidence during the trial. When it comes to documents, the rules of evidence require, when possible, that the original document be used. This is known as the Best Evidence Rule and was originally created to avoid any allegation that the state altered a document by producing a copy with features added or removed to make it appear that the defendant was guilty. But in these days of computers, PhotoShop, printers, and the Internet, it is sometimes difficult to decide what actually constitutes the "original" document. Suppose, for example, that part of the proof against the defendant involves e-mail messages that

FIGURE 7-8

Rule 702, Federal Rules of Evidence

If scientific, technical, or other specialized knowledge will assist the trier of fact to understand the evidence or to determine a fact in issue, a witness qualified as an expert by knowledge, skill, experience, training, or education, may testify thereto in the form of an opinion or otherwise, if (1) the testimony is based upon sufficient facts or data, (2) the testimony is the product of reliable principles and methods, and (3) the witness has applied the principles and methods reliably to the facts of the case.[4]

[3] 509 U.S. 579 (1993).
[4] Rule 702. FRCE.

she sent to the victim. What is the original evidence in this case: the actual encrypted e-mail or a printout of what the e-mail says? The rules of evidence allow for these situations by permitting the state to certify that a printout of an e-mail message is the original document. When the original is not available, other rules of evidence allow the state to use a copy of the document, as long as the prosecutor can prove through witness testimony that the copy is identical to the original document and that nothing has been altered in the copy. As a way to help the jury assimilate all of this information, the prosecutor may create another type of evidence: demonstrative evidence.

1. DEMONSTRATIVE EVIDENCE

As we saw in Chapter 3, demonstrative evidence refers to any charts or diagrams used by the attorneys or witnesses to help illustrate or explain testimony. Because the prosecutor or the defense attorney normally prepares these exhibits, they may not be admitted during the trial. Unlike physical, documentary, and testimonial evidence, demonstrative evidence does not go with the jury into the jury room during deliberations. Demonstrative evidence is created specifically to persuade the jury and normally consists of charts, diagrams, lists, or other displays created to emphasize one or more points of the case to the jury.

2. ADVANCED TECHNOLOGY TO PRESENT EVIDENCE

Advancements in technology have made the presentation of evidence much different than it was even two decades ago. Beginning with the widespread availability of video cameras and VCRs, modern jurors can expect to see video footage from surveillance cameras, computer-generated re-creations of the crime, ballistic tests and bullet vectors demonstrated in three dimensions, in-dash video recordings made from patrol cars, and a wide variety of demonstrative charts, diagrams, and maps. It is now quite common for prosecutors and defense attorneys to digitize all of the media involved in a case and store it on a flash drive or computer so that it can be pulled up with much greater ease than the traditional hard copies held in files in storage cabinets.

As you read this case excerpt, consider the issues surrounding identifying, or misidentifying, witnesses.

CASE EXCERPT

HOGAN v. STATE

908 P.2d 925, 927-931 (Wyo.,1995)

Macy, Justice.

Appellant Eugene Hogan, Jr. appeals from the judgment and sentence which was entered after a jury found him guilty of two counts of delivery of cocaine and one count of conspiracy to deliver narcotics.

We affirm.

ISSUES

Appellant presents the following issues for our review:

I. Whether the trial court erred by denying the request of defense counsel to allow the defendant to sit with another man for identification purposes by a witness since there was a substantial likelihood of irreparable misidentification?

II. Whether Appellant was denied his constitutional right to a speedy trial under the U.S. Constitution, Amendment 6 and the Wyoming Constitution, Article I, §10?

FACTS

In August of 1993, an informant, who was working on a controlled buy for the Laramie County sheriff's department, was instructed to purchase narcotics from Appellant. The informant knew who Appellant was because they had previously been introduced. On August 10, 1993, the informant went to Appellant's house to purchase some cocaine; however, Appellant did not have any at that time. Appellant told the informant that he would have some more available on August 12, 1993. On that date, the informant, who had been provided with money as well as with a listening device, went back to Appellant's home to buy some cocaine. Although the informant had enough money for only one gram of cocaine, Appellant told him that he could take two grams and pay for the second gram the next day. On August 13, 1993, Appellant went to the informant's house where he received payment for the second gram of cocaine.

From August 12, 1993, until August 23, 1993, the informant saw Appellant at least every other day. On August 23, 1993, the informant purchased more cocaine as well as marijuana from Appellant. The informant also inquired as to whether it would be possible for them to make a bigger deal at a later date. Appellant told him that it would be, and they tentatively made a deal for a quarter of a pound of cocaine. After the informant departed, the police arrested Appellant.

An information was filed, charging Appellant with one count of conspiring to deliver a controlled substance on August 10, 1993, one count of delivering a controlled substance on August 12, 1993, and one count of delivering a controlled substance on August 23, 1993. A preliminary hearing was scheduled for August 31, 1993, but Appellant waived that hearing. Appellant was released from custody on August 31, 1993. Although an arraignment had been scheduled for September 16, 1993, it did not occur, and Appellant never entered a plea on the initial charges which had been filed against him. On December 2, 1993, when it became apparent that a trial would be required, a new information was filed, charging Appellant with one count of delivering cocaine on August 12, 1993, one count of delivering cocaine on August 23, 1993, and one count of conspiring to deliver cocaine on August 23, 1993. The original information was dismissed the following day because it erroneously alleged that the conspiracy to deliver cocaine occurred on August *928 10th rather than on August 23rd. Appellant was arrested in mid-December. Following a preliminary hearing which was held on December 21, 1993, Appellant was bound over on all three counts and released on bond.

Appellant was arraigned on January 12, 1994. After he entered a not guilty plea, the trial court set March 21, 1994, as a jury trial date. Appellant filed a motion to dismiss on February 1, 1994, for denial of his right to have a speedy trial in which he alleged:

15. The total time that will have elapsed from Defendant's initial arrest on August 23, 1993, and his trial date on March 21, 1994, is 211 days. Time elapsed from his initial arraignment date on September 16, 1993, and the trial date, is 187 days. None of this delay has been caused by the Defendant.

16. The delay in this case is excessive and violates the Defendant's statutory and constitutional rights to a speedy trial.

The trial court denied this motion.

The trial began on May 9, 1994. At the conclusion of the trial, the jury found Appellant guilty of all three of the charged crimes. The trial court sentenced Appellant to serve a term in the Wyoming Department of Corrections of not less than four and one-half years nor more than six and one-half years on each count with the sentences to run concurrently. Appellant appeals from his judgment and sentence.

DISCUSSION

Speedy Trial

Appellant contends that he was denied his constitutional right to have a speedy trial. He asserts that W.R.Cr.P. 48(b)(2), which provides that "[a] criminal charge shall be brought to trial within 120 days following arraignment," identifies the wrong starting point for determining whether a defendant has been given a speedy trial and is, therefore, constitutionally inaccurate. He propounds that the starting point should be at the time when the arrest is made or when the information or indictment is filed. He also presents an extensive analysis of the four factors which we utilized to consider claimed violations of the speedy trial right when Rule 204 of the Uniform Rules for the District Courts of the State of Wyoming was in effect. When the United States Supreme Court adopted this analysis in Barker v. Wingo, 407 U.S. 514, 92 S.Ct. 2182, 33 L.Ed.2d 101 (1972), it stated:

> We do not establish procedural rules for the States, except when mandated by the Constitution. We find no constitutional basis for holding that the speedy trial right can be quantified into a specified number of days or months. The States, of course, are free to prescribe a reasonable period consistent with constitutional standards, but our approach must be less precise.

In accordance with W.R.Cr.P. 48, we calculate the length of a delay by excluding the time periods specified in W.R.Cr.P. 48(b)(3). McDermott v. State, 897 P.2d 1295, 1300 (Wyo.1995). After those time periods have been excluded, delays of fewer than 120 days are permissible. Id. Pursuant to W.R.Cr.P. 48(b)(2), the responsibility to try Appellant in a timely fashion did not attach until he had been arraigned. Id.

Appellant's arraignment occurred on January 12, 1994. This arraignment was on the charges which had been filed on December 2, 1993, and for which Appellant was ultimately convicted. While earlier charges were filed against Appellant, no arraignment was held on them prior to them being dismissed. Appellant's trial commenced on May 9, 1994—117 days after Appellant was arraigned. Since Appellant was brought to trial within 120 days after he was arraigned, his speedy trial right was not violated.

Appellant suggests that the guarantee of a speedy trial would not be protected if the right were to attach only at the time when the arraignment occurs and not at the time when the arrest is made or when the information or indictment is filed.

Wyoming has no statute of limitations for criminal offenses, and prosecution for such offenses may be commenced at any time during the life of the offender. However, when a delay in bringing charges results in prejudice to a defendant, due process considerations may arise. In order to require dismissal of a charge, it is necessary that a preindictment delay cause "substantial prejudice to [appellant's] rights to a fair trial and that the delay was an intentional device to gain tactical advantage over the accused." Story [v. State], 721 P.2d [1020,] 1027 [(Wyo.1986)], quoting from United States v. Marion, 404 U.S. 307, 324, 92 S.Ct. 455, 465, 30 L.Ed.2d 468 (1971). Substantial prejudice requires the showing of the loss of a witness, exhibit or other evidence, the presence of which would probably bring a different result.

Appellant contends that he was prejudiced because of the preindictment delay and, as support for that contention, he lists his pretrial anxiety, the loss of his job, having to send his son to live with a relative, and disruption of his life due to police surveillance and harassment. Conspicuously absent from this list is either a claim that Appellant was prejudiced in his ability to receive a fair trial because of the time which elapsed prior to his indictment or a claim that such a delay was an intentional device used by the State to gain a tactical advantage over him. Because Appellant failed to demonstrate either substantial prejudice or an intentional delay, we conclude that his due process right was not violated.

CONCLUSION

We hold that the trial court did not err when it denied Appellant's request to sit in the back of the courtroom with another man for identification purposes and that Appellant was not denied his right to have a speedy trial.

Affirmed.

CASE QUESTIONS

1 What was Hogan's dispute regarding the denial of his speedy trial rights?
2 Were the original drug charges dropped because of Hogan's delay?
3 What were the charges brought against Hogan?
4 What is Hogan's argument that he was prejudiced?
5 How did court rule on Hogan's argument?

CHAPTER SUMMARY

As we have seen in this chapter, prosecutors routinely evaluate cases pending on their trial calendars and attempt to determine which cases will plead guilty pursuant to plea bargains and which will likely to go trial. In addition to evaluating which cases are likely to go to trial, a prosecutor must also consider how she will prove a case to the jury. The prosecutor's burden of proof is to prove beyond a reasonable doubt that the defendant committed the crime. One factor weighing against the prosecutor is that the defendant enters the trial protected by the presumption of innocence. This presumption stays with the defendant unless and until the prosecutor proves that the defendant committed the crime. There are other presumptions that factor heavily in criminal law, including the presumption that the indictment was drawn correctly and the presumption that the defendant is sane. In contrast to a presumption, an inference is a conclusion that a jury may make, based on facts presented in the case. Jurors may infer that the defendant intended the natural consequences of his actions, and jurors may infer that witnesses are telling the truth.

A prosecutor must be sure that she proves each and every element of the crime to the jury's satisfaction. An element is an important feature of a crime, and the prosecution must present evidence and testimony to support each element. One element that is common to all criminal cases is venue. The prosecution must prove that the crime occurred within the geographic limits of the court's authority. If a prosecutor fails to prove any of the elements, then the case against the defendant can and will be dismissed. As a prosecutor prepares the case, she will meet with witnesses and go over their testimony, being careful not to coach them as to what they should say, but instead ensuring that they tell the truth. These days, prosecutors have additional tools that they can use to investigate not only defense witnesses but also their own witnesses. Some prosecutors make a habit of checking out Facebook or other social networking sites to make sure that their own witnesses do not have inappropriate or even criminal items shown there.

KEY TERMS

Key terms are listed here in order of appearance in chapter.

Plea bargain	Presumption	Venue
Burden of proof	Inference	Coaching
Burden of persuasion	Element	

REVIEW QUESTIONS

1. Explain how a prosecutor evaluates a pending trial docket to decide which cases will go to trial and which ones will plead guilty.
2. What is a plea bargain?
3. Is a plea bargain recognized as a contract between the prosecution and the defense? If so, how?
4. Explain the arguments of the critics of plea bargains.

5. How does a prosecutor go about prioritizing cases on the trial docket?
6. What bearing do the so-called "three strikes and you're out" laws have on potential trials?
7. Explain the burden of proof that the prosecutor has in a criminal trial.
8. What is the burden of persuasion, and how does it relate to the prosecutor's burden of proof?
9. What is the burden of proof in a criminal case?
10. What is a presumption, and what impact does it have on a criminal defendant?
11. Explain the difference between presumptions and inferences.
12. Explain the presumption of innocence.
13. What is an "element" of an offense?
14. What is venue, and why is it important to a criminal prosecution?
15. What is the difference between coaching a witness and preparing a witness to testify?
16. What are some of the issues that a prosecutor must consider when dealing with physical evidence?
17. What is demonstrative evidence?
18. Explain how a court might use the "important life decision" example as a way of defining reasonable doubt.
19. What is "qualifying" an expert witness?
20. How might a prosecutor use Internet resources, such as Facebook, to investigate witnesses for either the state or the defense?

WEB SURFING

Expert Law: Plea Bargains
http://www.expertlaw.com/library/criminal/plea_bargains.html

Legal Dictionary Online: Burden of Proof in Criminal Cases
http://legal-dictionary.thefreedictionary.com/burden+of+proof

Answers.com: Burden of Proof in Criminal Cases
http://wiki.answers.com/Q/What_is_the_burden_of_proof_in_a_criminal_case

EXERCISES

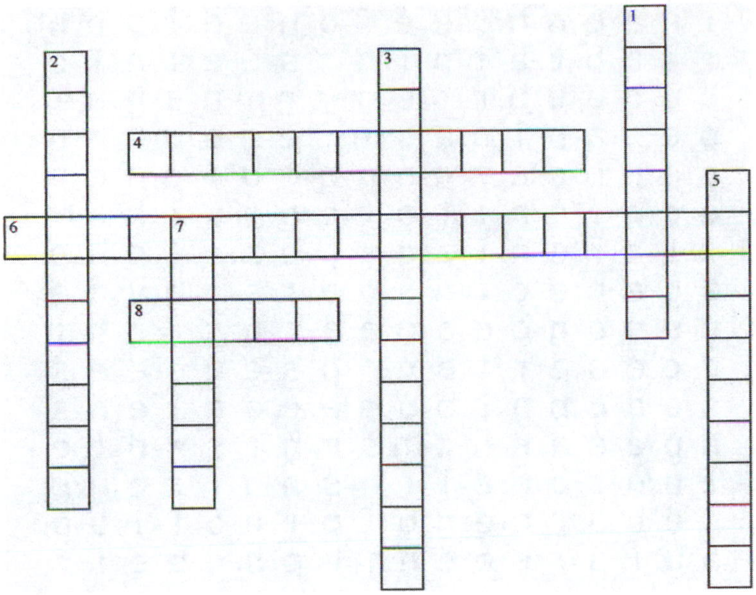

ACROSS

4. A prosecutor's recommendation for a somewhat lighter sentence than a defendant might normally receive in exchange for the defendant's plea of guilty to the offense charged
6. The obligation on the party who has the burden of proof to not only establish facts, but to convince the jury or judge that the facts are true and beyond dispute
8. The geographic area, often based on a counties boundaries, where a court may hear an action

DOWN

1. Telling a witness how he should answer specific questions without strict regard for the actual truth of the statement
2. A conclusion of fact that is based on the existence of another fact
3. The obligation on one party to produce sufficient evidence and testimony to establish facts that meet the elements of the crime charged
5. Facts that are probably true or facts that a jury can reasonably believe are true
7. A necessary and component part of the crime

o	e	d	u	n	o	p	a	e	p	r	f	n	b	e	f	f	h
b	i	b	e	v	f	r	e	p	l	l	e	o	u	p	b	r	a
p	n	t	i	d	a	n	v	u	u	r	u	n	r	n	e	n	p
r	n	e	e	p	h	r	e	e	f	g	n	e	d	l	g	p	n
r	c	a	b	t	a	i	p	i	n	r	s	u	e	i	n	f	c
b	e	o	o	u	b	r	t	e	n	u	r	m	n	s	n	u	i
o	e	b	a	p	i	o	a	s	m	f	e	g	o	o	p	n	u
c	e	p	b	c	e	r	c	p	n	n	e	u	f	p	n	e	a
e	o	h	f	o	h	i	t	o	t	e	o	r	p	l	h	a	m
r	t	e	r	e	n	i	a	g	r	a	b	a	e	l	p	h	p
a	g	e	n	e	o	r	n	a	b	a	r	s	r	n	v	d	e
u	e	e	o	n	o	g	a	g	a	a	c	u	s	r	c	h	m
c	c	e	o	e	r	f	a	n	n	p	a	e	u	b	e	e	s
n	e	d	o	b	n	r	o	u	e	e	e	a	a	l	e	n	s
h	p	e	e	a	n	n	c	m	s	n	h	r	s	r	n	t	e
t	u	o	r	b	n	e	i	r	h	s	n	n	i	r	e	n	e
c	o	b	u	r	d	e	n	o	f	p	r	o	o	f	i	u	o
o	u	i	n	r	e	e	e	n	m	e	p	b	n	e	e	r	r

plea bargain
burden of proof
burden of persuasion
presumption
inferences
element
venue
coaching

QUESTIONS FOR ANALYSIS

1 Do you have an account on Facebook or some other social network site? If so, are there items on it that you would prefer not to be shown to a jury if you were called to testify in a case?

2 Should plea bargains in cases be restricted a great deal more than they are now? Why or why not?

8

Preparing for the Trial: The Defense

Chapter Objectives

- Explain how defense attorneys prepare for their cases
- Describe the process that defense attorneys use to investigate their cases and how it differs from the investigative tools available to the state
- Explain various affirmative defenses such as alibi and insanity
- Define the notice requirements that a defense attorney must meet before presenting certain affirmative defenses
- Describe the various constitutional defenses available to a criminal defendant

I DEFENSE ATTORNEYS

Before we discuss the various things that a defense attorney will do when representing a client, we will first examine a very basic question: How does an attorney get paid? Then we'll address how and when the attorney-client relationship is created.

A. COMPENSATION

If this were a book about civil law, then we would spend a great deal of time discussing the various ways that attorneys are compensated. A civil attorney who represents plaintiffs, for example, might be compensated by receiving one-third of the total recovery from any verdict or settlement. In that situation, if the client receives nothing, then the attorney receives nothing. In other cases, lawyers charge an hourly fee. This fee can vary widely even among a small group of attorneys. It is not unheard of for some attorneys to receive rates as high as $500 per hour.

However, because this is a book about criminal law, we must address the compensation issues for defense attorneys, as shown in Figure 8-1. In this section we will assume that the attorney representing the defendant is a private attorney. If the defendant is represented by a member of the public defender's office, then that attorney is paid by the state or the local county in exactly the same way that the assistant district attorney is compensated. In fact, in counties and states that have the public defender system, the pay grades for prosecutors and defense attorneys are usually the same. There are also situations in which a jurisdiction may not have the resources to afford a separate public defender's office, so it relies on an appointed system. Under the appointment system, local, private attorneys are retained to represent defendants and are paid on an hourly basis. However, the hourly rate is nothing like what a civil attorney at a large firm might receive. In major cities, an appointed defense attorney might receive $50 an hour to represent a client. Although $50 an hour might sound like a lot of money, you must remember that out of this $50 the attorney must also pay the salary for his secretary, paralegal, and other support staff.

If the defendant hires an attorney to work for him or her, then the chances are that defense attorney will charge a flat, upfront fee instead of an hourly rate. The reasons for this are entirely practical. First of all, the defendant might be able—at this early stage of the case—to scrape together enough money to pay the attorney, either by borrowing money from the bank or taking it from savings or getting it from some other source. Those sources might not be available if the defendant is convicted and sent to prison. Because the statistics are lopsided, with prosecutors winning a majority of criminal trials, there is a very good chance that the defendant might be convicted. So, most defense attorneys who are hired by defendants charge an upfront fee. The amount of the fee varies depending on the nature of the crime and the experience level of the attorney. Attorneys with great experience and skill might charge up to $20,000 as an upfront fee for a major felony defense. The reasoning behind charging upfront fees for attorneys is painfully simple: If the attorney charges by the hour, there is a strong likelihood that the defendant may fall behind in his payments to the attorney, and if the defendant is convicted, it is unlikely that the attorney will receive any additional money. The defendant might reason that since he has been sent to prison, the attorney did not do such a good job, or even if the defendant believes that the attorney did do a good job, the defendant no longer has financial resources.

FIGURE 8-1

Typical Compensation Schemes for Defense Attorneys

- Public defender system
- Appointed system
- Hourly rate
- Flat fee

Paying the Defense Attorney

"I sometimes tell a client to have the money with him on the court date. If I show up and he doesn't have the money, I leave. It may sound a bit heartless, but I've been burned too many times by promises from clients to pay money and it never materializes. I have an entire office to support, so I can't afford to work for free."

B.J. Bernstein, Defense Attorney

PROFILING THE PROFESSIONAL

B. CREATING THE ATTORNEY-CLIENT RELATIONSHIP

One might be tempted to think that the attorney-client relationship between a defendant and her attorney is effectively established when the defendant pays the attorney's upfront fee. However, the case law on this makes clear that an attorney-client relationship is actually established in a different way. According to the courts, the attorney-client relationship is created when three specific events occur, none of which actually involves the payment of money. First, the defendant goes to the attorney and seeks advice or help in a case. Second, the advice or help sought is clearly within the scope of the attorney's expertise. Third, the attorney agrees to take the case, either by expressly stating it or by implication, such as starting an investigation into the case or contacting the prosecutor on the defendant's behalf.[1]

First Meeting with the Client

"When I first meet with the client, I usually want to know what it is that the government is alleging (about the crime), not the client's version. What is the government saying about the crime? Then I concentrate on getting the details: the police report, getting a feel for a client—for who they are—other than talking about the offense. When I ask questions, it's more of 'What is it that the police are saying? Did you talk to the police? Did they take anything? Was there any sort of search?' Sometimes, I stay away from the client's version until I've heard what the government has to say."

B.J. Bernstein, Criminal Defense Attorney

PROFILING THE PROFESSIONAL

[1] *State ex rel. Stivrins v. Flowers*, 273 Neb. 336, 729 N.W.2d 311 (2007).

INVESTIGATING THE CASE FROM THE DEFENSE VIEWPOINT

When it comes to investigating the case, the defense team does not have anything like the resources available to the government. The prosecution can call on crime scene technicians, police officers, detectives, forensic experts, and a whole host of others to help prepare for the case. The defense attorney does not have access to that huge apparatus. What the attorney lacks in resources, he must make up for in resourcefulness and creativity. The first, but not necessarily the best, source of information about the case is the client. The attorney will often question the client at length to discover the client's version of the cases. In the real world, defense attorneys know that their clients often lie to them, even though their conversation is protected by the attorney-client privilege. It is simply a matter of human nature that people tend to either downplay or completely obfuscate their actions when it puts them in a bad light. Also, the client may not fully trust the attorney, regardless of what the attorney says about protected communications.

After meeting with a client, the defense attorney will begin to build a picture of the case. That picture will then be compared to the one provided by the state in discovery materials. As we have seen in previous chapters, discovery in criminal cases has come a long way in recent years. In many states, defense attorneys now have access to police reports and witness statements. However, even this may not be enough to get a full picture of the case. Defense attorneys routinely contact police officers and other witnesses to discuss the case. However, they often run into a roadblock. Police officers know that they are under no obligation to speak to the defense attorney and have very little incentive to do so. The police officer knows that the defense attorney may try to make the police officer look foolish or incompetent when the officer is testifying in the trial, so there is very little reason for the officer to assist the defense attorney. The same situation may occur when the defense attorney attempts to contact the victim or other witnesses. Many of these individuals will be openly hostile to the defense attorney.

Although it may be beneficial to the defense to hire a private investigator and have this person interview all of the witnesses, there may not be enough money available to do so. In smaller cases, where the upfront fee is correspondingly lower, there is simply not enough money to pay for much outside help. In this situation the defense attorney must act like an investigator or ask a member of his staff to investigate the case.

PRETRIAL MOTIONS

Once the defense attorney has sufficiently investigated the case and reviewed any material provided by the state, he will undoubtedly file motions in the case. Among the more routine motions would be a motion to suppress evidence, including the defendant's statement or confession, and motions regarding specific evidence. The defense attorney might file a Bill of Particulars requesting additional information beyond what is provided in the indictment or accusation. But, as we saw in Chapter 5, there are many other motions that a defense attorney might file.

PROFILING THE PROFESSIONAL

Speedy Trial Demands

"I've only done it once or twice in years. A speedy trial demand means I'm ready to go to trial right now and it moves your case to the front of the line and the question is do you really want to be at the front of the line? A lot of prosecutors won't negotiate with you anymore when you have filed one. If your client is out on bond, then I'm not sure what the hurry is. Maybe there's a hurry because of their job, but more times than not, time is a defendant's friend. You've got to have a good reason. In the cases where I did file speedy trial demands, they were cases where the prosecutor indicted in order to avoid a preliminary hearing. When they indict, it does mean that they are ready. At least it should mean that they're ready. And in these cases they weren't. So it forced them to be sloppy on a lot of evidence and they just weren't ready for trial."

B.J. Bernstein, Criminal Defense Attorney

The number and variety of motions an attorney might file prior to trial is limited only by the rules of criminal procedure and the attorney's own creativity and resourcefulness. In major cases, it is not unheard of for an attorney to file dozens of motions. We discussed many of these motions in previous chapters. However, there is one listed above that we have not addressed previously: the defendant's motion to request state witnesses to speak with the defense attorney.

A. MOTION TO REQUEST STATE WITNESSES SPEAK WITH DEFENSE ATTORNEY

Although this is by no means a common motion, it is raised in enough cases to make it worthy of discussion. A defense attorney might file such a motion when he is running into active resistance from police officers or other state witnesses. It might seem, at first blush, that the prosecutor might fight this motion, but there are other considerations for a prosecutor. For one thing, if the witnesses refuse to cooperate with the defense attorney, then it is almost certain that this will come out during the trial. When a defense attorney accuses each of the witnesses of not cooperating with the defense and begins to suggest a concerted conspiracy of silence to hide some critical piece of evidence in the case, the prosecutor will undoubtedly wish that she had acquiesced to the defense attorney's request. Besides this consideration, a prosecutor might want the state's witnesses to discuss the case with the defense attorney prior to trial because it might actually push the case toward a plea bargain when the defendant's attorney realizes just how strong the case against his client is.

IV DEFENSES

One of the most common misconceptions about criminal law has to do with defenses. A defendant enters the courtroom protected by many different constitutional rights, including the presumption of innocence and the state's burden of proving the defendant guilty beyond a reasonable doubt, among others. When a defendant is charged with a crime, he has no obligation to say anything during the course of his trial. The defendant cannot be compelled to take the stand in his trial. A prosecutor cannot put the defendant on the stand and cross-examine him about what happened when the crime occurred. In fact, a prosecutor cannot even refer to the fact that the defendant has failed to deny the charge. Defendants are under no obligation to present any defense of any kind. They have the right to remain silent and present no defense to the state's accusations. However, that tactic is rarely successful. Defendants often want to present a defense, even to take the stand to present their version of the facts, and defense attorneys must consider all of these elements in formulating a defense. It is unlikely that a jury will find the defendant not guilty without some defense presented. The problem for the defense attorney is both ethical and practical. On the ethical side, a defense attorney cannot be party to perpetrating some fraud on the court, such as having the defendant or other witnesses to knowingly commit perjury. On the practical side, the defense attorney knows that if the only version the jury hears is the government's, the chances of a conviction are very high.

However, there are additional considerations for a defense attorney when addressing specific types of defenses. Although some are automatic, such as the constitutional rights that protect the defendant, some must be supported by evidence and witness testimony. These defenses, which require some affirmative action on the defendant's part, are referred to as *affirmative defenses.* Among the many affirmative defenses are self-defense, alibi, consent, and insanity. We will examine each of these defenses and then also address some additional constitutional defenses that a defendant can assert, including equal protection and due process. However, before we can address the topic of defenses, we must first discuss how an attorney prepares defense witnesses to testify during the defense portion of the trial.

A. PREPARING DEFENSE WITNESSES

We have already discussed how the prosecution prepares witnesses to testify at trial, and the defense goes through a similar procedure. However, the perspective of the defense witnesses is entirely different from that of the prosecution witnesses. The individuals who testify for the state are being used to establish the basic

Do	Don't
Review your statement	Guess
Dress professionally	Get angry
Make eye contact with the jurors	Use sarcasm
Be polite	Answer questions you don't understand
Tell the truth	

FIGURE 8-2
Ground Rules for Witnesses

elements of the offense and to prove beyond a reasonable doubt that the defendant committed the crime. Defense witnesses, on the other hand, are put on the stand to attack those elements and to sow doubt in the jurors' minds.

Preparing a witness for testifying at trial is one of the most important aspects of trial preparation and should never be skipped. Witnesses are often very nervous about testifying. They are afraid of looking foolish in front of a large group of strangers. They are afraid that the opposing attorney will yell at them or try to confuse or embarrass them. Although this does sometimes happen, the defense attorney can assure a defense witness that a judge will not allow this type of behavior for very long. Defense attorneys may go over the witness's written statement given to the police to make sure that the witness remembers all of the details of the original incident. It may be months or even years since the witness gave a statement, and some details may have become foggy. The defense attorney faces the same restrictions in preparing witnesses as does the prosecution. Defense attorneys are not permitted to coach witnesses any more than prosecutors are. As the defense attorney prepares the witness to testify during the trial, he will tell the witness some basic ground rules that all witnesses should follow. See Figure 8-2 for a list of ground rules for witnesses.

B. THE JURY'S ROLE IN WEIGHING DEFENSES

When it comes to defenses, the same rule applies as it does for the prosecution. The final decision about what and whom to believe rests with the jury. It is the jury's duty to decide if a defense is valid and creates a reasonable doubt.

C. DEFENDANT'S BURDEN OF PROOF IN PRESENTING A DEFENSE

In Chapter 7, we discussed the state's burden of proof at length. There, we saw that the government must prove that the defendant is guilty beyond a reasonable doubt. That burden does not shift during the trial. If a defendant presents a defense, the state is required to disprove it beyond a reasonable doubt. But this raises an even more basic question: Is any evidence enough to establish a defense? Does the defendant have any burden of proof in presenting a defense?

Preponderance of the evidence
A showing by one side in a civil suit that its version of the facts is more likely to be true than not.

The answer is clearly yes. However, unlike the state, the defendant does not have the heavy burden of proving a defense beyond a reasonable doubt. Instead, defendants have a lower standard: **preponderance of the evidence**. Preponderance of evidence is a burden of proof that requires a party to simply show that her version of facts is more likely to be true than not true. It is a much lower standard than proof beyond a reasonable doubt, but it is a high enough threshold to prevent the defense from simply stating a defense and providing no evidence to back it up.

Sidebar

In some states, the defendant's burden of proof in presenting a defense is "some" evidence or "any evidence" to support the affirmative defense.

D. SIMPLE DEFENSE VERSUS AFFIRMATIVE DEFENSE

Simple defense
A defense that is automatically triggered when a defendant is charged with a crime. A defendant is not required to submit any evidence or testimony to raise a simple defense.

Affirmative defense
A defense that is something more than a mere denial and requires that the defense present evidence and/or testimony to establish. An affirmative defense may offer mitigation or a legal excuse for the defendant's actions.

A defendant enters a criminal trial with certain defenses already in place. He is not required to raise them at the trial. These are the legal or constitutional defenses that all defendants have and are often referred to as **simple defenses**. Among these simple defenses is the right to be considered not guilty until his guilt is proven beyond a reasonable doubt. However, there are other defenses that the defendant must present evidence and testimony to support. These are the **affirmative defenses** and require the defense to make a presentation at trial and produce enough evidence to warrant a serious consideration by the judge and jury (see Figure 8-3). If a defendant wishes to raise the affirmative defense of alibi, for example, the defendant must present testimony that he was somewhere else when the crime occurred. It is not enough for a defense attorney to simply state that the defendant was not present when the crime occurred. The defense attorney must present testimony, either from the defendant or someone else, to substantiate this defense to a preponderance of the evidence. Affirmative defenses do not require that the defendant take the stand, but someone must. An affirmative defense attempts to explain, refute, or excuse the defendant's criminal conduct. If the jurors believe the affirmative defense to a preponderance of the evidence, then they would be authorized to find the defendant not guilty of the charges.

Mens rea
Guilty intent; the requirement that the defendant is aware of and conscious of his actions before a crime can be charged.

In many circumstances, when a defendant raises an affirmative defense, she is actually admitting to the criminal conduct but is attempting to mitigate or excuse it. As we will see when we discuss the insanity defense, for example, the defendant admits that she committed the act charged, but is not guilty because the defendant could not form ***mens rea*** at the time of the incident. Similarly, self-defense does not claim that the defendant did not commit the act of violence. Instead, it states that the defendant did injure or kill another, but the action was excused because the defendant was protecting himself or another person. Once an affirmative defense is presented, it is the duty of the prosecution to disprove the defense beyond a reasonable doubt. The burden in a criminal trial never shifts to the defendant to prove her innocence. Instead, the burden of proving the case beyond a reasonable doubt applies both to the state's case and to the defendant's affirmative defense.

Simple defense	Affirmative defense
Denial of the charge Triggered automatically	Requires presentation of evidence or testimony Must be raised and proved by the defense

FIGURE 8-3
"Simple" Defense Versus Affirmative Defense

Defenses from the Prosecutor's Perspective

PROFILING THE PROFESSIONAL

"When you're dealing with defenses, you have to put yourself in the defendant's (or defendant's attorney's) shoes. You have to see the case the way they see it, both the good and the bad. That way you can build a better case for the prosecution."

R. Keith Miles, Prosecutor

E. INCONSISTENT DEFENSES

Can a defendant raise inconsistent defenses? For instance, can a defendant raise the affirmative defenses of insanity and simple denial of the charge? These two defenses contradict each other. The defendant is essentially saying: "I didn't do it, but even if I did, I was legally insane at the time." Many jurisdictions allow defendants to present inconsistent defenses, no matter how inconsistent they are. However, that latitude is not as much of an advantage as it might seem. The defendant must still convince the jury that the defense is valid, and presenting conflicting defenses might simply confuse the jurors and have them negate both.

F. NOTICE REQUIREMENTS

In almost all jurisdictions, defendants are required to notify the state when they intend to bring certain affirmative defenses such as alibi or insanity. The defendant is required to serve written notice on the government that he intends to bring these defenses. This notice allows the state to prepare additional witnesses to refute the defense. There is also the idea that by serving notice on the state that the defendant is raising a certain defense, the state might be inclined to review its case more closely to see if in fact that defense is valid and the case against the defendant should be dismissed. Whether or not that last point is actually followed in the real world, there is no doubt that the state has the responsibility of presenting a rebuttal to an affirmative defense.

G. REBUTTAL: THE PROSECUTOR'S RESPONSIBILITY

Rebuttal
Evidence offered by a party that directly refutes evidence or pleading by the opposing party.

In almost all jurisdictions, the government is required to present evidence rebutting the affirmative defense. If the prosecution fails to rebut the evidence, then the defendant is entitled to a directed verdict in his favor. **Rebuttal** comes after the defense has rested its case. At that point, the prosecutor announces that she would like to present rebuttal testimony and evidence to disprove the affirmative defense. The prosecutor must present enough testimony to not only prove that the defendant committed the crime, but also that the affirmative defense is not applicable; the prosecutor must also meet the burden of proof beyond a reasonable doubt for both. For an example of how important the notice requirements can be, see this chapter's case excerpt.

H. SPECIFIC AFFIRMATIVE DEFENSES

Now that we have discussed the basic requirements of bringing an affirmative defense, we will examine specific types of affirmative defenses. As we will see as we discuss each affirmative defense in turn, there are specific elements that the defense must present. If this sounds familiar, it is identical to the process that the prosecutor follows in evaluating and proving the state's case against the defendant. Just as we saw in Chapter 7 when discussing prosecutors and the importance of proving the elements of the offense, defense attorneys must also ensure that they prove each element of their defense. Otherwise, the judge may refuse to instruct the jury about the defense, and they will be unable to adequately consider it during deliberations.

1. AGE

Actus reus
Guilty act.

When it comes to prosecuting individuals, their age can be a significant factor in whether criminal charges can be brought. Although there is no upper limit on a defendant's age and whether a criminal case can proceed, there is a lower limit. In most jurisdictions, a child below the age of seven is presumed to be incapable of forming *mens rea*. *Mens rea* is the mental component that is required in order to prove almost all crimes. Although with ***actus reus***, these two elements are the basic building blocks of any prosecution. *Actus reus* refers to the act of committing the crime. However, because children have not developed mentally, they are presumed to lack this ability below a certain age. (Seven is the most common age, but it is not universal.) What this essentially means is that any child age seven or younger who commits what would otherwise be a crime cannot be prosecuted. For children between the ages of 7 and 14, the presumption is rebuttable, meaning that the prosecution can present evidence that a particular child could form *mens rea*. Over the age of 14, a child is presumed to be able to form *mens rea*. We will see that *mens rea* plays a large role in another affirmative defense that we will discuss later in this chapter: insanity. Children over the age of 14 are generally handled through juvenile court, which we will discuss in Chapter 12.

2. ALIBI

Alibi is the defense that asserts that the defendant was not present when the crime occurred. Unlike many other affirmative defenses, alibi does not admit to the underlying crime and then seek to mitigate or excuse it. When a defendant raises the defense of alibi, the defendant is claiming that she was somewhere else when the crime occurred and therefore cannot be guilty. Alibi is a **complete defense**, meaning that if the defendant presents sufficient proof, the jury is not only authorized but obligated to reach a verdict of not guilty. A complete defense is one that shows that the defendant is not guilty of the crime and leaves the jury with no other option than finding the defendant not guilty.

Complete defense
A defense that would completely exonerate the defendant of the crime charged, assuming the defendant presents sufficient evidence to meet his burden of proof (usually preponderance of the evidence).

3. BATTERED WOMAN'S SYNDROME

Battered woman's syndrome is not recognized in all jurisdictions and has had some controversy attached to it. Essentially, battered woman's syndrome is a legal defense that is an offshoot of self-defense. The controversial aspect to battered woman's syndrome is that unlike self-defense, where the person being attacked immediately moves to protect herself, battered women's syndrome allows a battered spouse or significant other to retaliate against repeated abuse at a time when the person is not actually being attacked. The most common example of battered woman's syndrome is when a woman who has been repeatedly battered waits until her attacker falls asleep and then attacks him, sometimes even killing him. What makes this controversial is that in self-defense, the attack and response are simultaneous. An attack is met with a counterattack. In many of the jurisdictions that question the use of battered woman's syndrome, they point to the fact that when the victim does retaliate, it is when the abuser is most vulnerable. Battered woman's syndrome has been the focus of several cases in which the defense was questionable and may have simply been a smoke screen put up by a defendant who murdered her significant other and then tried to claim that she had endured years of abuse and finally responded. Like most affirmative defenses, the defendant who uses battered woman's syndrome admits that she attacked her abuser, but seeks to have this attack mitigated or excused because she had endured a prolonged period of abuse, and waiting until her abuser was incapacitated was the only way that she could effectively fight back.

Battered woman's syndrome
An affirmative defense that asks the jury to excuse a woman's attack on her alleged long-time abuser or asks the judge to mitigate her sentence in reflection of the fact that she was responding to a long period of abuse at the hands of the "victim."

One of the most notorious cases that involved the battered woman's syndrome defense took place in the early 1990s. Lorena Bobbitt claimed that she and her husband, John Bobbitt, had a volatile marriage during which she was sexually, physically and emotionally abused. According to Lorena, after returning home intoxicated one night, John Bobbitt sexually assaulted her. Once he had fallen asleep, she used a carving knife to sever his penis. During her trial, the defense team argued temporary insanity as a result of battered woman's syndrome, which resulted from long-term physical and emotional abuse. Furthermore, several witnesses provided testimony that supported Lorena's claims of abuse. The jury found her not guilty by reason of insanity, which caused her to succumb to an irresistible impulse to wound her husband sexually. Under state law, Lorena had to undergo a 45-day mental evaluation at a hospital before being released.

Sidebar

Using battered woman's syndrome, a woman can seek to have her crime of battering or even murdering her purported attacker mitigated or excused by presenting evidence that she has been the victim of repeated domestic violence on the part of the man.

FIGURE 8-4

Coercion As a Defense

A justification defense of coercion is available to show that a criminal act is performed under such coercion that the person reasonably believes that performing the act is the only way to prevent his imminent death or great bodily injury. In order to assert a statutory affirmative defense, such as coercion, the defendant must admit all of the elements of the crime except intent; evidence of coercion is then presented to justify, excuse or mitigate the crime by showing no criminal intent. OCGA §16-3-26.[2]

4. COERCION

The affirmative defense of coercion alleges that although the defendant committed the crime, he was forced to do so by someone else. In essence, the defendant must admit that he participated in the crime but had no alternative because someone else was threatening him with severe bodily injury or even death. The threat to the defendant must be something that a reasonable person would deem to be a drastic threat. In a Maryland case, the coercion defense fell flat. An 18-year-old man was called by his older brother to pick him up. While in the car, the brother told him to pick up two other friends as well. When the other friends got into the car, one had a shotgun and the other a handgun. The young man was then ordered to drive to a nearby McDonald's, which they intended to rob. Fearful for his own safety, the young man complied and drove to McDonald's, and the brother and his friends went inside and robbed the restaurant. The key flaw in mounting a coercion defense in this case was that the young man had the opportunity to drive away while the others were inside, but he did not. See Figure 8-4 for a statute on coercion.

EXAMPLE

Rick and his friend Sam visit a convenience store. Rick pulls out a gun and tells Sam that he intends to rob the convenience store and that if Sam doesn't go along, Rick will shoot him. Sam assists in the robbery, and they both flee. Does Sam have the defense of coercion?

Answer: Yes. Because Sam was faced with death, he can claim coercion.

There are many jurisdictions that recognize the affirmative defense of coercion, but many limit its application to specific types of crimes. Coercion cannot, for instance, be used to excuse the defendant's killing another person. The affirmative defense of coercion does not allow one person to kill another to prevent being killed himself.[3]

[2] *Hightower v. State*, 224 Ga. App. 703, 705(2), 481 S.E.2d 867 (1997).
[3] *State v. Getsy*, 84 Ohio St. 3d 180, 702 N.E.2d 866 (1998).

5. CONSENT

When a defendant raises the affirmative defense of consent, she is saying that the victim agreed to the crime and therefore there can be no crime. In a battery, for instance, if the victim consents to be struck, then there is no crime because the victim has raised no objection by agreeing to the injury. Consent is raised most often in rape prosecutions in which a defendant claims that the victim consented to sexual contact and therefore there can be no crime.

EXAMPLE

In the movie *Fight Club*, Brad Pitt's character asks Edward Norton's character to hit him in the face "as hard as you can." If Pitt's character were later to seek charges against Norton's character, could he claim the defense of consent?

Answer: Yes, Norton's character could successfully claim consent.

Consent as a defense cannot be used in all situations. A person cannot consent to murder, for instance. In addition to certain crimes not being covered by consent, there are also certain victims who cannot give consent. Children, for example, are limited in the kind of consent they may give. Since they lack the level of maturity and experience that adults have, statutes prohibit them from giving legal consent to many actions. In most jurisdictions, for example, a child below the age of 12 (in almost all jurisdictions) cannot give consent to any type of sexual activity with an adult.

In addition to the previous two examples of exceptions to when consent can be used, there is the additional requirement that the person who gives consent must understand what she is consenting to, and must knowingly agree to take on the possibility of injury, whether financial, physical, or emotional. Since this is the rule, it becomes clear why other individuals are legally incapable of consenting to other activities. Mentally disabled people, for instance, are protected under the law in most states by statutes that limit the kind of consent that they can give.

Consent is also not a defense in a crime like statutory rape, where one partner is legally incapable of giving consent. Third parties cannot consent for others. A husband cannot give consent to another man to have sex with his wife. In other situations, the law recognizes that people are not given authority to allow another person to commit a crime. Consent law also requires that consent must be given freely and voluntarily. Without such a showing, consent is not a valid defense.

EXAMPLE

A man pulls a gun on a woman who has just gotten some money from the ATM. He points the gun in her face and asks, "Do you give me consent to take your money?" She nods and he takes her money and flees. When he is caught, he raises the defense of consent. Will he be successful?

Answer: No. Consent that is obtained by coercion or threat of violence is no consent at all.

6. DURESS

A claim of duress is one in which the defendant claims that some other person used intimidation, psychological control, or other means short of outright threats to force a defendant to commit a crime. Unlike coercion, where there is a direct correlation between the crime and the threat of physical violence to the defendant, duress operates more as subtle mental manipulation—even what some might term verbal and mental torture. As such, it is a great deal harder to prove than coercion, where the equation "do this or die" is fairly straightforward. Duress comes about through weeks or months of nonstop mental cruelty or manipulation until the defendant believes that she has no other choice than to obey the wishes of another. Unlike coercion, there is no specific point at which the defendant can show the jury that it was at this precise instant when she felt overwhelmed. Instead, duress is a process that takes time. Just as we saw with coercion, however, the duress must be something that a reasonable, objective person would also believe would eventually force someone to commit a crime.

EXAMPLE

Every night, Martha's mother locks her in a closet for being "bad." In this case, *bad* is defined as not stealing from the local convenience store. When Martha finally breaks down and steals a small item from the store, she is "rewarded" by being able to sleep in her own bed. The next time that Martha is caught, she raises the defense of duress. Will she be successful?

Answer: Most likely. Assuming that Martha can prove that she was forced to sleep in a closet and endure other forms of verbal and mental abuse, her defense may be sufficient for the jury to find her not guilty.

EXAMPLE

Ted steals a car and when he is caught, he explains to the police that his friends were all calling him "chicken" because he would not go along with their plans to steal automobiles. Ted felt that this constant haranguing questioned his manhood and made him feel very insecure. He also raises the defense of duress. Will he be successful?

Answer: No. As we have already seen, duress is evaluated from the perspective of what an objective person would consider mental manipulation or abuse. Calling someone "chicken" hardly amounts to that level of psychological strain.

7. ENTRAPMENT

Entrapment is an interesting defense in that the defendant claims that he was tricked or manipulated into committing a crime by the police. Unlike coercion or duress, entrapment can be carried out only by law enforcement officers. When a person is entrapped, he has been given both the idea for the crime and the means to carry it out by law enforcement or prosecutors. Essentially, the defendant is saying that the police made him do it. The idea behind making entrapment a valid defense is that we, as a society, do not want the police in the business of thinking up crimes and then encouraging others to carry them out. Because the government should not be in the business of creating crime, jurors are authorized to punish the government for doing so by finding the defendant not guilty.

But entrapment can be a confusing defense. Defendants often claim that they have been entrapped when police work as undercover police officers, sometimes even providing defendants with drugs so that they can continue the illusion that the undercover officer is actually a fellow criminal. The question often becomes: When do the government's actions cross the line between acceptable police work and entrapment?

There are two ways of testing whether entrapment exists in a particular case. This involves answering two separate questions:

1. Did the idea for the crime originate with the police?
2. Did the police provide the defendant the means to carry the crime out?

If the answer to both questions is yes, then there is a solid case for entrapment. If the answer to either question is no, then there is no case of entrapment.

As we have seen with all affirmative defenses, the prosecution must disprove entrapment beyond a reasonable doubt, assuming that the defendant has met the relatively low burden of presenting it. When a defense of entrapment is presented, the government must present rebuttal testimony refuting that the idea of the crime originated with the police or that the police provided the means to the defendant to consummate the crime. The most common way to rebut a defense of entrapment is to show that the defendant was already disposed to commit the crime, and the police simply provided the defendant with the opportunity to put his wish into action. Some states have a further requirement in order to disprove entrapment beyond a reasonable doubt: The state must prove that it did not overcome the defendant's free will and force him to carry out the crime.[4]

EXAMPLE

Mel is an undercover police officer who is pretending to be a college student. He has joined a militant college group that espouses anarchy as a viable political system. One night, while they are all talking about the best way to spread the word about the benefits of an anarchic political system, Mel suggests that they bomb the university's administrative office. He eventually convinces the group to go along and then obtains dynamite and brings it to the next meeting. As the group is discussing the merits of blowing up the building, the police arrive and arrest everyone, charging them with conspiracy to commit terrorism. Has the group been entrapped?

---

[4] *Quick v. State*, 660 N.E.2d 598 (1996).

Answer: Yes. In this case, both the idea of the crime (to blow up the building) and the means (the dynamite) originated with the police, specifically an undercover police officer. Had Mel simply provided the dynamite after the group had decided on its own to blow up a college building, there would be no valid case for entrapment.

8. INSANITY

When it comes to affirmative defenses, insanity is one of the most complicated and often the most misunderstood. The essential question any time that a defense of insanity is raised is whether the defendant meets the legal test of insanity: that he did not know the difference between right and wrong. A person can suffer from any number of different psychological problems, including schizophrenia and multiple-personality disorder and still not meet the legal test for insanity.

A defendant presents an insanity defense by presenting expert testimony during the defense case to show that the defendant did not know or understand the difference between right and wrong when he committed the crime. This requires either a psychiatrist or a psychologist to testify that at the time the defendant committed the crime he met the legal standard for insanity.

There are many misconceptions about the defense of insanity. One common misconception is that people who have a mental illness will automatically be considered not guilty by reason of insanity. This is not true. People with multiple personalities, people who hear voices, and people who have hallucinations have all been held to be legally sane. Another common misconception about the defense of insanity is that if the defense is raised successfully, and a verdict of not guilty by reason of insanity is entered, the defendant is then released. This is also not true. If a defendant has been found not guilty by reason of insanity, the defendant is usually placed in a mental hospital for the criminally insane.

a. How Insanity Affects *Mens Rea* Analysis

As we have seen with most affirmative defenses, a defendant who raises the insanity defense must admit that he actually committed the crime but was legally insane at the time that it occurred. Unlike many other affirmative defenses, insanity is a complete defense and akin to our discussion about underage children. When we discussed prosecuting children under the age of seven, we saw that society considers that they have not developed sufficient mental capabilities to form *mens rea*. In the insanity defense, the defendant claims that because of mental problems or brain disease, the defendant was also incapable of forming *mens rea*. Just as we saw with alibi, insanity is a complete defense. Once proven, the jury is required to find the defendant not guilty by reason of insanity—although in some states there is another alternative, discussed below.

b. A Brief History of the Insanity Defense: M'Naghten Test

The ancient Romans recognized that insanity was a defense to crime and recognized it as a valid defense. However, under the English and American legal systems, the pendulum has swung very far in both directions, with occasional periods during which insanity was considered liberally for most crimes and other times when proving legal sanity was virtually impossible.

Courts have been wrestling with the insanity defense for centuries. As time has passed, different standards for insanity have come into vogue and then disappeared. One of the earliest was the M'Naghten test. This test was an early attempt to establish a workable scheme to determine who was and was not legally insane.

In 1843, M'Naghten attempted to kill Sir Robert Peel, the current prime minister of England. Instead, he killed Peel's private secretary, a man named Edward Drummond. He was found not guilty by reason of insanity, and this controversial verdict started a national debate in both England and the United States over what the definition of legal insanity should be. The findings of a British court of inquiry into the case established the first conclusive test for legal insanity:

> "To establish a defense on the ground of insanity, it must be clearly proved that, at the time of the committing of the act, the party accused was labouring under such a defect of reason, from disease of the mind, as not to know the nature and quality of the act he was doing; or, if he did know it, that he did not know he was doing what was wrong."
>
> M'Naghten's Case, 10 Clark & Finnelly 200, 210, 8 Eng Rep 718, 722 (HL 1843).

Since the M'Naghten case, there have been many modifications to the insanity defense. Various states have sought their own standards, and the Model Penal Code has also weighed in on the issue.

c. Modern Definitions of Insanity After M'Naghten

In most states, the modern definition of insanity is either the standard M'Naghten test or some variant on the definition shown in Figure 8-5.

A growing dissatisfaction with the plea of not guilty by reason of insanity brought about legislative initiatives in many jurisdictions that modified this defense. In many states, for example, a new verdict was created: guilty but mentally ill. When the jury returns this verdict, the defendant will be incarcerated in a regular prison facility but must have some access to psychiatric or psychological services and treatment.

FIGURE 8-5

Durham Test for Insanity

A defendant is considered to be legally insane when one of the following is true:

- He cannot distinguish between right or wrong.
- He suffers from an irresistible impulse that precludes him from choosing between right and wrong.
- His or her lawful act is the product of a mental disease or defect.

Before this modification, when the defense of insanity was raised, the jury had three possible verdict choices:

Before Changes	After Changes
Guilty	Guilty
Not guilty	Not guilty
Not guilty by reason of insanity	Not guilty by reason of insanity
	Guilty but mentally ill

As is true with all affirmative defenses, even the insanity defense, the defendant must agree to the defense being offered. Although that might fly in the face of the entire reason for bringing the insanity defense, that the defendant does not understand the difference between right and wrong, it is still up to the defendant to agree to bring this defense or refuse to allow his attorney to offer it.

d. When Was the Defendant Considered to Be Insane?

There are really two different types of insanity pleas. A defendant may plead insanity by providing proof by a preponderance of evidence that at the time of the crime he was legally insane. But a defendant may also raise the "special plea" of insanity at the time of the trial. Although these two defenses sound very similar, in practice they are quite different. When a defendant pleads insanity at the time of the trial, he is alleging that he is not competent to understand the legal process and cannot assist in his defense. However, when a defendant raises the defense of insanity at the time that the crime was committed, the defendant is maintaining that he cannot be guilty of a crime. Defendants who claim that they are insane at the time of trial do not get the benefit of the insanity defense. The jury is not authorized to find them not guilty by reason of insanity, because they are not alleging that they were insane at the time that the crime was committed. A defendant who is not competent to stand trial may be remanded into a state facility until such time that he is able to stand trial. In many cases, a defendant may claim both forms: insanity at the time of the crime and insanity at the time of the trial. The court will wait and make further determinations in the future. If, at some time, the defendant is declared to be fit for trial, then the trial will proceed. The defendant can then raise any affirmative defense he or she wishes, including legal insanity.

The defense of insanity at the time of trial was attempted in the Elizabeth Smart kidnapping case. In 2002, Smart was kidnapped at the age of 14 and held captive by Brian David Mitchell and Wanda Barzee for nine months. At first, a forensic psychiatrist found that both Mitchell and Barzee were unfit to stand trial. Mitchell, in particular, was diagnosed as a paranoid schizophrenic, based on his belief that he was divinely inspired and on a par with Jesus or God. However, a second forensic psychiatrist determined that Mitchell was a malingerer, faking his illness in order to avoid trial. Eventually, a U.S. district judge ruled that both Mitchell and Barzee were competent to stand trial for kidnapping and unlawful transportation of a minor across state lines for the purpose of illegal sexual activity. Barzee pleaded guilty, and Mitchell was convicted.

e. Raising the Insanity Defense

The defendant who wishes to use the defense of insanity must serve notice on the state prior to trial that she plans to do so. This notice allows the state to bring in its own experts to evaluate the defendant and offer their own opinion about the state of the defendant's sanity at the time that the crime occurred. At the trial, the defense will present its own expert witnesses to testify that the defendant was not legally sane at the time that she committed the crime, and the state will then, in rebuttal, present evidence that the defendant was legally sane when the defendant committed the crime. In the end, it becomes a battle of the experts, and the jury is left to decide which expert to believe. If they believe the defense expert, then they must find the defendant either not guilty by reason of insanity or, in the states that have this verdict alternative, guilty but mentally ill.

Having said all of this, the insanity defense is rarely used and is even less likely to be successful. Part of this rests with the burden placed on the defense to present believable evidence that the defendant did not know the difference between right and wrong when the crime occurred. Any action that a defendant took to conceal the crime, dispose of evidence, or flee indicates that the defendant understood all too well that what she did was wrong.

Sidebar

The insanity defense is rarely used, and even when it is, it is usually not successful.

f. Burden of Proof for the Defendant When Raising the Insanity Defense

As is true with many other affirmative defenses, the defendant who raises the defense of insanity must present enough evidence to establish by a preponderance of evidence that she is legally insane. In some jurisdictions the standard the defendant must meet is "clear and convincing" evidence of legal insanity. Once the defendant has presented this evidence, the prosecution must rebut the defendant's evidence. The government must show that the defendant was legally sane at the time of the crime.

g. Diminished Capacity

The defense of **diminished capacity** is a form of insanity defense. Although it is not recognized in all jurisdictions, the defense of diminished capacity allows a defendant to offer testimony and evidence about his mental condition. This evidence is intended to mitigate or excuse the defendant's guilt in the crime. Often, diminished capacity defenses focus on the *mens rea* element of a crime. A defendant presents evidence of lower-than-normal IQ or slow mental development as a

Diminished capacity
Inability of the defendant to understand the actions that he took and why his actions constituted a crime.

way to show the jury that he lacked the ability to form *mens rea.* In specific intent cases, such as murder, diminished capacity may be used as a defense to show that the defendant lacked the ability to form specific intent and therefore could not be guilty of first-degree murder.[5] The problem with diminished capacity defenses is defining exactly what a diminished capacity is. For instance, courts have held that a defendant does not fall under the category of diminished capacity if he suffers from mood swings, feelings of insecurity, overwhelming fear of disease, or inability to care about others.[6]

h. Irresistible Impulse

Irresistible impulse is an offshoot as a refinement of the M'Naghten test that provides that a defendant can be found legally insane if, even though he knew the difference between right and wrong, he was unable to control himself from committing the crime. The impulse, in essence, is so powerful that it overcomes the individual's will. A defendant who brings this defense must show that he has the lost the power to choose right from wrong, not that he did not know the difference between right and wrong.

9. INTOXICATION

Voluntary intoxication is not a defense to most crimes. Permitting a defendant to avoid responsibility for a crime by getting drunk would not serve society's interests. However, there are times when voluntary intoxication does affect criminal liability. There are instances where voluntary intoxication might help reduce a crime from the most severe to a lesser-included offense. For instance, in the crime of murder in the first degree, the state must prove that the defendant specifically intended to cause the death of another human being with malice and premeditation. A person who is severely intoxicated, even if this intoxication is the result of his own actions, may cause the state some trouble in proving premeditation. The defendant might have been acting out of some warped sense of right and wrong. This does not mean that the defendant cannot be charged with murder; it simply means that it might reduce a charge of first-degree murder to second-degree murder. However, except for this narrow exception, voluntary intoxication is not a defense to a crime and will lessen neither the defendant's culpability nor the ultimate sentence.

a. "Involuntary" Intoxication May Be a Defense

Although voluntary intoxication is not a defense to crime, involuntary intoxication may be. Involuntary intoxication results when a person is overcome by fumes or

---

[5] *State v. Warden,* 133 Wash. 2d 559 (1997).

[6] *State v. Wilburn,* 249 Kan. 678, 822 P.2d 609 (1991).

chemicals to such an extent that he is no longer capable of rational thought. When the defendant is overcome with these substances, and has not voluntary induced this state, he may not be criminally liable. Situations that bring about involuntary intoxication are rare and might include a worker in a factory where dangerous chemicals have been accidentally released or the defendant who has been unknowingly exposed to fumes or toxins.

10. MISTAKE

When a defendant raises the defense of mistake, he is saying that although he committed the crime, he was not aware that it was a crime. We have all heard the statement that ignorance of the law is no excuse. Mistake is an affirmative defense that attempts to override that maxim. As we have seen several times throughout this chapter, many affirmative defenses go towards the *mens rea* part of a crime, either attempting to show that the defendant had no *mens reas* (age, insanity) or that the defendant had the requisite *mens rea,* but his actions should be excused for some other reason. But *mens rea* has never required that the prosecution prove that the defendant intended to commit a crime. That is reserved only for specific-intent crimes like murder or rape. All other crimes simply require a showing that the defendant was aware of his actions and acted voluntarily. Suppose that a defendant states to the jury that he believed he was committing a legal action that turned out to be illegal. Is that a crime? The answer in almost every instance is a clear yes. The only time that mistake can be a successful defense is when it negates the defendant's intent. If the mistake can actually be shown to prove that the defendant did not have *mens rea,* then mistake can work successfully. However, most criminal situations do not lend themselves to such a claim. Mistake is also not available as a defense for certain crimes, such as statutory rape. In that crime, the defendant is charged with having sexual relations with a female who is under a certain age. Even if he had good reason to believe that the female was over 18 years of age, he will not be permitted to present the defense of mistake. Mistake is also not available to a defendant who sets out to injure or kill a specific person and kills another person instead. In this case, mistake will not mitigate or excuse his actions.

EXAMPLE

Morris has recently arrived in the United States from a different country. Where he comes from, it is not a crime to strike your wife. During an argument, Morris slaps his wife for what he considers to be a disobedient statement. Several witnesses report him to the local police. Morris explains to the officers that he has not committed a crime. They inform him that striking anyone, including your spouse, is a crime in the United States. Morris states that he didn't know that and he will never do it again, now that he knows. Can he be prosecuted for battery?

Answer: Yes. Despite the fact that the action Morris took may or may not be legal in his own country, he is now in the United States and must abide by its laws. This is true even if he truly believed that his actions were legal.

EXAMPLE

Rick and Diane throw a party at their house. Unfortunately, everyone has too much to drink, including Diane's twin sister. Diane's sister collapses in Rick and Diane's bed and passes out. Later, Rick comes to bed in the darkened room and begins to fondle the woman he believes is his wife. Diane's sister wakes up and accuses Rick of trying to rape her. Can Rick be prosecuted for attempted rape or sexual battery?

Answer: No. If Rick genuinely believed that the woman in his bed was his wife and all indications certainly point to that as a believable assumption, then Rick has no *mens rea* and has a genuine defense of mistake.

11. MUTUAL COMBAT

The affirmative defense of mutual combat arises when the defendant and the victim agree to fight one another. Similar to consent, when a victim agrees to enter into a fight, he essentially surrenders his right to bring charges for battery against the other fighter. However, mutual combat has some strict limitations. If the defendant exceeds the understanding of what weapons will be used in the fight, or uses excessive force, mutual combat as a defense may not be available.

EXAMPLE

Two men are in a bar and begin to argue. The argument leads to pushing and shoving, and the two men decide to "take it outside." Once outside, however, one man pulls out a knife and stabs the other man, causing him severe injuries but not killing him. Does the man with the knife have a valid defense of mutual combat?

Answer: No. Mutual combat assumes that both parties have the same weapons and defenses. There was nothing to indicate that either man was armed when they both went outside, but when the other man pulled a knife, that exceeded the implied terms of the fight. The defense of mutual combat will not be available to the man with the knife.[7]

12. NECESSITY

The affirmative defense of necessity is similar to duress. When a defendant claims necessity, he admits that he committed the crime, but in this case, he did so in order to avoid some catastrophe or some force of nature. A common example of necessity is when someone breaks into a cabin to avoid a blizzard. Normally, he would be guilty of trespass or criminal damages to property; however, the offense is excused by his need to stay alive. In this case, breaking into the cabin was the lesser of two evils: committing a crime or dying. In applying the defense of necessity, most jurisdictions require that the danger to the defendant outweigh the damage he does in committing the crime. A defendant could not use the defense of necessity in attempting to excuse a murder, for example, because all jurisdictions have held that no danger outweighs the value of another person's life.

[7] *Martin v. State*, 258 Ga. 300, 368 S.E.2d 515 (1988).

13. SELF-DEFENSE

Self-defense is, perhaps second only to insanity, the most misunderstood of defenses. Under the law, a person always has the right to defend himself against a physical threat. However, there are severe limitations on this affirmative defense. In most situations, the response of the person raising the claim of self-defense must be comparable to the threat. This means that when someone is threatening the defendant with bare fists, the defendant is not permitted to retaliate with a weapon. The claim of self-defense seeks to excuse the defendant's actions by showing that they were necessary to keep the defendant alive. In order to use self-defense, the defendant must admit that he used force, but only for protection. When self-defense is raised, most jurisdictions require the jury to make a determination as to whether or not the defendant acted reasonably when he used force. If the jury finds that the defendant did not act reasonably, the jury could refuse to take self-defense into account.[8]

What if the victim had a reputation for being a violent and aggressive person? Could the defendant present such evidence to prove that the defendant acted reasonably? The answer is: maybe. In most jurisdictions, if the defendant was aware of the victim's violent history, it may be admissible. However, if the defendant did not know the victim's history, it probably would not be admissible. The reason for this discrepancy is simple. Self-defense has a great deal to do with what was in the defendant's mind at the time of the attack. If the defendant didn't know that the victim was a violent person, then he couldn't have based his actions on this fact.

Does self-defense apply to protecting other people? Under the common law, a person could only defend another person with whom he had a close, legally recognized relationship. Parents could defend children; husbands could defend wives. But at common law, a stranger could not use force to defend another stranger. That rule is no longer followed in most jurisdictions. Like self-defense, however, the other person must be faced with the immediate threat of bodily injury before the stranger acted to defend him. The threat must be one that a reasonable person would perceive as a threat.

Violence, especially deadly force, is not permitted to protect property, only people. If a person is stealing Joe's car, Joe does not have the right to use deadly force to protect his property. In fact, deadly force can be used only when a person is presented with deadly force. It cannot be used to protect property, no matter how precious or expensive the property is.

a. Defendant As Aggressor

A defendant cannot use the defense of self-defense when she is the person who started the fight. Aggressors are not permitted to raise the claim of self-defense when they attack a person and that person fights back. There are also other times when a defendant cannot use self-defense. Individuals who are trained in the

[8] *State v. Adams*, 52 Conn. App. 643, 727 A.2d 780 (1999).

martial arts or are professional fighters or have advanced military training may be considered to be using deadly force even when they respond with their bare hands. These individuals must be much more cautious before they engage in physical confrontations because their greater skill and training makes their hands and feet "deadly weapons" as far as self-defense is concerned.

b. Rebutting a Claim of Self-Defense

Like all affirmative defenses, the state has the burden of disproving one or more of the elements of the self-defense beyond a reasonable doubt. To do this, the state must present evidence in rebuttal showing that the defendant's actions were not justified, either because the defendant used excessive force or because the defendant was the aggressor.

14. UNUSUAL DEFENSES

At various points, defendants have come up with a wide variety of novel and interesting defenses. Among the more unusual and generally ineffective defenses are claims that antidepressant drugs caused the defendant to black out and commit murders.[9] Other defenses have attempted to show that the defendant had watched too much violent television programming, was addicted to sugar, and suffered from premenstrual syndrome, among others. These novel defenses have rarely been successful. A case that was successful and garnered intense publicity was when Dan White, a former San Francisco supervisor, assassinated Mayor George Moscone and Supervisor Harvey Milk in 1978. At trial, the defense claimed that White suffered from diminished capacity because his overconsumption of sugary foods and drinks resulted in severe depression. In this case, the so-called Twinkie Defense worked. White was convicted of the lesser charge of voluntary manslaughter instead of first-degree murder. Ironically, the public outcry over the verdict led to the elimination of diminished-capacity law in California.

V CONSTITUTIONAL DEFENSES

The Fifth Amendment, shown in Figure 8-6, provides numerous protections to a person accused of a crime. However, since this amendment is part of the U.S. Constitution, a question that lingered in the republic for decades after the founding of our country was whether this amendment applied to the states. The Civil War helped to answer that question. The Fourteenth Amendment, shown in Figure 8-7, voted into existence as a direct result of the Civil War, decreed that the United States Constitution—and most of the Bill of Rights—would apply to all states.

---

[9] *State v. Clemons*, 82 Ohio St. 3d 438, 696 N.E.2d 1009 (1998).

No person shall be held to answer for a capital, or otherwise infamous crime, unless on a presentment or indictment of a Grand Jury, except in cases arising in the land or naval forces, or in the Militia, when in actual service in time of War or public danger; nor shall any person be subject for the same offence to be twice put in jeopardy of life or limb; nor shall be compelled in any criminal case to be a witness against himself, nor be deprived of life, liberty, or property, without due process of law; nor shall private property be taken for public use, without just compensation.

FIGURE 8-6

The Fifth Amendment

A. EQUAL PROTECTION

The Fifth and Fourteenth Amendments require that all citizens be treated fairly. As far as criminal law is concerned, this means that people falling into different socioeconomic, religious, or racial categories cannot be treated differently under the law. Any law that contains classifications based on these factors is immediately suspect and may be found unconstitutional.

B. DUE PROCESS

The due process clause requires that the same procedures be used in all criminal cases. The rules do not change when someone is "obviously" guilty as opposed to someone who "may" be guilty.

EXAMPLE

Ron was arrested last night and gave a full confession to murdering his wife. He wants to plead guilty and he says that he wants to receive the death penalty. Can the state bypass the initial appearance, the preliminary hearing, and the arraignment, among other items, and move directly to the sentencing phase?

Answer: No. Due process requires that the rules should be followed in every case, even when a defendant has confessed and is obviously guilty. Ron may, after all, change his mind later in the process, and the safest course to follow (and the one that meets constitutional muster) is to follow criminal procedure in this case the same way that the state follows it in other cases.

All persons born or naturalized in the United States, and subject to the jurisdiction thereof, are citizens of the United States and of the State wherein they reside. No State shall make or enforce any law which shall abridge the privileges or immunities of citizens of the United States; nor shall any State deprive any person of life, liberty, or property, without due process of law; nor deny to any person within its jurisdiction the equal protection of the laws.

FIGURE 8-7

The Fourteenth Amendment, Section 1

C. DOUBLE JEOPARDY

The Fifth Amendment creates several rights in very few words. Among those rights is the protection of double jeopardy. At its simplest, the Fifth Amendment prohibits a person from being tried twice for the same crime if that person was found not guilty in the first trial. This is true even if the state later discovers new evidence that conclusively proves that the defendant committed the crime. The defendant, once tried and found not guilty, can even admit to committing the crime, and the government can still not prosecute him. Of course, there are limits to this right, just as there are for all others. Although a defendant cannot be tried again for the same crime, a different jurisdiction, such as the federal government, might try the defendant for a different crime. In the example above, involving Ron's murder charge against his wife, suppose that the jury found him not guilty? In that case, the federal government might charge him with denying his wife her constitutional rights (by killing her). It is not the same charge and it is not brought by the same jurisdiction, so there is no prohibition against a new case proceeding. However, the federal charge will not carry anything like the type of sentence that Ron might have received had he been found guilty of murder.

An excellent example is the O. J. Simpson case. Simpson was acquitted of two counts of murder in the deaths of his wife, Nicole, and her friend, Ron Goldman. After the acquittal, the families of Nicole Simpson and Ron Goldman sued Simpson for damages in a civil trial. The jury found that there was a preponderance of evidence to hold Simpson liable for the two deaths and awarded damages of $33.5 million. The two trials did not amount to double jeopardy, because the first trial was in criminal court for murder, and the second trial was in civil court for damages.

One of the key points in analyzing double jeopardy is answering this question: When does it apply? Clearly, a defendant cannot be retried if the jury finds him not guilty. However, what if the jury cannot reach a verdict and a mistrial is declared? In the case of a mistrial, the parties are put back into a posture as though the trial had never occurred. Obviously, it is very important to a criminal defendant when this right of double jeopardy "attaches."

Various states have approached the problem of when the protection of double jeopardy attaches. For instance, what if a prosecutor, realizing that his case is not going very well, deliberately causes a mistrial? Should he be free to try the defendant again? The general rule is that double jeopardy attaches when the jury is sworn and enters the jury box. A clever defendant, knowing this, might try to cause a mistrial. Many states have addressed this issue by declaring that if the prosecution deliberately causes a mistrial, the case cannot be retried, but if the defendant deliberately causes a mistrial, the case can be retried.

Once a defendant has been found guilty and brings an appeal, this appeal is not a violation of the Fifth Amendment, because an appeal is not a new trial. It is a review of the first trial. This is true even if the appellate court orders a new trial because of some defect in the original case. In that eventuality, the original trial and its result are thrown out, and the parties must proceed as if the first trial never happened and try the case all over again. This means that the same witnesses will be called and the same evidence introduced. If several years have passed since the first trial (which is very common), it may be difficult or impossible for the state to retry the defendant.

D. VAGUENESS AND OVERBREADTH

The same constitutional protections that we have seen above also apply to claims that a particular statute is vague or overbroad. A defendant may challenge the statute under which she has been charged by claiming that the statute is worded in such a vague manner that people of common intelligence would have to guess at its meaning. The underlying principle in criminal law is that people must be able to figure out what is and is not illegal. When a statute fails to make this notice clear, a court may declare it unconstitutional.

In a similar vein, a court may strike down a statute if it is overbroad. A statute that is overbroad is one that makes constitutionally protected and *unprotected* activities equally illegal. A statute that criminalizes the homeless, for example, when they carry out inoffensive conduct, is considered overbroad.[10]

E. BILLS OF ATTAINDER AND EX POST FACTO LAWS

A bill of attainder is a legislative action attempting to short-circuit a criminal trial and declare an individual guilty of a crime (usually treason). Bills of attainder are not permitted in the United States. Challenges to a law based on a claim that it is a bill of attainder are extremely rare. Instead, it is far more common to base a claim on ex post facto laws.

1. EX POST FACTO

An ex post facto law is one that criminalizes behavior or increases punishment for an action *after* it has already occurred. In many cases, a person may carry out an activity that is not technically illegal. For instance, when the crime of computer hacking first began, most states had no statute on the books that made this illegal. The prohibition against ex post facto laws prevents the legislature from making that action illegal, after the fact, just to punish that individual. The legislature can, and often does, address the situation by enacting laws, but these laws only apply to people who commit the crime *after* the statute has been enacted. Ex post facto defenses also apply to sentences. A person's sentence must reflect the law at the time he committed the action. The legislature cannot, in a fit of outrage, seek to enhance the punishment for a particularly gruesome crime. The legislature can only enhance the sentence for others who commit it. The constitutional limit of

---

[10] *Pottinger v. Miami*, 810 F. Supp. 1551.

ex post facto means that these new statutes cannot be applied to a defendant who committed the crime before the new law was created.

VI SHOULD THE DEFENDANT TESTIFY?

The final decision that the defense team must consider is whether to put the defendant on the stand to testify in his own trial. Although it might seem obvious that all defendants should testify, if for no other reason than to let the jury hear the defendant deny the charge, there are several factors that weigh against putting the defendant on the stand. Although the defense attorney can control the questioning during direct examination, the defendant would then be subject to cross-examination by the prosecutor. The prosecutor will, no doubt, go after the defendant on any discrepancy between the defendant's version of the case and the victim's description. Prosecutors are usually very good at cross-examining witnesses—after all, they do it all the time. A good cross-examination can destroy all of the careful work that a defense attorney has put into creating a valid affirmative defense. But there is one other reason to avoid putting the defendant on the stand: his criminal record.

A. THE DEFENDANT'S CHARACTER IN EVIDENCE

Under the federal rules of criminal procedure and many states' rules, the moment that the defendant takes the stand, the defendant can be cross-examined about his criminal record. Up to this point, the jury will have no idea that the defendant has a criminal record. The prosecutor and state's witnesses are forbidden to mention the fact, and if they do, even inadvertently, the judge will declare a mistrial. However, all of that goes out the window when the defendant takes the stand to testify in his own trial. One of the first actions a prosecutor may take on cross-examination is to go over the defendant's criminal history, point by point, so that the jury understands that the defendant has extensive convictions (if that happens to be the case). Not all states follow this pattern, however. In some states, a defendant must make some statement that puts his criminal record into dispute. Attorneys refer to this as putting the "defendant's character in evidence." Until the defendant makes some statement that opens the door to his criminal history, prosecutors in these states are forbidden to bring up the defendant's criminal record. However, regardless of the rules about putting the defendant's character in evidence, most defense attorneys advise their clients not to testify. They know too well that a skilled prosecutor can tear the defendant's story to ribbons, which may even be the key to the defendant's conviction.

As you're reading the following case excerpt, pay close attention to the concept of alibi charge. Evaluate the defendant's request in light of the legal definition of alibi as well as the rules for a valid alibi charge.

COM. v. POINDEXTER

646 A.2d 1211 (1994)

CASE EXCERPT

CIRILLO, Judge.

This is an appeal from the judgment of sentence entered in the Court of Common Pleas of Allegheny County. We affirm.

A jury found defendant Rufus Poindexter guilty of one count of rape, two counts of involuntary deviate sexual intercourse, one count of statutory rape, and one count of corruption of minors. Poindexter filed post-trial motions for a new trial and an arrest of judgment. New counsel, Robert M. Barrett, was then secured and an additional motion for a new trial was filed.

The Honorable Walter R. Little denied Poindexter's post-trial motions on August 16, 1993. Poindexter was immediately sentenced as follows: on the rape conviction, not less than five nor more than fifteen years incarceration; on the involuntary deviate sexual intercourse conviction, not less than five nor more than fifteen years incarceration, concurrent with that imposed on the rape conviction; on the corruption of minors conviction, incarceration of not less than one nor more than five years, to run consecutive to the sentence imposed on the rape conviction; and on the second involuntary deviate sexual intercourse conviction, not less than five nor more than fifteen years of imprisonment, concurrent with that imposed on the rape conviction. A finding of guilt with no further penalty was entered with respect to the statutory rape conviction.

After sentencing, Poindexter timely filed a notice of appeal from the judgment of sentence. Poindexter presents the following issues for our review:

Whether the trial court erred in failing to grant a request for an alibi charge?

Poindexter's contention is that the trial court erred in failing to grant his request for an alibi charge. Specifically, Poindexter claims that, despite failing to provide the prosecution with adequate notice of his intention to pursue an alibi defense, the court was nonetheless required to charge the jury with an alibi instruction, as evidence of Poindexter's alibi was introduced at trial. We disagree.

The Pennsylvania Supreme Court has defined alibi as "a defense that places the defendant at the relevant time in a different place than the scene involved and so removed therefrom as to render it impossible for him to be the guilty party." Commonwealth v. Roxberry, 529 Pa. 160, 163, 602 A.2d 826, 827 (1992).

An alibi instruction is required if the defendant presents evidence which covers the time period when the crime was committed and which puts him at a different location than that of the crime scene. It is not necessary for an alibi defense to be corroborated in order to constitute an alibi. See Roxberry, 529 Pa. at 165, 602 A.2d at 828; Commonwealth v. Saunders, 529 Pa. 140, 602 A.2d 816 (1991); Commonwealth v. Willis, 520 Pa. 289, 553 A.2d 959 (1989) (all requiring an alibi instruction when the alibi defense had been presented solely by the unsupported testimony of the defendant). There is no minimum or threshold quantum of physical separation necessary for a defense to constitute an alibi, so long as the separation makes it impossible for the defendant to have committed the crime. Id.

It will be the duty of the trial judge to carefully instruct the jury as to the relationship of the evidence of the prosecution and the evidence of the defendant as each bears upon the essential elements of the crime charged. Where an alibi defense is presented, such an instruction is necessary due to the danger that the failure to prove the defense will be taken by the jury as a sign of the defendant's guilt. The instruction on alibi is to emphasize that the defendant is not required to disprove any elements of the crime charged, but that the defense's evidence of alibi, even if not wholly believed, may create a reasonable doubt.

The right to present evidence of an alibi and to receive a jury instruction therefrom, however, is not absolute. In order to obtain this right, a defendant must comply with the notice requirement set forth in Rule 305 of the Pennsylvania Rules of Criminal Procedure. Rule 305 provides that if a defendant intends to offer the defense of alibi at trial, the defendant must file of record notice prior to trial with the prosecuting attorney. Such notice must contain specific information as to the place or places where defendant claims to have been at the time of the alleged offense and the names and addresses of witnesses whom the defendant intends to call in support of such claim. Pa.R.Crim.P. 305(C)(1)(a). Furthermore, Rule 305 also provides, in part:

> If the defendant fails to file and serve notice of alibi defense as required by this rule, or omits any witness from such notice, the court at trial may exclude the testimony of any omitted witness, or may exclude entirely any evidence offered by the defendant for the purpose of proving the defense, except testimony by the defendant, or may grant a continuance to enable the Commonwealth to investigate such evidence, or may make such other order as the interests of justice require. Pa.R.Crim.P. 305(C)(1)(d).

Accordingly, Rule 305 enables the trial court, when the notice requirement is not met, to take such measures as preventing an alibi witness from testifying and to deny a request for an alibi instruction. Rule 305 is "designed to enhance the search for truth in the criminal trial by insuring both the defendant and the state ample opportunity to investigate certain facts crucial to the determination of guilt or innocence."

In Commonwealth v. Anthony, 376 Pa.Super. 623, 546 A.2d 1122 (1988), the defendant presented a defense of alibi. Not only did he testify to his whereabouts, but he attempted to call two other people as witnesses to corroborate his story. Id. at 627, 546 A.2d at 1124. The defendant, in that case, failed to give adequate notice of his defense until the day of the trial. The court prohibited the alibi witness from testifying, concluding that the defendant failed to give adequate notice of his intent to present a defense of alibi, thus denying the Commonwealth the opportunity to investigate the alibi. Accordingly, because the court had the discretion to exclude that testimony under Pa.R.Crim.P. 305(C)(1)(d), we concluded that the court did not err in prohibiting the alibi witnesses from testifying. Id. See also Commonwealth v. Zimmerman, 391 Pa.Super. 569, 575-78, 571 A.2d 1062, 1065-67 (1992) (holding that defendant violated Rule 305, failing to timely file a notice of an alibi defense, and was properly precluded from introducing alibi evidence).

In the case at hand, Poindexter failed to provide notice, prior to trial, of his intention to present the defense of alibi to the prosecution. Despite such failure, Poindexter elicited testimony at trial as to the incident occurring on December 25th. The record discloses that the testimony of Poindexter does not establish a defense of alibi for the crime on December 25th. The victim testified that the sexual assault occurred in Poindexter's home after 4:00 P.M. on December 25, 1992. Poindexter testified that he was out with friends all night on Christmas Eve until Christmas morning. He further stated that he was in and out of his home, 446 Rosedale, all day on the 25th, but that he returned to his home and went to sleep around 4 P.M.

Concerning the December 25th incident, Poindexter's own testimony, during trial, placed him in his home at the time the incident occurred on December 25th. Therefore, due to Poindexter's own admission that did not place him away from the scene of the crime at the relevant time, and so removed therefrom as to render it impossible for him to be the guilty party, he was not entitled to an alibi instruction with respect to the December 25th charge.

As to the incident on December 27, 1992, Poindexter was more successful at establishing a potential alibi. The victim testified that her mother went to Poindexter's mother's house to bake a cake. She stated that when her mother left, Poindexter made her suck his "private part" and put his "private part" in her "private part" and in her "butt." On December 29, 1992, the victim told Officer Billups, at Children's Hospital, that between 11 P.M. and 11:30 P.M. on the 27th, after her mother left for Poindexter's mother's house, Poindexter assaulted her.

At trial, Poindexter presented the testimony of Debra Fisher, his ex-wife. Both Poindexter and Ms. Fisher testified at trial that Poindexter, Barbara Ramsey, and Debra Fisher were at Ms. Fisher's home from approximately 10:00 or 10:30 on the evening until 12:30 or 12:45 in the morning. According to Fisher's testimony, Poindexter arrived with Barbara Ramsey at 10:00 or 10:30 in the evening to bring a birthday cake for Poindexter's son. Fisher testified that the victim was not with the couple. Ms. Fisher also stated that she was sure of the time they had left, because she was having company at 1:00 A.M. and she wanted Poindexter and Ms. Ramsey out of her home.

Poindexter stated that on the 27th of December, he was at his mother's house preparing for his son's birthday party. He said he went down to his mother's house about 7:00 P.M. Poindexter then testified that he and Barbara Ramsey left his mother's house around 9:00 P.M. and headed for Debra Fisher's house. He stated that the victim remained at his mother's home until they returned from Ms. Fisher's house at 1:00 A.M. He then gave the key to the apartment to Barbara Ramsey, and Ms. Ramsey and the victim walked to Poindexter's home. Poindexter further testified that he did not return to his home until approximately 2:00 in the morning because he stayed at his mother's and cleaned up the mess from baking the cake.

As to the crime committed on December 25th, as stated earlier, we agree with the court that Poindexter's alibi evidence did not place him away from the scene of the crime at the relevant time and he, therefore, was not entitled to an alibi instruction for that incident. However, we disagree with the court concerning Poindexter's alibi evidence for December 27th. In Repaci, supra, we stated that the evaluation of evidence for an alibi requires a court to take all pertinent testimony as true. Repaci, 419 Pa.Super. at 595, 615 A.2d at 798. It does not, however, require us to treat testimony, which is offered with uncertainty, as if it were certain. Id. In Repaci, we stated that "if the alibi witness had testified that he had seen defendant in the sub shop between 10:00 P.M. and 10:30 P.M., it would be the trial court's and our responsibility to view that evidence as if it were true, in order to determine if that version of the facts would preclude the possibility that appellee was the guilty party." Id.

In the instant case, Ms. Fisher testified that Poindexter was at her home from 10:00 in the evening on December 27th until around 12:30 or 12:45 the next morning. Poindexter corroborated the testimony that he was at Ms. Fisher's home from approximately 10:00 P.M. on the 27th to 12:30 or 1:00 the next morning. The victim testified and the police officers confirmed her testimony, that around 11:00 or 11:30 on the evening of the 27th, the victim was sexually assaulted.

We are required to take all pertinent testimony as true in order to determine if that version of the facts would preclude the possibility that Poindexter is the guilty party. The testimony, taken as whole, presents evidence which covers the time period when the crime was allegedly committed and which puts Poindexter at a different location than that of the crime. Such testimony constitutes evidence of alibi.

At the close of testimony, after the charge to the jury, Poindexter requested that the jury be instructed as to the defense of alibi. Judge Little summarily denied this request for an alibi instruction to the jury citing Rule 305 of the Rules of Criminal Procedure, failure to give notice of any alibi defense. Specifically, Judge Little stated in the record:

THE COURT: You never gave the Commonwealth notice of any alibi defense. You know the rules of discovery; 305, 306 and 307.

MR. HOUCK: Still request one, your Honor.

THE COURT: How can you request an alibi notice when you did not follow the rules and give the Commonwealth notice of alibi?

MR. HOUCK: My argument was that he was not present and that was his testimony.

THE COURT: But you never presented that alibi, notice of alibi testimony to the Commonwealth which you're required to do under the rules; okay?

We find that this ruling was entirely within the discretion and authority of the trial court. Rule 305(C)(1)(d) clearly enables the trial court to take whatever action is within the interests of justice, when no notice is properly provided as to the alibi defense. Judge Little, therefore, acted properly in denying Poindexter's request for an alibi instruction. Zimmerman, supra; Anthony, supra.

In the opinion written pursuant to Pa.R.A.P. 1925(a), the trial court misapprehended the facts in determining that Poindexter's testimony precluded him from receiving an alibi instruction. Poindexter's testimony, along with that of his witness, did provide an alibi. However, Poindexter failed to give notice of an alibi defense, a violation of Rule 305. On these grounds, it is clear that the court was not in error when it denied Poindexter's request for an alibi instruction.

Judgment of sentence affirmed.

CASE QUESTIONS

1 What were the charges against Poindexter?
2 Should the trial court have overturned the decision based on proof of Poindexter's alibi?
3 Did Poindexter have reasonable grounds to request an alibi defense?
4 Is an alibi notice required to have an alibi defense?
5 Was the trial court in error by not providing Poindexter with an alibi charge?

CHAPTER SUMMARY

In this chapter, we have seen how defense attorneys prepare for trial. One of the most important aspects of representing a client is when and how the attorney-client relationship with the defendant is formed. That relationship does not necessarily depend on the payment of a fee. Instead, it is established when an attorney gives the defendant legal advice and agrees to represent the client. Defense attorneys must do a great deal of preparatory work in order to be ready to defend a case. Pretrial investigation will center on the witnesses and evidence, as well as the defendant's version of the case, but it will also consist of numerous pretrial motions that the defense may file in order to learn more about the case. Defense attorneys routinely file motions seeking to lower the defendant's bond so that he may remain free prior to trial and so that they can continue to earn a living and help the defense attorney prepare the case. The defense may also consider filing other motions, such as a demand for a speedy trial, which puts the prosecution into the difficult position of either trying the defendant within this term of court or the next or the defendant will automatically be acquitted. Defense attorneys may also file motions for change of venue when a case has received a great deal of pretrial publicity.

As the trial comes closer, the defense attorney will meet with any defense witnesses and prepare them for testifying at trial. The defense team must consider what type of defense it will raise during the trial, knowing that, unlike the prosecution, their burden for raising a defense is often a simple preponderance of the evidence, not proof beyond a reasonable doubt. There are numerous types of defenses that a defendant can bring. Some are automatic and are referred to as simple defenses. These are the defenses that are provided for in the U.S. and state Constitutions, and consist of defenses such as equal protection and due process under the law. However, a defense attorney might also bring an affirmative defense, such as alibi or insanity. In that situation, the attorney must present evidence to support the defense. In order to bring an affirmative defense at trial, a defense attorney must file notice on the prosecution that it intends to raise a specific defense.

KEY TERMS

Key terms are listed here in order of appearance in chapter.

Preponderance of evidence
Simple defense
Affirmative defense
Mens rea
Rebuttal
Actus reus
Complete defense
Battered woman's syndrome
Diminished capacity

REVIEW QUESTIONS

1. How is the process of investigating a case different for the defense and the prosecution?
2. What is a simple defense?
3. Provide a list of at least five affirmative defenses that a criminal defendant might raise in a case.
4. What is the defendant's burden of proof in presenting a defense? Explain.
5. Is the defendant required to give the prosecutor notice when the defendant intends to raise particular defenses? If so, which defenses?
6. What is rebuttal, and why might a prosecutor use it?
7. Under what circumstances is a defendant allowed to claim self-defense?
8. When is a person authorized to use deadly force?
9. Is consent a defense to all crimes?
10. Explain the difference between duress and necessity.
11. What are some of the considerations the defense team must go through before putting the defendant on the stand?
12. What is the legal definition of insanity?
13. Explain entrapment.
14. Is voluntary intoxication a complete defense? Why or why not?
15. When is the attorney-client relationship created between a defendant and a private attorney?
16. Explain the various ways in which a defense attorney might be compensated for her representation.

WEB SURFING

Ohio Public Defender System
http://www.opd.ohio.gov/

'Lectric Law Library:Attorney-Client Relationship
http://www.lectlaw.com/def/a113.htm

California Constitution, including Speedy Trial Demand
http://www.leginfo.ca.gov/.const/.article_1

EXERCISES

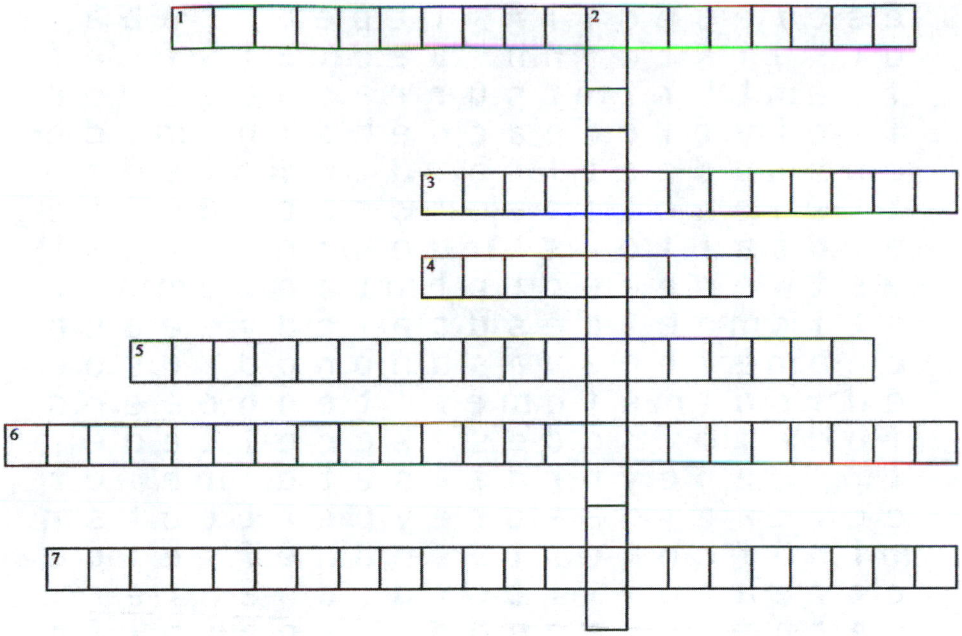

ACROSS

1. Inability of the defendant to understand the actions that he took and why his actions constituted a crime
3. A defense that is automatically triggered when a defendant is charged with a crime
4. Evidence offered by a party that directly refutes evidence or pleading by the opposing party
5. A defense that is something more than a mere denial and requires that the defense present evidence and/or testimony to establish
6. The greater weight of evidence, more than likely to be true
7. An affirmative defense that asks the jury to excuse a woman's attack on her supposed long-time abuser or asks the judge to mitigate her sentence in reflection of the fact that she was responding to a long period of abuse at the hands of the "victim"

DOWN

2. A defense that would completely exonerate the defendant of the crime charged, assuming the defendant presents sufficient evidence to meet his burden of proof

```
e a r f o c o d a c t m t b f n d t t s s e l
e c n e d i v e f o e c n a r e d n o p e r p
b e e p b s v t f e s p r t t e e l e e i e e
e s e r e u e d i i n f i t p e d e t n b a i
o r s a i s t d r n n ' a e e m a i s f e d f
f c e m t b r t m t p u r r a d a e e e r e c
i s o i y t i c a p a c d e h s i n i m i d n
e n s m p d e e t l t a m d t h m e i s d e p
t f w o p n c t i s e e m w s c c l d d ' t e
e f d c a l l o v s t m e o b r n a e v p s t
v s t w e n e e e c t p t m f a e e c m m s o
a t i c m d e t d e s d s a i e d y e e a e n
e e a m e f b h e v a s d n o n o d r o s u o
e d m s p i m e f d m r v ' t e n n c a e e d
f b d e i l i s e d e s e s e c e l e e d e t
t m r e e n e y n r d f a s e t e i m e l e t
e c r e a e i d s e c r e y p e t t t e t s m
m i n h i c n a e r l a s n d n e f m e l p e
c t r e a l o i i f t c t d s d o e n f e r m
b e t h m s b c e e e d e r e e e e m o i f e
a d t m n t m e b i t n e o f n n r e o a e f
e u d o s t e d u r m s s m p f d l t e c s s
a d f v e i o s m l m a d e o v o d f s n m e
```

preponderance of evidence
simple defense
affirmative defense
rebuttal
complete defense
battered woman's syndrome
diminished capacity

QUESTIONS FOR ANALYSIS

1 Should all jurisdictions, even rural ones, be required to have public defenders instead of using appointed systems to represent criminal defendants? What are some arguments for and against such a system?

2 Why is the defendant required to give the prosecution notice of alibi or insanity defenses? Aren't such defenses obvious to the prosecutor, and shouldn't the prosecutor already be prepared to deal with these defenses by the time of the trial?

3 Should the insanity defense be abolished? Is there a continued need for this defense?

Trial

9

Chapter Objectives

- **Explain the various rights that a defendant has during his trial**
- **Explain how the court must balance the right of the press against the right of the defendant to a fair trial**
- **Describe when and where a defendant has the right to be represented by an attorney**
- **Explain the basic layout of a trial courtroom**
- **List and describe the various phases of a jury trial**

I RIGHTS ASSOCIATED WITH TRIALS

In this first section, we will examine the rights associated with a jury trial. As we have already seen, a defendant enters a trial protected by certain constitutional guarantees and presumptions. The defendant is presumed innocent unless and until the prosecution presents sufficient evidence to prove beyond a reasonable doubt that the defendant committed the crime. Beyond this presumption, however, there are specific constitutional protections that all defendants have before and during a trial. Once we have discussed these rights, we will explain the basic layout of a courtroom and then describe the typical phases of a trial, from jury selection through the return of the jury's verdict. We will discuss sentencing and related issues in the next chapter.

A. THE RIGHT TO A PUBLIC TRIAL

In addition to a speedy trial, as we have seen, the Sixth Amendment also provides that a trial must be conducted in public. The Supreme Court has stated that the right to a public trial is one of the most important guarantees to a criminal defendant. "Without the freedom to attend such trials, which people have

PROFILING THE PROFESSIONAL

The "CSI" Effect

"Juries want more; they've always wanted more. But now they really want more because they see it on TV. I talk to the juries about it and tell them that they use tests on those shows that don't exist. I also have the people from the Crime Lab talk about it when they testify. They'll say, 'We don't have tests like that. There's no such test.' Or, if there is a test, 'It doesn't do what the TV people say it does.' They had a whole prosecutor's conference a couple of years ago about the 'CSI effect.' We had a statewide meeting and the forensics people came in and said, 'Here are the things that we can do and here are the things that we can't do.' You have to deal with the jurors and what they see on TV and it does affect them."

Debra Sullivan, Assistant District Attorney

exercised for centuries, important aspects of freedom of speech and of the press could be eviscerated."[1] Secret trials are the staple of totalitarian governments the world over. Opening a criminal trial to the public is a simple and efficient way to ensure that justice is served. When judges and prosecutors know that their actions can be monitored by any member of the public or the press, they tend to behave more responsibly.

It is possible to attend almost any trial. There are some proceedings that are closed to the public, such as juvenile hearings, but the vast majority of trials are open to anyone who wishes to attend, and the only limitation is space, which is allotted on a first-come, first-served basis. It is extremely rare to close even portions of a trial to the public. A judge is permitted to briefly close a trial only under extraordinary circumstances. Even though a trial is open to the public, there is nothing to prevent the judge from prohibiting specific individuals from appearing at trial, such as anyone who has threatened a witness or who engages in disruptive or violent behavior.[2]

There are only a few instances in which a trial judge is allowed to close a jury trial to the public, and even in these instances the judge may do so for only a brief period of time. The judge must show a "compelling interest" to close a portion of the trial from the public. The two most common instances involve testimony by rape victims or testimony by children about sexual acts committed on them. There is no standing rule that requires a trial to be closed at a certain point; indeed, the preference under American law is for all trials to remain open. For instance, in a case in which a state passed a statute that required a trial to be closed whenever a child sexual assault victim testified, the U.S. Supreme Court ruled that that is an infraction of the defendant's right to a public trial, and before any such closing is made, the judge must weigh the state's compelling interest (in this case, protecting

---

[1] *Richmond Newspapers, Inc. v. Virginia,* 100 S. Ct. 2814 (1980).
[2] *Estes v. Texas,* 381 U.S. 532 (1965).

the identity of the child) against the defendant's constitutional right to have an open and public trial. In that situation, the rule that required closure in all such cases was ruled to be unconstitutional.

It is not simply the trial that must remain open to the public, but also the jury selection process as well.[3] If jury selection involves some sensitive issues, the jurors can be questioned in the judge's chambers. There are also practical issues to be considered. In some instances, the size of the courtroom itself is the limiting factor, not the parties' intention of closing the trial—when a large jury pool is summoned for a case, there may not be available seating for anyone to sit and view the selection process.

Interestingly enough, the rule about open trials also applies to preliminary hearings and many other hearings, including motions, where important issues are decided. The only time the Supreme Court has allowed a preliminary hearing to be closed to the public is when the hearing may actually impinge on the defendant's right to a fair trial, such as when the case involves intensive pretrial publicity.[4]

In the 2010 trial of Steven Hayes, who was convicted of invading a Cheshire, Connecticut, home and killing a mother and her two daughters, the defense requested a closed court during pretrial arguments on whether the books Hayes had read while in prison could be admitted into evidence. Hayes's attorneys said that several of the books he had checked out from the prison library were "salacious and criminally malevolent in the extreme." The books' content, the attorneys claimed, was inflammatory and prejudicial to the defendant and would compromise his right to a fair trial. The judge ruled that the constitutional right of openness had not been overcome, and he refused to close the courtroom.

1. THE RIGHT OF THE PRESS

According to the First Amendment, "Congress shall make no law abridging the freedom of speech, or of the press." Because criminal trials are open to the public, they are also open to the press. But press coverage brings with it a whole host of other issues that are not seen when members of the general public are in attendance at a public trial. It is not uncommon for intensive press coverage to make it difficult for a defendant to receive a fair trial. As a result, there is an inherent conflict between two constitutional values: the right of the defendant to receive a fair trial and the freedom of the press. Neither right is ascendant over the other. In each case, the judge must weigh the constitutional values and reach some type of accommodation to balance the freedom of the press with the defendant's right to a fair trial. A judge cannot, for example, bar any press coverage of the trial, but a judge can prevent news organizations from bringing in cameras to televise or photograph the trial.[5] The defendant's right to a fair trial does not always

Sidebar

The right to a fair trial does not automatically take precedence over the freedom of the press and vice versa. In any criminal trial that the press is covering, the judge faces a delicate balancing act between the rights of the accused and the right of the press. Most trials receive no media attention at all, while others become "trials of the century" with nonstop, wall-to-wall coverage that can tax the patience of everyone involved.

[3] *Press Enterprise Co. v. Superior Court (Press Enterprise I)*, 464 U.S. 501 (1984).
[4] *Press Enterprise Co. v. Superior Court (Press Enterprise II)*, 478 U.S. 1 (1986).
[5] *Bridges v. California*, 314 U.S. 252 (1941).

trump the freedom of the press, so a judge must take both concerns into account in conducting the trial.

PROFILING THE PROFESSIONAL

Dealing with the Press

"Sometimes the hardest part of a trial isn't the trial. It's dealing with the press. They want access. They want a story. There's only so much that you can tell them during the case, but you don't want to simply give a 'no comment' and move on, especially if the other side is talking to the press. You have to walk a tightrope between protecting your client's interests and not saying too much to the press."

Prosecutor

Although we have seen that the press cannot be barred from the courtroom, this does not mean that the press has any greater freedom than any other member of the public. Reporters are not permitted access to the jurors during the trial any more than a member of the public would be. Even when the jurors are not sequestered and are allowed to go home at night during the course of the trial, they are instructed not to speak with the press about the case. If they do, then they risk being removed from the jury or even held in contempt by the judge. During breaks in the trial, when jurors are moving around the courthouse or even while they are out having lunch, none of the parties, witnesses, or reporters are allowed to speak with the jurors. This rule is strictly enforced. Jurors often wear badges that identify them as jurors on an active case, and that serves as a warning to all persons that the jurors should not be approached and asked questions about the trial. Jurors are informed that they should not discuss the case with anyone during the trial, not even their spouses. Only when the case is concluded are the jurors allowed the freedom to discuss the case among themselves while they decide their verdict. Once the case is concluded and the jury has returned its verdict, the jurors are then free to discuss the case with anyone they choose. They are also free to refuse to discuss the case, as they see fit. In some high-profile cases, members of the jury have written books about their experiences, but in the vast majority of jury trials, there is no press coverage, no throng of spectators, and no audience for a tell-all book about the proceedings.

Both the prosecutor and the defense attorney will instruct their witnesses to have no contact with the jury during the case. They may go so far as to advise their witnesses against even greeting the jurors or answering simple questions such as, "What time is it?" Attorneys for both sides want to avoid even the appearance that one of their witnesses is attempting to communicate with a juror during the trial.

Jury tampering/embracery The crime of attempting to influence a juror or jurors in their deliberations on a case.

If a person does approach a juror during the course of the trial and attempts to persuade the juror to vote a certain way, this is a crime known as **jury tampering** (or by the older name of **embracery**). In some states, the crime of embracery is a felony, but in most it is normally a misdemeanor carrying a maximum sentence of one year in prison.

B. THE RIGHT TO A JURY TRIAL

The Sixth Amendment guarantees that individuals who are charged with certain crimes must be given a jury trial. This does not mean, however, that everyone charged with any type of criminal offense must receive a jury trial. Instead, the Supreme Court has interpreted this amendment to mean that jury trials are warranted in some types of cases, but not in others. For instance, there are no jury trials in juvenile cases, primarily because the hearings are not considered to be adversarial or criminal. As we will see in Chapter 12, the entire juvenile court system is built around a different concept than what underpins the rest of criminal law: the rehabilitation of the juvenile.

Trials are also not guaranteed under the Sixth Amendment for petty offenses. The Supreme Court has interpreted that amendment to be reserved for "serious offenses." In that lexicon, a serious offense is one in which the potential sentence is more than six months in custody.[6] If the potential punishment for an offense is less than six months, a state does not have to provide a jury trial for the defendant.[7] This ruling applies even in situations in which the defendant is charged with several crimes, none of which can be punished by more than six months in custody but taken as consecutive sentences could result in the defendant serving more than six months in prison.

In order to determine whether a defendant's charge is considered a serious offense and therefore one in which he must receive a jury trial, the court will consider the maximum sentence allowed by law. Almost all statutes that criminalize behavior list not only the elements of each offense, but the range of punishments for those offenses (see Figure 9-1). In that situation, the judge would simply refer to the applicable statute to decide whether a jury trial is warranted. However, there are situations in which the state legislature has made a certain action criminal but has failed to provide a maximum sentence for the offense. In that case, the judge must determine what the possible maximum sentence is by researching similar offenses or by referring to common law (see Figure 9-2).

Sidebar

"In all criminal prosecutions, the accused shall enjoy the right to a speedy and public trial, by an impartial jury of the State and district wherein the crime shall have been committed. . . ." (Sixth Amendment, U.S. Constitution)

EXAMPLE

Ann is charged with theft of services. There is no maximum sentence stated for the offense, and the trial judge rules that the charge is petty and therefore no jury will be impaneled. Instead, Ann is permitted only a bench trial, where the judge decides both the issues of law and the verdict. After her conviction, Ann is sentenced to 12 months in the prison system. She appeals her conviction on the grounds that she should have been given a jury trial. How is the appellate court likely to rule?

Answer: The appellate court will almost certainly rule that Ann's conviction should be overturned and that she should be retried, this time with a jury. The fact that there was no maximum sentence stated in the statutes does not allow a judge to arbitrarily decide to exclude the possibility of a jury trial, especially where the judge by his own actions demonstrates that the maximum sentence is clearly beyond the six-month threshold.[8]

[6] *Lewis v. U.S.*, 518 U.S. 322, 116 S. Ct. 2163, 35 L. Ed. 2d 590 (1996).
[7] *Baldwin v. New York*, 399 U.S. 66 (1970).
[8] *Codispoti v. Pennsylvania*, 418 U.S. 506, 94 S. Ct. 2707 (1974).

FIGURE 9-1

Felony Trial Rates for 13 States*

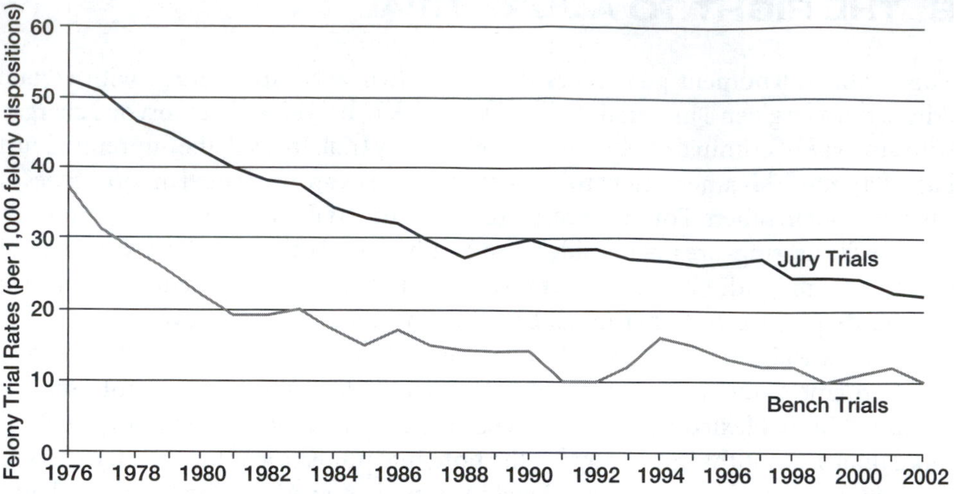

Note: The use of trial rates, which are calculated by dividing the total number of felony jury (or bench) trials by the total number of felony dispositions, and then multiplying by 1,000, standardizes the variations that are inherent in states of different sizes and with different disposition trends, thus allowing for better comparisons to be made among states.

*California, Texas, New York, Florida, Illinois, Pennsylvania, Ohio, Michigan, New Jersey, Georgia, North Carolina, Virginia, Massachusetts

Source: Examining Trial Trends in State Courts: 1976-2002. Ostrom, National Center for State Courts. 2004.

1. THE NUMBER OF JURORS USED IN A TRIAL

Anyone who has watched TV police dramas knows that a jury has 12 members. However, that common conception is not always true. Many states allow 6-person juries for misdemeanors, while sticking with 12 jurors for felonies. In fact, there is no particular significance to the number 12, either. The U.S. Constitution guarantees the right to a jury trial but does not set any minimum or maximum number of jurors. The Supreme Court has gone so far as to state that "the 12-person requirement . . . is not an indispensable component of the right to trial by jury." However, tradition weighs heavily in favor of 12-person juries, and despite the fact that the Constitution does not require 12 jurors to sit on a felony case, all states follow this rule. This does raise an interesting question: Where did the requirement of 12-person juries come from in the first place?

As we have seen, the American judicial system is based in large part on the English system. When our country declared its independence from the nation of Britain, we did not declare ourselves free of the English system of jurisprudence. In fact, most early states adopted English common law in its entirety, taking advantage of centuries of scholarly thought and legal decisions. Twelve-person juries are a part of that heritage. But when and where did the English system adopt the practice of having 12 people serve on a jury?

FIGURE 9-2

Percent Decrease in Felony Jury Trial Rates

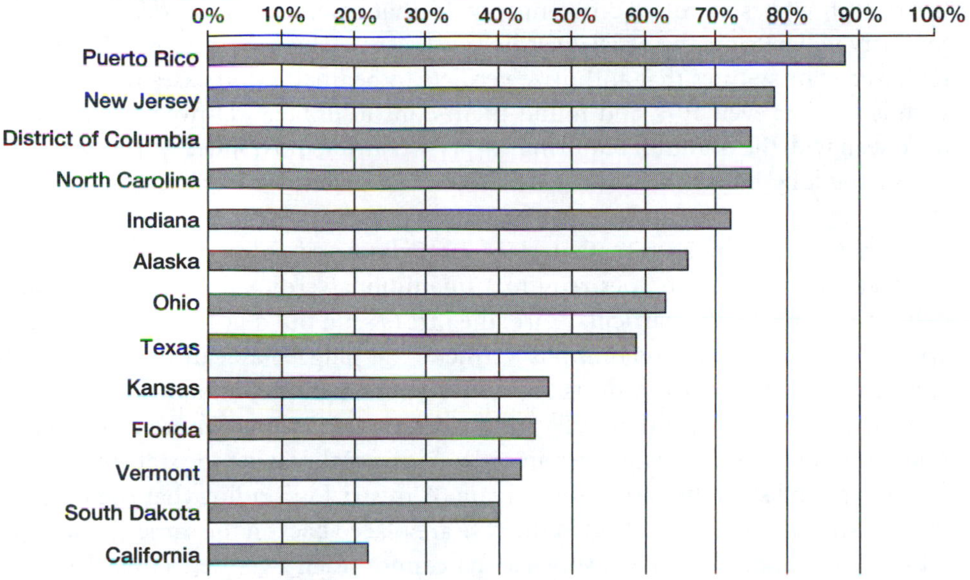

Note: The jury trial rate (calculated per 1,000 dispositions) decreased for each state in the sample, with Puerto Rico experiencing the greatest decline and California experiencing the least.

Source: Examining Trial Trends in State Courts: 1976-2002. Ostrom, National Center for State Courts. 2004.

In the past, jury service was limited to men only and, in most situations, men who held property or met some other financial test. In 1164 Henry II decreed that a jury of 12 men should decide certain cases involving claims between the church and state, thus laying the foundation for a tradition that has continued for nearly a thousand years.[9] One could argue that 12 has always been a number of special significance, perhaps also seen as lucky or having some other natural or supernatural qualities. The number of jurors may have been suggested by ancient Roman law, which was written out in the Twelve Tables.[10] It certainly was not based on the system created by the ancient Greeks, who used hundreds of jurors to hear individual cases. For whatever reason, 12 became the number associated with jury trials and has remained so ever since.

Now that we have established that there is nothing particularly noteworthy or constitutionally viable about the number of jurors who hear a case, it may also come as a surprise to learn that another common perception about jury trials is also not true. The common belief is that a criminal jury must reach a unanimous verdict. Although this is actual law in many states, some states do not impose that requirement in most felony and misdemeanor trials. In fact, some states will allow a case to conclude when 11 members wish to vote one verdict and

[9] *Foundations of Modern Jurisprudence*, William Seal Carpenter, 1958, p. 114.
[10] *The Grandeur That Was Rome*, J.C. Stobart, 4th Ed. 1961.

the twelfth wishes to vote a different way. In that case, the verdict decided by the majority will become the official verdict in the case. The U.S. Supreme Court has reviewed state statutes that authorize verdicts to be finalized in cases in which the vote is 11-1 or even 10-2 and found them constitutional.[11] However, just as we have seen with the tradition requiring 12-person juries, most states will continue to follow the long-entrenched practice of requiring unanimous verdicts in criminal trials.

Sidebar

The U.S. Supreme Court has held that unanimous verdicts in six-person juries are required, reasoning that with so few jurors, allowing them to split their decision would be an infraction of a defendant's right to a fair trial.[12]

What occurs in a state that does not allow for split verdicts? Suppose, for example, that a state does require a unanimous verdict, and during the jury deliberation phase of a particular case, the jurors send out a note stating that they are not able to reach a unanimous verdict. The judge may call the jurors out, admonish them to reach a decision, whatever it might be, and then send them back to deliberate. But if they still cannot reach a verdict, they are referred to as a **hung jury**, and the court will enter an order of **mistrial**, leaving the state to bring in a new jury and start the case all over again. A mistrial is a ruling that the trial is a nullity, and all persons involved in the case are placed back in the same situation as if the trial had never occurred. When a jury cannot reach a verdict, a mistrial is not a violation of a defendant's Fifth Amendment right of double jeopardy, which protects a person from being tried twice for the same offense, for the simple reason that the order of mistrial officially removes any legal significance for the first trial, so it is as if the trial never happened and the prosecution is free to start over.

Hung jury
A jury that cannot reach a unanimous verdict.

Mistrial
An order that a trial is terminated because of a hung jury or for some other action that occurred during the trial. A mistrial is the legal equivalent of a nullity, and all parties must behave as though the trial did not occur.

One might be tempted to think that a finding of mistrial over a hung jury would be perceived as a "win" for the defense, but most defense attorneys would not view the situation so blithely. They realize that a mistrial means that their client may be tried again, and just like actors who rehearse to perfect a performance, the state's witnesses have now had a complete run-through of their testimony and will no doubt give a better performance the second time around. However, a mistrial might be a victory in one sense: The state may decide that it does not make sense to waste any more time or resources retrying this case when there are so many other cases still pending. A mistrial may be all that the prosecutor needs to justify dismissing the case and moving on to a new one.

a. Investigating the Jury Pool

Because the jurors are so important to the jury trial process, both the prosecution and the defense will want to know as much about the individual jurors as possible. Defense attorneys and prosecutors will often obtain a list of people who have been called in to serve on jury trials. In high-profile cases, defense attorneys will often hire private investigators to prepare background material on all of these people. However, in most cases, the economics involved do not make this feasible, either for the prosecution or the defense. The number of people summoned for jury duty could be in the hundreds, and there is simply no way to investigate all of these people. Instead, defense attorneys will rely on some basic information provided in

[11] *Apodaca v. Oregon*, 406 U.S. 404, 92 S. Ct. 1628, 32 L. Ed. 2d 184 (1972).
[12] *Burch v. Louisiana*, 441 U.S. 130, 139, 99 S. Ct. 1623, 60 L. Ed. 2d 96 (1979).

the jury questionnaires and whatever additional information they can glean from public records. Most of the following questions can be answered by simply visiting the court clerk's office or the land record office:

- Where does a prospective juror live? (They may be familiar with the crime scene area.)
- Has the prospective juror ever been sued? (This will indicate at least some familiarity with the court system.)
- Does the prospective juror have a criminal record? (Individuals with felonies will be disqualified from serving on the jury. However, a prospective juror with a misdemeanor record might also be someone that the prosecution would remove from the panel during jury selection.)

2. THE DEFENDANT'S PRESENCE AT THE TRIAL

Although there are instances in which a trial may be conducted against an individual when she is not present, or **in absentia**, it is much more common and in many instances required for the defendant to be present during all phases of a jury trial. What happens in situations in which the defendant absconds before the trial begins? In that situation, the court will continue the defendant's case until such time as the defendant is arrested and brought back before the court.

In absentia
(Latin) Refers to a trial conducted when the defendant is not present.

What happens when a defendant is so unruly that his presence disrupts the trial? Suppose, for example, that the defendant continually interrupts the witnesses, yells, or acts in a threatening manner? In that situation, the trial judge is authorized to bind and gag the defendant or to remove the defendant and keep him nearby.[13] The defendant can be informed about the various stages of the trial by his attorney or can listen (or watch) the trial through a closed-circuit system. This is a better alternative to gagging or binding the defendant to prevent him from acting out in court. In fact, if the defendant is put in restraints, he must be done so in such a manner that the jury cannot see that the defendant is shackled. Given the choice between handcuffing the defendant to his chair and simply removing him to a nearby cell where he can listen to the proceedings over an intercom, most judges would opt for the latter choice.

In *Illinois v. Allen*, the U.S. Supreme Court case that upheld this option, the defendant, William Allen, was on trial for armed robbery and insisted on representing himself. During jury selection, he argued with the trial judge abusively and disrespectfully. At one point he told the judge, "When I go out for lunchtime, you're going to be a corpse here." Allen then tore a file and scattered the papers on the floor. The judge warned Allen that another outbreak would result in his being removed from the courtroom. Allen continued to argue with the judge, and the judge ordered the trial to go on without Allen's presence. He was convicted of armed robbery. He appealed, claiming that his constitutional right to confront

[13] *Illinois v. Allen*, 397 U.S. 337, 90 S. Ct. 1057, 25 L. Ed. 2d 353 (1970).

witnesses against him was violated because of his removal from the courtroom. The U.S. Supreme Court's decision held that a person's constitutional right to be present at trial can be forfeited if it is abused for the purpose of frustrating the trial.

In minor cases, such as misdemeanor charges, the defendant can waive her presence during the trial, but only with the judge's permission. Most states have statutes or court rules that allow a defendant to waive her presence for certain minor offenses. However, this rule does not apply to felonies and certainly never to capital murder cases (where the death penalty can be imposed). Although a defendant cannot waive her presence at a felony jury trial, some states do allow the defendant to waive her presence during earlier stages in the prosecution, such as a preliminary hearing or arraignment.

If the defendant is not permitted to waive her presence during the jury trial, but is not available when the trial is scheduled to begin, a court must wait until the defendant is present before the jury trial can commence. Although many foreign countries allow defendants to be tried in absentia, this is a very rare phenomenon in the U.S. court system. However, there is one situation in which a trial may proceed without the defendant: when the defendant absconds.

Once the trial is underway, a defendant who is out on bond is free to come and go, just like the witnesses and attorneys. Suppose, for example, that a defendant who is free on bond decides to flee the jurisdiction once his trial has begun. Must the judge declare a mistrial? When the case is a misdemeanor, the judge may opt to continue the case against the defendant in absentia. However, if the defendant absconds during a felony case, the court may call a recess to see if the defendant can be arrested and brought back to the courtroom; if the defendant cannot be located, the most common result is for the judge to declare a mistrial and wait for the defendant to be rearrested and a new trial scheduled. In such a situation, the judge would issue a **bench warrant** for the defendant's arrest, and that would authorize any law enforcement officer to seize the defendant and bring him back to the courtroom so that the trial could continue. A bench warrant will often contain a "no bond" provision, which prevents the defendant from obtaining a bail bond before the next trial date. It would not make much sense to allow a defendant who has absconded on his first bond to be able to make bail again.

Bench warrant
A court order directing law enforcement to arrest a specific individual and to hold him until a specific court date.

One final provision about the defendant is what he wears when he appears before the jury. It is common practice for jails to confiscate all of a defendant's personal items, including his clothing, and hold it in safekeeping. In such situations, defendants are issued uniforms, often brightly colored so that they may be identifiable at a distance. However, a defendant has the right to appear before the jury without a prison uniform. In fact, numerous appellate court decisions have held that putting a defendant on trial in prison garb would jeopardize his right to a fair trial.[14] Instead, the state must provide the defendant with suitable clothing if he has none of his own. In many cases, the defense attorney might provide her client with suitable clothing for the duration of the trial.

[14] *Estelle v. Williams*, 425 U.S. 501 (1976).

C. THE RIGHT TO CONFRONT WITNESSES

The right of a criminal defendant to confront witnesses and also to cross-examine them is considered to be one of the fundamental rights guaranteed by the U.S. Constitution. Without the ability to confront witnesses and ask them questions, there can be no due process.[15]

EXAMPLE

During John's trial, he received information that the state's witness against him, Maria, had been offered a deal whereby she will avoid being prosecuted as a fourth-time felon, which would result in a mandatory sentence of 20 years, and instead will be prosecuted for a misdemeanor and receive a one-year sentence. John's attorney wishes to cross-examine Maria about her plea agreement with the state, but the judge refuses to allow this testimony. How is the appellate court likely to rule on this denial of John's right to cross-examine the states witness?

Answer: The appellate court will likely rule that the trial judge's decision was an improper restriction of the defendant's right to cross-examine witnesses.[16]

The provisions of the Sixth Amendment, especially the right to confront witnesses in a criminal trial, have been made applicable to the states through the passage of the Fourteenth Amendment.[17] It is common for courts to say that the right of the defendant to face-to-face confrontation of a witness is one of the most important rights guaranteed under the U.S. Constitution, but this right is not absolute. Like many other rights, it must be balanced against other interests. There are several situations in which a defendant does not have the right of face-to-face confrontation but instead can watch the victim's testimony through closed-circuit television, or watch as a child victim is seated at a small table in front of the jury box, where he may testify directly to the jury and not directly to the defendant.

The so-called confrontation clause of the Sixth Amendment actually provides two rights: (1) the right of the defendant to confront witnesses against him and (2) the right to cross-examine these witnesses.[18] Included in this concept is the idea that a defendant can use cross-examination to develop evidence of a witness's biases or even a motive that the witness might have to lie about the events.[19] Defendants have the right to cross-examine the state's witnesses in order to show that the witness is biased or prejudiced or that the witness simply does not have personal knowledge of the facts to which he is testifying.[20]

Although the defendant has the right to a cross-examination, this does not mean that the cross-examination must accomplish all of the defendant's desires or even meet with the defendant's satisfaction. Such a standard might be difficult, if

[15] *Chambers v. Mississippi*, 410 U.S. 284, 93 S. Ct. 1038, 35 L. Ed. 2d 297 (1973).
[16] *Burbank v. Cain*, 535 F.3d 350 (5th Cir. 2008).
[17] *Shorter v. U.S.*, 792 A.2d 228 (D.C. 2001).
[18] *U.S. v. Eagle*, 498 F.3d 885, 74 Fed. R. Evid. Serv. 257 (8th Cir. 2007).
[19] *Commerford v. State*, 728 So. 2d 796 (Fla. Dist. Ct. App. 4th Dist. 1999).
[20] *Com. v. Avalos*, 454 Mass. 1, 906 N.E.2d 987 (2009).

not impossible, to meet. Instead, the defendant is guaranteed the opportunity to a full and effective cross-examination. What she does with that opportunity is left to the defendant and the defense attorney. Defendants are not given the opportunity to avoid all of the rules of evidence or even to range across any and all topics in hopes of finding some kind of bias on the part of the witness. The judge has the responsibility of moving the case along, and if it appears that a defendant has asked all relevant questions, the judge may suspend any further cross-examination of a witness and ask the state to call its next witness.[21]

Finally, the right to confront witnesses changes with the status of the defendant. During a jury trial, the defendant has the right to confront witnesses as part of the guarantees of the due process clause of the Constitution. However, when the defendant is convicted, a probationer's constitutional right of confrontation is considerably less. At a probation revocation hearing, the state has a relaxed standard and can use witness statements, hearsay, and other documentary evidence that might not be admissible during trial.

D. THE RIGHT TO AN ATTORNEY

For decades the Sixth Amendment's guarantee of the right to "the Assistance of Counsel" was narrowly interpreted to mean that a defendant could hire any attorney she could afford. If defendants could not afford one, then they would have to represent themselves. The first change to this area of law came in a recognition that in cases in which the defendant faced the death penalty, not allowing her an attorney was tantamount to an automatic guilty verdict. But that was not the only change in the interpretation of the Sixth Amendment. In a series of decisions, the U.S. Supreme Court, especially the Warren Court in the 1960s, addressed the issue of when a person should be allowed to have an attorney and, more importantly, when the state must provide counsel if the defendant could not afford to hire one. The most famous—and in many ways, the most popular—U.S. Supreme Court case in this field is *Gideon v. Wainwright.*

1. *GIDEON v. WAINWRIGHT*

Clarence Earl Gideon was charged with a felony in the state of Florida. He represented himself at trial because he could not afford to hire his own attorney. At that time, Florida appointed counsel only in death penalty cases, not in generic felony cases. Gideon had no legal education or experience, so it was no wonder that he was convicted and sentenced to five years in prison on breaking and entering charges.

What makes the *Gideon* case so important is that Gideon decided to challenge Florida law and, in writing his own appeal, he made the case that a felony sentence

---

[21] *U.S. v. Orisnord,* 483 F.3d 1169 (11th Cir. 2007).

is serious enough to warrant the protections of the Sixth Amendment. The U.S. Supreme Court agreed with him and entered a ruling that had far-reaching effects throughout the American judicial system.

The court ruled in favor of Gideon, saying that "assistance of counsel is one of the safeguards of the Sixth Amendment deemed necessary to insure fundamental human rights of life and liberty. . . . The Sixth Amendment stands as a constant admonition that if the constitutional safeguards it provides be lost, justice will not . . . be done."[22] The Court ruled that Gideon should be retried and that the state of Florida should provide him with an attorney, paid for by the state. With his new attorney, Gideon was found not guilty in the second trial and set free.

Gideon was the first in a series of U.S. Supreme Court decisions that expanded the guarantees of the Sixth Amendment's right to counsel and helped solidify the public defender and appointed systems that we discussed in Chapter 2. As the law now stands, any person facing a potential maximum sentence of greater than six months in prison must have representation. If the person cannot afford to hire an attorney, then the state must provide one for him.

2. PRO SE REPRESENTATION

Even after the safeguards of *Gideon* and other cases were firmly installed into the American criminal justice system, a defendant did not lose the right to represent himself. When a person conducts a trial and acts as his own attorney, this is referred to as **pro se** representation. The defendant is free to decline the services of the attorney provided by the state and represent himself. However, such a tactic is rarely successful. In fact, a pro se defendant often does himself more harm than good. A person might, reasonably enough, conclude that no one could better represent his interests than himself, but in law, that conclusion is faulty. A pro se defendant is not familiar with the rules of evidence or the proper way to subpoena witnesses and evidence. He does not know the correct way to give an opening statement or how to conduct a case. The pro se defendant also has a very skilled and experienced opponent in the person of the prosecutor. This mismatch usually results as you might expect: The pro se defendant is found guilty.

Pro se
(Latin) By oneself, a person who chooses to represent himself in a legal proceeding.

E. THE RIGHT TO A SPEEDY TRIAL

We discussed the Sixth Amendment's guarantee of the right to a speedy trial in depth in Chapter 6. As we saw there, a defendant may file a formal demand to receive a speedy trial.

[22] *Gideon v. Wainwright*, 372 U.S. 335, 343, 83 S. Ct. 792, 796 (U.S. Fla. 1963).

F. THE RIGHT TO PRESENT WITNESS TESTIMONY AND EVIDENCE

So far, we have discussed several important constitutional rights that a defendant has when she is charged with a crime and the case is slated for trial. As we saw earlier, most commentators consider the right to cross-examine and confront the witnesses against the defendant to be one of the most important, but the right to present witness testimony and physical evidence must surely be in the top three of important rights guaranteed to a defendant. The American judicial system specifically carved out the right for defendants to present testimony and evidence after considering other historical instances in which defendants were denied this right. A defendant has the right to take the stand and tell her side of the story (although in most cases the defendant does not do so). The defendant also has the right to subpoena other witnesses to testify, and this subpoena carries the same weight as the subpoena issued by the government to compel witness testimony on its behalf. Without this right, it would be difficult to claim that a defendant can receive a fair trial.

If a defendant issues a subpoena, the state may challenge it. For instance, if the defendant's subpoena is too broad or calls for violating an evidentiary privilege, the defendant can no more receive this information than can the state.

EXAMPLE

Tim is on trial for murder and wants to subpoena a popular movie star who portrayed a character in a movie that Tim claims was the inspiration for his own crime spree. He is representing himself, and he obtains a subpoena form and actually has it served on the movie star. The state objects to the subpoena, calling it overbroad and irrelevant since the star has no personal knowledge of the case whatsoever. How is the court likely to rule?

Answer: The court will undoubtedly quash the subpoena in the same way that it would if the state had requested irrelevant, duplicative, or privileged testimony. In this case, the court will likely rule that the defendant's subpoena is for a witness who can provide no relevant information on the case, and therefore the subpoena is quashed.

As we have seen, the right to present evidence and testimony is a critical one for the defendant, and that includes the defendant's own testimony. Given the fact that the defendant is permitted to testify in her own trial, why do most defendants choose not to take the stand? There are several reasons, some of which we covered in Chapter 8. First of all, in many jurisdictions, the moment that the defendant takes the stand, the prosecutor is allowed to cross-examine the defendant about her criminal record. In those jurisdictions, the defendant's voluntary testimony places her "character in evidence," and allows the prosecutor to reveal to the jury that the defendant has committed other crimes. However, this rule is not followed universally, and even in jurisdictions that do not automatically allow a prosecutor to bring up a defendant's criminal record when she testifies, defendants still routinely waive their right to testify. Why should this be so? The answer is simple: The defendant will be subject to cross-examination by the prosecutor. There are many defendants who doubtlessly enter into a trial with a firm conviction to take the stand and tell the jury that they did not commit the crime, but after watching the prosecutor in action cross-examining other witnesses, the defendant may rethink this strategy. Prosecutors cross-examine witnesses all the time and, as a result, they get very good at it. A defendant may not wish to pit her skills against that of the prosecutor. The defendant's attorney may also counsel the defendant to remain silent during the trial, fearing that the defendant might reveal some inconsistency during her testimony that would only convince the jury of the defendant's guilt instead of urging them to acquit. However, the decision of whether to take the stand is always the defendant's.

EXAMPLE

In the movie *The Untouchables*, Robert De Niro portrays the historic figure Al Capone. In the movie version, Capone's attorney not only refuses to allow him to testify but, right in the middle of the trial, enters a plea of guilty on Capone's behalf. Are either of these actions permissible?

Answer: No. The defendant is being represented by the attorney, not controlled by the attorney. If the defendant wishes to take the stand during his trial, the defense attorney may advise against it, but the attorney cannot refuse the defendant's request. Similarly, only the defendant can decide to enter a guilty plea. Attorneys cannot surrender their client's constitutional rights without their clients' assent.

The defendant's right to remain silent and not testify is zealously protected by both the defense attorney and the judge. The rules on this point are clear: A prosecutor is not permitted to point out to the jury that the defendant has remained silent. A prosecutor cannot even suggest the question that if the prosecution's version is not correct, why hasn't the defendant taken the stand to refute it? The defendant's right to remain silent is so valued that if any prosecutor were to make such a statement, the court would undoubtedly order an immediate mistrial and might also take the prosecutor to task for ignoring one of the basic tenets of American criminal law.

PROFILING THE PROFESSIONAL

Investigating Witnesses: Facebook

"When I meet with clients I discuss their Facebook pages and their Twitter accounts. I look at their Facebook pages, especially the young ones. You want to see what's on there, what they're doing. You'll see various things, like I had a young woman who was accused of being part of an armed robbery and she was, but we were trying to give evidence from the other side. She was friends with these other guys and I took the Facebook page to the prosecutor and showed him that these guys were holding guns and money. There's just a lot in there. People put all kinds of things on their Facebook pages."

B.J. Bernstein, Defense Attorney

THE COURTROOM LAYOUT

Although courthouses and courtrooms vary dramatically across the country, a courtroom that hears jury cases will have some elements in common, no matter what the architectural theme of the courthouse. All jury trial courtrooms have jury boxes, witness stands, tables for attorneys, and so on. Not all courtrooms are equipped or designed to have jury trials, though. In fact, the ones that are reserved for juries are relatively few. A courthouse has many other rooms where other types of legal proceedings are held, such as bench trials and motions. Because these courtrooms are not designed to conduct jury trials, they do not have many of the elements that one would find in a jury courtroom. The most obvious of these is the jury box.

PROFILING THE PROFESSIONAL

Using Technology in Old Courthouses

"Our courtrooms aren't really set up for much technology. We wish we would be. We wish we could show things to the jury, but the old courtrooms just aren't set up for that, but they're trying. I have an ongoing bet with the DA about who's going to use Power Point in their closing argument first. I had one all ready to go and they pled guilty right in the middle of the trial. Our courtrooms just aren't set up for it. The jury would have to look off to the side to see what you were displaying. It's just not set up well for that. Some courtrooms are set up a lot better. My Power Point would be more about the charges and the elements than about the other side's argument. I've got a pretty good idea where I'm going to be going, so there usually aren't too many surprises. With felonies, you usually have a lot more information up front. With misdemeanors, you don't get as much information. Of course, every trial goes in different directions than you think. Even as well prepared as you can be, sometimes things come up and you have to deal with them."

Debra Sullivan, Assistant District Attorney

A. THE JURY BOX

The jury box is the area in which the jurors who have been selected in the voir dire process (discussed later in this chapter) are seated during the trial. They are restricted to this area and are not allowed to leave it and roam around the courtroom or interact with any other witnesses or attorneys during the trial. When the judge calls a recess or the trial has finished for the day, the bailiff will guide the jurors back to a jury room. If they are on a recess, this is the area where they can relax and talk. They are forbidden to discuss the case until the end of the trial, but whether that rule is strictly followed is a matter of some debate. Although all felony cases require 12 jurors, the jury box usually has extra seats for alternate jurors. As we will see later in this chapter, an alternate juror (or two) is often selected in cases where there is a chance that the trial will last for several days or weeks, and having an extra juror on hand is convenient if one of the main jurors becomes sick or otherwise incapacitated and must be released from the trial. Alternate jurors are not allowed to deliberate at the end of the trial, but they do sit and hear all evidence and arguments.

1. THE JURY ROOM

The jury room is usually a small room adjacent to the courtroom where the jury will go on recesses and where they will retire to consider their verdict in the case. Jury rooms are not known for their comfort or luxury. This is done purposefully. No one wants the jurors to enjoy the jury room too much; they might be tempted to stay in there longer. Instead, if the room is cramped, with uncomfortable seating and no window, there is a good chance that the jurors will reach a quick verdict and conclude the case. Televisions, cell phones, media players, and other electronic devices are all barred from the jury room. The room is private, and no one but the jurors and the bailiff are permitted to enter. The jurors are not permitted access to outside media for fear that they might base their verdict on coverage in the news and not on what they heard in the courtroom.

B. THE WITNESS STAND

Witness stands are always located next to the judge's bench. The witness stand is often a seat inside a closed area with one side open to admit the witness. Most modern courtrooms have microphones set up at face level for the witnesses, even though the witness stand is close to the jury box. The microphone enables everyone in the courtroom to hear the witness testify and also to record the testimony even as a court reporter takes down every word in the exchange between the attorneys and the witness.

C. THE JUDGE'S BENCH

The judge sits on an elevated platform called the bench. It is always the highest position in the courtroom and helps to emphasize the judge's power and authority. The judge's bench is always positioned so that the judge can get a clear view of the entire courtroom, including the jury box, witness stand, and attorneys' tables. In modern courtrooms, the judge may have a laptop available at the bench with real-time transcription of the testimony as it is being taken down by the court reporter. The judge may also use the laptop to access legal databases should a question of law come up during the trial. When the judge calls the attorneys to the bench during the trial, it is called a bench conference. In situations in which the judge acts as the fact finder and there is no jury, the trial is referred to as a **bench trial**. A defendant might decide to waive a jury trial in favor of a bench trial when there is little issue of the defendant's guilt but he has no desire to enter a plea of guilty to the charge (see Figure 9-3).

Bench trial
A trial where the judge decides both questions of law and the final verdict in the case; no jury is present.

FIGURE 9-3

Total Criminal and Bench Trials in 23 States

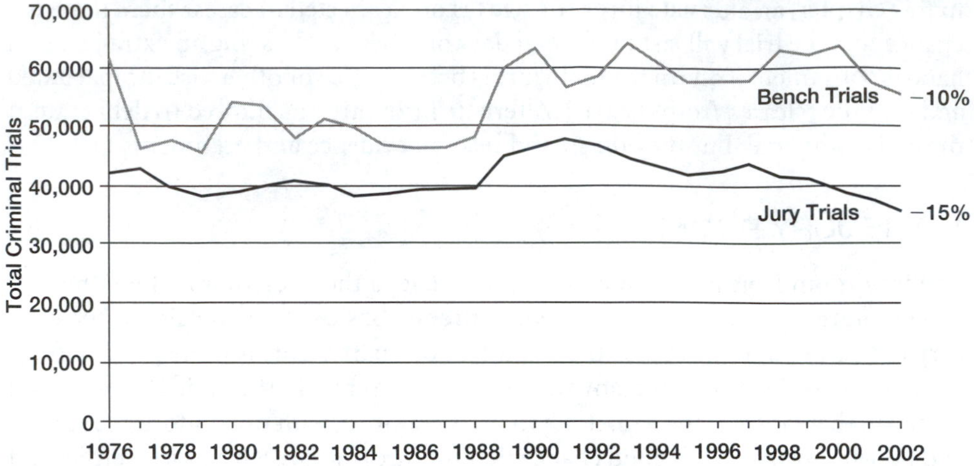

Note: The definition of what constitutes a trial, either jury or bench, may vary by state.

Source: Examining Trial Trends in State Courts: 1976-2002. Ostrom, National Center for State Courts. 2004.

D. CLERK'S AND COURT REPORTER'S TABLES

Clerk
A court official who maintains records of dispositions in both civil and criminal cases.

Usually located in front of or on the far side of the bench are spaces for the court reporter and the **clerk** of court. The court reporter usually occupies a central position in the courtroom since every word spoken in the courtroom must be taken down by the court reporter. There is usually a table or other space set aside for the clerk of court. This space is empty during a trial, as the clerk is normally present only for calendar calls or sentencing hearings, when the details of a case must be recorded in the pertinent file.

D. ATTORNEYS' TABLES

At least two tables are set aside for the attorneys. One table is used by the prosecution, while the other is reserved for the defense. There is a long-standing tradition that the prosecution uses the table closest to the jury box. The one farthest from the jury box is for the defense. In most jurisdictions, there are no court rules that mandate this arrangement.

Just like the judge's bench, modern courtrooms have Ethernet or wireless capabilities for attorneys so that they can access their computer files during the trial or even conduct some quick online legal research. Like the judge, they also have real-time transcription on their laptops from the court reporter's machine, and this allows them to review testimony while the trial is proceeding and even to cross-examine witnesses about previous statements made in the case.

E. THE BAR

The courtroom is the area (sometimes referred to as the arena) that consists of the jury box, the witness stand, the judge's bench, and attorney's tables. This is separated from public seating by some form of partition, commonly referred to as the **bar**. It sets off the public section of the courtroom—the gallery—from the area reserved for the parties. This also helps explain some of the terminology used in law, such as the fact that only members of "the bar" and witnesses summoned by the attorneys are permitted into this area.

Bar
A physical barrier that separates the trial area from the public gallery.

The organization of the courtroom helps to emphasize the importance and solemnity of the proceedings. In some areas, older courtrooms are things of beauty and look more like movie sets than practical places to hold trials. Like old movie theaters, they recall bygone eras when a jury trial might be the only source of entertainment in the entire district.

THE TRIAL

Before the trial can begin, the state and the defendant must **join issue**. This is an ancient procedure in which the defendant officially enters his plea of not guilty and the state shows that it is ready to try the defendant for the crimes charged. Once issue has been joined, jury selection begins.

Join issue
To officially submit the case to a jury for a determination and verdict.

A. VOIR DIRE (JURY SELECTION)

Jury selection is also known as **voir dire**. This is a French phrase meaning *look-speak*, and that is what actually happens during jury selection. Members of the community are brought into a courtroom and asked questions by both the prosecutor and defense attorney. Their responses are noted and used to determine which members of the panel will be removed from the panel and which will stay. This group of citizens, from whom a jury is selected, is known as the **panel**, or **venire**.

Voir dire
(French) To look, to speak. The process of questioning jurors about their potential biases in the case.

Panel/venire
A group of people who have been called for jury duty; the final jury will be selected from this group.

Although in the past there were many restrictions to jury service, including the deliberate exclusion of women and minorities from panels, modern practice allows almost anyone to serve on a jury. The only people who are barred from jury duty are those who have been convicted of a felony, minors, or anyone who cannot or will not follow the judge's orders and the law.

Panel members are selected from a wide variety of sources. Although it was true in the past that the jury administrators would cull voter registration rolls for names of people to be summoned for jury duty, modern practice has expanded this to DMV records, tax records, and other public records.

The process of selecting a jury varies from state to state and even from county to county, but some provisions occur in all jury selection. For instance, there is always a session during which general questions are asked of the entire panel. These often consist of questions designed to make sure that everyone who is present is legally qualified to serve on the jury. The judge or the prosecutor might ask the panel if there are any convicted felons seated in the panel or anyone under the age of 18. Beyond that, general questions might include more nuanced ones about whether panel members can follow the judge's directions and the law. Panel members will also be asked a series of broad-based questions to make sure that no members are biased or prejudiced against one side or the other. In some states, attorneys question the potential jurors; in others, and in federal court, the judge asks all of the questions. Before the attorneys ask general questions, they may make a few preliminary comments to the panel. The prosecutor, who usually goes first, may explain just what the jury selection process is and then proceed to ask general questions. Undoubtedly, the judge will also explain the jury selection process to the panel members to help them understand what is happening.

Once the prosecutor has finished with her general questions, the defense attorney will also have the opportunity to address the panel and ask general questions. The attorneys will likely have very different general questions for the panel. For instance, if the case involves domestic violence or some other form of violence, the prosecutor might ask the panel if anyone believes that it is appropriate to resort to violence to settle disputes. The defense attorney in the case might ask questions from an entirely different viewpoint, such as, "Is there anyone here who would always believe a police officer over any other kind of witness?"

In recent years, many of the most common general questions asked by attorneys have been reduced to juror questionnaires and given to the panel members when they are summoned for jury duty. Each panel member's answers are provided to the prosecutor and defense attorney, which frequently helps speed up the jury selection process. One of the most common questions is: Have you ever been the victim of a crime? Both attorneys will want to know the answer to that question. The prosecutor would like to know because this person might be more willing to return a guilty verdict than someone who has not been the victim of a crime; the defense attorney might wish to strike that person during selection for the same reason.

General questioning often has a second, more subtle purpose: educating the jury. An attorney might phrase a question in such a way as to suggest a possible way of looking at the case at the same time that he is also requesting information. Consider the following examples:

- Does anyone here believe that the narcotic cocaine should be legalized?
- Is there anyone here who believes that it is okay to drink and drive?

The chance that someone would actually answer yes to either of these questions is remote, so why would an attorney ask them? There are two reasons. First, there might be a chance that someone actually does believe the sentiment expressed in the questions and, if so, that person will be eliminated by the prosecution during the final selection process. But, perhaps more importantly, the prosecutor wants the entire panel to start thinking about crime. The prosecutor knows that her 12 jurors are sitting on the panel; they just have not been selected yet. Having the panel members start to think about crime and verdicts gets them in the proper frame of mind to serve as jurors. These questions promote the idea of law and order.

Once general questioning is over, the attorneys are then allowed to move on to individual questions. Here, they follow up on any indications or answers that panel members gave in general questioning. The attorneys may wish to know more specifics about a panel member's response to a general question and also to try to evaluate the person more closely to determine whether he would make a good juror for the prosecution or defense. Just as we saw with general questioning, the prosecutor goes first in asking individual questions. Attorneys often see this as an opportunity for establishing a personal rapport with the panel members. This rapport may carry over to the trial if this panel member ends up as a juror on the case. Attorneys also wish to see how interested the panel members are—for instance, whether they make eye contact and the myriad of other body language clues that people give off. Jury selection often boils down to a gut-instinct appraisal of a person, and in that respect it is more art than science. Barring any openly hostile panel members, whom the attorney will eliminate, in the end the attorney removes people often based on nothing more than a negative feeling about a particular panel member.

1. STRIKING THE JURY

When we use the phrase *jury selection*, we are not being accurate. Attorneys do not select the jurors that they want. Instead, they remove panel members that they do not want until only 12 remain. The process of removing panel members is called *striking a jury*. When a panel member is struck, this person will not serve on the jury. Panel members may be struck in two different ways: (1) challenge for cause and (2) peremptory strike.

A **challenge for cause** is the process of removing a panel member because the person has demonstrated some prejudice to one of the parties or has indicated that she will not follow the judge's instructions. When either the state or the defense uncovers any of these attitudes, that party normally moves to have the panel member dismissed for cause. A challenge for cause does not count against a side's number of peremptory strikes.

Challenge for cause
A formal objection to the qualifications or attitude of a prospective juror.

A **peremptory challenge** is the right of either party to strike a panel member for almost any reason. One of the attorneys may not like the way that the person answers a question, or the attorney just has a gut feeling about the panel member. Peremptory strikes do not have to be justified, except in certain instances (set out below). Both sides are given a specific number of peremptory strikes. When they have used up their number of strikes, they are not permitted to remove any more panel members. The defense, in many jurisdictions, has twice as many peremptory strikes as the state. If, say, 48 panel members are brought into the courtroom and questioned, the defense attorney would have the right to remove 24 and the prosecutor 12. Once these 36 people are removed, 12 remain to serve on the jury.

Peremptory challenge
A strike of a juror for any reason, except one based on race or sex.

In the last 20 years, the power of peremptory strikes has been significantly curtailed. In a U.S. Supreme Court, *Batson v. Kentucky*, 476 U.S. 79 (1986), the Court ruled that peremptory strikes could not be used by a prosecutor to remove all African-American panel members simply because of their race. The Court reasoned that because the court system is a function of the government, funded by the government, it could not be used to further discriminatory practices. The *Batson* decision has been extended to other types of discriminatory peremptory strikes. For instance, *Batson*-type decisions have forbidden striking panel members on the basis of any racial affiliation, as well as gender-based discrimination. Given such case law, it is an open question how many other types of peremptory challenges will remain.

Courts handle the process of striking the jury in different ways, but there are two generally accepted procedures. In the first scenario, the clerk of court reads off each panel member's name, and that person stands. The prosecutor will either strike this juror (using one of her peremptory strikes) or accept the juror. This is done out loud. The prosecutor may say, "The state strikes this juror" or, a little more politely, "The state excuses this juror." This eliminates the panel member from serving on the jury. If the state accepts the juror, then the defendant has the right to strike the panel member. If the defendant accepts, this person becomes a member of the trial jury. Each panel member's name will be called until 12 jurors have been selected. If either the prosecutor or the defense attorney uses all of his allotted peremptory strikes, he has lost the right to strike any more panel members.

In some jurisdictions, striking the jury is done on paper with "silent strikes." Under this system, the attorneys do not announce their acceptance or rejection of the panel member out loud. Instead, they simply mark the panel list with their strikes. The list is handed back and forth between each attorney until 12 jurors have been selected. Many judges prefer the silent strike because it moves the jury selection along at a faster pace and causes less inconvenience for the panel members.

In addition to selecting 12 members of the jury, the court may select one or more alternate jurors. Although alternates are not used in most trials, there are times when a trial is projected to last several days or even weeks. In that situation, it is wise to select one or two alternate jurors who would take the place of one of the 12 jurors, should he get sick or otherwise be unable to carry on in the trial. Alternate jurors sit in the jury box during the trial but do not retire with the 12 main jurors at the end to deliberate. Alternate jurors are normally released when the case is over and the jury retires to the jury room to reach a verdict. The process of selecting alternate jurors is exactly like the process for selecting the 12 main jurors. Once the twelfth juror has been selected, the judge will announce that selection will continue for one or two alternates. The prosecutor and the defendant have the right to use additional peremptory strikes to eliminate panel members, just as they did when selecting the main jury. Once accepted, these alternate jurors join the main group in the jury box. Jury selection has now concluded.

When a jury has been selected and seated in the jury box, the rest of the panel is excused. The people who were not selected to serve on the jury return to the jury administration area, where they may be released from any further jury duty or be called to sit on another panel in a different case. The jurors who have been selected to sit on the trial will now be given badges identifying them as jurors in an ongoing trial. They will be given pads and pencils to take notes. The judge will also give them some preliminary instructions, such as informing them about their duties in the trial. One of the most important instructions that a judge gives the jurors is that they must wait until the end of the case before they reach a decision about the defendant's guilt or innocence. The judge tells the jurors that they will hear testimony from witnesses and will also see physical and other evidence that is admitted during the trial. They are not to make up their minds about the guilt or innocence of the defendant until all evidence and testimony has been tendered. Whether jurors actually follow that dictum has come under a great deal of debate in recent years, with studies showing that many jurors begin to make up their minds as early as opening statements and have almost always reached a final conclusion long before the trial is over.

The judge will also tell the newly sworn-in jurors that they are forbidden to discuss the details of the case with anyone, even each other, while the case is pending. They may not talk about the case with friends or family and may not discuss the case with the media or anyone else. In fact, most judges tell the jurors that if anyone approaches them and questions them about the case or tries to persuade them, they should report that fact to the judge immediately, and the judge will launch an investigation into the possibility of jury tampering.

Jurors are also told to avoid watching media accounts of the trial (if any) and reading anything about the case in newspapers or online. (In the vast majority of cases, there will be no media attention at all.) In addition to these instructions, the judge will tell the jury that neither the attorneys nor the witnesses in the case are allowed to speak with them outside the courtroom. Most attorneys take this instruction so seriously that they will not even greet a juror if they should see one in the hallway during a break in the trial.

2. SEQUESTERING THE JURY

In some trials, where the publicity is intense, jurors may be sequestered. To **sequester** a jury is to cut them off from all outside information and even prevent them from going home in the evenings at the end of each day of the trial. Sequestered jurors are put up, at the state's expense, at a hotel, where they can be monitored. Many times, televisions, radios, and any device that can provide information about the trial is confiscated until the trial ends. Jurors may watch DVDs or listen to music on media players, but they are not allowed to watch press coverage of the trial or hear anything about the case until it has ended. Sequestering a jury is an expensive proposition, and that, along with the fact that most criminal cases receive little or no attention from the media, explains why sequestering a jury is such a rare event. However, a judge will order it if she believes that it is necessary in order for the defendant to receive a fair trial.

Sequester
To cut off from contact; to prevent jurors in a case from reading, watching, or listening to any media accounts of the trial and from returning home until the trial is over.

No better example of the need for sequestering a jury was, once again, during the O.J. Simpson trial. The media frenzy surrounding the case was likened to a 24/7 circus, and the judge knew there was little chance that the 12 jurors and 12 alternates would be able to avoid hearing or reading media reports. The jury was sequestered for nearly nine months, a longer period of sequestration than during the 1970-71 trial of the Charles Manson family, whose jury was sequestered for 225 days.

B. OPENING STATEMENTS

After jury selection, the next phase of the trial is opening statements. Both the prosecutor and the defense attorney are permitted to make brief introductory remarks to the jury to explain what they will see and hear and also to urge them to return a verdict for their side.

Opening statements are outlines of the facts and evidence that the attorney expects the jurors to see and hear. The attorney will often explain how the trial will proceed, what witnesses will take the stand, and what evidence will be presented. Unlike what is seen on television, an opening statement is not a persuasive argument. It is intended only as a mechanism for the attorneys to explain the trial process. In fact, it is improper for an attorney to attempt a persuasive argument during opening statements. Instead, the attorneys will outline each of their cases and ask the jury to return a verdict. For the prosecutor, the verdict requested will always be a finding of guilt on all counts against the defendant. Defense attorneys often ask the jurors to keep an open mind throughout the case and to remember that there are two sides to every story. Because the state will go first, the defense attorney will remind the jurors that they should not reach a conclusion in the case until they have heard from the defense in the case.

C. PRESENTING THE CASE TO THE JURY

Case in chief
The body of evidence and testimony offered by a party during its presentation of a jury trial.

After opening statements, the prosecutor will begin her case in chief. The **case in chief** refers to the entire body of evidence and testimony that the prosecution will present. Testimony will come in the form of direct examination of witnesses. The case in chief is the prosecution's attempt to prove beyond a reasonable doubt that the defendant is guilty.

1. DIRECT EXAMINATION

Direct examination
The questions asked of a witness by the attorney who has called him to the stand.

When the defense attorney concludes his opening statement, the judge will turn to the prosecutor and say, "Call your first witness." This is the government's cue to begin its case in chief. The prosecutor will call her first witness to the stand and the witness will be sworn. Once sworn, the witness takes the stand and is asked questions by the prosecutor in what is referred to as **direct examination.** The questions that the prosecutor asks on direct examination attempt to prove the elements of the offense, establish the basic facts of the case, and provide a platform for the prosecutor to introduce evidence that also establishes the defendant's guilt beyond a reasonable doubt.

The witnesses who testify on direct examination are generally considered to be friendly to that side. State's witnesses often include police officers, coroners, victims, etc. Because these witnesses are friendly to the side calling them, attorneys are not allowed to ask leading questions on direct examination. A leading question is a question that suggests an answer. Compare the two questions in Figure 9-4.

FIGURE 9-4

Leading Versus Nonleading Questions

- **Leading question:** You saw the defendant with a knife, didn't you?
- **Nonleading question:** What did you see in the defendant's hands?

As the prosecutor questions each witness on direct examination, she may also introduce evidence during the examination. As we saw in Chapter 3, evidence must be admitted before it can be seen or handled by the jury. When the prosecutor has finished asking the witness questions, she usually says something like, "No further questions." This statement allows the defense attorney to cross-examine the witness.

2. CROSS-EXAMINATION

When the attorney who has called the witness to the stand has completed direct examination, the next phase is **cross-examination**. There is no requirement that all witnesses must be cross-examined, but most are. As we saw earlier in this chapter, the right to cross-examine witnesses arises under the Sixth Amendment as part of the confrontation clause. Later, if the defense attorney presents any witnesses for his case in chief, the prosecutor will have the right to cross-examine those witnesses.

Cross-examination
Asking questions of a witness to determine bias, lack of knowledge, prejudice, or some other failing.

A cross-examination is very different from a direct examination. On direct examination, an attorney is not permitted to ask leading questions. During cross-examination, an attorney not only has the right to ask leading questions, but is in fact encouraged to do so. Direct examination puts the witness in the spotlight; cross-examination puts the attorney in the spotlight. Direct examination seeks to establish a fact; cross-examination seeks to destroy the fact or at least question the witness's recollection, bias, or temperament. When the defense attorney cross-examines the state's witnesses, he will attempt to discredit the witness's testimony or to use it to develop points favorable to the defense. When the prosecutor cross-examines the defendant's witnesses, her main goal will be to discredit the witness, show a bias, or develop points helpful to the state. Cross-examination is both an art and a skill. Attorneys spend many years developing good cross-examination skills.

The rules of cross-examination are very simple. Attorneys are allowed to question a witness's credibility, test for bias, or simply show that the witness has no relevant information. Another basic rule of cross-examination is that the attorney will try to limit the witness to yes or no answers and avoid asking open-ended questions (see Figure 9-5). The attorney does this in the way that he phrases the question. By attempting to limit the witness to answering a question with a yes or no, the attorney can concentrate on specific points in the case and then cease questioning the witness.

Attorneys often use cross-examination as a way of developing a particular theme for the trial. The defense attorney may emphasize the fact that there is some question about the eyewitness identification of the defendant, for example, or establish some evidence of alibi. Defense attorneys rarely use the tactics portrayed on TV or in movies, such as screaming at witnesses or physically intimidating them. These tactics rarely work and often turn the jury against the defense

Yes or no question: Were you standing in the hallway when the defendant came out of the room?
Open-ended question: Where were you when the defendant came out of the room?

FIGURE 9-5
Examples of Yes or No Questions Versus Open-Ended Questions

attorney and, by extension, against the defendant. Instead, most attorneys focus on the details of the question, not the loudness of the delivery.

As we have already seen earlier in this chapter, the defendant does not have an absolute right to confront the witnesses against him. In cases involving children as witnesses, it is common for the witness to testify in another room and have the entire direct and cross-examination shown to the jury on closed-circuit television. In other situations, the Supreme Court has ruled that the child may not have to testify at all if the child's statements about abuse fall into one of the clearly established exceptions to the use of hearsay.[23] Instead, a person to whom the child spoke may repeat what the child said.

3. REDIRECT EXAMINATION

At the conclusion of each cross-examination, the attorney who originally presented the witness on direct examination has the right to ask question on redirect examination. Such questioning is usually limited to points raised on cross-examination and is not designed to allow the attorney to repeat the entire direct examination. The attorney will simply ask questions to help clear up any apparent contradictions the witness may have made during the cross-examination.

4. CONCLUDING THE GOVERNMENT'S PRESENTATION

After the prosecution has presented all of its witnesses and evidence, the government will make the following announcement (or something similar) to the court, "Your Honor, the state rests." Resting the case means that the state believes it has presented enough testimony and evidence to prove beyond a reasonable doubt that the defendant is guilty.

5. MOTION FOR DIRECTED VERDICT

Directed verdict
A ruling by a judge that there is not sufficient evidence of the defendant's guilt to present to the jury.

When the state rests, the defense is authorized to present its case in chief, but before that happens, the defense attorney almost always makes a motion for directed verdict. A motion for **directed verdict** requests the court to enter a verdict of not guilty on some or all of the charges against the defendant. The basis of the motion is that the state has failed to meet its burden of proof on the charges and that there is not sufficient evidence for the jury to even consider the case in deliberations at the end of the trial. Normally, the court will grant such a motion only if the prosecution has failed to present any evidence to support the various charges against the defendant. If it is a question of the sufficiency of the evidence, that is solely the province of the jurors, and they must make their own determination about guilt or innocence. However, there is no reason for a defense attorney to not make such a motion. In the best case, the court may grant a directed verdict of acquittal for some or all of the charges. In the worst case, the defense is exactly where it was already: ready to present its case in chief.

---

[23] *White v. Illinois*, 502 U.S. 346 (1992).

E. PRESENTING THE DEFENDANT'S CASE TO THE JURY

A defendant has the right to remain silent throughout the trial and present no defense of any kind. The presumption of innocence acts as a catch-all defense, but, in many cases, the defense may wish to present some other evidence. The jury will certainly want to hear what the defense has to say about the points raised by the prosecution in its case in chief, and simply denying the state's proof and remaining silent, although constitutionally valid, is not a satisfying option for the jury or the defendant. However, a defense attorney may be constrained in what he can do during the defense case in chief. For instance, there may not be any witnesses who can support the defendant's version of the case. As we have already discussed, there are some serious drawbacks to putting the defendant on the stand to tell his side of the story, no matter how much the jury might wish to hear the defendant deny the charge. The defense may attempt to mitigate the defendant's guilt by calling sympathetic witnesses, such as the defendant's family members, but if they have no relevant information about the case, the judge will not allow this kind of testimony. Without the option of putting the defendant on the stand, and with no other witnesses to support the defense case, the defendant's attorney may be in the unenviable position of opening and closing the defense case in the same moment.

During the jury instruction phase of the trial, the jurors will be told that they may not make any negative inference from the defendant's failure to take the stand in order to deny the allegations against him. Whether the jurors actually heed that instruction is another matter. Most of us want to hear an accused person emphatically deny his guilt, but the practical world of criminal jury trials often makes that impossible.

F. REBUTTAL

Once the defendant has rested his case, the prosecution must decide whether to present rebuttal testimony. **Rebuttal** is used to attack a point raised during the defense. If the defense's case raises no new issues, there is little need for the prosecutor to go back over its testimony and present the same witnesses who testified during the prosecution's case in chief. However, at times the prosecution must present a rebuttal, such as when the defense is insanity or alibi. We will discuss those issues in a later chapter, but when such defenses are raised, the jury will be instructed that as long as the defense has raised some evidence to support its defense, the prosecution must rebut the testimony or the jury will be compelled to find the defendant not guilty. But even where the defense has raised several critical issues, the court may limit how much evidence the prosecution can use to rebut the claims. By this point in the trial, the jury has heard all the testimony, and the prosecution may need only a brief rebuttal to show how the defense theory is wrong or does not apply to the facts of the case.

Rebuttal
Evidence offered by a party that directly refutes evidence or pleading by the opposing party.

G. CLOSING ARGUMENTS

Closing argument
A summation of the case, during which each attorney seeks to convince the jury to return a verdict favorable to his side.

When all testimony has been heard and all evidence admitted, including any on rebuttal, the trial moves to the **closing argument** phase. Usually, there is a brief recess while the attorneys prepare their closing arguments and meet with the judge to discuss the jury instructions.

In a closing argument, both attorneys will urge the jury to return a verdict in their favor. The prosecutor will argue that the state has proven beyond a reasonable doubt that the defendant is guilty of each of the elements of the crime. The defense attorney will argue, just as forcefully, that the state has failed to meet its burden, either because they have prosecuted the wrong person or because the defendant is legally insane, whatever the defense in the case was. The defense attorney will ask the jurors to consider the case closely and to decide that the state has failed to prove the case to the high standard of proof beyond a reasonable doubt.

We have all seen closing arguments on TV and in movies. These are uniformly brilliant, dramatic, and brief. In the real world, an attorney may have one or two hours to deliver a closing argument. In previous decades, some closing arguments lasted for days. Research conducted in the past few years suggests that the closing argument, for all its drama, may have very little to do with the jury's decision. Often, the individual jurors have already made up their minds by the time of the closing argument, and the attorney's appeal will either reinforce that decision or simply be ignored. This is not to say that a brilliant closing argument cannot win a case. In some situations, it probably does. However, the idea that the jurors have not thought through the facts of the case prior to the closing argument and reached some type of conclusion, even tenuous, is hard to believe. Attorneys have wide latitude in how they conduct a closing argument. This is one of the few phases of a jury trial where fictional attorneys and real attorneys often cross paths. Attorneys may give a prepared speech to the jury, or they may speak extemporaneously. They may reenact the crime. They may appeal to the highest virtues of mankind or to the lowest and meanest of emotions. Attorneys are even allowed to argue theories that are inconsistent, even illogical. What they cannot do is to refer to evidence that was never admitted during trial, nor can they make up or suggest new evidence. Aside from that, an attorney has a great deal of leeway in how he appeals to the jurors.

A question often arises in jury trials: Which party gets to give a closing argument first? Most jurisdictions follow the rule that if the defendant presented any evidence, then the state has the right to give the closing argument first and then a brief chance to rebut the defense argument after the defense attorney has given his closing argument. Many prosecutors waive this second chance at argument, believing that the jury is getting tired and has heard enough. If the defendant presents no evidence or testimony, then the defense attorney gets the right to address the jury first and then rebut any argument that the prosecutor gives. The defense attorney has the same concerns as the prosecutor: How far to go? The defense attorney wants the jury to vote to acquit, but the attorney must walk a thin line between zealously advocating for his client and alienating the jury by addressing them twice. Often, the momentum or overall feel of the trial will dictate the actions of both attorneys.

H. JURY INSTRUCTIONS

When the closing arguments are completed, the judge will instruct the jurors about the law that applies in the particular case. **Jury instructions** give the jurors the statutory guidelines and elements of the offense with which the defendant is charged and also direct them in practical matters, such as how to select a foreperson and how to complete the verdict. The judge will instruct the jury about the state's burden of proving the case beyond a reasonable doubt and will tell the jurors that even if they believe that the defendant has committed the crime, if they also believe that the state has failed to prove it beyond a reasonable doubt, they must vote to acquit the defendant. Beyond this, there may be other jury instructions. The tradition has been, for hundreds of years, for the judge to read all of these instructions to the jury, probably stemming from a time when most people were illiterate. However, these days, it is often excruciating for the jurors to sit and listen to what could be several hours of a judge reading jury instructions to them, to say nothing of how much of the charge the jurors will actually remember. Instead, some judges simply provide a copy of the entire jury instructions to each juror to allow them to read it themselves. No matter how the jury is "charged" with the law, the judge always instructs them to consider the instructions as a whole and not single out any one part and give it higher priority or importance than any other part.

Jury instructions
A judge's directions to the jury about the law that pertains to the issues in the trial and the jury's function once they retire to the jury room.

The jury instruction phase of the trial comes after the closing arguments, but the decision about what jury instructions to give was likely to have been hotly contested before the closing arguments were ever given. Once the defense has concluded its case and the prosecution presented any rebuttal, the judge will call for a recess during which she meets with both the defense attorney and the prosecutor and goes over the jury instructions that she intends to read to the jury. Both attorneys are permitted to offer their own versions of particular charges, and there are often objections by one side to the other's jury instructions. In addition to the parties' suggested jury charges, there are also standard jury instructions that a judge must give in every jury trial. When the judge makes a final decision about which instructions will be given to the jury and which will not, the judge allows the attorneys to enter their objections to the proposed charge and then allows the attorneys a brief recess to prepare their closing arguments. The attorney will need to know what instructions the judge plans to give because they will refer to some of them during their closing argument.

I. THE VERDICT

When the jury reaches its **verdict** in the case, it summons the bailiff to pass on this information to the judge. Returning a verdict in a criminal case varies considerably from jurisdiction to jurisdiction. In some states, the judge may have the foreperson hand the verdict form over, and the judge will review it and then read it aloud. In other cases, the judge may review the verdict and hand it to the prosecutor to read. There are also jurisdictions in which the jury foreperson reads the verdict aloud in court. If the verdict is guilty, then the judge will enter a judgment that the defendant was found guilty and will either sentence the defendant immediately or defer sentencing to some later date. If the defendant is found not guilty, then he

Verdict
The jury's finding in a trial.

will be released. The returning of a verdict in a criminal case is one of the most dramatic moments in law.

In the case excerpt you are about to read, race is a prominent factor in both the crime committed and in the striking of a jury member. Keep this in mind as you're reading, and pay close attention to the questioning of the jury member and her responses.

CASE EXCERPT

COM. v. BENOIT

452 Mass. 212, 892 N.E.2d 314 (2008)

Botsford, J.

The defendant was convicted of murder in the second degree by a jury in the Superior Court. On appeal, he argues that (1) the Commonwealth's peremptory challenge to the only eligible African-American juror violated his Federal and State constitutional rights because the prosecutor's proffered reasons supporting the challenge were inadequate; We granted his application for direct appellate review. Because we conclude that the Commonwealth did not meet its burden of demonstrating a race-neutral, individualized basis for its peremptory challenge, we reverse the defendant's conviction.

Peremptory challenge.

a. Background. The defendant was tried on a single indictment charging him with murder in the first degree of Anthony Hopkins. The events giving rise to the charge occurred in Pittsfield on May 30, 2005. The defendant, who is black, was seventeen years of age; the victim, who was white, was eighteen years of age.

By the time the trial began in January, 2007, there was no dispute between the Commonwealth and the defendant that the victim had died as a result of stab wounds inflicted by the defendant with a knife during a fight between the two young men outside of the victim's home in Pittsfield. There was also no dispute that race was likely to arise at least as a tangential issue at trial. In particular, at the time of his arrest on May 30, 2005, some hours after the fight with and resulting death of the victim, the defendant gave a statement to the police in which he said that immediately before the actual physical confrontation between him and the victim began, the victim "was on his porch saying that, 'I'm going to stab you nigger, this and that.'" The Commonwealth was intending to introduce the defendant's statement in evidence at trial. In addition, the Commonwealth had given notice that it would seek to introduce evidence of an earlier statement of the defendant to his brother, describing an encounter between the victim and the defendant approximately one year before the confrontation leading to the victim's death. The defendant had stated to his brother that in that earlier encounter, the victim, accompanied by one friend who was white, had called the defendant, who was with three friends who were black, names, like "nigger this, nigger that," causing a fight to erupt, and in that fight the victim ultimately "got the best of" the defendant and his friends.

Trial commenced on January 2, 2007. Because the case involved the killing of a white man by a black man, individual voir dire was required.

The juror in question was juror no. 47. At the time the judge questioned her individually, she was the only black juror remaining in the venire. In response to the judge's question, the juror stated that she had read about the case in the newspaper, and had

heard about it over the radio, but did not really remember any details. She indicated that she had not formed any opinions from what she read or heard that would prevent her from being fair, but also stated, "I really wish I wouldn't have to [serve as a juror on the case]. . . . You hear so much on TV with murders and read so much in the paper, after a while it kind of stresses you out a little bit." Nonetheless, when the judge told her that "fair and open minded people [are needed] to hear these types of cases," the juror stated that she could decide the case based on the evidence and not on what she had read or heard. She also stated that she would have no difficulty being fair and impartial about the case, and could make judgments about the credibility of black and white witnesses fairly and without race being a factor. The judge's last question to the juror confirmed that she worked at a school as a teacher's assistant. The judge then found the juror to be indifferent, and asked the juror to step outside for a moment. The prosecutor thereupon asked the judge to ask further questions of the juror about her work as a teacher's assistant at a "school for handicapped and learning disabilities," and about the juror's level of stress, commenting, "Obviously, she doesn't want to do this because she gets stressed out. My fear is that stressed out factor and how stressed out does she get." The judge acquiesced in the prosecutor's request, and had the juror brought back for further questioning. In this second inquiry, in answer to the judge's questions about her job, the juror described the children with whom she worked at the school and what she did there, and the judge then asked some questions about stress. The juror began by stating that she hated violence, but in response to a specific question whether dealing with stress would be a problem for her if she were a juror, she responded, "No. I just want to do the right thing, that's all. You know what I'm saying? I'd talk it over with the other jurors and see, should we put, prosecute this person? You know what I'm saying? We are sitting right there together. I wouldn't talk outside to them." The juror indicated that she had been a juror before, and described that prior case as one involving drugs and the sexual abuse of a child. The judge then asked whether serving as a juror on that case had been a stressful experience, and the following exchange took place:

The juror: "Well, I got myself together. But I felt sorry for the girl. If one of my—"

The judge: "I don't want to talk about the case. I want to talk about the effect it had on you. Was it too stressful for you?"

The juror: "No. What I was saying now, I just felt sorry for the girl. We solved the case. He was guilty. He raped the child. He was bothering with the girl and the grandmother wasn't aware. He was living in the home. It was sick."

The judge: "Now, the deceased in this case was a white male and the defendant is a black male. Is there anything at all about those facts by themselves that would make it difficult or impossible for you to be a fair and impartial juror?"

The juror: "No, because you go by what is right and what is wrong."

The judge: "Okay. Would you tend to believe the testimony of a black witness over a white witness, or vice versa, just because of the race of the people involved?"

The juror: "Not really, no."

The judge: "When you say 'not really,' what do you mean by that? Would it be a factor at all in who to believe?"

The juror: "No, because you are not supposed to go on the witness stand on a jury and lie."

The judge: "I'm asking you, if you were a juror and you had a white witness saying one thing and a black witness saying something totally different, would you tend to believe one or the other because of the person's race?"

The juror: "No, that shouldn't have nothing to do with it. No."

The judge again found the juror indifferent, and asked her once more to step outside. The prosecutor then exercised a peremptory challenge of the juror, and the defense counsel objected on the grounds that this was the single black juror in the pool, that a pattern of race-based challenges had been established, and that race might be an issue in the case. When the judge followed with a request to the prosecutor to respond, the prosecutor justified his challenge:

The prosecutor: "Your Honor, well, just so the record is clear, I think that in the jury pool there was another African American female that was excused for other reasons."

The judge: "That's correct."

The prosecutor: "Your Honor, I would suggest to the Court that this is a proper challenge. It's not one that I make lightly because I have obviously anticipated this objection may be raised, which is why I asked the Court to make further inquiry. I do have some concerns with her responses in terms of sympathy for parties, understandably based upon her occupation. The fact that she made a reference to a prior case where she said she actually had sympathy for one of the parties, or one of the principals, I should say, in that case, causes me some concern in this respect. I think she even volunteered what her thinking process would be in terms if she would go back to the jury and ask, 'Should we prosecute this?' She didn't finish the sentence, but I think that causes me some hesitation as well as to—the question is not, should she prosecute it, obviously, the question is whether or not the facts have been presented and the Commonwealth has satisfied its burden. I think those reasons, Your Honor, give the Commonwealth legitimate cause to exercise a peremptory challenge."

The judge responded to this statement as follows:

The judge: "Well, I think that I'm constrained to find because she is the only African American juror who was not excused earlier who has come forward. I think the law is that one can be a pattern. So I think I'm constrained to make that finding.

"However, I'm also satisfied that the Commonwealth's reasons for challenge is [sic] not race based. That there are race neutral reasons which the Commonwealth has articulated which justify the challenge. Therefore, the objection is overruled, but the defendant's rights are saved. She may be excused."

b. Discussion. "The use of peremptory challenges to exclude prospective jurors solely because of bias presumed to derive from their membership in discrete community groups is prohibited both by art. 12 [of the Massachusetts Declaration of Rights] and the equal protection clause [of the United States Constitution], see *Batson v. Kentucky*, 476 U.S. 79, 84-88, 106 S.Ct. 1712, 90 L.Ed.2d 69 (1986)." There is a presumption that the exercise of a peremptory challenge is proper. That presumption may be rebutted, however, if it is shown that (1) there is a pattern of excluding members of a discrete group; and (2) it is likely that individuals are being excluded solely because of their membership in this group. A single peremptory challenge may be sufficient to make a prima facie showing that rebuts the presumption of proper use.

The United States Supreme Court has stated that a basis for denying peremptory challenges is the right of jurors "to participate in the administration of the law." The Court has concluded that classifications based on "impermissible stereotypes" violate the equal protection clause and that discrimination in jury selection harms the individual jurors "wrongfully excluded from participation in the judicial process" as well as the litigants and the community. A defendant in a criminal case can raise the third-party equal protection claims of jurors. Regardless of the perspective from which the problem is viewed, the result appears to be the same.

Following Soares, this court has laid out in many cases both the legal principles that apply and the specific procedural steps that must be followed by a trial judge (and counsel) when there is a claim that one party is using a peremptory challenge to exclude a member of a protected class. Specifically, our procedures direct that when an issue of improper use of a peremptory challenge is raised, "the trial judge should make a finding as to whether the requisite prima facie showing of impropriety has been made." When the defendant does make such a showing, the burden shifts to the Commonwealth to "provide a group-neutral reason for challenging the venireperson in question. The prosecutor must give a 'clear and reasonably specific' explanation of his 'legitimate reasons' for exercising the challenges." Once the prosecutor states his reasons, the judge is obligated "to make an independent evaluation of the prosecutor's reasons and to determine specifically whether the explanation was bona fide or a pretext. . . . This latter step involves more than a rubber stamping of the proffered reasons; it requires a meaningful consideration whether the challenge has a substantive basis or is impermissibly linked to race." That is, the inquiry must determine whether the prosecutor's explanation is "belatedly contrived to avoid admitting facts of group discrimination." In Maldonado, supra at 464-466, 788 N.E.2d 968, the court explained in more detail what is meant by "bona fide," and, of particular relevance here, also explained why a specific determination by the trial judge on this subject is essential:

> "The determination whether an explanation is 'bona fide' entails a critical evaluation of both the soundness of the proffered explanation and whether the explanation (no matter how 'sound' it might appear) is the actual motivating force behind the challenging party's decision. . . . In other words, the judge must decide whether the explanation is both 'adequate' and 'genuine.' . . .
>
> "An explanation is adequate if it is 'clear and reasonably specific,' 'personal to the juror and not based on the juror's group affiliation' (in this case race) . . . and related to the particular case being tried. . . . Challenges based on subjective data such as a juror's looks or gestures, or a party's 'gut' feeling should rarely be accepted as adequate because such explanations can easily be used as pretexts for discrimination. . . . An explanation is genuine if it is in fact the reason for the exercise of the challenge. The mere denial of an improper motive is inadequate to establish the genuineness of the explanation. . . .
>
> "Once a trial judge has ruled that a prima facie showing of the improper use of a peremptory challenge has been made, the need for specific findings by the judge as to whether the explanation offered by the challenging party is both adequate and genuine becomes readily apparent. On appeal, the appellate court must be able to ascertain that the judge considered both the adequacy and the genuineness of the proffered explanation, and did not conflate the two into a simple consideration of whether the explanation was 'reasonable' or 'group neutral.' While the soundness of the proffered explanation may be a strong indicator of its genuineness, the two prongs of the analysis are not identical. The appellate court must also be able to ascertain that the consideration afforded to both adequacy and genuineness was itself adequate and proper. . . . Finally, while appellate courts may be equipped to some extent to assess the adequacy of an explanation, they are particularly ill-equipped to assess its genuineness. . . . For these important reasons, it is imperative that the

record explicitly contain the judge's separate findings as to both adequacy and genuineness and, if necessary, an explanation of those findings."

The challenge here involved a black or African-American juror—the only eligible African-American juror in the venire—and race is one of the discrete groups to which the Soares principles apply. Once the prosecutor challenged the juror and defense counsel objected, the judge asked the prosecutor to justify the challenge. In doing so, the judge did not follow exactly the procedures called for in our cases, because he did not make an actual or explicit finding that a prima facie showing of impropriety had been made before requiring the prosecutor's justification; as the judge's statements quoted supra reflect, that explicit finding came after the explanation was given. Nevertheless, we view the judge's direct request for an explanation from the prosecutor as an implicit finding, at the appropriate time, of a pattern of improper exclusion.

Once the judge determined a pattern had been shown, he was obligated to make a specific determination or specific findings, in some form, that the prosecutor's proffered justification was both adequate and genuine. The necessary determination must be clear from the record. The dissent suggests that the court today is going beyond our prior cases, and demanding that trial judges provide explicit subsidiary findings about adequacy and genuineness "such as they might furnish on a motion to suppress or in a nonjury trial." We impose no such requirement. We simply adhere to what we stated in Maldonado, supra. While it obviously would provide greater guidance to the parties and a reviewing court when a judge expressly states his or her findings about the sufficiency and genuineness of a proffered justification, we do not intend to exalt form over substance. The point that Maldonado makes, and we repeat, is that in this sensitive area, it is necessary for an appellate court to be able to "ascertain that the judge considered both the adequacy and the genuineness of [counsel's] proffered explanation, and did not conflate the two into a simple consideration of whether the explanation was 'reasonable' or 'group neutral.'" Clearly, the ability of the appellate court to do so in a specific case will depend on what the record reveals—in terms of the reasons stated by the counsel or party seeking to exercise the peremptory challenge; the interchange, if any, between the judge and counsel about those reasons; and the statements (whether or not in the form of findings), if any, the judge made in accepting or rejecting the peremptory challenge. We have upheld decisions to approve and to deny peremptory challenges even without explicit findings when the record as a whole permits us to do so. In some cases, however, the record will not permit the appellate court to ascertain that the judge gave "meaningful consideration," to adequacy and genuineness unless the judge also includes "an explanation of those findings."

This is one of those cases. The judge's findings concerning the prosecutor's stated reasons for his challenge, fairly read, do not contain, implicitly or otherwise, the kind of independent evaluation and determination of the adequacy and genuineness of the prosecutor's reasons that Maldonado and our earlier cases call for. Rather, the findings simply state conclusions: that the challenge was "not race based," and that "there were race neutral reasons" for it. Furthermore, in characterizing the prosecutor's reasons as "race neutral" the judge never clarified to which of the prosecutor's several proffered reasons he was referring—a significant problem in light of the vague and in one respect illogical nature of the prosecutor's statement (a point later discussed). In the circumstances, there is little substantive distinction between this case and those cases where the judges allowed a challenge without making any findings at all. Accordingly, the court is not in a position to give deference to the judge's findings.

Where the necessary findings by the judge are absent, as an appellate court we must consider more directly the adequacy and genuineness of the prosecutor's stated reasons, rather than confine ourselves to a review of the judge's findings. The prosecutor here first argued his concern that the juror was likely to have sympathy "for parties," based on the juror's indication that she had sympathy for one of the "principals" in a prior case on which she had served as a juror. The Commonwealth suggests that this statement represented an expression of legitimate concern by the prosecutor that the juror would align herself with the defendant. The present case also had a victim—Anthony Hopkins—and it is illogical to conclude that a person who indicates that she felt sympathy for the victim in a prior criminal case is likely to identify or align her sympathies with the defendant in this case. "Common sense suggests that the prosecutor may not have been acting fairly when, after questioning one juror's antipathy to the police, he challenged [the one black juror in the venire] on the basis that she might be prejudiced in favor of the police"

The prosecutor went on to reference the juror's statement that if she were a juror on the present case, she would talk over the case with the other jurors, and consider together with them whether they should "prosecute" the defendant. The prosecutor did not explain precisely what he thought this statement by the juror meant, but he seemed to suggest either that it is a further expression of sympathy by the juror, or that it signifies the juror would not be likely to carry out her appropriate responsibility of deciding whether the Commonwealth had met its burden of proving its case. It appears reasonably clear, however, that the juror either made a slip of the tongue or was unfamiliar with criminal law terms, and that the word she meant to use was "convict"—in other words, she was saying that she would discuss the case with her fellow jurors, and consider with them whether they should "convict" the defendant. The juror's slip of the tongue, or her lack of working knowledge of the vocabulary of criminal law, simply does not qualify as a valid, race-neutral basis on which to exercise a peremptory challenge here.

The prosecutor also made passing reference to the juror's "occupation." We have held that a juror's occupation may be a sufficient and valid basis on which to justify the exercise of a peremptory challenge. Nonetheless, where a question has been validly raised about the propriety of a party's use of a peremptory challenge, the claim of occupation as legitimate disqualifier should be carefully scrutinized. This was not done in the present case. The juror gave no answers to the questions posed to her that would suggest her occupation was going to interfere with her expressed desire to "do the right thing" or that would detract from her indication that she had successfully served as a juror on at least one criminal case in the past.

The issue of race plays an important role in the assessment of the jury selection process in this case. Our decisions have specified that in assessing whether a challenged peremptory challenge has been improperly exercised, significant factors to consider are "not only the numbers and percentage of group members excluded, but also common group membership of the defendant and the jurors excluded, and of the victim and the remaining jurors." Like the Fryar case, this case had a single black juror in the venire and involved a serious criminal charge (murder) with a black defendant and a white victim. In these circumstances, the prosecutor's stated reasons for his challenge, considered separately or together, do not satisfy the Commonwealth's burden "of countering the prima facie finding of improper use by proffering a 'bona fide,' race-neutral explanation for its peremptory challenge."

This court has frequently articulated the procedures to be followed when there is a question raised about the improper use of a peremptory challenge, and has also emphasized the need for independent and specific inquiries to be conducted by judges who are put in the position of deciding the bona fides of a party's exercise of such a challenge; Maldonado, supra, which contains perhaps the most detailed discussion of this issue, was not entering an uncharted territory. There is no question that the jury selection process is often pressured and difficult, and we have no reason to doubt the desire and good faith attempts of the judge and all the attorneys in this case to conduct the process in a manner that was fair to all concerned. However, the defendant has an unquestionable right to be tried before a jury that has been selected in a manner that is free from discrimination, and this right was not adequately protected in the present case. The defendant's conviction must be reversed.

Conclusion. The defendant's conviction is reversed, the verdict set aside, and the case remanded to the Superior Court for a new trial.

So ordered.

CASE QUESTIONS

1 What were the charges against the defendant?
2 Was race a factor in the killing?
3 What issue arose with juror no. 47?
4 What did the prosecutor do once the questioning of juror no. 47 was concluded? What action did the defense attorney take?
5 What ruling did the court enter in this case and why?

CHAPTER SUMMARY

In this chapter we have seen that there are numerous rights associated with a jury trial. Among these rights are the right to a public trial, the right to a jury trial, and the defendant's right to confront witnesses. The rights of the defendant are not absolute. Frequently, a judge must balance one constitutional right against another, such as when a judge balances the First Amendment protections of the press against the Sixth Amendment's guarantee of a fair and impartial jury. If the jury is unable to reach a verdict at the conclusion of a jury trial, it is referred to as a hung jury and the judge will declare a mistrial.

The famous United States Supreme Court case of *Gideon v. Wainwright* expanded the rights of defendants so that anyone charged with a serious offense would be entitled to an attorney. A serious offense is defined as any sentence for which the maximum possible sentence is six months or more.

Wherever jury trials are held, there are common features to the courtroom layout. These include a jury box, where the jury sits during the trial; a witness stand for witnesses who are called to testify; and the judge's bench, where the judge sits during the course of the trial. In addition, there are tables for both the prosecution and the defense as well as for the clerk of court. A court reporter will usually maintain a central position in the courtroom so that he may take down everything that is being said.

The actual jury trial begins with the jury selection process. Instead of picking jurors to sit on the trial, attorneys instead remove members of the panel until 12 jurors remain. Some panel members may be removed from the panel by a challenge for cause when an attorney can show that a panel member will not follow the court's instructions or the law in the case. Attorneys are also allowed peremptory jury strikes, which allow them to remove members of the panel for almost any reason. The case of *Batson v. Kentucky* has restricted the use of peremptory jury strikes by forbidding parties to use their peremptory jury strikes to remove members of specific racial groups and religious groups, and even by gender. Peremptory jury strikes in the wake of *Batson v. Kentucky* must be neutral and not based on some racial or ethnic stereotype.

After jury selection, the attorneys address the 12 members of the jury in opening statements, in which they outline what they intend to prove during the case. The prosecutor goes first and gives the jury an overview of the state's case against the defendant. The defense attorney will then address the jury and explain what the defense in the case will be. After opening statements, the prosecution's case in chief begins with the calling of witnesses and the presentation of evidence. After each witness is questioned on direct examination, the defense attorney has the right of cross-examination. During cross-examination, the attorney will attempt to show that the witness has some bias or prejudice or simply lacks sufficient knowledge to inform the jury about the facts in the case. Once the state has presented all of its witnesses and evidence, the state rests its case. At that point, it is common for the defense attorney to bring a motion for directed verdict. This motion alleges that the state has failed to prove the allegations against the defendant and requests the court to enter a verdict of not guilty before the case ever goes to the jury. If the motion for directed verdict is not granted, the defense must now present its case in chief. The defense will proceed in almost exactly the same way that the prosecution did. The defense is allowed to call witnesses and to present evidence. At the conclusion of the trial, attorneys for both the state and the defense will give closing arguments, and then the jury retires to decide the verdict in the case.

KEY TERMS

Key terms are listed here in order of appearance in chapter.

- Jury tampering/embracery
- Hung jury
- Mistrial
- In absentia
- Bench warrant
- Pro se
- Bench trial
- Clerk
- Bar
- Join issue
- Voir dire
- Panel/venire
- Challenge for cause
- Peremptory challenge
- Sequester
- Case in chief
- Direct examination
- Cross-examination
- Directed verdict
- Rebuttal
- Closing argument
- Jury instructions
- Verdict

REVIEW QUESTIONS

1. Under what circumstances is a judge allowed to close a jury trial to the public?
2. At what point during a prosecution is a defendant entitled to an attorney?
3. Why are there 12 jurors in most felony cases?
4. Are there situations in which nonunanimous verdicts are permitted?
5. What is the crime of jury tampering?
6. According to the Supreme Court, what type of offense requires a jury trial?
7. What is a hung jury?
8. What is a mistrial?
9. Can a jury trial be held against a defendant if he is not present when the trial begins?
10. Explain the process used to select a jury.
11. What is the difference between peremptory jury strikes and challenges for cause?
12. What effect has *Batson v. Kentucky* had on the use of peremptory jury strikes?
13. How has *Gideon v. Wainwright* affected the availability of counsel for people charged with serious offenses?
14. Explain the purpose of the opening statement.
15. What is the state's case in chief?
16. What is the difference between direct examination and cross-examination?
17. Explain a motion for directed verdict.
18. What are jury instructions?

WEB SURFING

Nolo: Criminal Trial Procedures
http://www.nolo.com/legal-encyclopedia/article-29509.html

FindLaw: Right to a Speedy Jury Trial
http://criminal.findlaw.com/crimes/criminal_rights/speedy_jury_trial/

Courtroom Layout
http://www.utd.uscourts.gov/documents/Outreach/Courtroom_Layout.pdf

Ohio Judicial System
http://www.supremecourt.ohio.gov/JudSystem/trialCourts/

EXERCISES

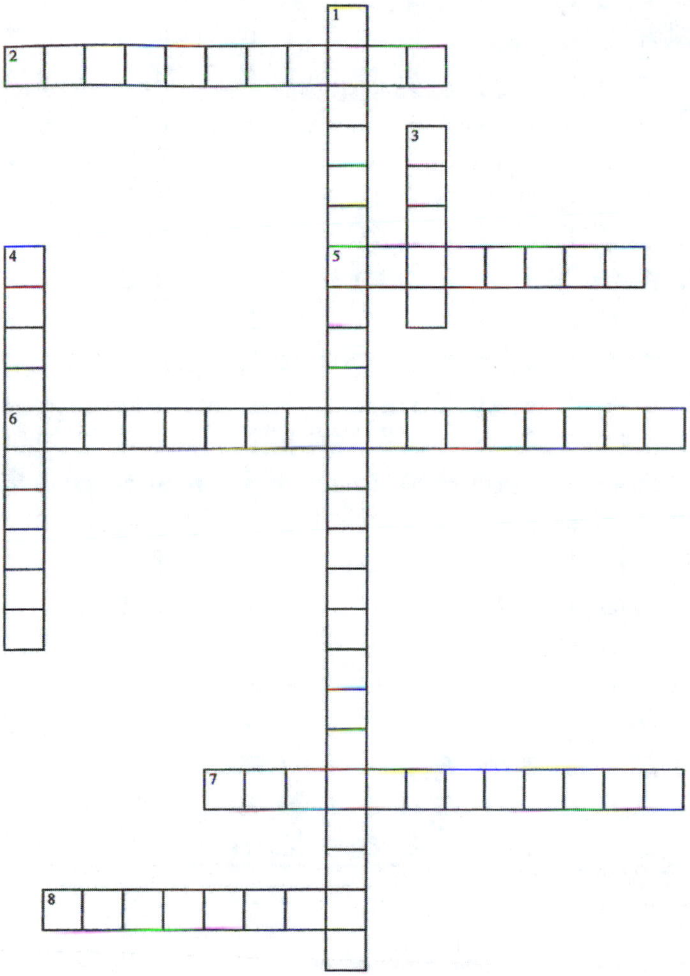

ACROSS

2. The time period set aside by the court to hear specific types of cases
5. An order that a trial is terminated because of a hung jury or for some other action that occurred during the trial
6. A motion that seeks to require the defendant's case to be heard during the pending term of court or before the expiration of the next term
7. A warrant for the defendant's arrest that is issued by a judge
8. A jury that cannot reach a unanimous verdict

DOWN

1. The crime of attempting to influence jurors in their deliberations on a case
3. A person who chooses to represent himself in a legal proceeding
4. The defendant is not present

e	h	r	n	c	s	r	a	r	f	(	p	e	d	n	m	y	j	a	i	i	h	(	a
t	n	m	h	i	m	e	m	r	)	e	c	o	p	i	)	a	e	e	n	h	l	)	g
r	s	t	a	r	e	o	)	c	r	t	o	a	n	n	h	i	h	a	e	r	t	f	d
i	m	r	t	h	s	e	t	n	u	l	i	d	r	c	u	t	a	c	b	h	n	i	t
j	a	m	y	s	a	u	r	e	l	e	p	a	t	o	i	p	i	w	y	i	j	r	r
w	e	s	b	h	p	b	u	u	y	r	r	f	e	y	r	(	m	r	g	e	i	m	a
n	u	r	a	r	t	e	r	m	o	f	c	o	u	r	t	s	a	t	y	a	c	u	b
)	m	i	a	i	t	n	e	s	b	a	n	i	e	u	r	e	p	p	a	s	e	o	r
o	p	s	u	t	i	c	e	d	r	n	g	r	r	j	r	o	d	a	n	a	e	e	n
g	r	t	d	h	m	h	l	u	y	b	m	h	g	g	i	o	a	y	y	e	w	m	y
h	u	p	g	d	c	w	u	h	r	t	r	r	e	n	i	n	m	g	e	n	j	)	b
a	n	b	a	r	n	a	t	e	r	u	r	d	o	u	c	j	t	m	r	m	m	s	u
e	h	s	b	i	t	r	e	p	w	u	r	i	r	h	e	a	m	r	j	r	a	b	d
e	n	d	s	t	m	r	t	o	b	r	i	y	a	h	)	n	a	c	e	(	r	t	r
m	h	g	m	e	e	a	e	m	e	b	d	p	o	l	n	s	s	p	a	b	n	c	s
i	y	u	m	t	a	n	h	i	p	(	p	m	b	a	d	t	u	u	r	n	i	u	n
a	l	e	e	n	m	t	r	i	h	g	b	g	n	i	n	e	a	o	s	h	t	m	r
)	y	r	e	c	a	r	b	m	e	(	g	n	i	r	e	p	m	a	t	y	r	u	j
s	t	s	n	j	s	u	i	r	e	m	p	d	m	t	c	r	t	a	r	n	o	m	s
a	i	e	m	i	n	o	r	n	i	u	y	d	n	s	t	a	i	p	n	d	o	s	a
d	u	t	s	e	c	g	n	t	e	)	r	t	d	i	m	j	t	s	i	d	i	t	r
n	y	y	i	p	t	m	s	w	r	r	s	(	d	m	b	i	c	i	r	a	o	i	c
a	p	e	a	s	c	b	t	m	b	d	a	r	e	a	a	i	m	n	p	n	e	)	m
y	r	r	a	c	u	r	t	e	d	a	a	s	r	m	a	r	u	t	a	l	r	e	c

jury tampering (embracery)
hung jury
mistrial
in absentia
bench warrant
pro se

QUESTIONS FOR ANALYSIS

1 Should all use of peremptory strikes be barred? Should the prosecution and defense be forced to accept the first 12 people on the panel who have not been challenged for cause?

2 Are all of the steps in a jury trial really necessary? Can you think of some way to streamline the process?

3 In your opinion, should the defendant's right to a fair trial always take precedence over the freedom of the press? Why or why not?

10

Sentencing

Chapter Objectives

- **Define the different types of pleas the defendant can enter in a criminal case**
- **Explain the judge's role in sentencing, including how broad the judge's discretion is in imposing a sentence**
- **Explain plea bargaining**
- **Describe the constitutional limits on criminal sentences in the United States**
- **List and explain the procedures involved in imposing the death penalty**

INTRODUCTION TO SENTENCING

A defendant who is found not guilty after a jury trial is released (assuming that there are no other charges pending against him), and the case is conclusively finished. A prosecutor cannot appeal a not guilty verdict, and the protections of the Fifth Amendment's double-jeopardy provision bar any new charge based on the facts for which the defendant has been found not guilty. Because there are no further proceedings in cases in which defendants are found not guilty, in this chapter we will concentrate on the sentencing and appeals phase of criminal prosecutions—that is, the issues around defendants who either decide to plead guilty or are found guilty at the end of a trial.

At first blush, one might think that the sentencing is a simple process; however, that is not the case. Whether we discuss the intricacies of an *Alford* plea, a nolo contendere plea, a plea bargain, or a situation in which the defendant has been found guilty after a trial, numerous issues arise in the sentencing phase. Add to that the fact that in almost all cases in which a defendant has been found guilty after a trial, he will certainly appeal, and you have a setting ripe for discussion.

In this chapter, we will address the question of plea bargaining first, because the vast majority of criminal cases are resolved by a criminal defendant pleading guilty to some or all of the charges pending in exchange for a lower recommended sentence by the prosecutor. After we discuss the various ways in which a plea bargain can proceed, we will then address the issue of sentencing after a trial.

A. HOW A DEFENDANT ENTERS A GUILTY PLEA

Before we can address the process involved in entering a guilty plea, we must first address a basic question: What is the significance of a pleading guilty? At its simplest, a plea of guilty is the defendant's admission that she committed the crime with which she has been charged.[1] Once the plea is made and accepted by the court, and the defendant begins serving her sentence, the defendant is barred from retracting it. A person accused of a crime always has the right to plead guilty to it—in some states, even when the crime is capital murder and the defendant is facing a possible death sentence.[2]

Even though a defendant has the right to plead guilty, the judge is not compelled to accept the plea. Why would such a rule exist? Consider the following scenario:

> Tom has been charged with multiple counts of indecent exposure in local parks. During his court hearings, Tom refuses any counsel and demands that he be allowed to represent himself pro se. However, his behavior becomes increasingly bizarre, and when Tom suddenly announces that he wants to plead guilty to "everything," the judge refuses to accept the plea. Instead, the judge orders that Tom be committed to a mental health facility and be evaluated before he will be allowed to continue to represent himself.

A judge may also reject a defendant's guilty plea if the defendant claims that he did not commit the crime. A defendant cannot have it both ways: He either admits guilt and accepts the sentence of the court or pleads not guilty and goes to trial. With the sole exception of *Alford* pleas (discussed below), a defendant cannot both maintain his innocence and plead guilty to the infraction.

1. ESTABLISHING THE VOLUNTARINESS OF THE PLEA

Before a judge can accept a defendant's plea, the judge must make a determination that the plea is given voluntarily and not as the result of coercion, threats, or other inducements.[3] A guilty plea must be given knowingly and voluntarily. In order to establish the voluntary nature of the plea, the judge (or the prosecutor) will question the defendant on the record to determine that the plea has not been forced. In some misdemeanor cases, the defendant may simply initial statements on a plea form that state, "This plea is not the result of force, threat, or coercion." In felony cases, the traditional method of accepting a guilty plea is to do so in open court, with the entire proceeding taken down by a court reporter and subsequently made part of the record. In order to establish that a guilty plea is voluntarily and knowingly given, many courts have established a standard set of questions that defendants must answer, out loud, in open court. If a defendant refuses to respond to any of the questions or retracts any statement, the court will reject the defendant's guilty plea and set the case for a trial. Defendants are not railroaded into pleading guilty by overzealous judges or prosecutors, despite what we may often see

---

[1] *State v. Merino*, 81 Haw. 198, 915 P.2d 672 (1996).
[2] *People v. Coates*, 337 Mich. 56, 59 N.W.2d 83 (1953).
[3] *Woods v. Rhay*, 68 Wash. 2d 601, 414 P.2d 601 (1966).

portrayed on television and in movies. See Figure 10-1 for a list of questions that the defendant must answer.

If a defendant gives an equivocal answer to one of the plea interrogatories set out in Figure 10-1, then the judge will be required to suspend the sentencing. During the suspension, the defendant will have the opportunity to speak to his or her counsel and then restart the sentencing phase again. If the defendant continues to make statements that seem to indicate he or she is not guilty of the crime, then the judge must halt the sentencing process, enter a plea of not guilty and place the defendant's case back on the active trial roster.

FIGURE 10-1

Guilty Plea Interrogatories for Defendant

1. State your name.
2. How old are you?
3. Are you now under the influence of alcohol, medicine, drugs, or any other substance?
4. Can you read and write?
5. Have you read and examined the indictment charging you in this case?
6. Do you understand that you are charged with the following offenses? [List each one on the indictment.]
7. Do you understand that there are certain rights that you would have at trial and that by pleading guilty you give up those rights? Do you understand that you are giving up the right to:

- A trial by a jury?
- Be presumed innocent?
- Confront the witnesses against you?
- Subpoena any witnesses to appear on your behalf?
- Testify yourself and offer other evidence?
- Have an attorney represent you during your trial?

8. Do you understand that if you plead not guilty or if you remain silent and enter no plea at all you will have the right to a trial by jury?
9. Do you understand that for the offense of ____________ you can be sentenced to a maximum sentence of from __________ to ___________ years and a fine of $____________?
10. The State has recommended a sentence to the judge of __________________. Other than this recommendation, has anyone made any promises to cause you to plead guilty?
11. Do you understand that the judge is not required to follow this recommendation but can give you any sentence allowed by law?
12. Has anyone used any force or threats against you to cause you to plead guilty?
13. Are you satisfied with the services of your attorney in this case?
14. Do you understand all of the questions that you have answered so far?
15. Understanding all of your rights, do you want to enter a plea of guilty to the offense(s) listed in the indictment?
16. Is your decision to plead guilty made freely and voluntarily?
17. Did you in fact commit the offense of __________ as it is stated in the indictment?

EXAMPLE

During Andrew's questioning concerning his guilty plea, Andrew states, "Sure, I'll plead to it, even though I'm not guilty." What should a judge do at this point?

Answer: The judge really has no option. If the defendant indicates that he is not guilty, then the judge must suspend the sentencing phase, remove the defendant's plea of guilty from the record, and schedule the case for trial.[4]

If the defendant can establish that she was coerced, threatened, or intimidated into giving a guilty plea, then the court may allow the defendant to rescind the guilty plea. However, the level of coercion must be such that it overcomes the defendant's will or prevents her from reasoning out the possible options. Negotiations during a plea bargain do not normally rise to that level of coercion; simply because the defendant is faced with two equally unappealing prospects (a lengthy sentence as part of a plea bargain or the chance of being found guilty at a jury trial and receiving the maximum legal sentence), that is not considered coercion.

Here are some other factors that a judge must consider before accepting a defendant's plea:

- the amount of time the defendant has had to consult with her attorney
- whether there are available alternatives to prison
- the seriousness of the offense
- whether the defendant seems confused or undecided
- whether the judge believes that there are some outside factors compelling the defendant to plead guilty[5]

EXAMPLE

Judy has been charged with second-degree murder and child endangerment. She pleaded guilty last month when her case was scheduled for trial. During the sentencing phase, the judge asked all of the questions set out in Figure 10-1. However, yesterday Judy filed a motion to withdraw her guilty plea, claiming that at the time that she entered her plea she was under the influence of medication that caused her to be confused and not understand what she was doing. Based on what we have discussed so far in this chapter, can you predict what the trial court will do?

Answer: The judge is likely to rule that Judy's guilty plea remains on the record. After all, the judge did question her at the time and had the opportunity to evaluate her. One of the questions that the judge specifically asked was whether Judy was under the influence of any medication or other drugs, to which she replied, "No." The fact that Judy now regrets the decision to plead guilty is not legally sufficient for the judge to withdraw it.[6]

---

[4] *Chizen v. Hunter*, 809 F.2d 560 (9th Cir. 1986).
[5] *State v. Ford*, 125 Wash. 2d 919, 891 P.2d 712 (1995).
[6] *State v. Stith*, 108 Conn. App. 126, 946 A.2d 1274 (2008).

B. TYPES OF PLEAS

A defendant can enter numerous types of pleas in a criminal case. If the defendant pleads not guilty, then she will have a trial. The defendant can request a jury trial for all serious offenses but may receive only a bench trial for minor offenses. However, if the defendant chooses not to take the case to trial, she can enter a wide variety of guilty pleas.

1. NOLO CONTENDERE

A plea of **nolo contendere** literally means, "I do not contest." For purposes of sentencing, a plea of nolo contendere has the same requirements and the same implications as a guilty plea. If that is the case, why would a person bother to present such a plea? In some instances, a plea of nolo contendere can prevent points from being assessed against the defendant's driver's license. For that reason, pleas of nolo contendere are routinely accepted in first-offense cases of driving under the influence of alcohol (DUI). Because a plea of nolo contendere does not admit guilt, a defendant may also wish to use this plea instead a plea of guilty because of a pending civil case. Because a nolo plea does not admit guilt, this plea cannot be used against the defendant in a civil case in the same way that a guilty plea can. A certified copy of a defendant's guilty plea to a traffic violation may be the only thing that a plaintiff in a civil case needs to prove that the defendant is liable for medical and property damages. A nolo plea cannot be used in that manner.

Nolo contendere
(Latin) I do not contest. A plea offered in a criminal case in which the defendant does not contest his guilt and asks for the court's mercy.

It should be noted that many states do not allow a defendant to use the plea of nolo contendere or, if they do, limit its use to specific types of offenses, usually minor traffic violations or a first-offense DUI. The judge always has the option to accept or reject a nolo contendere plea. If the judge rejects the plea, then the defendant must either change the plea to guilty or proceed to trial on a plea of not guilty.

2. *ALFORD* PLEA

An ***Alford* plea** allows a defendant an alternative to pleading either guilty or not guilty. Under an *Alford* plea, a defendant can continue to maintain his innocence but tender a guilty plea and be sentenced as though he had said he was guilty. A defendant might decide to use an *Alford* plea when the government's case against him seems very strong and his possible defenses very weak. The Supreme Court first recognized the possibility of a defendant choosing to plead guilty while protesting his innocence in the case of *North Carolina v. Alford*, 91 S.Ct. 160 (1970), and it has since been referred to as an *Alford* plea.

***Alford* plea**
A plea that allows a defendant to enter a guilty plea, but basing the plea on the amount and quantity of evidence against him instead of on the defendant's belief in his actual guilt.

Alford pleas are common, although there are no statistics that reveal exactly how often they are used. Judges and legal scholars alike support the use of the *Alford* plea as an efficient, constitutional way of resolving cases. Furthermore, when defendants enter an *Alford* plea, it can be a benefit when they seek future employment. They can explain to their potential employer that they were innocent, but the evidence was stacked against them.

3. CONDITIONAL PLEA

In some states, a defendant is allowed to enter what is referred to as a conditional plea. This is an alternative to an *Alford* plea, and in many ways they are very similar. A defendant enters a plea of guilty, including a condition that although he continues to maintain his innocence, the facts and the law are such that the chances of him actually winning at trial are virtually nil. In the face of such overwhelming evidence, the defendant enters a conditional plea of guilty. The practical consequences of a conditional plea, an *Alford* plea, and a guilty plea are all identical. For purposes of crime records, employment applications, security clearance, and any other jobs that require someone without a criminal record, the person who has entered a conditional plea is considered to have pled guilty—exactly as the person who offered an *Alford* plea of guilty.

4. FIRST OFFENDER TREATMENT

Another possible outcome for a defendant who decides to plead guilty is a request to be enrolled in the state's First Offender Program. All states have some form of this program, although it is not available for all types of crimes. Generally, First Offender Programs are reserved for youthful offenders for relatively minor crimes. Rather than have these people carry a criminal conviction for the rest of their lives, a judge might decide to enroll them in the First Offender Program. Under the terms of the program, a defendant must sign an agreement to complete various activities. If he is successful, at the completion of the First Offender Program, the judge will rescind the defendant's guilty plea. At this point, a defendant can truthfully say that he has not been convicted of a crime. The judge will order that the defendant's conviction be expunged from the record. However, in order to earn this generous benefit, a defendant will have to complete some or all of the following:

- Attend education classes.
- Complete substantial amounts of community service.
- Pay all fines and restitution to victims.
- Attend psychological, drug, or narcotics counseling on a regular basis.
- Commit no further crimes during his time in the First Offender Program.

If the defendant does not complete these activities, he will be resentenced with a felony conviction and a possible prison sentence.

PLEA BARGAINING

The vast majority of criminal cases end in some kind of negotiated plea of guilty. The process of plea bargaining has been going on for hundreds of years in this country, although it has not always gone by that name. As noted in Chapter 7, a plea bargain is essentially an agreement between the defendant and the state.

The prosecutor promises that she will recommend a lower sentence than what the defendant might ordinarily receive in exchange for the defendant's promise to plead guilty. Plea bargaining works differently in different areas. In some states and on the federal level, prosecutors cannot recommend a specific sentence, because sentencing guidelines demand specific sentences for specific crimes, but prosecutors can negotiate the number and type of charges that they will bring against a defendant. In other states, a plea bargain is as simple as first stated: The state (in the person of the prosecutor) makes a promise to the defendant to recommend a sentence in exchange for a guilty plea.

In most jurisdictions, the judge has specific restrictions on the ultimate **sentence** that he can impose on the defendant. In some states, for example, a conviction for armed robbery could carry a maximum sentence of 20 years. Following a conviction for this crime, the judge could not impose a sentence that exceeds this period, even if the judge wanted to set an example for the community by imposing an especially harsh sentence. Later in this chapter we will address additional constitutional prohibitions that a judge faces when imposing a sentence.

Sentence
The punishment, such as a prison sentence and/or fine, that is imposed on a convicted defendant by a judge.

Although the prosecutor can make a recommendation to the judge about the defendant's sentence—at least in those states that do not follow mandatory sentencing guidelines—the judge is the final authority in the sentence that the defendant receives. The state's recommendation may seem inadequate to a judge, and the judge will announce to the defendant that he does not intend to follow the recommendation. The judge is not compelled to tell the defendant what sentence he is inclined to give. However, the defendant does have one option: When the judge announces an intention not to follow the recommendation, the defendant is free to withdraw his guilty plea and proceed to trial instead. The defendant's attorney may meet with the prosecution again to determine a new plea bargain in hopes that the judge will accept a different arrangement.

A. FEDERAL SENTENCING NEGOTIATIONS

On the federal level, it is common for a prosecutor to dismiss one or more of the charges against the defendant in order to help persuade her to enter a guilty plea. Federal prosecutors do this because, under the Federal Sentencing Guidelines, they have very little latitude in the kinds of recommended sentences they can give. On the state level, prosecutors have much more autonomy—at least in states that have not followed the federal lead and enacted sentencing guidelines.

1. FEDERAL SENTENCING GUIDELINES

In 1984, after finding that there were large discrepancies in the length of sentences that defendants received for the same crime in different parts of the country, the U.S. Congress created a sentencing commission. The commission's job was to develop a set of Federal Sentencing Guidelines for sentencing all federal offenders.

These guidelines became the law of the federal courts in 1987 and withstood a constitutional challenge in 1989.[7] However, one can hardly claim that the Federal Sentencing Guidelines were a success. They have been attacked from all sides—by defense attorneys and prosecutors and even by federal judges.

A big change came in the use of Federal Sentencing Guidelines in the Supreme Court case of *U.S. v. Booker*, 543 US 220 (2005). That case held that the mandatory provisions of the Federal Sentencing Guidelines were unconstitutional because they took power away from juries to determine key facts in a case and gave that responsibility solely to the federal judge. However, the Supreme Court did not rule that the Federal Sentencing Guidelines are unconstitutional in all ways. They may be used as guidelines for judges when they impose sentences. The basic claim raised in the *Booker* case was that the judge made additional factual findings during the defendant's sentencing phase concerning facts that the jury had not considered in the case in chief. This put the judge in the impermissible position of being both fact finder and judge in a jury trial. In the aftermath of the *Booker* case, the Federal Sentencing Guidelines are no longer considered mandatory but do provide guidance for federal prosecutors and judges.

B. STATE PLEA NEGOTIATIONS

On the state level, prosecutors face the same pressures as federal prosecutors. As we will discuss later in this section, there is a genuine need to reduce caseloads on both the state and federal level. States have addressed this problem in different ways. Some states allow a judge great latitude in the sentence that she may impose, risking a claim of disproportionate sentencing. Other states have attempted to follow the federal model and enacted their own state sentencing guidelines.

1. STATE SENTENCING GUIDELINES

Many states have followed the federal model by enacting sentencing guidelines for individuals convicted of crimes. These sentencing guidelines have been imposed, in many situations, as a way of reaching more uniform results in length of prison term and fine imposed. Essentially, these statutes take away some of the judge's discretion in imposing a sentence and require specific sentences for specific crimes.

The rationale for sentencing guidelines is that they provide more consistent sentences. When a judge has wide discretion in the sentence that she can impose, the judge may give a sentence that is considerably less or considerably more than the sentences other individuals have received for the same offense. This gives the criminal justice system the appearance of being arbitrary and capricious. Under sentencing guidelines, or structured sentencing as it is sometimes called, judges have far less discretion in the sentence imposed on the defendant. When the judge is confronted with a defendant convicted of a crime, the judge must refer to a schedule that determines the sentence, based on the kind of infraction and the

---

[7] *Mistretta v. U.S.* 488 U.S. 361 (1989).

defendant's prior criminal record. In many cases, the guidelines were imposed by legislatures eager to show a "get tough on crime" stance.[8]

2. CONSECUTIVE VERSUS CONCURRENT PRISON SENTENCES

When the judge sentences a defendant to a term in prison, he may order that the sentence be served consecutively to other prison terms or concurrently with other terms. A **consecutive prison sentence** is one that is added to a current prison term. For example, if a defendant has been sentenced to a five-year prison term on one offense, then her new sentence will begin when the first prison term has ended. Judges sentence defendants to consecutive sentences when they want to increase the overall time that a defendant will serve in custody. A **concurrent prison sentence**, on the other hand, is one that will be served at the same time as any other prison term. Obviously, a defendant would prefer to serve concurrent sentences rather than consecutive sentences.

Consecutive prison sentences
Sentences that require a defendant to begin serving time for subsequent charges only after his first sentence is completed.

Concurrent prison sentences
Sentences that permit a defendant to serve time on all of his pending charges at the same time.

C. THE CONTROVERSY SURROUNDING PLEA BARGAINS

Many claim that allowing defendants to plead guilty to lesser sentences does nothing to advance the cause of justice and merely sets up a system in which an offender is doomed to become a repeat offender. Critics argue that prison conditions should be worsened so that no one would want to risk becoming a recidivist. However, others argue that without plea bargaining, the criminal justice system in the United States would grind to a halt. There are simply too many cases for every defendant to receive a jury trial. If prosecutors did not offer some incentive to defendants to get them to plead guilty, then they would all opt for a jury trial. There is already considerable delay between a defendant's arrest and her trial, and this gap would only become longer as more and more defendants requested jury trials. There is also the question of economics. All of those jurors must be paid, even if it is only $25 per day. Moreover, in high-profile cases, jurors may be sequestered, meaning that they would be sent to hotels at night during the trial instead of being allowed to go home and possibly see news coverage of the trial that could affect their verdict.

Despite the naysayers, plea bargains are a daily fact of every prosecutor's life, and through skillful negotiation, a prosecutor might reduce her monthly trial docket by as much as 90 percent through plea bargains.

Of course, there are some cases in which plea bargains are simply not appropriate. In states that have enacted "three strikes and you're out" provisions (discussed below), a defendant faces a mandatory life sentence on a third felony conviction. There is no offer that a prosecutor can make to induce the defendant

---

[8] *Fear of Judging: Sentencing Guidelines in the Federal Courts*, Kate Stith and Jose A. Cabranes. Chicago: The University of Chicago Press, 1998.

FIGURE 10-2

Amendment VIII, U.S. Constitution

> **Excessive bail shall not be required, nor excessive fines imposed, nor cruel and unusual punishments inflicted.**

to plead guilty. The sentence is mandatory and the prosecutor cannot alter it. In other cases, such as capital murder cases in which a defendant is facing a possible death sentence, there is also very little room—and often very little inclination—for a prosecutor to offer a defendant a deal.

D. CONSTITUTIONAL LIMITATIONS ON CRIMINAL SENTENCES

In addition to maximum permissible sentences mandated by the state legislature, judges face other limitations on the types of sentences that they are permitted to mete out. The U.S. Constitution, for instance, addresses the issue of criminal sentencing in the Eighth Amendment, shown in Figure 10-2. This Amendment was made applicable to the states through the enactment of the Fourteenth Amendment.

Although the wording of the Eighth Amendment is notably brief, it does create several important limitations on the powers of judges to fashion sentences in criminal cases, including the prohibition that a judge may not set excessive bail (addressed in Chapter 4) nor institute any sentence that is considered to be "cruel and unusual." This phrase has been given extensive attention by the U.S. Supreme Court over the years, so we can create a fairly comprehensive list of what sentences and actions constitute a violation of the Eighth Amendment and what do not. The amendment itself obviously does not define what the words *cruel and unusual* actually mean, so it has fallen to appellate courts to interpret the intention of the founding fathers. In its earliest interpretations, the Court ruled that the Eighth Amendment prohibits torture and requires that sentences must be proportional to the crime (see Figure 10-3).

1. TORTURE

A prisoner cannot be sentenced to a period of incarceration that involves periodic sessions of anything that might be deemed torture. In recent years, the term *torture* has been examined extensively in the media and by legal experts in the use of questionable interrogation tactics used on foreign nationals seized by the military. Waterboarding, for instance, which is the practice of strapping an individual down to a board and pushing his head under water for a period of time (or simulating drowning by other means) may not be defined as torture under some international treaties, but it would definitely count as a violation of the Eighth Amendment for anyone sentenced in the United States.

Much attention has been given in recent years to the alleged torture of detainees at the Guantanamo Bay facility in Cuba. Although waterboarding is clearly

Court decisions have established that none of the following are permissible forms of punishment:

- Torture
- Corporal punishment
- Excessive fines
- Disproportionate sentencing

FIGURE 10-3

Eighth Amendment Prohibitions on Sentencing

considered torture (and thus unconstitutional) if perpetrated on someone in the United States, the status of the detainees as foreign nationals with suspected ties to terrorism places the issue in a decidedly gray area. As with many issues, the legality of waterboarding in this case is often subject to political interpretation.

2. CORPORAL PUNISHMENT

Corporal punishment is considered something less than torture. Where torture may cause permanent physical or psychological damage, corporal punishment is closer to spanking or slapping. This, too, is forbidden under the Eighth Amendment. Interestingly enough, although courts have interpreted the Eighth Amendment to bar torture and corporal punishment, the death penalty is not considered to be cruel and unusual punishment. We will discuss the death penalty in greater depth later in this chapter.

3. EXCESSIVE FINES

The Eighth Amendment not only forbids cruel and unusual punishment, it also prohibits excessive fines. Many states have enacted minimum fines that a convicted defendant must pay as part of his sentence. For instance, some states require a minimum fine of $1,000 on a third DUI conviction in a five-year period. Other offenses, such as trafficking in narcotics, carry much stiffer fines. Fines for some narcotics offenses are $250,000 or higher in some states. However, the fine must still be proportional to the nature of the offense. A minor offense cannot be assessed a huge fine.

Once a defendant is sentenced and begins serving his sentence on probation, the defendant must make regular payments on the fine to the probation office. When a probationer fails to make payments on the outstanding fine, the probation officer assigned to the defendant's case can bring an action to revoke the defendant's probation and, if granted, will result in the defendant returning to prison for some period of time, including the balance of his sentence.

If a defendant is serving time in prison, he cannot be compelled to pay a fine; a defendant can be required to pay fines or other courts costs only once he has been released and has obtained employment.

4. DISPROPORTIONATE SENTENCING

The U.S. Supreme Court has mandated that a sentence must be proportional to the crime to satisfy the Eighth Amendment. For instance, without some other aggravating circumstance, a life sentence for a petty infraction would be out of proportion and would be a violation of the Eighth Amendment.[9] Generally, the more serious the crime, the longer the defendant's sentence will be. Violent crimes are punished by longer prison sentences than nonviolent offenses. However, this principle has undergone a certain amount of manipulation with the enactment of the so-called three-strikes laws.

a. "Three Strikes and You're Out"

The so-called three-strikes statutes generally require a lengthy prison sentence (sometimes even life in prison) for a third felony conviction. These statutes have been deemed constitutional by the Supreme Court because they place conditions on imposing such a severe sentence (namely, two prior felony convictions before the statute is triggered). In practice, this could mean that a defendant's third felony conviction could be for a relatively minor felony, yet still satisfy the minimum requirements of the statute and trigger a mandatory life sentence.

EXAMPLE

Bill has two prior felony convictions, one for car theft and another for armed robbery. While he is in a local store, he decides to steal a DVD player that is worth $150. State law makes theft by shoplifting any item with a value greater than $100 a felony. When Bill is convicted of theft by shoplifting, will he get the standard two-year sentence that is the maximum for this offense, or will he be sentenced to life based on "three strikes and you're out"?

Answer: Bill will be sentenced to life in prison. His third conviction was a felony and therefore his sentence qualifies under the three-strikes laws.

Not all states follow a strict three-strikes pattern (see Figure 10-4). Some states require that the three felonies must involve violent crimes before the defendant can be sentenced to life in prison. Other states go in a different direction; in Georgia, for instance, a second felony conviction involving violent crime results in an automatic life sentence.

As drastic as these sentences appear, there are some practical difficulties in maintaining such a regimen. For one thing, there are numerous federal lawsuits pending that have been filed by inmates challenging the number of prisoners assigned to cells. Overcrowding in our nation's prisons is a very serious problem, and parole boards across the nation have been forced to release many of the three-strikes prisoners simply because there is no room to house them all. The parole boards try to release only the nonviolent repeat offenders, but even that is not always possible. As a result, you can have the almost surreal experience outlined in the following scenario.

---

[9] *Solem v. Helm*, 463 U.S. 277, 103 S. Ct. 3001, 77 L. Ed. 2d 637 (1983).

(2) Any person who has been convicted of a serious violent felony in this state or who has been convicted under the laws of any other state or of the United States of a crime which if committed in this state would be a serious violent felony and who after such first conviction subsequently commits and is convicted of a serious violent felony for which such person is not sentenced to death shall be sentenced to imprisonment for *life without parole*. Any such sentence of life without parole shall not be suspended, stayed, probated, deferred, or withheld, and any such person sentenced pursuant to this paragraph shall not be eligible for any form of pardon, parole, or early release administered by the State Board of Pardons and Paroles or for any earned time, early release, work release, leave, or any other sentence-reducing measures under programs administered by the Department of Corrections, the effect of which would be to reduce the sentence of life imprisonment without possibility of parole, except as may be authorized by any existing or future provisions of the Constitution. [Emphasis added by author].[10]

FIGURE 10-4

Punishment of Repeat Offenders; Punishment and Eligibility for Parole of Persons Convicted of Fourth Felony Offense Georgia

Life Sentences

"I tried a guy. I'll call him Joe. This guy had a prior possession of cocaine conviction. He comes before me and he's looking at life. We're a 'one strike and you're out' state. So, on the first offense, he got probation. On the second offense, which was identical to the first, he's facing life. Naturally, we take the case to trial. He's figuring, 'What have I got to lose?' He gets convicted in about 90 minutes. Two years later, I'm calling the docket and there's Joe again. I couldn't believe it. I walked over to him and said, 'Hey, aren't you supposed to be serving a life sentence?' He just looks at me. 'They let me out,' he says. So, Joe had already been sentenced to a life sentence, been released, and had time to commit another narcotics offense and land back in front of me again, all in less than two years. And, you guessed it; he was facing another mandatory life sentence."

Prosecutor

PROFILING THE PROFESSIONAL

E. INNOVATIVE SENTENCES

Because of prison overcrowding issues, judges have begun to entertain alternatives to prison sentences, especially for nonviolent offenders. Some judges have become quite innovative in structuring sentences that will not involve placing the defendant inside a prison. We will now take a look at some of the more popular of these innovative sentences.

[10] O.C.G.A. § 17-10-7.

1. HOUSE ARREST AND ELECTRONIC MONITORING

In appropriate cases, a judge may order that a defendant be held under house arrest. Several private companies specialize in monitoring services, some of which use advanced technology such as electronic ankle bracelets and computer terminals to confirm that a defendant remains within the confines of his home. If the defendant leaves a specified area, then an alarm will sound and the company will be alerted.

Computers have now been added to the arsenal of monitoring devices for people serving sentences on probation or under house arrest. A computer randomly calls the person to make sure that she is in fact at home. Some units have cameras and even breathalyzers so that a probation officer can see the person as well as obtain a random breath sample (for instance, when the defendant is known to abuse alcohol). The business of monitoring has expanded with the availability of technology. Now, even convicts who have permission to go to work every day and then return to a prison facility can be monitored on a second-by-second basis and, if they deviate from their prescribed routes, can be contacted immediately. This technology can be imbedded in smart phones, essentially a person's location to be monitored at any time of the day or night.

2. SUSPENDED SENTENCES WITH CONDITIONS

A judge may also order a defendant to serve a suspended sentence, which is essentially no sentence at all. A defendant sentenced to a suspended sentence is still technically convicted of a crime but does not serve any time in prison and will probably not pay a fine. Actually suspending a defendant's sentence is rare, but suspending on certain conditions is not. Suppose that the judge does not believe that the defendant poses a threat to himself or others and that placing him in prison would serve no good societal purpose. However, the defendant does have a problem; he may be dependent on drugs or have issues with violence. A judge might sentence the defendant to a suspended sentence on the condition that the defendant attend a certain number of Alcoholics Anonymous meetings or receive psychiatric counseling. If the defendant fails to abide by the conditions, the judge may always bring the defendant back to court, remove the suspension, and impose a full sentence.

Some of the most common conditions imposed this way include staying away from a victim in a domestic violence case, seeking counseling for violent outbursts, entrance into a substance abuse program, or even giving monthly presentations to local high school and middle school classes about the dangers of drugs or of not seeking counseling for mental problems.

3. PRIVATE PRISONS

Although it might have been unthinkable 50 years ago, there are now companies that specialize in maintaining prisons for intermediate and low-level offenders. Private companies have seen a potential for turning a profit by running prisons more efficiently than the state. While some private companies have supplanted probation or parole officers, others have built and maintain medium-security prison facilities. Instead of sentencing a defendant to an overcrowded state facility, a judge might decide to place a defendant into a private prison. Some estimates place as many as 100,000 inmates currently serving in private prison facilities (see Figure 10-5).

A common hope among policymakers is that governments will save money by housing prisoners in private prisons. Whether this is true is debatable. Also at issue

FIGURE 10-5

Number of Felony Convictions for Persons Sentenced in State Courts

Most serious conviction offense	Total	Percent of felons sentenced for— One felony conviction	Two felony convictions	Three or more felony convictions
All offenses	100%	77	15	7
Violent offenses	100%	71	19	11
Murder/ Nonnegligent manslaughter	100%	60	22	18
Sexual assault[a]	100%	65	20	15
Robbery	100%	66	21	13
Aggravated assault	100%	73	18	9
Other violent[b]	100%	83	13	4
Property offenses	100%	72	18	10
Burglary	100%	62	23	15
Larceny	100%	84	12	4
Fraud/Forgery[c]	100%	67	20	13
Drug offenses	100%	80	14	6
Possession	100%	88	10	2
Trafficking	100%	73	18	9
Weapon offenses	100%	78	17	5
Other specified offenses[d]	100%	90	8	2

Note: Data on number of conviction offenses were reported for 100% of convicted felons. The number of convictions is based on current convictions only. Detail may not sum to total because of rounding.

[a]Includes rape.

[b]Includes offenses such as negligent manslaughter and kidnapping.

[c]Includes embezzelment.

[d]Comprises nonviolent offenses such as vandalism and receiving stolen property.

Source: Felony Sentences in State Courts, 2006—Statistical Tables. Bureau of Justice Statistics, U.S. Department of Justice. Revised 11/22/10.

is the possibility that private firms attempt to lower operating costs by sacrificing service quality, especially considering that public safety and the lives of staff and inmate are at risk. Inmates at some of these private institutions have claimed that their constitutional rights are routinely violated. Stories abound of substandard health care, recurrent violent episodes, criminal activities, and escapes. Whether these stories are merely anecdotal or symptomatic of a disturbing trend is not known.

Private industry has also gotten into the business of monitoring probationers. In some states, private companies monitor all people sentenced on misdemeanor cases, while state probation officers monitor convicted felons.

Sidebar

Great Britain has a much higher percentage of its inmates in private prisons than the United States.

4. REGISTERED SEX OFFENDER PROGRAMS

When a person is convicted of one of a set of specific statutes, he is required to register as a sex offender in his community. Requiring sex offenders to declare themselves to local law enforcement and even to their neighbors may be embarrassing but has been held to be constitutional. Many states maintain online databases of registered sex offenders that include their full names, photographs, current addresses, and occupations. Many registered sex offenders are prohibited from coming within 1,000 feet of a school area and face many other prohibitions. Crimes that can cause a person to become a registered sex offender differ from state to state, but most obviously involve some type of sexual offense, including public indecency, child molestation, and rape, to name just a few.

5. INTENSIVE PROBATION

In some cases a judge might want more extensive contact with the defendant over the course of her probation, especially to ensure that the defendant is abiding by the terms of the sentence, which might include not using any narcotics, not associating with other known felons, getting and maintaining work, and abiding by any other terms that the judge might impose. Regular probation, as we will discuss later in this chapter, takes care of some of those items, but a judge has a third option between incarceration and normal probation: intensive probation.

Intensive probation provides strict control, monitoring, and surveillance of a defendant (at this point referred to as a *probationer*) during the entire course of her probated sentence. Any violation of the terms of intensive probation could mean that the defendant's probation is revoked, and she will be sent to prison to serve out the balance of the sentence. Defendants serving under the terms of intensive probation are subject to random drug tests, unannounced searches of their homes, regular checkups at their jobs to see if they are reporting and working as they should be, and a host of other features that truly merit the term *intensive.* Under most intensive probation terms, a defendant will be visited at least four times per week by a probation officer. The defendant must be employed and will submit her entire paycheck to the probation office, which will deduct any payments for fines, court fees, and restitution to victims and then pay the defendant the balance. If a defendant does not violate the terms and conditions of intensive probation, she can petition for conversion to standard probation. It is up to the judge to determine whether the defendant should be transferred from the intensive probation program to regular probation.

SENTENCING AFTER TRIAL

So far, our discussion has centered on defendants who choose to plead guilty prior to trial, either to take advantage of a plea bargain offered by the prosecutor or because the amount of evidence against them makes it obvious that a trial would be a waste of time. However, what happens to defendants who choose to plead not guilty and proceed to trial? If that person is found not guilty, then he will be released. But for the balance of this chapter, we will assume that the defendant has been found guilty either at a jury or bench trial. What happens once the jury returns with a guilty verdict?

A. DEFENDANT IS FOUND GUILTY

Assuming that nothing improper has occurred during the jury deliberation process, once the jury decides on a unanimous verdict, the jury foreperson communicates that fact to the bailiff. The jury foreperson writes the jury's verdict on the indictment or other charging document, and the judge summons the jury back into the courtroom to announce the verdict. The judge often reviews the jury's verdict first, to make sure that the jury has followed proper procedure and has not done something improper, such as a clear showing that the verdict was not unanimous or that some other impropriety occurred. (Some states do allow nonunanimous verdicts in certain types of cases, with the jury allowed to return a verdict if 11 out of the 12 agree on a particular verdict.)

B. ENTRY OF THE VERDICT AS THE JUDGMENT OF THE COURT

Once the jury has returned its verdict of guilty, the judge must then enter the verdict as the judgment of the court. Although this may seem like a mere bookkeeping item, there are times when the judge takes issue with the jury's verdict. No judge is empowered to overturn a jury's not guilty verdict, but some states do give the power to a judge to overturn a guilty verdict. In such a situation, the verdict of the jury would be guilty, but the judgment of the court would be not guilty.

C. JUDGE'S DISCRETION IN SENTENCING

As we have already seen, sentencing guidelines were imposed as a way of curbing a judge's discretion. Many people had become uncomfortable with the wide latitude that a judge enjoyed in imposing a sentence, and some studies had suggested that the color of the defendant's skin might be a stronger indicator of whether a defendant will serve a long prison sentence than the underlying facts of the crime. However, as we have seen, sentencing guidelines have met with several restrictions, and judges retain the discretion that they once had before the guidelines were introduced. But there are many states that never adopted sentencing guidelines in the first place. Just how much discretion does a judge have in fashioning a sentence after a defendant has been found guilty? The answer to that question is that a judge has broad discretion. As long as the judge acts within the confines of the minimum and maximum sentences prescribed by state law and does not exceed the mandates of the Eighth Amendment, the judge can sentence a defendant to all kinds of punishments. Here are the most common alternatives for a judge:

- Probation/parole
- Life in prison
- Life in prison without the possibility of parole
- Determinate sentence of incarceration

You will notice that death sentences are not listed under the most common sentencing alternatives for judges. Death penalties are not common, and we devote an entire section to the subject of death penalties later in this chapter.

1. PROBATION/PAROLE

Probation
Allowing a person convicted of a criminal offense to avoid serving a jail sentence, so long as she abides by certain conditions (usually including being supervised by a probation officer).

Parole
The supervised portion of a convict's sentence that he serves once he has been released from prison.

Before the 1980s, when big changes were enacted, especially on the federal level, there was a clear distinction between the terms *probation* and *parole.* A sentence served on **probation** was one in which the defendant was not incarcerated after trial but was instead allowed to return home to live and to work in the community, but was required to have regular visits with a probation officer who would double-check to make sure that the defendant was making payments on his fine, court fees, and restitution. The probation officer would also ensure that the defendant had not committed any new offenses or violated any other terms of probation. **Parole** on the other hand, used to mean that after a person was released from prison, he would have to make regular reports to a parole officer, pay fines, court costs, and restitution and abide by another terms of his release. There was, and remains, an understandable confusion over the two terms, and the fact that the federal government and some states have categorically eliminated parole for convicts while still maintaining probation offices has not made the situation any clearer (see Figure 10-6).

These days, there is a strong chance that if a person has committed her first offense, and the offense was relatively minor, she will not be sent to prison. The prison system in every state is already overcrowded, so the justice system is looking for alternatives to prison time already. A person who has been convicted after trial might receive a probated sentence or might be sent into any of a number of diversionary programs, including halfway houses, community service projects, and other alternatives that we have already discussed.

	Number convicted		Percent sentenced to prison		Mean prison term imposed in months	
	2005	1995	2005	1995	2005	1995
All offenses	78,042	47,556	79.0%	67.1%	61 mo.	63 mo.
Violent	2,900	2,658	86.1	86.6	96	101
Property	12,861	13,484	53.3	50.1	26	26
Fraud	10,459	9,847	56.7	53.2	25	20
Other	2,402	3,367	38.9	41.9	32	45
Drug	27,452	16,728	90.1	86.9	83	83
Public order	8,796	8,538	47.5	31.9	50	27
Regulatory	1,102	1,492	32.3	32.2	31	26
Other	7,694	7,046	49.7	31.9	52	28
Weapons	8,963	3,116	92.2	90.7	84	89
Immigration	17,070	3,007	88.5	90.6	25	23
Southwest U.S. border district						
Yes	22,875	8,143	87.7%	78.4%	35 mo.	40 mo.
No	55,167	39,413	75.4	64.7	74	68
District size						
Small	4,390	3,064	76.2%	67.0%	70 mo.	62 mo.
Medium	33,209	30,076	79.6	65.4	67	60
Large	40,443	14,416	78.9	70.5	55	67

Source: Felony Sentences in State Courts, 2006—Statistical Tables. Bureau of Justice Statistics, U.S. Department of Justice. Revised 11/22/10.

FIGURE 10-6

Defendants Convicted and Sentenced to a Federal Prison Term

a. Probation Revocation Hearings

When a probationer violates one or more conditions of his probation, the probation officer is authorized to file a petition with the original sentencing judge, asking that the probation be revoked. In many states, prosecutors can also file such petitions. Probation revocation hearings are similar to trials. The state presents evidence to justify revoking the defendant's probation, and the defense is permitted to present evidence to show that the defendant should be allowed to continue on probation.

b. Pardons and Commutations

State governors and the president are authorized to issue pardons for people convicted of crime. A **pardon** rescinds a conviction. Usually, a pardon is issued only when there is some question about the defendant's guilt or other concerns about justice in the case. The power to issue pardons is considered to be an

Pardon
A president's or governor's release of a person from punishment for a crime.

executive privilege and cannot be rescinded by the other branches of government. In recent years, a few questionable pardon cases on the national level have brought this fairly low-key executive privilege into the limelight. For example, President Richard Nixon famously pardoned Jimmy Hoffa, the former Teamsters president, giving rise to numerous conspiracy theories about Nixon's ties to organized crime. President Bill Clinton granted nearly 400 pardons during his two terms in office. The grand prize for pardons goes to President Franklin D. Roosevelt, who was responsible for a whopping 3,687 pardons during his 12 years in office.

Executives are also empowered to reduce an overall sentence. For example, President George W. Bush failed to pardon I. Lewis "Scooter" Libby, but he commuted Libby's sentence for his role in leaking the identity of a CIA agent. Although Libby did not receive a pardon, his **commutation** generated heated protests because of his close ties to the White House. To commute a death sentence would be to reduce it to life in prison.

Commutation
Changing a criminal punishment to one less severe.

c. Early Release

Most jurisdictions have provisions that allow a prisoner to be released prior to serving his full sentence. For instance, in many states there is a provision called "day for a day." If the prisoner abides by the rules and has good behavior, the state will take away one day of his sentence for every day that he has been a model prisoner. In those jurisdictions, a prisoner serving a six-year sentence could be released in three years. If the prisoner becomes a trustee at the facility, or gets a job with a certain amount of responsibility, he might get even greater than day for a day. In jurisdictions that have imposed sentencing guidelines, however, these programs have often been done away with. On the federal level, for example, a sentence of six years means that the prisoner will serve six years and no less.

2. LIFE IN PRISON

If the defendant's crime is severe enough, he might face a maximum sentence of life in prison. In some states, a judge has the discretion of ordering a sentence of anywhere from 20 years to life for specific offenses. Obviously, these sentences are reserved for the most severe crimes, such as manslaughter or sale and distribution of large quantities of narcotics, and for repeat offenders. We have already discussed the possibility that a defendant may be sentenced to life under the three-strikes provisions that many states enacted.

There is a common misperception of what a life sentence constitutes. On the federal level, for instance, if a person is given a life sentence, it usually means that that person will serve the balance of his life in prison. In some states, however, a life sentence could have the practical effect of only a few years served. Persons sentenced to life may, in some states, qualify for parole hearings within one or two years of being sentenced, while most allow a defendant to petition for parole or probation within seven years. This has led to a common misapprehension of the law that a life sentence means only seven years. In fact, a person may petition for release in most states within seven years of sentencing, but that does not mean that he will be released.

3. LIFE SENTENCE WITHOUT THE POSSIBILITY OF PAROLE

The U.S. Supreme Court has also held that sentences of life without parole do not violate the Eighth Amendment for certain offenses. These include murder, kidnapping, bank robbery, narcotic offenses, and aggravated rape. Except for murder, life sentences without parole are authorized only when the listed crime involves violence or repeated convictions.

4. DETERMINATE YEARS SENTENCING

In many cases, a judge has little or no discretion in sentencing a defendant when she has been found guilty of a specific crime. Some narcotics offenses, for example, carry mandatory minimum sentences of 25 years in custody. The judge has no option but to impose that sentence when the jury finds the defendant guilty of that charge. Many types of offenses now carry mandatory minimum sentences, including narcotics cases and aggravated assault on a police officer, to name just two.

D. SENTENCING HEARINGS

Before a judge imposes a sentence, the defendant has the right to request a sentencing hearing during which the defendant can present evidence that might mitigate his final sentence. This hearing is like a minitrial. Witnesses may testify, and both sides may introduce evidence to support their positions. The prosecutor also has the right to present evidence showing the defendant in a bad light, and such evidence might urge the judge to order a harsher sentence. Finally, sentencing hearings are also where victims have the right to make a statement to the court in a victim impact statement. We will examine all three of these phases of a sentencing hearing.

1. DEFENDANT'S PRESENTATION OF EVIDENCE TO MITIGATE THE SENTENCE

The defense is permitted to present evidence during a sentencing hearing in mitigation of the defendant's sentence. For instance, the defense may show that the defendant has a poor education or a bad childhood to help explain why the defendant resorted to crime. In addition to family life and education, the defense might introduce evidence of the defendant's mental stability or intelligence. The defendant may even take the stand and testify about the circumstances of his life as a way to explain why he committed the crime.

2. STATE'S PRESENTATION OF EVIDENCE IN AGGRAVATION OF THE DEFENDANT'S SENTENCE

During a sentencing hearing, the prosecutor may seek to introduce a wide range of evidence to justify a harsher sentence for the defendant. For example, the prosecution might show that:

- The defendant has prior criminal convictions.
- The defendant's actions have had an adverse impact on the victim or victim's family.
- The defendant poses a significant threat to the community or is likely to commit more crimes in the future.

3. VICTIM IMPACT STATEMENTS

Many states have enacted statutes that allow victims of specific kinds of crime to recover money from state or federal funds. These funds are designed to help defray some of the costs associated with obtaining replacement goods (or to meet insurance deductibles when insurance coverage exists).

Victim impact statement
A right given to victims of a crime or the victim's relatives to explain to the court the impact that the crime has had on the person or the family; the victim also has the right to ask the judge to impose the maximum possible sentence allowed by law.

Another victims' right initiative has been statutes that allow a victim to have some personal input at the defendant's sentencing hearing. A victim is permitted and often encouraged to file such a statement that can be read at the hearing and is made a part of the defendant's file. A **victim impact statement** allows the victim to tell the judge what effect the defendant's crime has had on the victim's life. Victim impact statements are often an important part of the healing process that occurs in the aftermath of a crime, especially a violent crime.

PROFILING THE PROFESSIONAL

Victim Impact Statements

"In the old days, the victim would never get up because nobody asked them if they want to say something. Now the law requires prosecutors to ask victims if they want to say something during sentencing. They have the right to speak. The judge can't deny it. In the old days, a lot of judges would ignore victims. It creates an emotional atmosphere in the courtroom and a lot of the old-time judges found that uncomfortable and were hesitant about that."

Debra Sullivan, Assistant District Attorney

IV THE DEATH PENALTY

Originally, the Eighth Amendment's prohibition of cruel and unusual punishment was enacted to prohibit torture. The Eighth Amendment does not forbid a sentence of death; it simply means that the sentence must be carried out with as little pain as possible. Most "innovations" in the mechanisms of executing human beings have been created as supposedly painless methods of ending a human being's life. Thomas Edison's support of the use of the electric chair arguably stemmed from his belief that the method was less painful than hanging, although some alleged that he also saw it as another method of promoting the use of electricity in the early days of the twentieth century. The French use of the guillotine was also promoted as a more humane method of execution. These days, most states in the United States that impose the death penalty have moved toward lethal injection as the latest step in making the execution of a person as pain free as possible. However, there are still states that authorize death by firing squad and the gas chamber.

A. PROCEDURES IN DEATH PENALTY CASES

Issues surrounding the imposition of the death penalty could fill an entire volume. Sentencing a person to execution at the hands of the state has always been considered to be the most extreme sanction in law. As such, death penalty cases, known as capital murder cases, have different safeguards and procedures than are seen in other charges. For example, death penalty cases actually have two trials: one to determine guilt, the other to determine the sentence. Death penalty cases are often fast-tracked during the appellate procedure. They are also reviewed by the state governor for clemency.

B. SENTENCING IN DEATH PENALTY CASES

Sentencing in death penalty cases raises a whole host of crucial issues. Death penalty trials are always **bifurcated**, meaning that there are two trials. When a defendant is charged with capital murder and the government announces its intention to seek the death penalty, special rules are triggered to protect the defendant. The bifurcated trial consists of the guilt phase, where the jury decides whether the defendant is guilty of the crime, and the sentencing phase, where the judge or jury is called upon to decide whether the defendant's actions warrant a death sentence. In most jurisdictions the only crime that warrants a death sentence is murder. Although in the past it was possible to be sentenced to death for crimes such as rape, most jurisdictions limit a death sentence to cases involving homicide. In some states only a jury can decide to impose a death sentence. In other jurisdictions, the judge decides to impose death. In either situation, the fact finder must not only decide that the defendant is guilty of the crime but also decide that the defendant's actions warrant a death sentence. The only way to reach this conclusion is to find that certain aggravating factors were present. Simply killing another person is not enough to warrant a death sentence. In order for

Bifurcated trial
Separate trials for different issues in the same prosecution; the most common use of a bifurcated jury trial is a first trial to decide whether the defendant is guilty of murder and then a second trial to determine the defendant's sentence: life, life without parole, or death.

a defendant to be sentenced to death, the murder must have been committed during the commission of another crime (such as rape) or in a particularly gruesome way.

C. MORATORIUMS ON DEATH PENALTY SENTENCES

In the wake of recent cases in which DNA evidence has shown that the defendant who was sentenced to death could not have committed the offense, many groups and even some state governments have called for a moratorium on death penalties. By suspending any executions, these groups argue, the criminal justice system can regain some of its credibility by confirming that those who are scheduled to die have had every opportunity to overturn their sentences. Governor George Ryan of Illinois instituted a moratorium on death penalties in his state in the wake of over half the death row convictions being overturned by the state and U.S. Supreme Courts. Many European countries have total bans on the death penalty. The U.S. Supreme Court struck down state death penalty laws in 1972 but reinstated them once the states adopted new procedures. Still, 15 states have abolished the death penalty entirely.

D. NEW BILLS BARRING EXECUTION OF THE MENTALLY HANDICAPPED

Several states have recently passed legislation barring the execution of the mentally retarded. Some states, such as Georgia, have prohibited executing the mentally handicapped for decades. In 2001, Governor Jeb Bush signed such a law into effect for the state of Florida. Some states, such as Texas, have consistently failed to enact such a provision. In fact, the state of Texas has performed more executions than any other state.

V CORRECTIONAL FACILITIES

There are many different types of prisons. Depending on the nature of the offense and the defendant's prior record, time may be served in a maximum-, medium-, or minimum-security facility. The differences in these institutions are profound. A maximum-security facility houses some of the worst offenders, such as rapists and murderers, while a minimum-security facility is home to nonviolent offenders. Medium-security facilities might house those convicted of aggravated battery or major theft felonies and those who have committed robbery with violence but have not seriously injured their victims. Maximum-security facilities often have double rows of razor wire–topped fencing and guard towers manned by armed security guards who are authorized to shoot anyone attempting to escape. Minimum-security facilities, on the other hand, often look more like dormitories, have less security, and rarely suffer from escape attempts.

A. BOOT CAMPS

Another form of punishment is so-called boot camp. Someone who has been sentenced to a boot camp is normally sent there for a maximum period of 90 days. The conditions are stricter than what is seen in most prisons. Modeled on military boot camps, prisoners at such facilities must abide by a strict code of conduct. The advantage for a prisoner is that with successful completion of the boot camp program, the prisoner will be released much sooner than he would have been normally. Of course, if the defendant cannot follow the rules, his sentence will not be shortened, and he will be sent to a conventional maximum-security facility to serve out the balance of the sentence. Boot camp facilities are reserved for youthful offenders, under the theory that there may be a way to save young offenders from becoming lifelong criminals.

PROFILING THE PROFESSIONAL

Corrections Officer

"They [the prisoners] lack a little bit of privacy, but for the most part they do what they want. They work. They make money. They watch TV. They lift weights. It seems like every one of them in there is getting bigger and bigger. They've done away with weights in a lot of states; I think they should do away with them in ours."

Corrections officer at a maximum-security facility

B. PRISONER RIGHTS

Sidebar

"At least 80 percent of all criminal jury trials worldwide take place in the United States."[11]

Several federal and U.S. Supreme Court decisions have stated that prisons must maintain an adequate law library. Because a criminal defendant incarcerated in the prison system has a great deal of time on his hands, it is very common for a defendant to learn a lot about the law during a lengthy incarceration. Some inmates become experts at the appellate process and are often referred to as jailhouse lawyers. These individuals have developed an expertise in the area of appellate law and often assist other inmates with their knowledge. Most attorneys are reluctant to take cases on appeal, primarily since they often don't get paid. Because of this many convicted prisoners end up representing themselves on appeal.

[11] *Beyond A Reasonable Doubt: Inside the American Jury System.* By Melvin Bernard Zerman, Thomas Y. Crawl Publishers, New York, Copyright, 1981.

In the following case, look out for the court's discussion about concurrent and consecutive prisons sentences and the type of discretion that a judge has in ordering them.

CASE EXCERPT

STATE v. HAIRSTON

118 Ohio St.3d 289, 888 N.E.2d 1073 (2008)

SYLLABUS OF THE COURT

Where none of the individual sentences imposed on an offender are grossly disproportionate to their respective offenses, an aggregate prison term resulting from consecutive imposition of those sentences does not constitute cruel and unusual punishment.

Ron O'Brien, Franklin County Prosecuting Attorney, and Steven L. Taylor, Assistant Prosecuting Attorney, for appellee.

Clark Law Office and Toki M. Clark, Columbus, for appellant.

O'Donnell, J.

The sole issue before this court concerns whether the aggregate, 134-year prison term imposed on Marquis Hairston constitutes cruel and unusual punishment in violation of the Eighth Amendment to the United States Constitution and Section 9, Article I of the Ohio Constitution. Because this aggregate term of incarceration resulted from Hairston's guilty pleas to four counts of aggravated robbery, four counts of kidnapping, three counts of aggravated burglary, all with firearm specifications, and three counts of having a weapon while under disability, and because none of his individual sentences are grossly disproportionate to their respective offenses, we conclude that his aggregate sentence is not unconstitutional. Thus, we affirm the judgment of the court of appeals.

FACTS AND PROCEDURAL HISTORY

In the fall of 2005, a series of home burglaries caused concern among inhabitants of German Village, a neighborhood located just south of downtown Columbus.

At 7:00 A.M., on September 27, 2005, Marquis Hairston and two other males entered the home of Cynthia Green. She first saw them in the hallway adjacent to her bathroom as she prepared to take a shower. At gunpoint, they took her to the bedroom and forced her to remove her clothing and to kneel on her bedroom floor while they ransacked her home. One of the males, holding a gun to her head, began to tease her, saying "safety on, safety off" as the others loaded cash, jewelry, phones, stereo equipment, a laptop computer, and her clothing into her car. Then they gagged her by stuffing a pair of socks into her mouth, tied her to a chair, and left in her car. She eventually freed herself by using a pair of manicure scissors to cut her restraints and called the police.

Two weeks later, at 6:00 A.M. on October 10, 2005, Gary Michael Reames and his fiancée, Melanie Pinkerton, awoke to investigate why their dogs were barking and discovered two men in the hallway outside their bedroom—one holding a gun and the other holding a butcher knife. The men screamed obscenities and ordered Reames and Pinkerton to get down on their knees. While one of the men held them at gunpoint, the second man ransacked their home, taking cash, jewelry, and credit cards to Pinkerton's

BMW. After loading the car, they ordered Reames and Pinkerton to take off their clothes, tied them to chairs in the hallway, and gagged them. After the men left in her car, Pinkerton freed herself, untied Reames, and called the police.

At about 6:45 in the morning on October 25, 2005, John Maransky, after showering and dressing for work, walked downstairs to his living room, where two men confronted him at gunpoint and ordered him to get down on the floor. One of the men held him at gunpoint while the other ransacked his home and took electronic equipment and other items outside to his car. The gunman threatened to shoot him if he tried to do anything. Once they finished loading his car, the men took Maransky to the basement, ordered him to strip, hogtied him, and stuffed a glove into his mouth. After they left, Maransky freed himself and called the police.

A week later, on November 2, 2005, Maransky discovered several of his stolen belongings at the E-Z Cash Pawnshop, located near the German Village neighborhood. He called the police, and officer Brenda Walker responded and spoke with the pawnshop clerk, who identified Hairston and his brother, Louis, as the individuals who had pawned Maransky's items. Thereafter, Pinkerton identified Marquis Hairston from a photo array as the perpetrator of the crimes. Based on this information, officers arrested Hairston on November 3, 2005, and, during a videotaped interrogation, he admitted his involvement in all three burglaries.

The state subsequently indicted him on 26 counts, including charges of robbery, aggravated robbery, burglary, aggravated burglary, kidnapping, theft, receiving stolen property, and having a weapon while under disability. Following Hairston's pleas of not guilty to all charges, the court began a jury trial on March 29, 2006. On the third day of trial, however, Hairston pleaded guilty to four counts of aggravated robbery, three counts of aggravated burglary, four counts of kidnapping, all with firearm specifications, and three counts of having a weapon while under disability. The state agreed to nolle the remaining counts.

At the sentencing hearing, the state requested maximum, consecutive sentences, asserting that Hairston had been imprisoned on two previous occasions for similar offenses and pointing out that he had burglarized Green's home just seven days after being released from prison. Each victim gave a statement to the court explaining the impact that the crimes had on their lives. Defense counsel urged the court to consider that Hairston was only 24 years old at the time of the offenses, that he had completed his GED while previously incarcerated, that he had not fired the gun, and that he claimed he had not caused the victims to suffer any serious physical harm.

The court referred to the purposes of sentencing—to protect the public and to punish the offender—and noted that Hairston had previously been incarcerated on two separate occasions for robbery and burglary, that there was no indication that he would have stopped committing these crimes had he not been caught, and that he had not expressed remorse for his behavior. The court also recognized the effect that Hairston's crimes had on the victims and on the community in general. Based on these considerations, the court imposed maximum, consecutive sentences for each of the 14 felony offenses and the gun specifications, resulting in an aggregate prison term of 134 years.

Hairston appealed to the Tenth District Court of Appeals, arguing, inter alia, that the aggregate sentence constitutes cruel and unusual punishment. The court of appeals rejected that argument and affirmed the trial court. *State v. Hairston*, Franklin App. No. 06AP-420, 2007-Ohio-143, 2007 WL 96971. On Hairston's further appeal to this court, we agreed to consider the following proposition of law: "A violation of the Eighth

Amendment to the United States Constitution occurs where a Defendant is sentenced to 134 years incarceration for three aggravated robberies where injuries are non-life threatening." 113 Ohio St.3d 1512, 2007-Ohio-2208, 866 N.E.2d 511.

Hairston argues that his sentence violates the Eighth Amendment because it is grossly disproportionate to the aggregate nature of his crimes and shocking to a reasonable person and to the community's sense of justice. He further maintains that his offense warrants less punishment than more serious offenses, such as rape, sexual abuse, or murder. The state contends that Hairston's aggregate sentence is not unconstitutional, because the term of incarceration for each offense is within the statutory range and because the court has discretion to impose those terms consecutively.

CRUEL AND UNUSUAL PUNISHMENT

The Eighth Amendment to the United States Constitution applies to the states pursuant to the Fourteenth Amendment. See *Robinson v. California* (1962), 370 U.S. 660, 82 S.Ct. 1417, 8 L.Ed.2d 758. The amendment provides: "Excessive bail shall not be required, nor excessive fines imposed, nor cruel and unusual punishments inflicted." Section 9, Article I of the Ohio Constitution sets forth the same restriction: "Excessive bail shall not be required; nor excessive fines imposed; nor cruel and unusual punishments inflicted."

In *State v. Weitbrecht* (1999), 86 Ohio St.3d 368, 715 N.E.2d 167, we applied Justice Kennedy's Eighth Amendment analysis in his concurring opinion in *Harmelin v. Michigan* (1991), 501 U.S. 957, 997, 111 S.Ct. 2680, 115 L.Ed.2d 836. We quoted with approval his conclusion that "'the Eighth Amendment does not require strict proportionality between crime and sentence. Rather, it forbids only extreme sentences that are "grossly disproportionate" to the crime.'" *Weitbrecht*, 86 Ohio St.3d at 373, 715 N.E.2d 167, quoting *Harmelin*, 501 U.S. at 1001, 111 S.Ct. 2680, 115 L.Ed.2d 836 (Kennedy, J., concurring in part and in judgment). We further emphasized that "'only in the rare case in which a threshold comparison of the crime committed and the sentence imposed leads to an inference of gross disproportionality'" may a court compare the punishment under review to punishments imposed in Ohio or in other jurisdictions. Id. at 373, 715 N.E.2d 167, fn. 4, quoting *Harmelin*, 501 U.S. at 1005, 111 S.Ct. 2680, 115 L.Ed.2d 836 (Kennedy, J., concurring in part and in judgment).

With respect to the question of gross disproportionality, we reiterated in *Weitbrecht* that "'cases in which cruel and unusual punishments have been found are limited to those involving sanctions which under the circumstances would be considered shocking to any reasonable person,'" and furthermore that "'the penalty must be so greatly disproportionate to the offense as to shock the sense of justice of the community.'" Id. at 371, 715 N.E.2d 167, quoting McDougle v. Maxwell (1964), 1 Ohio St.2d 68, 70, 30 O.O.2d 38, 203 N.E.2d 334, and citing *State v. Chaffin* (1972), 30 Ohio St.2d 13, 59 O.O.2d 51, 282 N.E.2d 46, paragraph three of the syllabus.

GROSS-DISPROPORTIONALITY REVIEW OF AGGREGATE PRISON TERMS

Focusing on his aggregate term of incarceration, Hairston claims that the trial court imposed a 134-year sentence that is shocking to a reasonable person and to the community's sense of justice and thus is grossly disproportionate to the totality of his crimes.

In *State v. Saxon*, 109 Ohio St.3d 176, 2006-Ohio-1245, 846 N.E.2d 824, however, we held that "a sentence is the sanction or combination of sanctions imposed for each separate, individual offense." Id., paragraph one of the syllabus. We stated, "Ohio's felony-sentencing scheme is clearly designed to focus the judge's attention on one offense at a time," and "only after the judge has imposed a separate prison term for each offense may the judge then consider in his discretion whether the offender should serve those terms concurrently or consecutively." Because Hairston pleaded guilty to 14 separate felonies and three separate gun specifications, the court imposed 14 separate sentences to be served consecutively, and the cumulative length of his incarceration is therefore attributable to the number of offenses he committed.

When considering whether a cumulative prison term imposed for multiple offenses is cruel and unusual punishment, several federal courts of appeals have concluded that the Eighth Amendment proportionality review does not apply to cumulative sentences. For example, in *United States v. Aiello* (C.A.2, 1988), 864 F.2d 257, the court considered an Eighth Amendment challenge to a sentence of life imprisonment without parole, plus consecutive terms totaling 140 years, imposed for 11 felony counts related to a drug-trafficking enterprise. The court rejected the challenge, stating, "Eighth Amendment analysis focuses on the sentence imposed for each specific crime, not on the cumulative sentence." Id. at 265, citing *O'Neil v. Vermont* (1892), 144 U.S. 323, 331, 12 S.Ct. 693, 36 L.Ed. 450. See also *Hawkins v. Hargett* (C.A.10, 1999), 200 F.3d 1279, 1285, fn. 5 ("The Eighth Amendment analysis focuses on the sentence imposed for each specific crime, not on the cumulative sentence for multiple crimes"); *Pearson v. Ramos* (C.A.7, 2001), 237 F.3d 881, 886 ("it is wrong to treat stacked sanctions as a single sanction because to do so produces the ridiculous consequence of enabling a prisoner, simply by recidivating, to generate a colorable Eighth Amendment claim"); *United States v. Schell* (C.A.10, 1982), 692 F.2d 672, 675 (rejecting an Eighth Amendment challenge to a sentence imposing two ten-year prison terms, to run consecutively to a prior, 95-year prison term, because it would require the court to find that "virtually any sentence, however short, becomes cruel and unusual punishment when the defendant was already scheduled to serve lengthy sentences for prior convictions").

Several of our sister states have reached similar conclusions. In *State v. Berger* (2006), 212 Ariz. 473, 134 P.3d 378, for instance, the court rejected an Eighth Amendment challenge to a cumulative prison term of 200 years resulting from ten-year terms imposed consecutively for each of 20 counts of possessing child pornography. The court stated that "'a defendant has no constitutional right to concurrent sentences for two separate crimes involving separate acts.'" Id. at 479, 134 P.3d 378, quoting *State v. Jonas* (1990), 164 Ariz. 242, 249, 792 P.2d 705. It further reasoned that "if the sentence for a particular offense is not disproportionately long, it does not become so merely because it is consecutive to another sentence for a separate offense or because the consecutive sentences are lengthy in aggregate." Id.

In *Close v. People* (Colo.2002), 48 P.3d 528, 540, the Colorado Supreme Court rejected an Eighth Amendment challenge to a cumulative prison term of 60 years imposed on a teenager who had vandalized and stolen speakers from a car, and assaulted and ethnically intimidated several foreign students. The court held that the cumulative 60-year sentence imposed was not subject to proportionality review, noting that "if a proportionality review were to consider the cumulative effect of all the sentences imposed, the result would be the possibility that a defendant could generate an Eighth Amendment disproportionality claim simply because that defendant had engaged in repeated criminal activity." Id. at 539. See also *State v. August* (Iowa, 1999), 589 N.W.2d 740, 744 ("there is nothing cruel and unusual about punishing a person committing two crimes more severely than a person committing only one crime, which is the effect of consecutive sentencing"; *State v. Buchhold*, 2007 SD 15, 727 N.W.2d 816 (consecutive sentences are not subject to Eighth Amendment analysis).

In accordance with this analysis, we conclude that for purposes of the Eighth Amendment and Section 9, Article I of the Ohio Constitution, proportionality review should focus on individual sentences rather than on the cumulative impact of multiple sentences imposed consecutively. Where none of the individual sentences imposed on an offender are grossly disproportionate to their respective offenses, an aggregate prison term resulting from consecutive imposition of those sentences does not constitute cruel and unusual punishment.

Here, each of Hairston's individual prison terms is within the range authorized by the General Assembly. We have expressly held that trial courts have discretion to impose a prison sentence within the statutory range for the offense. *State v. Foster*, 109 Ohio St.3d 1, 2006-Ohio-856, 845 N.E.2d 470, paragraph seven of the syllabus. And, in McDougle, we stated that "as a general rule, a sentence that falls within the terms of a valid statute cannot amount to a cruel and unusual punishment." 1 Ohio St.2d at 69, 30 O.O.2d 38, 203 N.E.2d 334, citing *Martin v. United States* (C.A.9, 1963), 317 F.2d 753 (overruled on other grounds, *United States v. Bishop* (1973), 412 U.S. 346, 93 S.Ct. 2008, 36 L.Ed.2d 941); *Pependrea v. United States* (C.A.9, 1960), 275 F.2d 325; and *United States v. Rosenberg* (C.A.2, 1952), 195 F.2d 583.

Moreover, Hairston has not challenged any of the statutes upon which his sentences were based; had he done so, however, we have instructed that "reviewing courts should grant substantial deference to the broad authority that legislatures possess in determining the types and limits of punishments for crimes." *Weitbrecht*, 86 Ohio St.3d at 373-374, 715 N.E.2d 167, citing *Solem*, 463 U.S. at 290, 103 S.Ct. 3001, 77 L.Ed.2d 637, and *Harmelin*, 501 U.S. at 999, 111 S.Ct. 2680, 115 L.Ed.2d 836 (Kennedy, J., concurring in part and in judgment). Hairston also asserts that publicity about the length of his incarceration supports his assertion that the sentence is shocking to the community. However, even assuming that to be true, it is not the aggregate term of incarceration but, rather, the individual sentences that are relevant for purposes of Eighth Amendment analysis.

Because the individual sentences imposed by the court are within the range of penalties authorized by the legislature, they are not grossly disproportionate or shocking to a reasonable person or to the community's sense of justice and do not constitute cruel and unusual punishment. Accordingly, Hairston's aggregate prison term of 134 years, which resulted from the consecutive imposition of the individual sentences, does not violate the Eighth Amendment to the United States Constitution or Section 9, Article I of the Ohio Constitution.

CONCLUSION

The United States Supreme Court has emphasized that "'Eighth Amendment judgments should not be, or appear to be, merely the subjective views of individual Justices; judgment should be informed by objective factors to the maximum possible extent.'" *Rummel v. Estelle* (1980), 445 U.S. 263, 274, 100 S.Ct. 1133, 63 L.Ed.2d 382, quoting *Coker v. Georgia* (1977), 433 U.S. 584, 592, 97 S.Ct. 2861, 53 L.Ed.2d 982 (plurality opinion). And, as Justice Kennedy stated in his opinion in Harmelin, "the fixing of prison terms for specific crimes involves a substantive penological judgment that, as a general matter, is 'properly within the province of legislatures, not courts.'" *Harmelin*, 501 U.S. at 998, 111 S.Ct. 2680, 115 L.Ed.2d 836 (Kennedy, J., concurring in part and in judgment), quoting *Rummel*, 445 U.S. at 275-276, 100 S.Ct. 1133, 63 L.Ed.2d 382; see also *Gore v. United States* (1958), 357 U.S. 386, 393, 78 S.Ct. 1280, 2 L.Ed.2d 1405; *Solem*, 463 U.S. at 290, 103 S.Ct. 3001, 77 L.Ed.2d 637; *Weems v. United States* (1910), 217 U.S. 349, 379, 30 S.Ct. 544, 54 L.Ed. 793. Thus we are bound to give substantial deference to the General Assembly, which has established a specific range of punishment for every offense and authorized consecutive sentences for multiple offenses. *Weitbrecht*, 86 Ohio St.3d at 373-374, 715 N.E.2d 167.

Finally, we note that this case should not be heralded as a signal for future sentencing courts to impose maximum, consecutive terms of incarceration in all cases. Although Foster eliminated judicial fact-finding, courts have not been relieved of the obligation to consider the overriding purposes of felony sentencing, the seriousness and recidivism factors, or the other relevant considerations set forth in R.C. 2929.11, 2929.12, and 2929.13. When imposing sentence, courts must be faithful to the law, must not be swayed by public clamor, media attention, fear of criticism, or partisan interest, and must be mindful of the obligation to treat litigants and lawyers with dignity and courtesy.

Although the trial court here imposed an aggregate prison term that is not likely to be served, the singular conclusion we reach today is that this punishment does not constitute cruel and unusual punishment.

Judgment affirmed.

Moyer, C.J., and Lundberg Stratton, O'Connor, and Cupp, J.J., concur.
Pfeifer and Lanziger, J.J., concur separately.

CASE QUESTIONS

1. What is the sole issue in this case?
2. What was the defendant's pattern in these break-ins and burglaries?
3. Did Hairston take his case to a jury trial? If so, what happened?
4. What did the state recommend during the sentencing hearing?
5. What ruling did the judge make at the sentencing hearing?
6. According to the court, what is the rule about sentencing and proportionality to the crime?

CHAPTER SUMMARY

In this chapter, we have seen the many different types of pleas that can be raised in a criminal case. If a defendant pleads not guilty, he will have a trial. However, a defendant can enter several different types of guilty pleas if he does not wish to take the case to trial. For instance, a defendant can plead guilty and allow the judge to impose whatever legal sentence is permissible. However, most defendants plead guilty as a result of a plea bargain between the prosecutor and the defendant. Plea bargaining has sometimes been controversial. A prosecutor offers a defendant the promise of a recommendation to the judge to lower sentence than the defendant might otherwise receive in exchange for the defendant's plea of guilty. Given the enormous caseloads facing the criminal justice system, plea bargains have become a necessity.

There are strict constitutional limits on the types of sentences that can be imposed on an individual. The Eighth Amendment prohibits cruel and unusual punishment in sentencing, although that phrase has not been construed to mean that death sentences violate the Constitution. Sentences in the United States cannot contain provisions for torture or corporal punishment. A defendant may be sentenced to any of a number of different types of correctional facilities. Maximum-security facilities house the worst offenders in United States, while minimum-security facilities hold nonviolent offenders who have been sentenced on relatively minor charges. Over the years, courts have come up with innovative ways of sentencing individuals. It is now possible to have a defendant sentenced to house arrest or electronic monitoring as well as intensive probation.

Finally, there is the issue of the death penalty. As we have seen, the death penalty is not imposed in all murder cases. In fact, only a small minority of people charged with murder in the first degree are eligible to receive the death penalty. A person who is sentenced to death must have not only committed a murder but also have done so in a particularly gruesome or horrible way that justifies the imposition of death.

KEY TERMS

Key terms are listed here in order of appearance in chapter.

Nolo contendere
Alford plea
Sentence
Consecutive prison sentences
Concurrent prison sentences
Probation
Parole
Pardon
Commutation
Victim impact statement
Bifurcated trial

REVIEW QUESTIONS

1 What is an *Alford* plea?
2 What is the significance of a plea of nolo contendere, and why would a defendant wish to use this plea?
3 What must the judge establish before he accepts a defendant's plea of guilty?
4 What are plea interrogatories, and why are they important?
5 If a defendant changes his mind halfway through the guilty plea process, what will the judge do?

6 What are some of the questions that a defendant will be asked during his guilty plea?
7 What conditions would allow a judge to rescind a defendant's guilty plea?
8 What is the First Offender Program?
9 What is the basic arrangement in a plea bargain?
10 Why do some people consider plea bargains to be controversial?
11 Who has the power to impose a sentence on a criminal defendant?
12 What are the Federal Sentencing Guidelines?
13 How have the Federal Sentencing Guidelines been limited by U.S. Supreme Court cases?
14 What is the difference between concurrent and consecutive prison sentences?
15 Which amendment prohibits cruel and unusual punishment?
16 What would be an example of cruel and unusual punishment?
17 Explain the "three strikes and you're out" rule.
18 Explain house arrest.
19 What is the registered sex offender program?
20 What is a bifurcated trial, and how does it apply to death penalty cases?
21 Explain intensive probation.
22 What is a sentencing hearing?
23 What is a victim impact statement?
24 Describe the different types of correctional facilities.
25 Does everyone who is convicted of murder in the first degree receive the death penalty? Why or why not?

WEB SURFING

Texas Sentencing Issues
http://www.courts.state.tx.us/pubs/courtex/jan07.pdf

United States Sentencing Commission
http://www.ussc.gov/

Florida Sentencing Guidelines
http://www.dc.state.fl.us/pub/sg_annual/0001/intro.html

Federal Bureau of Prisons: Types of Prisons
http://www.bop.gov/locations/institutions/

EXERCISES

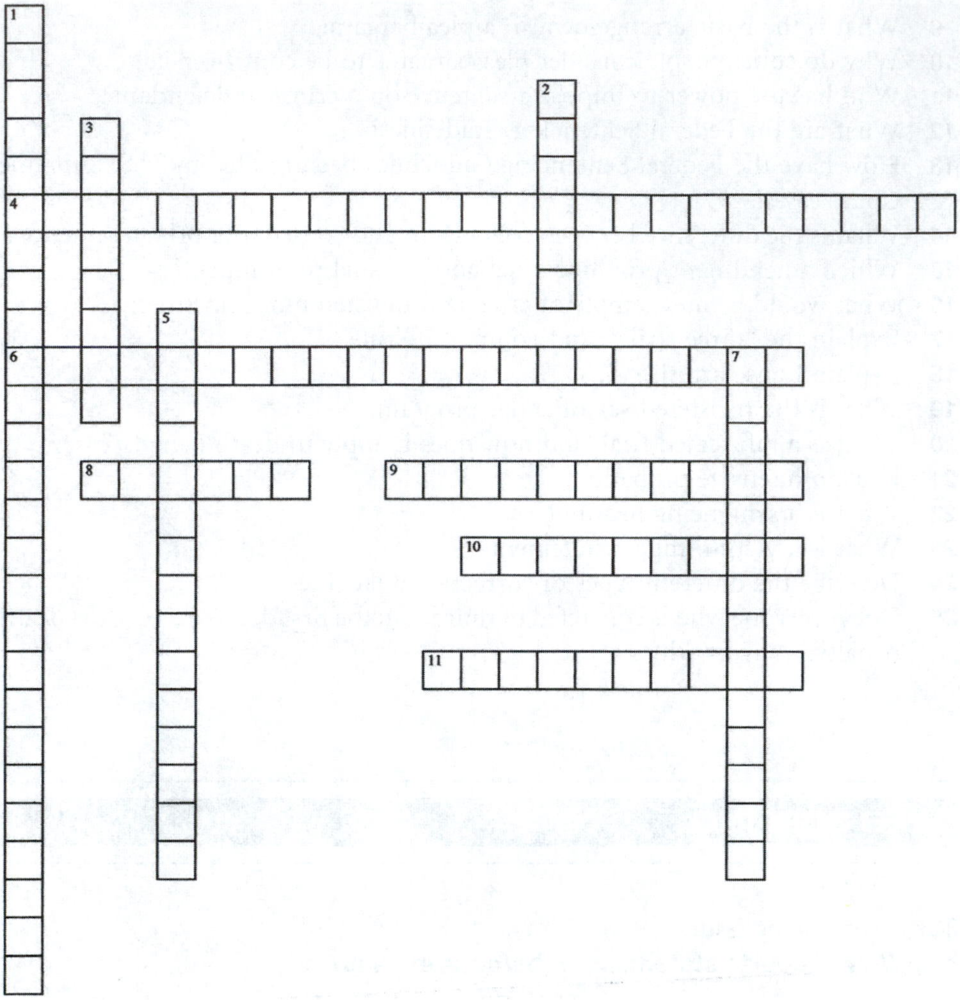

ACROSS

4. A sentence that permits a defendant to serve time on all of his pending charges at the same time
6. A right given to victims of a crime or the victim's relatives to explain to the court the impact that the crime has had on the person or the family
8. A president's or governor's release of a person from punishment for a crime
9. Changing a criminal punishment to one less severe

DOWN

1. A provision in the defendant's sentence that provides that once his first sentence is completed, the defendant will then begin serving time on any subsequent charges
2. The supervised portion of a convict's sentence that he serves once the convict has been released from prison
3. The punishment, such as a prison sentence and/or fine that is imposed on a convicted defendant by a judge

10. Allowing a person convicted of a criminal offense to avoid serving a jail sentence, so long as he abides by certain conditions (usually including being supervised by a probation officer)

11. A plea that allows a defendant to enter a guilty plea, but basing the plea on the amount and quantity of evidence against him, instead of the defendant's belief in his actual guilt

5. Separate trials for different issues in the same prosecution

7. A plea offered in a criminal case where the defendant does not contest his guilt and asks for the court's mercy

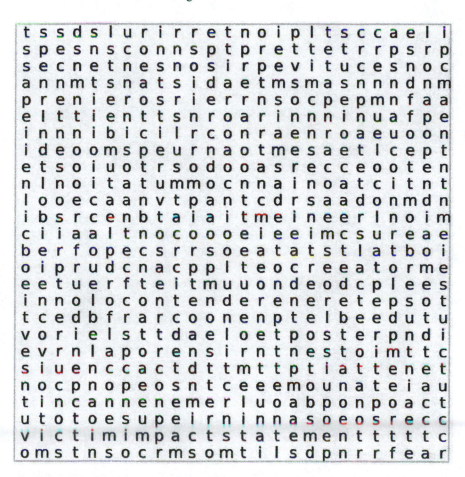

t	s	s	d	s	l	u	r	i	r	r	e	t	n	o	i	p	l	t	s	c	c	a	e	l	i
s	p	e	s	n	s	c	o	n	n	s	p	t	p	r	e	t	t	e	t	r	r	p	s	r	p
s	e	c	n	e	t	n	e	s	n	o	s	i	r	p	e	v	i	t	u	c	e	s	n	o	c
a	n	n	m	t	s	n	a	t	s	i	d	a	e	t	m	s	m	a	s	n	n	n	d	n	m
p	r	e	n	i	e	r	o	s	r	i	e	r	r	n	s	o	c	p	e	p	m	n	f	a	a
e	l	t	t	i	e	n	t	t	s	n	r	o	a	r	i	n	n	n	i	n	u	a	f	p	e
i	n	n	n	i	b	i	c	i	l	r	c	o	n	r	a	e	n	r	o	a	e	u	o	o	n
i	d	e	o	o	m	s	p	e	u	r	n	a	o	t	m	e	s	a	e	t	l	c	e	p	t
e	t	s	o	i	u	o	t	r	s	o	d	o	o	a	s	r	e	c	c	e	o	o	t	e	n
n	l	n	o	i	t	a	t	u	m	m	o	c	n	n	a	i	n	o	a	t	c	i	t	n	t
l	o	o	e	c	a	a	n	v	t	p	a	n	t	c	d	r	s	a	a	d	o	n	m	d	n
i	b	s	r	c	e	n	b	t	a	i	a	i	t	m	e	i	n	e	e	r	l	n	o	i	m
c	i	i	a	a	l	t	n	o	c	o	o	o	e	i	e	e	i	m	c	s	u	r	e	a	e
b	e	r	f	o	p	e	c	s	r	r	s	o	e	a	t	a	t	s	t	l	a	t	b	o	i
o	i	p	r	u	d	c	n	a	c	p	p	l	t	e	o	c	r	e	e	a	t	o	r	m	e
e	e	t	u	e	r	f	t	e	i	t	m	u	u	o	n	d	e	o	d	c	p	l	e	e	s
i	n	n	o	l	o	c	o	n	t	e	n	d	e	r	e	n	e	r	e	t	e	p	s	o	t
t	c	e	d	b	f	r	a	r	c	o	o	n	e	n	p	t	e	l	b	e	e	d	u	t	u
v	o	r	i	e	l	s	t	t	d	a	e	l	o	e	t	p	o	s	t	e	r	p	n	d	i
e	v	r	n	l	a	p	o	r	e	n	s	i	r	n	t	n	e	s	t	o	i	m	t	t	c
s	i	u	e	n	c	c	a	c	t	d	t	t	m	t	t	p	t	i	a	t	t	e	n	e	t
n	o	c	p	n	o	p	e	o	s	n	t	c	e	e	e	m	o	u	n	a	t	e	i	a	u
t	i	n	c	a	n	n	e	n	e	m	e	r	l	u	o	a	b	p	o	n	p	o	a	c	t
u	t	o	t	o	e	s	u	p	e	i	r	n	i	n	n	a	s	o	e	o	s	r	e	c	c
v	i	c	t	i	m	i	m	p	a	c	t	s	t	a	t	e	m	e	n	t	t	t	t	t	c
o	m	s	t	n	s	o	c	r	m	s	o	m	t	i	l	s	d	p	n	r	r	f	e	a	r

nolo contendere
alford plea
sentence
consecutive prison sentences
concurrent prison sentences
probation
parole
pardon
commutation
victim impact statement
bifurcated trial

QUESTIONS FOR ANALYSIS

1. Can you create an argument for making sentences in this country harsher? Essentially, you are arguing for a repeal of the Eighth Amendment. What would be the basis of your argument?
2. Should the death penalty be considered cruel and unusual punishment no matter what the circumstances of the crime? Why or why not?

11 Appeals

Chapter Objectives

- Explain the purpose of a motion for a new trial
- Define when and under what circumstances a person might bring a habeas corpus petition
- List and explain the various actions that an appellate court can take in a case pending before it
- Describe the basic components of an appellate brief
- Explain what certiorari is and why it is important

I INTRODUCTION TO THE APPELLATE PROCESS

When the defendant loses at trial, he or she is permitted to **appeal** the conviction to a higher court. The same cannot be said for the prosecutor. Barring an adverse ruling on a pretrial motion, the government is not permitted to appeal a finding of not guilty by a jury. How the defendant actually goes about bringing an appeal, along with the procedures for doing so, varies from jurisdiction to jurisdiction. In this chapter, we will assume, for the sake of clarity, that a defendant has been found guilty in a state court of a major felony (sexual assault, for example). We will limit our discussion to major convictions because there is more uniformity from state to state in felony appeals than in misdemeanor and traffic cases. In this chapter we will also examine the issues surrounding the appellate process at the federal level.

Appeal
A request for an appellate court to review the actions and ruling of a lower court in order to correct mistakes and remedy an injustice.

Once the jury has returned its verdict and the judge has entered it as the judgment of the court, the defendant must begin consideration of bringing an appeal. He does not have a great deal of time—in most states, a defendant must begin the appellate process within ten days of the entry of the judgment or else the defendant waives the right to bring any appeal. In criminal cases, the first step in the appellate process is not an appeal. Instead, it is a motion for a new trial.

A. MOTION FOR A NEW TRIAL

Motion for a new trial
A defendant's request that the trial judge set aside the jury's verdict and order a new trial; the request is based on alleged improper, unfair, and prejudicial rulings.

The appeal process begins shortly after the trial ends. In many jurisdictions, the defendant begins the appellate process by filing a **motion for a new trial**. This motion points to specific problems and irregularities that occurred in the trial that, according to the defendant, justify her demand for a new trial. In most jurisdictions the same judge who presided at the trial also hears the motion for new trial. If the judge grants the request, then a new trial is ordered and the entire trial process begins again as though the first trial never occurred. If the judge denies the request, then the defendant's appellate rights are triggered. In the vast majority of cases, a defendant's motion for a new trial is denied. Because for now we are assuming that this is a state prosecution, the defendant may now bring her appeal in the state appellate court system. In many states the first layer of the appellate court is referred to as the court of appeals; even though not all states follow that pattern, we will use that name for the rest of the discussion. Following the defendant's denial of her motion for a new trial, the defendant brings a notice of appeal.

EXAMPLE

More than ten days have elapsed since Keisha's conviction. The rules in the district are very specific. She must file within ten days or her appeal is waived. Keisha says that she wasn't aware of that rule. How is the court likely to rule?

Answer: Although one might be tempted to take a hard line on this request, most courts would probably allow Keisha to file her appeal anyway. Appealing a case is such an important right that most courts are very reluctant to dismiss a person's chance to appeal.

B. NOTICE OF APPEAL

Notice of appeal
The document giving official notice that a party intends to appeal; it is filed with the appellate court and served on the opposing party.

A **notice of appeal** puts the state on notice that the defendant intends to appeal his conviction to the court of appeals. The filing of a notice of appeal with the court of appeals not only places the prosecution on notice that the defendant intends to bring an appeal, but also triggers a series of procedural steps that must be followed in criminal appeals. For instance, most states provide a 30- to 60-day time period from the filing of the notice of appeal to the official docketing of the case before the court of appeals. If the defendant fails to register his case with the court, then the appeal may be dismissed. Docketing the case requires the completion of several forms and a request that the evidence used at trial and the transcript of the proceedings be transferred to the court of appeals. The rules and procedures used by appellate courts are very different from what is the norm in trial court. In the next section, we will examine the issues surrounding appellate jurisdiction.

III JURISDICTION AND PROCEDURAL STEPS IN APPELLATE COURTS

Whenever we encounter the term *jurisdiction* we are essentially talking about a court's power and authority. We have seen in earlier chapters that a trial court must have the appropriate original jurisdiction to hear a case. The same limitations are placed on appellate courts. An appellate court does not have the jurisdiction to make rulings in any prosecution until the jury has returned a verdict, the judge has entered a judgment, and the defendant has been sentenced (see Figure 11-1).

The organization of the American court system is typically presented as a pyramid, with trial courts forming the base and the state's highest court (often, but not always, called the state supreme court) occupying the pinnacle. In the middle of the pyramid is the intermediate appellate court, what we are referring to as the state court of appeals.

Before a case can move from the base of the judicial pyramid to the next highest level, the party bringing the appeal must establish that the appellate court has **jurisdiction** to hear the case. Jurisdiction is never assumed. It must be proved.

Jurisdiction
The persons about whom and the subject matters about which a court has the right and power to make decisions that are legally binding.

Before an appellate court will accept a case for review, the party bringing the appeal must establish that a final ruling has been made in the trial court and that there are no additional issues to be resolved in that court. The party must also establish that the ruling has an adverse impact on his life, liberty, or property. A criminal conviction qualifies in all of these areas.

FIGURE 11-1

Percent of Criminal Appeals Filed in U.S. District Court

	Percent of appeals		Average annual growth rate*	Appeals per 100 felony convictions	
	2005	1995		2005	1995
All offenses	14,644	10,162	4.1%	20	26
Violent	5.2%	7.6%	1.5	28	28
Property	14.7	19.3	2.3	19	16
Drug	40.5	49.1	3.2	22	29
Public order	7.2	9.7	2.1	18	26
Weapons	15.7	11.3	9.4	25	33
Immigration	16.6	3.0	25.3	14	9
Southwest U.S. border district					
Yes	19.2%	10.1%	11.2%	13	16
No	80.8	89.9	3.0	24	29
District size					
Small	6.8%	6.8%	3.3%	24	28
Medium	41.6	55.5	3.9	20	25
Large	51.6	37.7	4.5	20	29

*Calculated using each annual count from 1995 to 2005. District size is fixed by average U.S. resident population from 1995 to 2005 for computing the average growth rate by district size: 19 *large* districts (each with an average population of over 5 million residents), 58 *medium* districts (average population of 1 to 5 million residents), and 16 *small* districts (average population of under 1 million residents).

Source: *Federal Justice Statistics, 2005*, September 2008. NCJ 220383, Bureau of Justice Statistics, U.S. Department of Justice

Along with establishing jurisdiction for the state court of appeals, there are some additional changes that occur on appeal. One such change is that the parties are renamed. In the trial court, the state prosecuted the defendant. The parties were referred to as simply *the government* or *the state* versus *the defendant.* But appellate courts do not use that terminology. Instead, the party bringing an appeal is referred to as the **appellant.** The winning party in the lower court is referred to as the **appellee.**

Appellant
The party bringing the current appeal from an adverse ruling in a lower court.

Appellee
The party who won in the lower court.

A. THE RECORD

A notice of appeal not only informs the appellate court that an appeal will be brought and sets out the jurisdictional basis for the appeal, it also serves other functions. For one thing, the notice requests that the trial court forward the record to the appellate court. The **record** consists of all the evidence, motions, and other matters admitted at trial. This record, along with the transcript of the witness testimony, is then sent to the appellate court and remains there while the case is pending. See Figure 11-2.

Record
The official file containing the evidence, pleadings, motions, and the transcript of the trial, as well as any other documents regarding the case.

PROFILING THE PROFESSIONAL

Appeals from the Clerk's Perspective

"We send three copies of any exhibits that are in the file, and any copy of any documents that are with us. If there is physical evidence, it's bagged and sent, too. The court reporter prepares the transcript and sends that, too."

Mabel Lowman, Clerk of Superior Court

B. DOCKETING

When a case is filed with the appellate court, it receives a docket number similar to the case file number that it received when the prosecution originally filed the indictment against the defendant. The docket number is important because it must appear on all documents, notices, and briefs subsequently filed with the appellate court. Once a case has been properly docketed with the court and the appropriate record has been transferred to the court, the parties must then file their briefs. However, before we begin a discussion of how an appeal proceeds, we must

FIGURE 11-2

Rule 10, Federal Rules of Appellate Procedure

Rule 10. The Record on Appeal
(a) Composition of the Record on Appeal.
The following items constitute the record on appeal:
(1) the original papers and exhibits filed in the district court;
(2) the transcript of proceedings, if any; and
(3) a certified copy of the docket entries prepared by the district clerk.

first address a basic question: What is an appellate court authorized to do on an appeal?

PERMISSIBLE ACTIONS BY APPELLATE COURTS

Appellate courts only review the record of the case on appeal. Appellate justices do not retry the case. They do not hear sworn testimony of witnesses or closing arguments by attorneys. Appeals are not trials; they are reviews of the record and the proceedings to determine whether the lower court made an error. An appeal compares the actions of the lower court with the actions authorized by statutes and previous cases to determine whether an error of judgment or procedure occurred. If it did not, then there is very little that an appellate court can do. Although it runs counter to popular perception, appellate courts are extremely limited in what they can do with the case on appeal. In fact, we can summarize the actions of an appellate court into three main actions and one hybrid action:

- Affirm
- Reverse
- Remand
- Modify

When an appellate court **affirms** an appeal, it agrees with the lower court's decision in the case. If the appeal is **reversed**, it means that the appellate court is changing the decision of the lower court. A reversal at the first appellate court would mean that the defendant's conviction is invalidated and the defendant must be retried. To justify a reversal, the appellate court must point to some irregularity or legal violation that occurred in the trial. In cases in which an appeal results in a reversal, it is left up to the prosecution to decide whether to continue to appeal to a higher court or to retry the defendant. In most cases in which the appeal results in a decision of reversal, the state decides to appeal this case to the next higher court. If the court issues a **remand**, which is relatively rare, it states that the court does not have sufficient information to make a decision, and because it has no jurisdiction or facilities for conducting hearings, the case is sent back to the original trial court for additional hearings that are designed to answer specific questions offered by the appellate court. After the evidentiary hearing is held in the trial court, the case is then transferred back to the appellate court for additional review of the new record and transcript.

Appellate courts are also authorized to create a hybrid decision that partly affirms and partly reverses a lower court decision, often referred to as **modifying** the decision. This is common when there are numerous issues in the appeal. In such a situation, the court's ruling would be seen as modifying the lower court's ruling, perhaps not explicitly affirming or reversing, but presenting the case in a different light and altering the final judgment in the case accordingly. In a criminal case, for instance, the court might agree that the verdict was correct but that the sentencing phase was prejudicial (see Figure 11-3).

Affirm
A decision by an appellate court that the lower court's finding or verdict was legally valid and not tainted by prejudice or other legal impediment.

Reverse
To set aside. When an appellate court reverses a lower court, it issues a decision that the lower court's ruling was incorrect; if the lower court's finding was that the defendant was guilty, then the conviction is reversed and set aside.

Remand
Send back. For example, a higher court may remand a case to a lower court, directing the lower court to take some action.

Modify
To alter the lower court's decision without necessarily reversing or affirming it.

FIGURE 11-3

Types of Sentences Imposed on Felons

Type of conviction	Total	Life	Death	Others*
Total	100%	23	2	75
Trial	100%	41	6	53
Jury	100	41	7	52
Bench	100	22	0	78
Guilty plea	100%	12	1	87

Note: Zero represents no cases in sample.

*Includes a probationor an incarceration sentence expressed in days, months, or years.

Source: Felony Sentences in State Courts, 2006—Statistical Tables. Bureau of Justice Statistics, U.S. Department of Justice. Revised 11/22/10.

EXAMPLE

Emilio was convicted of burglary and has brought his own appeal. He claims that he has new evidence and that he wants the state court of appeals to hear this evidence. Will they?

Answer: No. At best, the court will remand the case back to the trial court to have a hearing on Emilio's "new" evidence. If the court determines that the evidence is not new, then nothing in the appeal changes. If the trial court finds that it really is new evidence, then they will notify the appellate court, which may use it as the basis to reverse Emilio's conviction.

IV PRESENTING AN APPEAL

Brief
A written argument presented to an appellate court that argues a position based on the facts of the case and the applicable law; a brief urges the appellate judges to adopt the party's position.

The parties present their arguments by means of **briefs**. Although there are provisions for the litigants to argue their cases before the justices, they must submit briefs in any event. Briefs are written arguments, based on facts and law, urging the court to rule in the party's favor. Both sides to an appeal file briefs. We will begin our discussion with the appellant's brief.

A. APPELLATE BRIEFS

The purpose of the appellant's brief is to explain the party's position and offer an argument. A brief is both a summary of the facts and law applicable to the case and a persuasive pitch to the court, asking the court to rule in the party's favor. Because we have assumed throughout this chapter that the appellant in the case is the defendant who has been convicted, the appellant's brief in this case will no doubt attempt to point out some improprieties, incorrect rulings, improper actions, and any other issues that the defendant believes are relevant and brought about his conviction. Appellate court briefs have a specified format, often set out in the state's rules of appellate procedure. They have strict requirements about page size, color, font size, and many other formatting issues. Although briefs are very important in

Appeals from the Defense Attorney's Perspective

PROFILING THE PROFESSIONAL

"Sometimes I handle my own appeals. For the most part, clients get a second attorney because they want to analyze it for a possible ineffective assistance of counsel claim. For other times you want to do the appeal yourself because the issue is so clear that it's more of a legal issue, that it's a bad law, that it's something that you feel very strongly about and you want to take it on up. For the most part, the client will probably say, 'I just lost with you, why would I want you to handle the appeal?' I don't do a lot of appeals; it's just every now and then."

Defense Attorney

appellate procedure, they are not the main focus of a course on court procedure and evidence. We will, therefore, spend relatively little time addressing the content of appellate briefs.

1. CONTENTS OF AN APPELLATE BRIEF

Whether the brief is filed by the defendant or the state, it must meet certain minimum requirements, as outlined below.

a. Title Page

A brief is required to have a title page, sometimes called a cover page. This title page lists the names of the parties, the appellate docket number, and the name of the court.

b. Statement of Facts

The appellate brief must contain a statement of facts. This statement summarizes the important details of the case and is presented by both parties. Significantly, the statements of fact prepared by either side vary considerably. Facts that are unfavorable to one side are underplayed, while they are emphasized by the opposing party. The statement of facts not only sets out specific incidents but also cross-references these details to the transcript of the trial. This makes it easier for the appellate justices to double-check facts and locate specific testimony.

c. Enumerations of Error

Each brief contains enumerations of error. For the appellant, these are specific points of contention that allege prejudicial and improper rulings by the court. The appellee's (state's) brief will contain allegations stating that each of the appellant's enumerations is without merit and that the trial court ruled correctly. The enumerations are usually set out in the brief in a single, bold-faced paragraph that briefly explains why the court's ruling was wrong or (from the appellee's viewpoint) right. Most appeals have several enumerations of error, with corresponding statements by the appellee denying the validity of each enumeration.

d. Argument

The title page, statement of facts, and enumerations of error all lead up to the main event of the brief: the argument. In this section, the parties set out the facts and the law to support their contentions.

e. Conclusion

The conclusion is normally a short statement that comes at the very end of the brief, in which each party restates its position and requests specific relief. For the appellant, that would be a reversal of the conviction. For the appellee, that would be that the court affirm the conviction.

EXAMPLE

Angel is very angry at the criminal justice system and has decided to file her own appeal. She handwrites it on ruled notebook paper and files it with the court. How is the court likely to react to this filing?

Answer: The court will undoubtedly reject the filing because it was not filed in accordance with the court rules.

B. ORAL ARGUMENT

Most appeals before state courts of appeal are conducted exclusively in writing. Although there are provisions that allow for oral argument before appellate courts, the vast majority of appellate litigants do not make this request. Oral argument is usually reserved for unusual cases in which the justices feel the need to ask additional questions of the attorneys about the consequences of a ruling. If oral argument is scheduled for a case on appeal, the attorneys representing the parties will appear before the appellate justices and present an argument. Attorneys cannot present new evidence or new witness testimony. In fact, there are no witness boxes or juries in an appellate court. The attorneys stand at podiums and address the justices, arguing the facts of their case and the applicable law. The justices may interrupt the attorneys at any time during the argument. There are also strict rules about how long the argument may take. Given the restrictions of oral argument, most attorneys waive it in favor of written briefs.

PROFILING THE PROFESSIONAL

Appeals from the Prosecutor's Perspective

"Here, fortunately, we have a person who does post-disposition work. It's very hard to deal with that kind of stuff when you're also dealing with court. Now, it might be difficult for someone who doesn't know anything about the case to come in fresh and start from scratch, but it's very difficult for a trial attorney to also handle appeals, too. Our jurisdiction, we purposefully sought out someone to do that work and free us up from having to do appeals, too. A lot of trial attorneys like to do trial work and the appellate writing stuff is not really what they're into. It's challenging; you're trying to do trial prep, preliminary hearings, and then you're also writing an appellate brief. Trying to go backwards and rethink the case—talk about time intensive! It chews up all of your time. The ones I've done have always been an interesting experience.

I've been before the court of appeals a couple of times. I did oral argument before the court of appeals with a defense attorney who'd been the district attorney for years. When we got to the court, all of the justices were greeting him by his first name. Okay, I thought, this is going to be interesting."

Debra Sullivan, Assistant District Attorney

V TAKING THE APPEAL TO A HIGHER COURT

As we saw in Chapter 1, all court systems, whether on the federal or state level, are arranged as a hierarchy. The trial courts, where witnesses testify, juries reach verdicts, and defendants are sentenced, occupy the bottom of this hierarchy. Defendants who appeal bring their cases to an intermediate appellate court, called a U.S. circuit court of appeal in the federal system and a state court of appeals on the state level (although not all states call their intermediate appellate court by that name).

At the top of this hierarchy on the federal level is the U.S. Supreme Court. States also have top courts, and they often share the same name as the top U.S. court, although in at least one state the top court is referred to as the state superior court, not the state supreme court. Although we examined the organization and structure of state and federal courts in Chapter 1, we did not spend any time addressing the issues surrounding how a party brings a case before the state or federal supreme court. (For purposes of clarity, we will refer to the highest state court as the *supreme court,* keeping in mind that although most states refer to this court by that name, not all do.)

A. CERTIORARI

Certiorari (cert)
(Latin) To make sure. Cert is a court's authority to decide which cases it will hear on appeal and which it will not.

Whenever a party loses before the court of appeals, that party has a right to continue on with the appellate process. However, appealing to the state supreme court is a good deal harder than appealing to the court of appeals. Unlike an appeal to the court of appeals, appeals to the state supreme court involve different procedural requirements. For one thing, almost all state supreme courts have the authority to decide which cases they will hear and which they will not. This authority is referred to as **certiorari** or, simply, **cert**. (Certiorari is almost universally referred to as *cert*, not only because the word itself is difficult to pronounce but also because appellate courts commonly abbreviate the term that way in reporting decisions, as in "petition for cert. denied.")

All litigants must pass this administrative hurdle before the court will consider the case. State supreme courts mirror the U.S. Supreme Court in that they all have the power to grant or deny cert, and in the vast majority of cases that petition for cert, the court refuses to grant it. Estimates are as low as 5 percent or less of the hundreds of cases that petition for cert to a state supreme court are granted cert.

1. STANDARDS USED TO DETERMINE GRANTING CERT

The U.S. and individual state supreme courts do not hear most of the cases that petition for cert. A petition for cert is filed by the party wishing the court to hear the appeal and sets out why this case is important and the impact that a ruling will have on case law interpretation or a provision of the state statute or constitution. The U.S. Supreme Court follows specific guidelines in granting cert, and states follow those standards closely. Before the U.S. Supreme Court will grant cert in a case, the litigants must show the following:

- The issues presented have been interpreted differently in various courts, causing a conflict among the federal circuits.
- The case involves an interpretation of the U.S. Constitution.
- One state has ruled a particular action legal, while another has ruled it illegal.
- The case involves issues of national importance.

You will notice that missing from that list is the fact that the case is important to the litigants to themselves. The U.S. Supreme Court, like state supreme courts, does not grant cert simply because the case has vital importance to the defendant or the state in an individual prosecution. In fact, the case must present issues that are important to the community at large, not just the litigants, to pass muster for granting cert.

The U.S. Supreme Court follows the "rule of four" in deciding whether or not to grant cert. If four out of the nine justices believe that cert should be granted, then the case will be heard. If that minimum is not reached, then the case is denied cert and the decision in the most recent appeal stands as the final decision in the appeal.

a. Granting Cert

When the state Supreme Court grants cert, it means that the court has agreed to hear the case. The appeal will now proceed in an almost identical fashion as the procedure followed in the state court of appeals. The parties will submit written briefs that include a statement of facts, an argument, and all the other features that we saw in our previous discussion of appellate briefs. Simply because a party has been granted cert does not mean that he will ultimately win the appeal. Granting cert simply authorizes the continuation of the appeal. The court is free to rule any way that it sees fit once it considers the merits of the case.

b. Denial of Cert

When the state supreme court denies cert, it means that the court has refused to hear the appeal. At this point, the appellate process is essentially over. The appellant can file a motion for rehearing, requesting the court to reconsider its ruling, but that is very unlikely. If the party has been denied cert before the state supreme court, then he has one more option: the U.S. Supreme Court. You will notice that a state case does not begin at the bottom of the federal system, moving through U.S. district court and moving up through the appropriate U.S. circuit court of appeals. Instead, a party that has been denied cert or who has lost in the state supreme court may file a writ of certiorari petition with the U.S. Supreme Court. However, if the state supreme court failed to grant cert, the chances that the U.S. Supreme Court will grant it are exceedingly small.

B. THE LENGTHY TIME FOR CASES TO PROCEED THROUGH THE APPELLATE PROCESS

Many people ask why it takes so long for a case to move through the appellate courts. In death penalty cases in particular, a person may be sentenced to die and not actually be executed for 15 or even 20 years. Why does the process take so long?

It is quite common for appeals in criminal cases to last for years. Although the process outlined above sounds relatively straightforward, in daily practice each of the steps takes months, sometimes years, to complete. Once a defendant is sentenced, he will file a motion for a new trial. It may be weeks before that motion is heard. If the motion is denied, then the defendant can file a notice of appeal. Pulling together all of the necessary information for the appeal can also take months. Once filed, the docketing process can take additional months. So, before even the first appeal in the case is heard, these time periods have already added up to a year or more. If the losing party wishes to continue the appellate process—and there is certainly no reason that a defendant would not wish to take advantage of every possible avenue for appeal—then getting the case heard before the state supreme court can take another year or two. It is not unusual, therefore, for a defendant's first appeal to last anywhere from two to three years. This is just the *first* appeal. Once a defendant has exhausted his first round of appeals, it is very common for him to bring another appeal. This new round of appeals may involve the federal court system in the form of a habeas corpus petition.

C. HABEAS CORPUS

Habeas corpus
(Latin) You have the body. A judicial order to a prison system ordering that the incarcerated person be brought to court for a hearing; a constitutional mechanism that allows convicts to challenge their sentences.

A **habeas corpus** action is an appeal using the federal court system, even if the original case began in state court. Habeas corpus is based on United States constitutional amendments requiring that a criminal defendant must be held for reasonable grounds. Although not originally designed to give a criminal defendant a second round of appeals, many criminal convictions are now routinely appealed using habeas corpus. In fact, a current issue is whether terrorists taken on the field of battle or seized overseas enjoy this right in the U.S. court system. An action for habeas corpus is based on centuries of legal tradition and has been suspended only once in the history of the United States. (Abraham Lincoln temporarily restricted the right during the Civil War.)

In a habeas corpus action a criminal defendant requests the federal court system to remove the defendant from a state prison system based on some alleged unconstitutional action that occurred in the trial. Since a habeas corpus action is brought in federal court, it will then follow the federal appellate court system, perhaps all the way up to the U.S. Supreme Court. Appeals through the federal court systems can sometimes take five to ten years. If you consider the amount of time that the first round of appeals can take and then add the term of years that a habeas action can take, it is easy to see why some criminal appeals can linger for a decade or more.

In the following case excerpt, the heart of the case is in the judge's refusal to charge the jury on involuntary manslaughter. Keep that issue in mind as you read the transcript of the appeal.

CASE EXCERPT

STATE v. BRAYBOY

387 S.C. 174, 691 S.E.2d 482, S.C.App., March 04, 2010 (NO. 4652)

HUFF, J.

John Brayboy was convicted of murder in the death of his girlfriend and was sentenced to forty years. Brayboy appeals, asserting the trial court erred in failing to charge the jury on involuntary manslaughter. We reverse and remand.

FACTUAL/PROCEDURAL BACKGROUND

Early in the morning on August 8, 2005, neighbors Towanda Means and her boyfriend, Roger Brewton, heard Brayboy and his live-in girlfriend, Simone Garrett, arguing in their home next door. Kenneth Holbert, who lived in the other side of a duplex shared with Brayboy and Simone, testified the arguing between Brayboy and Simone started as early as 4:00 or 5:00 the previous afternoon, continued until about midnight, and was heard again early that morning.

Towanda testified she was getting dressed for work that morning when she observed Simone on the front porch of the home she shared with Brayboy and Brayboy was four or five houses away at a stop sign. The two continued to argue back and forth. As Towanda was going back into her room to retrieve some shoes, she saw Brayboy walking back toward his home. Towanda continued to dress, and when she walked out of her door to go to work, she and Roger met Brayboy on their front porch. Brayboy asked to use the phone, and Towanda told him that she and Roger were not having "anything to do" with the argument, but they eventually provided Brayboy with a phone. At that point, Brayboy was nervous and upset, his hands were shaking, and he appeared to have been running. He fumbled with the phone trying to dial a number. Towanda asked Brayboy, "What did you do to her," and Brayboy replied, "Go check on my girl." Towanda, Roger, and Brayboy then went to Brayboy and Simone's home, where Towanda entered first, calling Simone's name. When Simone did not answer, Towanda continued through the home, up the steps, and into a bedroom where she discovered Simone laying in a puddle of blood between a bed and a wall.

Roger also testified he witnessed Brayboy and Simone arguing that morning on their porch. The pair continued to argue while Simone was on the porch and Brayboy walked to the stop sign. Brayboy commented to Roger that "all Simone wanted to do is put him in jail," and Roger told Brayboy he was doing the right thing by walking away. Brayboy turned around when Simone called him "a crack head smoking M.F.," and he started back toward their house. Roger stepped back into his home and told Towanda that Simone and Brayboy were still arguing. Within a minute, Brayboy was at Towanda and Roger's home asking to use the phone. Brayboy was nervous and frantic and fumbled with the phone as he tried to dial it. Towanda asked Brayboy what he had done to Simone, and all Brayboy said was "go check on my girl." Towanda and Brayboy started toward the house. By the time Roger got there, Towanda was upstairs and Brayboy was coming back out of the house. Roger asked Brayboy what he had done. He then heard Towanda scream and Brayboy started running. Roger ran up the stairs and saw Simone lying between the bed and the wall. Simone subsequently died as a result of a gunshot wound to the head.

Brayboy did not testify at trial. However, the State published to the jury and entered into evidence Brayboy's videotaped statement given to a detective on the day of the incident. The State also entered into evidence Brayboy's written statement, which had been reduced to writing by the detective during the taping of Brayboy's statement. Brayboy told the detective about the two arguing that morning. According to Brayboy, when Simone was on the porch she yelled at him that it was her home and he needed to come get his things. Brayboy told Simone he paid rent too, and he started walking back to the house. Simone entered the house and he entered the house as well. According to Brayboy, he walked upstairs and the arguing continued. Brayboy stated that Simone was backing up on the left side of the bed, and she then bent down like she was reaching for something. Simone picked up a gun from the floor. As Simone was coming up with the gun, Brayboy realized what she had in her hand and he ran up to her and pushed her. When he did so, the gun fell from Simone's hand to the floor between them and both Brayboy and Simone grabbed for it, with Brayboy successfully obtaining it. Brayboy explained that he and Simone were arguing and Simone was in his face. According to the written statement, Brayboy was "swinging the gun and Simone was in his face and the gun went off." In the video, Brayboy indicates that as he and Simone came up when he managed to grab the gun, Simone was in his face, swinging her arms and arguing, that Brayboy was also arguing, and the "next thing" Brayboy knew, as he was swinging his arms while he argued, the gun "just went off." Brayboy explained that Simone was "right in his face", that he "wasn't even thinking about the gun at the time, it was just in his hand" and that "he was just swinging and arguing and it just went off." Brayboy further stated in the video that he did not even remember the gun, and he was just swinging his arms and it went off.

At the close of the case, Brayboy requested the trial court charge the jury on accident and involuntary manslaughter. Brayboy asserted there was evidence in his statement that Simone pulled out the gun, they struggled over it, and he was able to obtain the gun and did so to defend himself. He therefore argued there was evidence from which the jury could find he was engaged in a lawful activity, but was negligent in the handling of the gun. The State opposed an instruction on involuntary manslaughter, arguing the case of *State v. Light*, 363 S.C. 325, 610 S.E.2d 504 (Ct.App.2005) rev'd, 378 S.C. 641, 664 S.E.2d 465 (2008), wherein this court affirmed the trial court's refusal to charge involuntary manslaughter in a similar matter, was on "all fours" with this case. The trial court agreed, and refused to charge involuntary manslaughter. The jury convicted Brayboy of murder, and this appeal follows.

LAW/ANALYSIS

Appellant argues the trial court erred in refusing to instruct the jury on involuntary manslaughter, as his statement shows he and Simone struggled over the gun, he was swinging the gun around while Simone was "up in his face," and he was armed in self-defense when the gun went off. He contends there is evidence from which the jury could determine he was acting recklessly with the firearm when he swung the gun, entitling him to a charge on involuntary manslaughter. The State contends, while appellant claimed he was entitled to the involuntary manslaughter charge because he was armed in self-defense at the time of the shooting, he could not meet the necessary prongs of a self-defense charge, as it was clear Simone no longer posed a threat of death or serious bodily injury to appellant once appellant disarmed her. The State further contends, pursuant to *State v. Reese*, 370 S.C. 31, 633 S.E.2d 898 (2006), overruled on other grounds by *State v. Belcher*, 385 S.C. 597, 685 S.E.2d 802 (2009), it is a felony for a person to present or point at another person a loaded or unloaded firearm and, as in Reese, "there is no doubt that appellant was presenting a firearm when he took the gun out and began waiving it around. Therefore, appellant was pointing or presenting a firearm, a felony, which would preclude an involuntary manslaughter charge." Id. at 36, 633 S.E.2d at 900-01. Thus, the State contends Brayboy was clearly engaged in the felony of pointing and presenting a firearm. The State further argues, pursuant to this court's opinion in Light I. Brayboy failed to present any evidence he was acting in reckless disregard for Simone's safety.

The law to be charged must be determined from the evidence presented at trial. *State v. Knoten*, 347 S.C. 296, 302, 555 S.E.2d 391, 394 (2001). A trial court commits reversible error if it fails to give a requested charge on an issue raised by the evidence. *State v. Hill*, 315 S.C. 260, 262, 433 S.E.2d 848, 849 (1993). In determining whether the evidence requires a charge on a lesser included offense, the court views the facts in a light most favorable to the defendant. See *Knoten*, 347 S.C. at 302, 555 S.E.2d at 394 (providing a court must view the facts in the light most favorable to a defendant when determining whether evidence required a charge on the lesser included offense of voluntary manslaughter alongside the charge of murder). Importantly, our courts have long emphasized that to warrant a court's eliminating the offense of manslaughter, it should very clearly appear that there is no evidence whatsoever tending to reduce the crime from murder to manslaughter. *State v. Cole*, 338 S.C. 97, 101, 525 S.E.2d 511, 513 (2000); *State v. Burriss*, 334 S.C. 256, 265, 513 S.E.2d 104, 109 (1999); *Casey v. State*, 305 S.C. 445, 447, 409 S.E.2d 391, 392 (1991). A request to charge a lesser included offense is properly refused only when there is no evidence that the defendant committed the lesser rather than the greater offense. *Casey*, 305 S.C. at 447, 409 S.E.2d at 392.

Involuntary manslaughter is (1) the unintentional killing of another without malice, but while engaged in an unlawful activity not naturally tending to cause death or great bodily harm or (2) the unintentional killing of another without malice, while engaged in a lawful activity with reckless disregard for the safety of others. *State v. Wharton*, 381 S.C. 209, 216, 672 S.E.2d 786, 789 (2009). "To constitute involuntary manslaughter, there must be a finding of criminal negligence, statutorily defined as a reckless disregard of the safety of others." *State v. Crosby*, 355 S.C. 47, 52, 584 S.E.2d 110, 112 (2003). "Recklessness is a state of mind in which the actor is aware of his or her conduct, yet consciously disregards a risk which his or her conduct is creating." *State v. Pittman*, 373 S.C. 527, 571, 647 S.E.2d 144, 167 (2007). "A person can be acting lawfully, even if he is in unlawful possession of a weapon, if he was entitled to arm himself in self-defense at the time of the shooting." *Crosby*, 355 S.C. at 52, 584 S.E.2d at 112. "The negligent handling of a loaded gun will support a charge of involuntary manslaughter." *State v. Mekler*, 379 S.C. 12, 15, 664 S.E.2d 477, 478 (2008). Additionally, evidence of a struggle over a weapon between a defendant and victim supports submission of an involuntary manslaughter charge. *Tisdale v. State*, 378 S.C. 122, 125, 662 S.E.2d 410, 412 (2008); *Casey*, 305 S.C. at 447, 409 S.E.2d at 392.

In Light I, this court found there was no evidence Light handled the gun with reckless disregard for the safety of others when he shot his girlfriend, and therefore the trial court properly refused to charge involuntary manslaughter. *Light I*, 363 S.C. at 331-32, 610 S.E.2d at 507-08. In July 2008, our supreme court reversed this court's decision in the matter. *State v. Light*, 378 S.C. 641, 664 S.E.2d 465 (2008) (Light II). There, the supreme court noted the facts showed that Light initially gave a statement to Texas authorities stating he emerged from the bathroom in his home to find the victim holding his .22 rifle, he tried to distract the victim, he remembered swinging his left arm to get the rifle out of her hand and when he did, the gun discharged. Id. at 644, 664 S.E.2d at 466. Light later altered his story, admitting he took the rifle from the victim before it was fired, the rifle was in his hand when it discharged, and "it was either the victim or him." Id. At trial, Light testified the victim was pointing the gun and screaming at him, he was afraid she was going to shoot him, and so he tried to knock the gun away with his left hand. Id. at 645-46, 664 S.E.2d at 467. After he jerked it away from her, he stumbled back several feet and the weapon discharged, "but it was not intentionally [sic]." Id. at 645-46, 664 S.E.2d at 467. The supreme court then held as follows:

> Although petitioner had inconsistent stories, we find he was entitled to a charge of involuntary manslaughter. . . . The Court of Appeals correctly found petitioner was lawfully armed in self-defense at the time of the shooting because, according to his testimony, petitioner took the loaded gun from [the victim] who was threatening him with it. There was also evidence petitioner recklessly handled the gun because, according to his testimony, it fired almost immediately after he took possession of it.

> As specifically stated in Burriss, the negligent handling of a loaded gun will support a finding of involuntary manslaughter. Further, the fact petitioner and [the victim] were struggling over the weapon is sufficient evidence to support an involuntary manslaughter charge to the jury. Accordingly, there was evidence to support a charge of involuntary manslaughter and, therefore, the trial court should have so charged the jury.

Id. at 648-49, 664 S.E.2d at 468-69. In a footnote to this holding, the court also noted there is a difference between being armed in self-defense and acting in self-defense, and that at the point of the analysis of determining whether one is armed in self-defense, the court is "concerned only with whether [the defendant] had a right to be armed for purposes of determining whether he was engaged in a lawful act, i.e. was lawfully armed, and not whether he actually acted in self-defense when the shooting occurred." Id. at 648 n. 6, 664 S.E.2d at 468 n. 6.

Here, considering the evidence in the light most favorable to Brayboy, we find there is evidence to support a charge on involuntary manslaughter such that the trial court erred in failing to so charge the jury. According to Brayboy's statement, Simone pulled the gun on Brayboy, Brayboy pushed Simone causing the gun to fall to the ground, the two both grabbed for the gun, Brayboy reached the gun first, they were both arguing and swinging their arms, and Simone was "up in Brayboy's face" when the gun discharged shortly after Brayboy grabbed the gun. There is evidence from the videotaped statement that the gun discharged when Brayboy swung his arm around, right after he picked it up, and he did not "even remember the gun" at the time. See *Crosby*, 355 S.C. at 53, 584 S.E.2d at 112 (finding involuntary manslaughter charge should have been given where defendant admitted he closed his eyes and pulled the trigger, but added that "he didn't even know he had pulled the trigger."). As in Light II, there is evidence the victim pulled out a gun, the defendant struggled with the victim to obtain the gun, and in the moments right after the defendant obtained possession of the gun, the weapon discharged. Accordingly, there is evidence from which the jury could determine Brayboy was lawfully armed in self-defense, and he negligently handled the loaded gun causing it to discharge.

There is no merit to the State's argument that Brayboy was not entitled to an involuntary manslaughter charge because he could not meet the necessary prongs of a self-defense charge. The supreme court's decision in Light II makes it clear the question is not whether one is acting in self-defense at the time of the shooting, but whether the defendant is lawfully armed at the time of the shooting. Therefore, whether a defendant is entitled to a self-defense charge is of no consequence. Additionally, the case of Reese, relied on by the State, is not controlling in this situation. In Reese, the defendant gave a statement to police admitting he shot the victim, but stated he did not go to her house with the intent to kill her. Rather, he was upset and crying and pulled the gun out and told the victim he was going to kill himself. While the victim was attempting to talk him out of killing himself, Reese claimed he was "moving the gun back and forth as a reaction" and the gun fired. *Reese*, 370 S.C. at 35, 633 S.E.2d at 900. Thus, the court found, "Although the jury could have found Reese's statement that he was moving the gun back and forth did not constitute pointing a firearm, and threatening suicide has not been classified as an unlawful act, there is no doubt that Reese was presenting a firearm when he took the gun out and began waiving it around." Id. at 36, 633 S.E.2d at 901. Because the defendant in

Reese produced the gun with which the victim was shot, he necessarily "presented" the firearm, an unlawful act. Here, as in Light II, the defendant did not "present" the gun. Therefore Reese is inapplicable.

CONCLUSION

We find, under the facts of this case, there is evidence from which the jury could determine Brayboy was lawfully armed in self-defense and negligently handled the loaded gun causing it to discharge, and he was therefore entitled to a charge on involuntary manslaughter. Accordingly, Appellant's murder conviction is REVERSED AND REMANDED.

THOMAS and KONDUROS, JJ., concur.

CASE QUESTIONS

1 What led to the killing of Simone in this case?
2 What instruction did Brayboy ask the judge to give at the conclusion of the case?
3 What error does Brayboy allege the trial judge committed?
4 What argument did the state make in response to Brayboy's contention?
5 What action did the court take after explaining its reasoning of the interplay between self-defense and reckless behavior?

CHAPTER SUMMARY

When a defendant loses at trial, he has the right to appeal the decision to an appellate court. The appeals process begins when the defendant files a motion for new trial. If that motion is denied, the party then has the right to file a notice of appeal and have the case transferred to the jurisdiction of the appellate court. In most states, and on the federal level, the first level of appellate court is called the court of appeals. Parties file appellate briefs to contest the decision in the trial court and to argue their positions on appeal. Appellate briefs have a standard format, with specific subsections appearing in all such briefs. These subsections include a statement of facts, argument, and enumerations of error.

Appellate courts are limited in the actions that they can take in an appeal. When an appellate court affirms the lower court's decision, it agrees with that court's decision and allows it to stand. However, when a court reverses a decision, it disagrees with the lower court's decision. Appellate courts can also modify lower court decisions or send the case back to the trial court for additional hearings in a remand.

Appellate courts form a hierarchy, with the most powerful court at the top and the trial courts at the bottom. On the state level, the highest court is usually called the state supreme court, and it has the final say about interpretations of state law. The U.S. Supreme Court is the highest court in the United States. It is the court of last resort for all types of appeals.

KEY TERMS

Key terms are listed here in order of appearance in chapter.

Appeal	Appellee	Modify
Motion for a new trial	Record	Brief
Notice of appeal	Affirm	Certiorari (cert)
Jurisdiction	Reverse	Habeas corpus
Appellant	Remand	

REVIEW QUESTIONS

1. What is a motion for new trial?
2. How do jurisdictional issues become important on an appeal?
3. What is a notice of appeal?
4. What is an appeal?
5. What is the appellate "record"?
6. What is a brief?
7. List the basic components of an appellate brief.
8. What is the purpose of a statement of facts in an appellate brief?
9. What is an enumeration of error?
10. What is oral argument?
11. Explain the limited powers of appellate courts.
12. What is the difference between affirming and reversing an appeal?
13. What is the purpose of a remand?
14. Explain the organization of state courts.
15. What is certiorari?
16. What is the basis for granting or denying certiorari?
17. What is the "record" as that term applies to appeals?
18. What is the name of the highest court in the United States?
19. Explain habeas corpus.
20. List and explain the terms that are used to describe the parties during the appellate process.

WEB SURFING

Cornell College, Department of Politics: Appellate Brief and Oral Argument
http://www.cornellcollege.edu/politics/courses/allin/365-366/appellate-brief-oral.shtml

Syracuse University: Appellate Briefs and Forms
http://www.law.syr.edu/Pdfs/0AppellBriefsAndFms.pdf

Alaska Court System: Preparing Appellate Briefs
http://www.courts.alaska.gov/shc/appeals/print_appealbriefs.pdf

U.S. Circuit Courts of Appeal
http://www.uscourts.gov/FederalCourts/UnderstandingtheFederalCourts/CourtofAppeals.aspx

EXERCISES

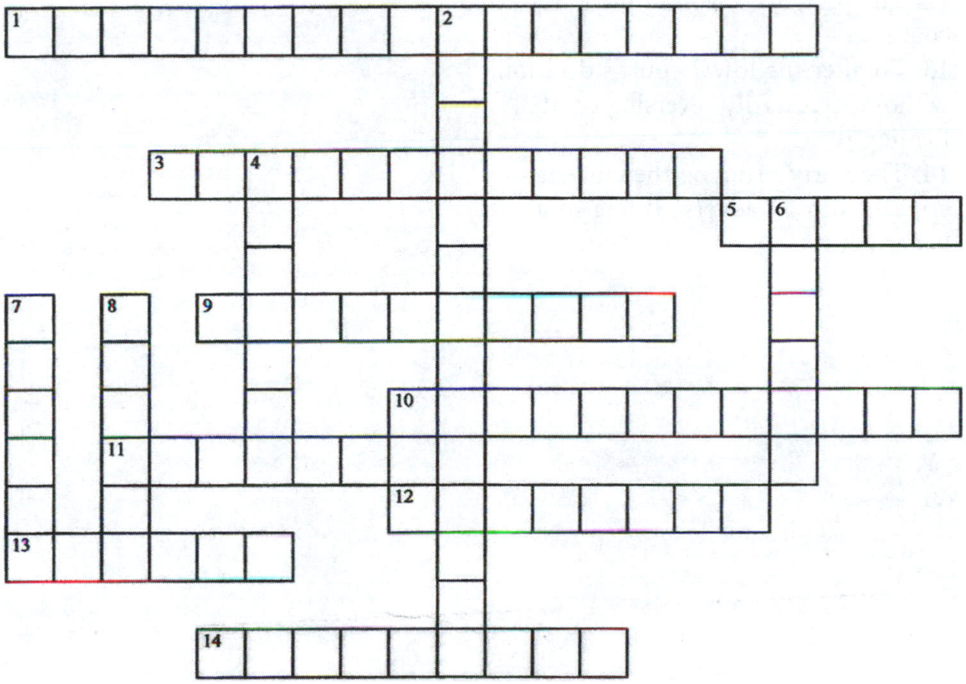

ACROSS

1. A defendant's request that the trial judge set aside the jury's verdict and order a new trial
3. The power and authority of a court to issue decisions on issues and to impose those decisions on the parties in the case

DOWN

2. The document giving official notice that a party intends to appeal
4. To set aside
6. The official file containing the evidence, pleadings, motions, and the transcript of the trial, as well as any other documents regarding the case

5. A written argument presented to an appellate court that argues a position based on the facts of the case and the applicable law
9. A court's authority to decide which cases it will hear on appeal and which it will not
10. A judicial order to a prison system ordering that the incarcerated person be brought to court for a hearing
11. Requesting an appellate court to review the actions and ruling of a lower court in order to correct mistakes and remedy an injustice
12. The party who won in the lower court
13. To alter the lower court's decision, without necessarily reversing or affirming it
14. The party bringing the current appeal from an adverse ruling in a lower court

7. A decision by an appellate court that the lower court's finding or verdict was legally valid and not tainted by prejudice or other legal impediment
8. To Send back

r	a	c	o	e	t	r	f	f	m	l	c	f	u	r	l	a
i	n	w	s	r	a	f	o	c	i	a	o	c	p	d	a	p
e	d	e	l	u	p	l	i	l	n	i	a	d	a	s	e	p
f	i	e	o	m	p	p	m	r	e	e	v	n	i	s	p	e
i	o	r	e	c	o	r	d	o	a	r	n	c	i	r	p	l
m	o	t	i	o	n	f	o	r	n	e	w	t	r	i	a	l
y	a	f	t	r	c	i	e	c	p	v	i	t	i	f	f	a
u	o	r	r	p	j	u	r	i	s	d	i	c	t	i	o	n
c	w	i	f	j	e	r	p	a	m	a	b	d	l	l	e	t
c	i	c	a	d	a	f	p	u	r	r	e	p	i	r	c	r
t	v	i	r	r	c	p	b	y	i	o	m	b	r	a	i	p
r	d	i	e	i	e	a	p	e	f	a	i	i	a	r	t	r
a	n	d	n	l	u	v	f	e	f	i	i	t	m	h	o	r
i	a	o	l	a	r	e	e	r	a	r	d	p	r	v	n	d
o	m	e	r	e	p	t	w	r	l	l	i	o	l	e	m	l
i	e	r	r	e	i	r	r	i	s	s	t	n	m	p	c	r
r	r	o	d	r	c	a	t	o	n	e	r	p	d	p	a	m

appeal
motion for new trial
notice of appeal
jurisdiction
appellant
appellee
record
affirm
reverse
remand
modify
brief
certiorari
habeas corpus

QUESTIONS FOR ANALYSIS

1 Should the criminal appeals process be more streamlined to cut down on the length of time that it takes for a case to be resolved? What suggestions would you make to cut down on the amount of time a case on appeal takes?

2 Should habeas corpus actions be permitted in cases in which defendants are seized outside the United States? Why or why not?

12

Juvenile Court

Chapter Objectives

- Explain the history of the development of juvenile courts in America
- Describe important U.S. Supreme Court decisions that have played a major role in the development of juvenile law
- List and explain the various ways that juvenile courts are organized around the United States
- Describe the basic steps in adjudicating a juvenile
- Explain the doctrine of *parens patriae*

I INTRODUCTION TO JUVENILE COURT

Juvenile courts are highly specialized and have limited jurisdiction. They hear cases separately from adult prosecutions, and the dispositions and even the procedures followed are very different from what is seen in adult court.[1] Why is this so? If we were to create the briefest possible summary of the differences between adult courts and juvenile courts, we could say that the purpose of adult courts is to punish, while the purpose of juvenile court is to rehabilitate. Because those two goals are often at cross purposes to one another, it became necessary to create a separate system to adjudicate children who had committed crimes. There is the inherent belief in most juvenile court statutes that a child may still be redeemable and may be able to become a productive member of society. The same attitude does not apply to adult prosecutions. Unlike adult court, the proceedings in juvenile courts, especially dealing with family issues, are considered to be noncriminal and actually based on civil law issues. Therefore, the rules of criminal procedure do not apply and, until a few decades ago, neither did most of the due process guarantees found in adult court.

[1] *In re Santillanes*, 47 N.M. 140, 138 P.2d 503 (1943).

The purpose of juvenile court is to protect delinquent, neglected, or dependent children.[2] Juvenile courts are the creations of state legislation, and this legislation provides two important aspects for juvenile offenders. In the first instance the purpose of juvenile court is to serve the best interests of the delinquent by providing care, guidance, rehabilitation, treatment, and any other support that would allow the child to become a law-abiding citizen. The second function is to provide for the safety and protection of the public from juvenile offenders.[3] This creates an interesting dual role that is not seen in adult courts. You could argue that sentencing for adults is designed to be punitive with some thought toward rehabilitation, but juvenile courts are specifically designed to help underage offenders and are not designed to be punitive by nature. Juvenile courts are supposed to be protective of their offenders and try to seek the best interests of both the child and society.[4]

PROFILING THE PROFESSIONAL

The Differences in Juvenile Court and Regular Court

"The language is different, they're adjudicated delinquent as opposed to guilty or not guilty. You have a judge instead of the jury deciding. The rules of evidence do apply, but the focus is trying to fix the situation for the child, depending on what they're charged with. It is a place where you're not just trying to get out of something, but they're trying to figure out how they can avoid this problem again in the future. The courts are overwhelmed."

B.J. Bernstein, Defense Attorney

A. A SHORT HISTORY OF JUVENILE COURT

The American juvenile system was originally based on the English model. Like so much of American law, the founders of our country adopted English common law and concepts almost wholesale. Among the many concepts derived from English law was a stern approach to juvenile delinquency. Some of these concepts remain embodied in our modern law. For instance, most states have a law creating the assumption that children under the age of seven are incapable of testifying or taking an oath because they lack the necessary mental development to do so. Children between the ages of 7 and 14, in most states, face a rebuttable presumption that they cannot testify or take an oath—that is, there is a presumption that they cannot testify unless and until the government can prove that they are competent to testify.

---

[2] *West Virginia Dept. of Health and Human Resources ex rel. Hisman v. Angela D.*, 203 W. Va. 335, 507 S.E.2d 698 (1998).

[3] *In re R.D.R.*, 2005 PA Super 204, 876 A.2d 1009 (2005).

[4] *In Interest of Brandon S.S.*, 179 Wis. 2d 114, 507 N.W.2d 94 (1993).

The flip side of being unable or incompetent to testify was the inability of the state to prosecute children. If a child does not have the necessary mental ability to testify, what does that mean to the *mens rea* analysis? As we know from earlier in the text, almost all crimes require two elements: intent and action, or *mens rea* and *actus reus*. The same presumptions that prevent children from testifying in court because of their age also prevented them from being prosecuted. What then should society do with juvenile offenders who cannot be prosecuted under an adult system? Before the creation of juvenile courts, children over the age of 14 in some states, 12 in others, were prosecuted as adults and were incarcerated with adults when they were found guilty. However, advocates for children in the late nineteenth and early twentieth centuries established time and time again that children incarcerated with adults were subject to all manner of abuse and demanded that a separate system be created not only to prosecute delinquent children but also to protect them. The other problem that existed prior to the creation of juvenile courts was that even though children as young as 14 could be prosecuted as adults, they enjoyed none of the constitutional protections that legal adults could rely on. As children, they were denied many of the due process rights that adult offenders had enjoyed for centuries.

The first court that we could recognize as an actual juvenile court was created in the state of Illinois in 1899 by the Illinois Juvenile Court Act. That court, like all of the courts that followed it, adopted a different philosophy from that used to prosecute adult offenders. Instead of creating adversarial court hearings, the court operated under the philosophy of ***parens patriae***. This term, taken from the Latin for "country as parent," acted not only to punish children but also to protect their interests and sometimes even to remove them from their family households in order to guarantee their safety. In this way, the government effectively became the parental authority for the child.

Parens patriae
(Latin) The country as parent; the philosophy that when parents or guardians fail a child, the government fills the gap by providing basic necessities, protection, education, and counseling, as needed.

By the early 1920s, most states had developed some form of juvenile justice system, even if some of the details had not quite been worked out. One of the details had to do with constitutional rights of juvenile offenders. With courts adopting the *parens patriae* philosophy, and acting as caretakers of juvenile offenders and neglected children, many commentators did not see the need for constitutional protections for children. However, as time went by, it became clear that some constitutional guarantees must be extended to juvenile offenders if for no other reason than simple fairness.

B. IMPORTANT U.S. SUPREME COURT CASES IN THE AREA OF JUVENILE LAW

Because juvenile courts were established in different ways in different states and because juvenile law itself was based more in civil law than in criminal law, many of the protections that adult defendants take for granted were not extended to juveniles accused of crimes. Over the years, the U.S. Supreme Court has ruled in several important cases to clarify the rights of juveniles and also to extend many, but not all, adult constitutional protections into juvenile courtrooms.

One seminal case, *In re Gault*, was particularly important because the U.S. Supreme Court ruled that a juvenile is entitled to specific due process protections, including the right to an attorney, the right to be notified of the charges pending against him, the right to confront witnesses against him, and the Fifth Amendment protection of the right against self-incrimination.[5]

Preponderance of the evidence
A showing by one side in a civil suit that its version of the facts is more likely to be true than not.

Also because juvenile proceedings are based more in civil law than in criminal law, the original burden of proof for juvenile offenders is **preponderance of the evidence**, which is a civil burden of proof rather than proof beyond a reasonable doubt, which is found in all adult criminal cases. Following on the *Gault* case, the court ruled in 1970 that proceedings in juvenile court of a criminal nature should require the same level of proof as that in adult courts, namely proof beyond a reasonable doubt. *In re Winship* held that the prior standard, preponderance of the evidence, was a violation of the Constitution.[6] Additional rights were also recognized in subsequent decisions, such as the right to judges who are fair, impartial, and detached.[7] However, this trend toward including more and more adult protections has not extended to all proceedings. For instance, there is no right to a jury trial in juvenile court.[8]

In the decision of *Roper v. Simmons*, the U.S. Supreme Court ruled that it is unconstitutional to execute a juvenile even when the juvenile's offense would be subject to capital punishment if it had been carried out by an adult.[9] This 2005 decision derailed many states' legislative initiatives to include more and more offenses that would permit an underage defendant to be transferred from juvenile court to adult court. (We will discuss trying juveniles as adults later in this chapter.)

C. THE ROLE OF THE FEDERAL GOVERNMENT IN JUVENILE JUSTICE

The federal government has taken a strong interest in juvenile delinquency proceedings and has attempted to be the standard bearer to provide an example that the states can follow. The Juvenile Delinquency Prevention and Control Act was passed in 1968 and encouraged states to develop their own juvenile programs. If they did, they would receive federal funding.[10] The act also encouraged treatment and services for juveniles, prohibited juveniles from being held in adult jails, and provided for monitoring the disproportionate percentage of minority juvenile offenders as compared to the adult population.

---

[5] 387 U.S. 1 (1967).
[6] 397 U.S. 358 (1970).
[7] *State ex rel. Ostoj v. McClernan*, 129 Mont. 160, 284 P.2d 252 (1955).
[8] *McKeiver v.Pennsylvania*, 403 U.S. 528 (1971).
[9] *Roper v. Simmons*, 543 U.S. 551 (2005).
[10] 42 U.S.C., Section 5601.

FIGURE 12-1

Model Juvenile Court Act

§1. Interpretation

This Act shall be construed to effectuate the following public purposes:

(1) to provide for the care, protection, and wholesome moral, mental, and physical development of children coming within its provisions;

(2) consistent with the protection of the public interest, to remove from children committing delinquent acts the taint of criminality and the consequences of criminal behavior and to substitute therefor a program of treatment, training, and rehabilitation;

(3) to achieve the foregoing purposes in a family environment whenever possible, separating the child from his parents only when necessary for his welfare or in the interest of public safety;

(4) to provide a simple judicial procedure through which this Act is executed and enforced and in which the parties are assured a fair hearing and their constitutional and other legal rights recognized and enforced; and

(5) to provide simple interstate procedures which permit resort to cooperative measures among the juvenile courts of the several states when required to effectuate the purposes of this Act.[11]

D. THE MODEL JUVENILE COURT ACT

In addition to federal legislation specifically governing juveniles, scholars and others have also created a Model Juvenile Court Act (see Figure 12-1). Like all model acts, the Model Juvenile Court Act seeks to create a uniform, effective, and fair system of legislation that can be adopted by states across the country. To date, only Georgia, North Dakota, and Pennsylvania have actually adopted the act.

III JURISDICTIONAL ISSUES AND JUVENILE COURT

The jurisdiction of juvenile court is statutorily set so that it covers any child who is listed as:

- Dependent or deprived
- Neglected or abused
- Victim of cruelty or abuse
- Delinquent
- "Status offender"[12]

[11] Model Juvenile Court Act §1.

[12] *In re Donald S.*, 206 Cal. App. 3d 134, 253 Cal. Rptr. 274 (2d Dist. 1988).

A. DEPENDENT OR DEPRIVED

Dependent
A court finding that a child's living conditions pose a substantial risk to the child or that the child is being neglected in his current home setting.

In order to determine whether a child is **dependent**, a juvenile judge must make a determination that the conditions or environment that the child is living in do not provide adequate parental care. Dependency does not focus on the fault of the parent or the caregiver. Instead, it focuses on whether the needs of the child are being met, despite the best efforts of the parent or guardian. A court may find that a child is dependent when his parents are unable to care for the child.

Similarly, a finding that a child is deprived also focuses on the child's living conditions and is closely associated with a finding of dependency. Deprived children lack necessary parental oversight, education, subsistence, or moral guidance, or they are abandoned.

B. NEGLECTED

States approach the question of who qualifies as a neglected or abused child in different ways. For the sake of clarity, we will use the Model Juvenile Court Act's definition of "neglected" child. Under the Model Act, a child is considered neglected when he is:

- A child who is without proper parental care or control, subsistence, education, or other care or control necessary for his or her physical, mental, or emotional health, or morals, and the deprivation is not due primarily to the lack of financial means of the child's parents, guardian, or other custodian;
- A child who has been placed for care or adoption in violation of the law; or
- An abandoned child.[13]

Investigations into neglected children focus on the actions and behaviors of the caregiver/parent/guardian. If the court determines that this person has failed to care for the child, has abused the child psychologically or physically, or has simply left the child in a condition in which the child is at substantial risk of harm, then the court will rule that the child is neglected. Such a ruling can justify removing the child from the home, or placing the child with protective services, a foster family or in some other institution where the child can be cared for.

C. VICTIM OF CRUELTY OR ABUSE

Abuse and cruelty to a child can affect an individual for the rest of her life. The long-term effects of abuse can be devastating both to the individual and to a family. The abused sometimes grow up to become abusers themselves, leading to a never-ending cycle. Given the nature of human beings, there are as many ways of abusing a child as there are abusers. What might be abuse in one context might not be abuse

[13] Model Juvenile Court Act §2(5).

in another. Because of this, cases of abuse or neglect are driven by the facts as the court finds them. Once a parent or guardian abuses a child, there is a very strong likelihood that it will happen again, and the juvenile court can take into account not only the facts of the current case but also all the surrounding circumstances, including past cases of abuse against the child.[14]

EXAMPLE

Melissa's parents are a member of a religious sect that does not believe in seeking medical treatment of any kind. Instead, their religion counsels that prayer and prayer alone will heal all of a person's ills. Melissa recently fell and broke her collarbone. When her teacher discovered that Melissa was in pain and had not received treatment, she contacted child protective services. CPS has filed a petition with the juvenile court requesting permission to have Melissa treated by a physician. How is the court likely to rule?

Answer: Although the First Amendment allows all U.S. citizens to worship freely, that right is not absolute. In cases in which a child may be endangered, a court is allowed to intervene for the health of the child regardless of the parents' religious beliefs.[15]

Interestingly, when the courts have intervened on behalf of an endangered unborn child, the results have been mixed. In the case of *In re Fetus Brown*, a pregnant woman underwent surgery during which blood loss caused her red blood count to drop to less than one-third the normal value for a woman at her stage of pregnancy. Because she was a Jehovah's Witness, she refused a blood transfusion even though her decision placed the fetus in grave danger. Doctors estimated that the fetus had only a 5 percent chance of survival without the transfusion. A hearing was held immediately, and the court named the hospital administrator temporary custodian of the fetus. Over the woman's violent objections—necessitating restraint and sedation—she was forced to receive several blood transfusions and then delivered a healthy baby a few days later. The woman subsequently filed an appeal to the court's decision, which the appellate court overturned. The rationale for the decision was that a blood transfusion was not a minimally invasive procedure and that the state "may not override a pregnant woman's competent treatment decision, including refusal of recommended invasive medical procedures, to potentially save the life of the viable fetus."[16]

D. DELINQUENT

Under juvenile law, **delinquency** is any action that would be a crime if it had been carried out by an adult but was instead committed by child (see Figure 12-2).

Delinquency
A criminal act committed by a minor.

[14] *In re N.G.*, 650 S.E.2d 45 (N.C. Ct. App. 2007).
[15] *In re M.*, 78 Misc. 2d 407, 357 N.Y.S.2d 354 (Fam. Ct. 1974).
[16] *In re Fetus Brown*, 689 N.E.2d 397, 400 (Ill. App. Ct. 1997).

FIGURE 12-2

Juvenile Cases Prosecuted in Criminal Courts

Juvenile cases prosecuted in criminal courts	All offices	Full-time offices by population served: Large (1 million or more)	Medium (250,000 to 999,999)	Small (Under 250,000)	Part-time offices
Percent of prosecutors' offices which prosecuted juvenile cases in criminal court	65%	95%	92%	65%	51%
Case total	23,194	4,335	5,330	12,571	959
Median number of cases per office	4	65	12	4	2
Percent of prosecutors' offices with—					
Specialized unit only	3%	30%	10%	2%	–
Designated attorney(s) only	34	14	25	40	25%
Specialized unit, with designated attorney	4	14	18	3	–
No specialized unit, with designated attorney	59	43	47	55	75
Written guidelines for handling juvenile cases in criminal court	13	58	32	12	5

Note: Data were available for 100% of the prosecutors' offices.
— Less than 0.5%.

Source: Prosecutors in State Courts, National Survey of Prosecutors, 2005. Bureau of Justice Statistics, U.S. Department of Justice, July 2006.

Delinquent acts include typical crimes such as shoplifting, robbery, possession and/or sale of narcotics, trespass, damage to property, and burglary, to name just a few (see Figure 12-3).

FIGURE 12-3

Nonfelony Cases Prosecuted by State Prosecutors' Offices

Type of nonfelony cases	Percent of offices				
	All offices	Full-time offices by population served: Large (1 million or more)	Medium (250,000 to 999,999)	Small (Under 250,000)	Part-time offices
Misdemeanor	95%	98%	85%	95%	100%
Juvenile matter	90	90	93	94	78
Traffic violations	88	63	63	88	100
Misdemeanor appeal	71	85	75	67	78
Representing the government in a civil lawsuit	60	46	23	57	81
Child support enforcement	57	37	40	54	73
Felony appeal	54	78	62	53	51

Note: Data were available on the percentage of offices handling misdemeanor cases, juvenile matters, representing government in civil cases, misdemeanor appeals, felony appeals, child support, and traffic violations for 99% of prosecutors' offices.
Source: Prosecutors in State Courts, National Survey of Prosecutors, 2005. Bureau of Justice Statistics, U.S. Department of Justice, July 2006.

Children who are found to be delinquent may be:

- Placed on probation
- Placed in a facility for delinquent children
- Committed to a state institution for delinquent children[17]

E. STATUS OFFENSES

A **status offense** is one that has no corollary in adult criminal law. Common status offenses include runaway child, truancy, unruliness, possession of alcohol, and curfew violations. Generally speaking, a child who is adjudicated as a status offender may end up in the same facility as one who has been adjudicated delinquent. However, the wisdom of that tradition has come under scrutiny. After all, status offenses are not necessarily crimes, but combining status offenders with juvenile

Status offense
An action that is prohibited for a child but is not necessarily a crime.

[17] Model Juvenile Court Act §31.

delinquents often has a negative effect on status offenders and opens them up to abuse by more violent juvenile offenders.

F. POWERS OF JUVENILE COURT JUDGES

Juvenile court judges are also authorized to order physical and/or psychological examinations of the child.[18] If a juvenile court judge finds that the child qualifies as deprived or neglected, the judge may order any of the following actions:

- Allow the child to remain with her parents while imposing strict conditions on those parents.
- Transfer the custody of the child to someone else for a temporary period of time.
- Transfer the child to a delinquent facility.[19]

G. JURISDICTION AND AGE OF THE CHILD

Before we can address the issue of the organization of juvenile court systems around the United States, we must first address a more basic question: How does juvenile court establish its jurisdiction—specifically what age does a child have to be before he falls within (or falls outside of) juvenile court jurisdiction? It is important for purposes of the juvenile court jurisdiction to determine the age of the child. Many states follow the pattern that the juvenile court has jurisdiction over the child until he turns 18 years old. But there is no clear pattern across the United States. In fact, there are some states where the cutoff age for juvenile court matters is as low as 15, with others coming in at 16 or 17.

There are additional concerns about the jurisdiction of juvenile courts. Some states base age-jurisdiction on the age of the child at the time of the crime, while others base it on the age of the child at the time of the hearing. In all cases, juvenile courts lose their authority to hear actions when the child turns 18. However, a child who has been adjudicated can be held in a juvenile facility for several years after reaching age 18.[20] For instance, under the Federal Juvenile Delinquency Act, the age of the child at the time the government institutes its adjudication controls, not the age of the child when the crime occurred.[21]

In many instances, when the juvenile has reached 18, or where there is some confusion about whether the case can proceed in juvenile court, the juvenile has the right to waive his right to juvenile proceedings and have the case handled in adult court. The only requirement is that the juvenile must voluntarily, knowingly, and willingly waive juvenile jurisdiction.

---

[18] Model Juvenile Court Act §28.
[19] Model Juvenile Court Act §30.
[20] *In re V.A.*, 140 S.W.3d 858 (Tex. App. Fort Worth 2004).
[21] *U.S. v. Hoo*, 825 F.2d 667 (2d Cir. 1987).

EXAMPLE

When Alex was arrested for burglary, he falsely gave his age as 20, even though he is 17 and would, under the laws of his state, fall under the jurisdiction of the juvenile court. Alex's case was brought in adult court, and Alex never told anyone what his real age is. Can Alex's conviction be overturned based on the fact that he was actually a juvenile when he was tried and not an adult as he claimed?

Answer: No. If a juvenile willfully misleads the court about his age, then he has essentially waived his right to juvenile court and must accept the judgment (and the sentence) of the adult court.

III ORGANIZATION OF THE JUVENILE COURT SYSTEM

Around the country, there are three general approaches to organizing and running juvenile courts. Some stand alone as independent court systems, while others are integrated and part of the overall adult court system. Finally, some are a hybrid, with some juvenile actions handled by adult courts and other issues transferred to a family court for disposition. We will examine each of these arrangements.

A. INDEPENDENT JUVENILE COURTS

States follow different patterns in the organization of their juvenile court system. A small number of states have a separate juvenile court system, with its own staff, judges, budget, and administration. Some states follow the pattern of combining juvenile court with general court so that on any given day a juvenile case might be heard followed by an adult case.

B. FAMILY COURTS

Family courts were created with the limited jurisdiction to oversee cases involving divorce, child custody, child support, alimony, adoption, and other issues. Family court may also consider issues of child support. A juvenile judge is authorized to impose child support payments on a parent, as long as the court takes into account the parent's ability to pay.[22]

1. TERMINATING PARENTAL RIGHTS

One of the powers of a juvenile court judge, and one that is often used in family courts, is the termination of parental rights. Cutting off a child from her biological parents is a drastic action, but one that is sometimes required for the health and

[22] *Matter of Welfare of C.S.H.*, 408 N.W.2d 225 (Minn. Ct. App. 1987).

safety of the child. Such actions are not taken lightly. When they become necessary, there are specific procedures in place that must be followed before a parent's rights can be terminated. The following procedures are required before parental rights can be terminated:

- Notice of the pending issues
- An opportunity to be heard before the court
- The right of the parents to introduce evidence and to present witness testimony
- The right to respond to the state's claims and evidence and
- A judge who is an impartial fact finder.[23]

C. INTEGRATED COURT SYSTEMS

The majority of states have opted for a third approach to juvenile administration. Juvenile cases are incorporated into the other cases that are also pending in front of superior or other courts. In these states, juvenile court is simply a division of the much larger superior court. Seen this way, juvenile court is very much like traffic court, magistrate court, or small claims court. Each of these courts has limited jurisdiction. Juvenile court is limited to issues dealing with neglected or abandoned children or children who have committed crimes. Given the vast differences between the states and how juvenile cases are processed, you should look to your own state statutes to see how your state handles juvenile court cases.

1. CAPTIONING OF CASES IN JUVENILE COURT

The differences between juvenile cases and adult cases can be seen even in the way that the cases are captioned and recorded in appellate reporters. In adult cases, for example, the defendant's last name is always provided in the caption of the case. Example: *State v. Smith.* However, this convention is not followed with juvenile court proceedings. Instead, you will see captions such as *In re Smith.* Here, the Latin phrase *In re* means *in the matter of.* This also signifies that a juvenile court proceeding is *about* the child, not against the child.

D. JUVENILE COURT RECORDS

Unlike adult court, the hearings and dispositions in juvenile court remain sealed and not open to the public. This secrecy is designed to protect the child and essentially to provide a clean slate for the child once he becomes a legal adult. Some commentators have criticized the secrecy surrounding juvenile court records when a former juvenile delinquent continues his criminal behavior into adulthood; without the ability to review juvenile court records, police

---

[23] *In re Priscilla D.*, 2010 ME 103, 5 A.3d 677 (Me. 2010).

officers are often limited in their investigations. This element of secrecy also applies to the actual hearings themselves. In most states, juvenile court hearings are not open to the public in the way that almost all adult court hearings are. Spectators can sit in on adult court proceedings for nearly any type of crime and are seldom barred from the court except in special circumstances (such as the testimony of a rape victim or the direct and cross-examination of an undercover police officer). But juvenile courts follow the opposite rule. Virtually every type of hearing in juvenile court is closed to the public. Like juvenile records, the idea behind closing juvenile hearings to the public is to protect the child from media and other scrutiny and to offer the child a chance to enter adult life without lingering stories of what he did as a juvenile.

The secrecy component of juvenile court has come into question in the past few decades with some high-profile juvenile cases, especially situations in which juvenile offenders committed crimes as adults that mirrored their infractions as juveniles. Some states have begun opening some juvenile hearings to the public, although in most states these hearings remain closed.

PROFILING THE PROFESSIONAL

Juvenile Court Secrecy

"Juvenile court is very, very confidential. No juvenile records can be released until ordered by a judge, usually when a person is facing probation for commitment, the probation officer is allowed to see the records. Nobody can look at the juvenile records. There is a courtroom court clerk present in juvenile court. We do juvenile court in the same court as we do other criminal cases. Monday, Tuesday, and Wednesday are usually set aside for adult court and then Thursday is for juveniles. Friday is child-support."

Mabel Lowman, Clerk of Court

E. JUVENILES TRIED AS ADULTS

States are also in disarray when it comes to the serious question of trying a child as an adult. All states have statutes that allow the transfer of a case out of juvenile court and into adult court when a child of a certain age commits a specific type of crime, usually rape or murder. The problem is the bottom cut-off age. In some states, a child as young as 13 can be tried as an adult if he has committed rape or murder, while in other states the youngest that a child can be tried as an adult is 16. Not only are there differences between the states about the age limit that a child can be tried as an adult, there is also considerable variation about how that process is carried out. In some states, for example, the district attorney has the right to certify that a specific child will be tried as an adult. In others, the decision is left to the juvenile court judge. Although many of these cases get a disproportionate amount of news coverage, the actual number of children who are tried as adults is very low. Fortunately, not that many children commit rapes and murders.

However, when they do, it's chilling. In Washington State, two 12-year-old friends, Jake Eakin and Evan Savoie, were arrested and charged with the murder of a 13-year-old boy, who was beaten and stabbed in 2003. Despite the young age of the defendants, the judge decided they should be tried as adults. (By the time the case went to trial, the boys were 15.) If they were found guilty, the judge declared that the crime was so gruesome he doubted the boys could be rehabilitated in the juvenile system. Eakin ultimately pleaded guilty to second-degree murder, was sentenced to 14 years, and testified against his friend. Savoie was found guilty of first-degree murder and sentenced to 26 years in prison.

PROFILING THE PROFESSIONAL

Trying Juveniles As Adults

"I do get a fair amount of juveniles who get tried as adults. The most common types of cases that we get a juvenile tried as an adult include murder, child molestation, kidnapping with bodily injury, and others. The district attorney can decide whether or not they go to juvenile court or whether they go to adult court. States do things differently. In my state, the DA has the authority to designate who will be tried as an adult. The youngest child I have ever represented who was tried as an adult was 15 years old."

B.J. Bernstein, Defense Attorney

IV JUVENILE COURT PROCEDURE

Because juvenile courts follow their own rules, independent of those found in adult courts, it should come as no surprise that the various procedural steps followed in juvenile court differ from those of their adult counterparts. There are four general procedural steps involved in most juvenile court cases, whether the action involves a petition for adjudication on delinquency or abuse:

- Summons (arrest)
- Intake
- Detention
- Judicial adjudication

A. SUMMONS (ARREST)

Summons
A court order for a person to appear at a specific time and place.

Police may arrest juveniles for crimes in the same manner that they arrest adults. An officer may take a juvenile into custody for a crime committed and then transport the juvenile to a different facility than that used for adults. No state allows juveniles and adults to mix together in holding cells. A **summons** is a court order for a juvenile (and his parents) to appear at a specific date and time. In some instances, the summons may be issued by the police in lieu of taking the juvenile into custody. In others, the juvenile may be held until the intake phase.

B. INTAKE

Intake is a procedural step during which the child is evaluated to determine whether she should be brought into the juvenile justice system. Most referrals come from police officers, but others are allowed to request intake for juvenile, including parents, teachers, and victims. In some cases, intake decisions are made by probation officers. During the intake process, one of two decisions will be made. If the case is petitioned, it means that the child will be handled by the juvenile court system. If the officials decide that intake is not necessary, they will file no petition, sometimes referred to as *nonpetitioned*. In many ways the petition resembles a prosecutor's accusation or indictment. In cases in which the juvenile is nonpetitioned, she may be diverted into a residential facility for juveniles, placed on probation and supervised by a probation officer, or issued a fine ordered to pay restitution for damages. Fifty percent of juvenile cases fall into the category of *nonpetitioned*, where they are handled informally and do not appear on the court's docket.

Intake
A juvenile court proceeding in which a judge determines whether the juvenile should be processed by the court or released.

C. DETENTION

While court officials are deciding whether to petition in a particular child case, the child may be held pending the decision. Children are usually detained only for serious offenses or when there is evidence that the child is a danger to himself or others. Once a child is detained, a hearing must be held within 24 to 48 hours to determine whether the child should continue in detention or be released.

D. JUDICIAL ADJUDICATION

Assuming that the case is petitioned, a juvenile court judge will not only hear the facts of the case and reach a decision, but will also decide issues of law. This process is not referred to as a finding of guilt or innocence, but instead as **adjudication**. As we have seen previously, there are no juries in juvenile court, so the judge serves the function instead. During the adjudication, the judge hears witness testimony and considers evidence offered by the prosecution and any rebuttal evidence offered by the defense. If the judge believes, beyond a reasonable doubt, that the child is responsible for the charges lodged against him, then the judge is entitled to make a judicial disposition that could include incarceration or other action. However, if the judge does not believe that there is proof beyond reasonable doubt, the case is listed as nonadjudicated, which is virtually identical to an acquittal in adult court. However, unlike acquittal in adult court, a judge may reach a decision of nonadjudication and still require the child to perform some action, including seeking counseling or paying restitution.

Adjudication
Similar to a trial in adult court, in an adjudication the juvenile court judge decides the culpability of the juvenile and then makes a decision about appropriate treatment or rehabilitation.

As you read the following case, notice references to the *Gault* case and how the question of proof beyond reasonable doubt, central to adult prosecutions, is related to a finding of delinquency.

CASE EXCERPT

In re Winship

397 U.S. 358, 90 S.Ct. 1068 (1970)

Mr. Justice Brennan delivered the opinion of the Court.

Constitutional questions decided by this Court concerning the juvenile process have centered on the adjudicatory stage at "which a determination is made as to whether a juvenile is a 'delinquent' as a result of alleged misconduct on his part, with the consequence that he may be committed to a state institution." *In re Gault*, 387 U.S. 1, 13, 87 S.Ct. 1428, 1436, 18 L.Ed.2d 527 (1967). Gault decided that, although the Fourteenth Amendment does not require that the hearing at this stage conform with all the requirements of a criminal trial or even of the usual administrative proceeding, the Due Process Clause does require application during the adjudicatory hearing of "the essentials of due process and fair treatment." Id., at 30, 87 S.Ct. at 1445. This case presents the single, narrow question whether proof beyond a reasonable doubt is among the "essentials of due process and fair treatment" required during the adjudicatory stage when a juvenile is charged with an act which would constitute a crime if committed by an adult.[1]

Section 712 of the New York Family Court Act defines a juvenile delinquent as "a person over seven and less than sixteen years of age who does any act which, if done by an adult, would constitute a crime." During a 1967 adjudicatory hearing, conducted pursuant to §742 of the Act, a judge in New York Family Court found that appellant, then a 12-year-old boy, had entered a locker and stolen $112 from a woman's pocketbook. The petition which charged appellant with delinquency alleged that his act, "if done by an adult, would constitute the crime or crimes of Larceny." The judge acknowledged that the proof might not establish guilt beyond a reasonable doubt, but rejected appellant's contention that such proof was required by the Fourteenth Amendment. The judge relied instead on §744(b) of the New York Family Court Act which provides that "(a)ny determination at the conclusion of (an adjudicatory) hearing that a (juvenile) did an act or acts

---

[1] Thus, we do not see how it can be said in dissent that this opinion "rests entirely on the assumption that all juvenile proceedings are 'criminal prosecutions,' hence subject to constitutional limitations." As in Gault, "we are not here concerned with . . . the pre-judicial stages of the juvenile process, nor do we direct our attention to the post-adjudicative or dispositional process." 387 U.S., at 13, 87 S.Ct., at 1436. In New York, the adjudicatory stage of a delinquency proceeding is clearly distinct from both the preliminary phase of the juvenile process and from its dispositional stage. See N.Y. Family Court Act §731-749. Similarly, we intimate no view concerning the constitutionality of the New York procedures governing children "in need of supervision." See id., at §§711, 712, 742-745. nor do we consider whether there are other "essentials of due process and fair treatment" required during the adjudicatory hearing of a delinquency proceeding. Finally, we have no occasion to consider appellant's argument that §744(b) is a violation of the Equal Protection Clause, as well as a denial of due process.

must be based on a preponderance of the evidence."[2] During a subsequent dispositional hearing, appellant was ordered placed in a training school for an initial period of 18 months, subject to annual extensions of his commitment until his 18th birthday-six years in appellant's case. The Appellate Division of the New York Supreme Court, First Judicial Department, affirmed without opinion, 30 A.D.2d 781, 291 N.Y.S.2d 1005 (1968). The New York Court of Appeals then affirmed by a four-to-three vote, expressly sustaining the constitutionality of §744(b), 24 N.Y.2d 196, 299 N.Y.S.2d 414, 247 N.W.2d 253 (1969). We noted probable jurisdiction 396 U.S. 885, 90 S.Ct. 179, 24 L.Ed.2d 160 (1969). We reverse.

I

The requirement that guilt of a criminal charge be established by proof beyond a reasonable doubt dates at least from our early years as a Nation. The "demand for a higher degree of persuasion in criminal cases was recurrently expressed from ancient times, (though) its crystallization into the formula 'beyond a reasonable doubt' seems to have occurred as late as 1798. It is now accepted in common law jurisdictions as the measure of persuasion by which the prosecution must convince the trier of all the essential elements of guilt." C. McCormick, Evidence §321, pp. 681-682 (1954); see also 9 J. Wigmore, Evidence, §2497 (3d ed. 1940). Although virtually unanimous adherence to the reasonable-doubt standard in common-law jurisdictions may not conclusively establish it as a requirement of due process, such adherence does "reflect a profound judgment about the way in which law should be enforced and justice administered." *Duncan v. Louisiana*, 391 U.S. 145, 155, 88 S.Ct. 1444, 1451, 20 L.Ed.2d 491 (1968).

Expressions in many opinions of this Court indicate that it has long been assumed that proof of a criminal charge beyond a reasonable doubt is constitutionally required. Mr. Justice Frankfurter stated that "(i)t is the duty of the Government to establish . . . guilt beyond a reasonable doubt. This notion-basic in our law and rightly one of the boasts of a free society-is a requirement and a safeguard of due process of law in the historic, procedural content of 'due process.'" *Leland v. Oregon*, supra, 343 U.S., at 802-803, 72 S.Ct., at 1009 (dissenting opinion). In a similar vein, the Court said in *Brinegar v. United States*, supra, 338 U.S., at 174, 69 S.Ct., at 1310, that "(g)uilt in a criminal case must be proved beyond a reasonable doubt and by evidence confined to that which long experience in the common-law tradition, to some extent embodied in the Constitution, has crystallized into rules of evidence consistent with that standard. These rules are historically grounded rights of our system, developed to safeguard men from dubious and unjust convictions, with resulting forfeitures of life, liberty and property." *Davis v. United States*, supra, 160 U.S., at 488, 16 S.Ct., at 358 stated that the requirement is implicit in "constitutions . . . (which) recognize the fundamental principles that are deemed essential for the protection of life and liberty." In Davis a

[2] The ruling appears in the following portion of the hearing transcript: Counsel: "Your Honor is making a finding by the preponderance of the evidence." Court: "Well, it convinces me."

Counsel: "It's not beyond a reasonable doubt, Your Honor."

Court: "That is true . . . . Our statute says a preponderance and a preponderance it is."

murder conviction was reversed because the trial judge instructed the jury that it was their duty to convict when the evidence was equally balanced regarding the sanity of the accused. This Court said: "On the contrary, he is entitled to an acquittal of the specific crime charged, if upon all the evidence, there is reasonable doubt whether he was capable in law of committing crime. No man should be deprived of his life under the forms of law unless the jurors who try him are able, upon their consciences, to say that the evidence before them . . . is sufficient to show beyond a reasonable doubt the existence of every fact necessary to constitute the crime charged." Id., at 484, 493, 16 S.Ct., at 357, 360.

The reasonable-doubt standard plays a vital role in the American scheme of criminal procedure. It is a prime instrument for reducing the risk of convictions resting on factual error. The standard provides concrete substance for the presumption of innocence-that bedrock "axiomatic and elementary" principle whose "enforcement lies at the foundation of the administration of our criminal law." *Coffin v. United States*, supra, 156 U.S., at 453, 15 S.Ct., at 403. As the dissenters in the New York Court of Appeals observed, and we agree, "a person accused of a crime . . . would be at a severe disadvantage, a disadvantage amounting to a lack of fundamental fairness, if he could be adjudged guilty and imprisoned for years on the strength of the same evidence as would suffice in a civil case." 24 N.Y.2d, at 205, 299 N.Y.S.2d, at 422, 247 N.E.2d, at 259.

The requirement of proof beyond a reasonable doubt has this vital role in our criminal procedure for cogent reasons. The accused during a criminal prosecution has at stake interest of immense importance, both because of the possibility that he may lose his liberty upon conviction and because of the certainty that he would be stigmatized by the conviction. Accordingly, a society that values the good name and freedom of every individual should not condemn a man for commission of a crime when there is reasonable doubt about his guilt. As we said in *Speiser v. Randall*, 357 U.S., at 525-526, 78 S.Ct., at 1342: "There is always in litigation a margin of error, representing error in factfinding, which both parties must take into account. Where one party has at stake an interest of transcending value-as a criminal defendant his liberty-this margin of error is reduced as to him by the process of placing on the other party the burden of . . . persuading the factfinder at the conclusion of the trial of his guilt beyond a reasonable doubt. Due process commands that no man shall lose his liberty unless the Government has borne the burden of . . . convincing the factfinder of his guilt." To this end, the reasonable-doubt standard is indispensable, for it "impresses on the trier of fact the necessity of reaching a subjective state of certitude of the facts in issue." Dorsen & Rezneck, In Re Gault and the Future of Juvenile Law, 1 Family Law Quarterly, No. 4, pp. 1, 26 (1967).

Moreover, use of the reasonable-doubt standard is indispensable to command the respect and confidence of the community in applications of the criminal law. It is critical that the moral force of the criminal law not be diluted by a standard of proof that leaves people in doubt whether innocent men are being condemned. It is also important in our free society that every individual going about his ordinary affairs have confidence that his government cannot adjudge him guilty of a criminal offense without convincing a proper factfinder of his guilt with utmost certainty.

Lest there remain any doubt about the constitutional stature of the reasonable-doubt standard, we explicitly hold that the Due Process Clause protects the accused against conviction except upon proof beyond a reasonable doubt of every fact necessary to constitute the crime with which he is charged.

II

We turn to the question whether juveniles, like adults, are constitutionally entitled to proof beyond a reasonable doubt when they are charged with violation of a criminal law. The same considerations that demand extreme caution in factfinding to protect the innocent adult apply as well to the innocent child. We do not find convincing the contrary arguments of the New York Court of Appeals, Gault rendered untenable much of the reasoning relied upon by that court to sustain the constitutionality of §744(b). The Court of Appeals indicated that a delinquency adjudication "is not a 'conviction' (§781); that it affects no right or privilege, including the right to hold public office or to obtain a license (§782); and a cloak of protective confidentiality is thrown around all the proceedings (§§783-784)." 24 N.Y.2d at 200, 299 N.Y.S.2d, at 417-418, 247 N.E.2d, at 255-256. The court said further: "The delinquency status is not made a crime; and the proceedings are not criminal. There is, hence, no deprivation of due process in the statutory provision (challenged by appellant)." 24 N.Y.2d, at 203, 299 N.Y.S.2d, at 420, 247 N.E.2d, at 257. In effect the Court of Appeals distinguished the proceedings in question here from a criminal prosecution by use of what Gault called the "'civil' label-of-convenience which has been attached to juvenile proceedings." 387 U.S., at 50, 87 S.Ct., at 1455. But Gault expressly rejected that distinction as a reason for holding the Due Process Clause inapplicable to a juvenile proceeding. 387 U.S., at 50-51, 87 S.Ct., at 1455, 1456. The Court of Appeals also attempted to justify the preponderance standard on the related ground that juvenile proceedings are designed "not to punish, but to save the child." 24 N.Y.2d, at 197, 299 N.Y.S.2d, at 415, 247 N.E.2d, at 254. Again, however, Gault expressly rejected this justification. 387 U.S., at 27, 87 S.Ct., at 1443. We made clear in that decision that civil labels and good intentions do not themselves obviate the need for criminal due process safeguards in juvenile courts, for "(a) proceeding where the issue is whether the child will be found to be 'delinquent' and subjected to the loss of his liberty for years is comparable in seriousness to a felony prosecution." Id., at 36, 87 S.Ct., at 1448.

Nor do we perceive any merit in the argument that to afford juveniles the protection of proof beyond a reasonable doubt would risk destruction of beneficial aspects of the juvenile process. Use of the reasonable-doubt standard during the adjudicatory hearing will not disturb New York's policies that a finding that a child has violated a criminal law does not constitute a criminal conviction, that such a finding does not deprive the child of his civil rights, and that juvenile proceedings are confidential. Nor will there be any effect on the informality, flexibility, or speed of the hearing at which the factfinding takes place. And the opportunity during the post-adjudicatory or dispositional hearing for a wide-ranging review of the child's social history and for his individualized treatment will remain unimpaired. Similarly, there will be no effect on the procedures distinctive to juvenile proceedings that are employed prior to the adjudicatory hearing.

The Court of Appeals observed that "a child's best interest is not necessarily, or even probably, promoted if he wins in the particular inquiry which may bring him to the juvenile court." 24 N.Y.2d, at 199, 299 N.Y.S.2d, at 417, 247 N.E.2d, at 255. It is true, of course, that the juvenile may be engaging in a general course of conduct inimical to his welfare that calls for judicial intervention.

But that intervention cannot take the form of subjecting the child to the stigma of a finding that he violated a criminal law[5] and to the possibility of institutional confinement on proof insufficient to convict him were he an adult.

We conclude, as we concluded regarding the essential due process safeguards applied in Gault, that the observance of the standard of proof beyond a reasonable doubt "will not compel the States to abandon or displace any of the substantive benefits of the juvenile process." Gault, supra, at 21, 87 S.Ct., at 1440.

Finally, we reject the Court of Appeals' suggestion that there is, in any event, only a "tenuous difference" between the reasonable-doubt and preponderance standards. The suggestion is singularly unpersuasive. In this very case, the trial judge's ability to distinguish between the two standards enabled him to make a finding of guilt that he conceded he might not have made under the standard of proof beyond a reasonable doubt. Indeed, the trial judge's action evidences the accuracy of the observation of commentators that "the preponderance test is susceptible to the misinterpretation that it calls on the trier of fact merely to perform an abstract weighing of the evidence in order to determine which side has produced the greater quantum, without regard to its effect in convincing his mind of the truth of the proposition asserted." Dorsen & Rezneck, supra, at 26-27.[6]

III

In sum, the constitutional safeguard of proof beyond a reasonable doubt is as much required during the adjudicatory stage of a delinquency proceeding as are those constitutional safeguards applied in Gault-notice of charges, right to counsel, the rights of confrontation and examination, and the privilege against self-incrimination. We therefore hold, in agreement with Chief Judge Fuld in dissent in the Court of Appeals, "that, where a 12-year-old child is charged with an act of stealing which renders him liable to confinement for as long as six years, then, as a matter of due process . . . the case against him must be proved beyond a reasonable doubt." 24 N.Y.2d, at 207, 299 N.Y.S.2d, at 423, 247 N.E.2d, at 260.

Reversed.

CASE QUESTIONS

1 What is the "single, narrow question" presented in this case?
2 How does New York define delinquency?
3 What standard of proof is followed in New York in order to determine delinquency?

---

[5] The more comprehensive and effective the procedures used to prevent public disclosure of the finding, the less the danger of stigma. As we indicated in Gault, however, often the "claim of secrecy . . . is more rhetoric than reality." 387 U.S., at 24, 87 S.Ct., at 1442.

[6] Compare this Court's rejection of the preponderance standard in deportation proceedings, where we ruled that the Government must support its allegations with "clear, unequivocal, and convincing evidence." *Woodby v. Immigration and Naturalization Service*, 385 U.S., 276, 285, 87 S.Ct. 483, 488, 17 L.Ed.2d 362 (1966). Although we ruled in Woodby that deportation is not tantamount to a criminal conviction, we found that since it could lead to "drastic deprivations," it is impermissible for a person to be "banished from this country upon no higher degree of proof than applies in a negligence case." Ibid.

4 According to the court, how far back does the principle of proof beyond a reasonable doubt go?
5 Why does the court say that proof beyond a reasonable doubt is vital in the American judicial system?

CHAPTER SUMMARY

In this chapter we have seen that juvenile law is very different from adult prosecutions. Although the early court systems in the United States tended to group juveniles with adults, over time activists and others urged the idea of splitting the two groups in order to protect juveniles. The purpose of juvenile court proceedings is to protect and rehabilitate juveniles. Courts have adopted the *parens patriae* philosophy that places the state as guardian over neglected, abused, or delinquent children. Several key U.S. Supreme Court cases have modified juvenile court procedures over the last 100 years. In recent decades, for example, the U.S. Supreme Court has ruled that the burden of proof in a juvenile case must be beyond a reasonable doubt and that juveniles are entitled to assistance of counsel, due process, and the right to confront witnesses, among other rights. Juvenile court dispositions do not focus on guilt. Instead, they categorize juveniles as dependent, neglected, delinquent, or status offenders. Delinquency is the corollary to a criminal conviction. Although juveniles are not sentenced, a finding of delinquency can result in their being detained and ordered to seek counseling and other rehabilitative services. Status offenders are juveniles who commit offenses that would not ordinarily be crimes if they were committed by adults. Examples of status offenses include curfew violations and truancy, among others.

Juvenile courts are arranged differently across the United States. Some juvenile courts stand alone with their own administrative staffs and separate court personnel. Other states operate juvenile court as a subsidiary of other adult courts, and a third approach is to fully incorporate juvenile court into all other functioning courts, in the same way that small claims and misdemeanor courts are incorporated into the court system. The procedure followed in juvenile court is also different from that found in adult courts. After arrest or summons, a decision about intake is made. Intake is the decision of whether to process the juvenile through juvenile court. If a petition for intake is granted, the juvenile can be detained and then finally adjudicated. Juveniles are not found guilty; they are simply adjudicated and then required to be counseled, released on probation, or held for a specific period of time. One of the most important aspects of juvenile court is to determine the jurisdiction of the court. Many states follow the rule that a person 17 and under automatically falls under the jurisdiction of juvenile court, but this is by no means universal. Some states cut off juvenile jurisdiction at age 16 or even 15.

KEY TERMS

Key terms are listed here in order of appearance in chapter.

Parens patriae
Preponderance of the evidence
Dependent
Delinquency
Status offense
Summons
Intake
Adjudication

REVIEW QUESTIONS

1. What were some of the problems in prosecuting delinquent juveniles prior to the 1800s?
2. Explain the importance of the case *In re Gault.*
3. What is the significance of the Juvenile Delinquency Prevention and Control Act?
4. What is recognized as the first modern juvenile court system, and when was it created?
5. What is the principle of *parens patriae*, and what significance does it have for juvenile courts?
6. How are the basic purposes of adult court and juvenile court different?
7. What was the original burden of proof in juvenile courts, and what is it now?
8. Explain the significance of the U.S. Supreme Court case of *In re Winship.*
9. What is significant about the case of *Roper v. Simmons*?
10. What is the Model Juvenile Court Act?
11. What is the definition of a dependent or deprived child?
12. Under the Model Juvenile Court Act, how does a child qualify as neglected or abused?
13. What is the definition of delinquency?
14. What are status offenses?
15. List and explain some of the powers of a juvenile court judge.
16. How does the age of a juvenile factor into a juvenile court's jurisdiction?
17. What are the three main ways in which juvenile courts are organized across the United States?
18. What procedures must be followed in terminating parental rights?
19. Why are juvenile court records kept secret?
20. Under what circumstances can a juvenile be tried as an adult?
21. What is the "intake" procedure?
22. What is adjudication?

WEB SURFING

National Criminal Justice Reference Service: Juvenile Justice
http://www.ncjrs.gov/app/topics/topic.aspx?topicid=122

Office of Juvenile Justice and Delinquency Prevention
http://www.ojjdp.gov/

EXERCISES

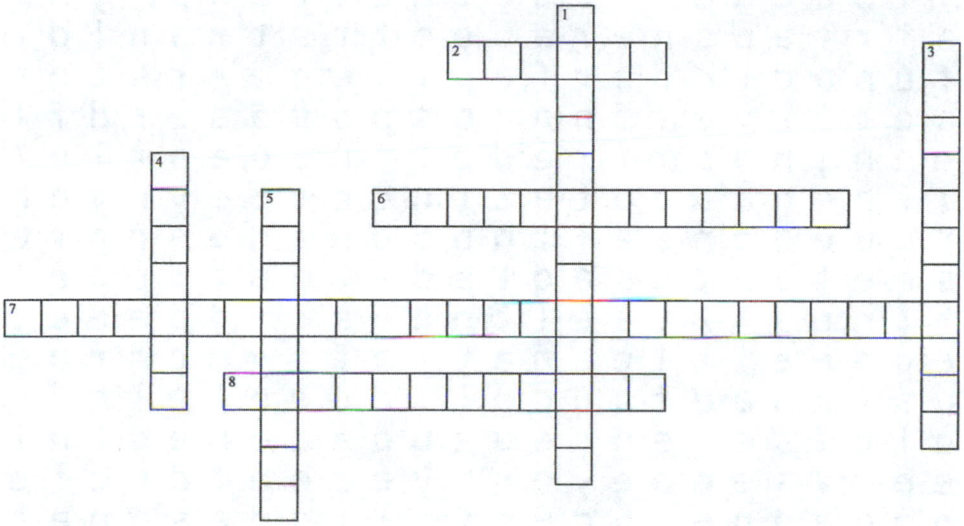

ACROSS

2. A juvenile court proceeding where a judge determines if the juvenile should be processed by the court or released
6. An action that is prohibited for a child, but is not necessarily a crime
7. A showing by one side in a civil suit that its version of the facts is more likely to be true than not
8. A proceeding where the juvenile court judge decides the culpability of the juvenile and then makes a decision about appropriate treatment or rehabilitation

DOWN

1. The philosophy that when parents or guardians fail a child, the government fills the gap by providing basic necessities, protection, education, and counseling, as needed
3. A minor who has committed a criminal act
4. A court order for a person to appear at a specific time and place
5. A court finding that a child's living conditions pose a substantial risk to the child or that the child is being neglected in his current home setting

l	e	c	u	n	u	a	t	m	f	e	o	t	k	e	e	s	s	o	k	e	n	k	d	e	d
e	c	r	u	i	e	i	n	n	p	h	d	k	i	e	u	e	n	l	e	o	h	s	p	t	u
t	n	i	r	e	e	v	n	a	o	d	n	t	f	p	p	o	t	i	d	i	s	i	t	t	t
r	e	o	c	j	a	i	s	e	e	t	n	p	a	e	n	d	a	e	v	d	e	o	a	f	f
e	d	r	i	i	n	i	a	d	e	e	t	t	f	u	n	i	i	n	d	t	e	q	e	u	n
e	i	d	i	t	p	n	e	e	o	n	r	e	n	p	p	e	d	t	r	l	t	p	p	d	s
e	v	p	a	i	a	y	p	d	d	n	t	a	c	a	e	e	s	d	n	l	j	a	e	c	r
p	e	k	i	u	l	c	n	a	c	m	k	o	j	f	l	o	r	p	t	c	c	a	e	p	f
t	e	i	s	u	p	s	i	o	t	e	e	t	n	i	f	n	o	a	p	q	e	r	m	e	n
n	h	e	e	t	c	s	u	d	u	o	i	n	n	n	j	c	d	a	e	v	e	a	e	e	t
u	t	d	p	e	a	i	t	u	u	d	o	q	q	n	s	e	d	d	a	v	e	e	n	d	f
e	f	n	j	f	e	t	p	n	u	j	u	e	d	e	a	r	l	d	n	a	u	a	a	r	a
a	o	m	i	o	e	e	u	e	s	e	d	d	e	t	d	c	t	t	a	a	p	m	y	n	n
a	e	a	i	r	t	a	p	s	n	e	r	a	p	e	o	t	r	s	t	r	a	n	i	d	r
a	c	f	u	p	a	d	t	c	o	s	r	f	e	p	i	k	e	p	e	e	r	s	c	d	s
s	n	a	e	r	i	a	y	e	m	f	n	n	n	o	s	p	o	d	d	a	e	r	d	f	l
u	a	e	n	n	j	n	d	s	m	f	f	e	d	e	t	f	u	s	o	a	o	r	i	e	t
i	r	i	t	e	a	n	a	a	u	d	t	e	e	t	n	c	e	c	p	e	y	n	y	n	n
e	e	p	o	u	e	e	e	n	s	a	i	t	n	p	o	d	n	a	e	o	e	c	p	r	e
i	d	s	e	e	t	a	e	t	n	s	a	q	t	s	d	t	t	q	p	t	l	p	d	e	f
l	n	t	f	n	e	s	l	k	t	e	e	i	t	n	e	o	s	c	c	d	p	e	e	e	e
e	o	e	c	n	e	e	i	t	l	e	e	n	a	t	j	a	f	c	y	n	c	n	r	o	d
m	p	e	s	f	k	n	a	d	f	c	u	c	o	i	i	d	c	e	e	r	n	i	n	f	r
s	e	o	i	p	t	s	e	s	e	n	n	e	u	e	u	d	a	e	e	n	e	c	t	n	i
n	r	e	e	t	v	s	e	e	o	e	y	e	n	e	y	e	r	e	e	f	d	v	e	i	e
t	p	n	o	p	a	o	p	e	n	q	d	e	e	t	s	r	f	d	d	e	s	d	n	a	t

parens patriae
preponderance of the evidence
dependent
delinquency
status offense
summons
intake
adjudication

QUESTIONS FOR ANALYSIS

1 Should all juvenile offenders above age 15 who break the law be treated as adults? Why or why not?

2 Is the basic philosophy of juvenile court, rehabilitation of youths, a realistic goal? Should juveniles be treated more like criminals, or does the current system strike the right balance?

Appendix: U.S. Constitution

We the People of the United States, in Order to form a more perfect Union, establish Justice, insure domestic Tranquility, provide for the common defence, promote the general Welfare, and secure the Blessings of Liberty to ourselves and our Posterity, do ordain and establish this Constitution for the United States of America.

ARTICLE I

SECTION 1

All legislative Powers herein granted shall be vested in a Congress of the United States, which shall consist of a Senate and House of Representatives.

SECTION 2

1: The House of Representatives shall be composed of Members chosen every second Year by the People of the several States, and the Electors in each State shall have the Qualifications requisite for Electors of the most numerous Branch of the State Legislature.

2: No Person shall be a Representative who shall not have attained to the Age of twenty five Years, and been seven Years a Citizen of the United States, and who shall not, when elected, be an Inhabitant of that State in which he shall be chosen.

3: Representatives and direct Taxes shall be apportioned among the several States which may be included within this Union, according to their respective Numbers, which shall be determined by adding to the whole Number of free Persons, including those bound to Service for a Term of Years, and excluding Indians not taxed, three fifths of all other Persons. The actual Enumeration shall be made within three Years after the first Meeting of the Congress of the United States, and within every subsequent Term of ten Years, in such Manner as they shall by Law direct. The Number of Representatives shall not exceed one for every thirty Thousand, but each State shall have at Least one Representative; and until such enumeration shall be made, the State of New Hampshire shall be entitled to chuse three, Massachusetts eight, Rhode-Island and Providence Plantations one, Connecticut five, New-York six, New Jersey four, Pennsylvania eight, Delaware one, Maryland six, Virginia ten, North Carolina five, South Carolina five, and Georgia three.

4: When vacancies happen in the Representation from any State, the Executive Authority thereof shall issue Writs of Election to fill such Vacancies.

5: The House of Representatives shall chuse their Speaker and other Officers; and shall have the sole Power of Impeachment.

SECTION 3

1: The Senate of the United States shall be composed of two Senators from each State, chosen by the Legislature thereof, for six Years; and each Senator shall have one Vote.

2: Immediately after they shall be assembled in Consequence of the first Election, they shall be divided as equally as may be into three Classes. The Seats of the Senators of the first Class shall be vacated at the Expiration of the second Year, of the second Class at the Expiration of the fourth Year, and of the third Class at the Expiration of the sixth Year, so that one third may be chosen every second Year; and if Vacancies happen by Resignation, or otherwise, during the Recess of the Legislature of any State, the Executive thereof may make temporary Appointments until the next Meeting of the Legislature, which shall then fill such Vacancies.

3: No Person shall be a Senator who shall not have attained to the Age of thirty Years, and been nine Years a Citizen of the United States, and who shall not, when elected, be an Inhabitant of that State for which he shall be chosen.

4: The Vice President of the United States shall be President of the Senate, but shall have no Vote, unless they be equally divided.

5: The Senate shall chuse their other Officers, and also a President pro tempore, in the Absence of the Vice President, or when he shall exercise the Office of President of the United States.

6: The Senate shall have the sole Power to try all Impeachments. When sitting for that Purpose, they shall be on Oath or Affirmation. When the President of the United States is tried, the Chief Justice shall preside: And no Person shall be convicted without the Concurrence of two thirds of the Members present.

7: Judgment in Cases of impeachment shall not extend further than to removal from Office, and disqualification to hold and enjoy any Office of honor, Trust or Profit under the United States: but the Party convicted shall nevertheless be liable and subject to Indictment, Trial, Judgment and Punishment, according to Law.

SECTION 4

1: The Times, Places and Manner of holding Elections for Senators and Representatives, shall be prescribed in each State by the Legislature thereof; but the Congress may at any time by Law make or alter such Regulations, except as to the Places of chusing Senators.

2: The Congress shall assemble at least once in every Year, and such Meeting shall be on the first Monday in December, unless they shall by Law appoint a different Day.

SECTION 5

1: Each House shall be the Judge of the Elections, Returns and Qualifications of its own Members, and a Majority of each shall constitute a Quorum to do Business; but a smaller Number may adjourn from day to day, and may be authorized to compel the Attendance of absent Members, in such Manner, and under such Penalties as each House may provide.

2: Each House may determine the Rules of its Proceedings, punish its Members for disorderly Behaviour, and, with the Concurrence of two thirds, expel a Member.

3: Each House shall keep a Journal of its Proceedings, and from time to time publish the same, excepting such Parts as may in their Judgment require Secrecy; and the Yeas and Nays of the Members of either House on any question shall, at the Desire of one fifth of those Present, be entered on the Journal.

4: Neither House, during the Session of Congress, shall, without the Consent of the other, adjourn for more than three days, nor to any other Place than that in which the two Houses shall be sitting.

SECTION 6

1: The Senators and Representatives shall receive a Compensation for their Services, to be ascertained by Law, and paid out of the Treasury of the United States. They shall in all Cases, except Treason, Felony and Breach of the Peace, be privileged from Arrest during their Attendance at the Session of their respective Houses, and in going to and returning from the same; and for any Speech or Debate in either House, they shall not be questioned in any other Place.

2: No Senator or Representative shall, during the Time for which he was elected, be appointed to any civil Office under the Authority of the United States, which shall have been created, or the Emoluments whereof shall have been encreased during such time; and no Person holding any Office under the United States, shall be a Member of either House during his Continuance in Office.

SECTION 7

1: All Bills for raising Revenue shall originate in the House of Representatives; but the Senate may propose or concur with Amendments as on other Bills.

2: Every Bill which shall have passed the House of Representatives and the Senate, shall, before it become a Law, be presented to the President of the United States; If he approve he shall sign it, but if not he shall return it, with his Objections to that

House in which it shall have originated, who shall enter the Objections at large on their Journal, and proceed to reconsider it. If after such Reconsideration two thirds of that House shall agree to pass the Bill, it shall be sent, together with the Objections, to the other House, by which it shall likewise be reconsidered, and if approved by two thirds of that House, it shall become a Law. But in all such Cases the Votes of both Houses shall be determined by yeas and Nays, and the Names of the Persons voting for and against the Bill shall be entered on the Journal of each House respectively. If any Bill shall not be returned by the President within ten Days (Sundays excepted) after it shall have been presented to him, the Same shall be a Law, in like Manner as if he had signed it, unless the Congress by their Adjournment prevent its Return, in which Case it shall not be a Law.

3: Every Order, Resolution, or Vote to which the Concurrence of the Senate and House of Representatives may be necessary (except on a question of Adjournment) shall be presented to the President of the United States; and before the Same shall take Effect, shall be approved by him, or being disapproved by him, shall be repassed by two thirds of the Senate and House of Representatives, according to the Rules and Limitations prescribed in the Case of a Bill.

SECTION 8

1: The Congress shall have Power To lay and collect Taxes, Duties, Imposts and Excises, to pay the Debts and provide for the common Defence and general Welfare of the United States; but all Duties, Imposts and Excises shall be uniform throughout the United States;

2: To borrow Money on the credit of the United States;

3: To regulate Commerce with foreign Nations, and among the several States, and with the Indian Tribes;

4: To establish an uniform Rule of Naturalization, and uniform Laws on the subject of Bankruptcies throughout the United States;

5: To coin Money, regulate the Value thereof, and of foreign Coin, and fix the Standard of Weights and Measures;

6: To provide for the Punishment of counterfeiting the Securities and current Coin of the United States;

7: To establish Post Offices and post Roads;

8: To promote the Progress of Science and useful Arts, by securing for limited Times to Authors and Inventors the exclusive Right to their respective Writings and Discoveries;

9: To constitute Tribunals inferior to the supreme Court;

10: To define and punish Piracies and Felonies committed on the high Seas, and Offences against the Law of Nations;

11: To declare War, grant Letters of Marque and Reprisal, and make Rules concerning Captures on Land and Water;

12: To raise and support Armies, but no Appropriation of Money to that Use shall be for a longer Term than two Years;

13: To provide and maintain a Navy;

14: To make Rules for the Government and Regulation of the land and naval Forces;

15: To provide for calling forth the Militia to execute the Laws of the Union, suppress Insurrections and repel Invasions;

16: To provide for organizing, arming, and disciplining, the Militia, and for governing such Part of them as may be employed in the Service of the United States, reserving to the States respectively, the Appointment of the Officers, and the Authority of training the Militia according to the discipline prescribed by Congress;

17: To exercise exclusive Legislation in all Cases whatsoever, over such District (not exceeding ten Miles square) as may, by Cession of particular States, and the Acceptance of Congress, become the Seat of the Government of the United States, and to exercise like Authority over all Places purchased by the Consent of the Legislature of the State in which the Same shall be, for the Erection of Forts, Magazines, Arsenals, dock-Yards, and other needful Buildings;—And

18: To make all Laws which shall be necessary and proper for carrying into Execution the foregoing Powers, and all other Powers vested by this Constitution in the Government of the United States, or in any Department or Officer thereof.

SECTION 9

1: The Migration or Importation of such Persons as any of the States now existing shall think proper to admit, shall not be prohibited by the Congress prior to the Year one thousand eight hundred and eight, but a Tax or duty may be imposed on such Importation, not exceeding ten dollars for each Person.

2: The Privilege of the Writ of Habeas Corpus shall not be suspended, unless when in Cases of Rebellion or Invasion the public Safety may require it.

3: No Bill of Attainder or ex post facto Law shall be passed.

4: No Capitation, or other direct, Tax shall be laid, unless in Proportion to the Census or Enumeration herein before directed to be taken.

5: No Tax or Duty shall be laid on Articles exported from any State.

6: No Preference shall be given by any Regulation of Commerce or Revenue to the Ports of one State over those of another: nor shall Vessels bound to, or from, one State, be obliged to enter, clear, or pay Duties in another.

7: No Money shall be drawn from the Treasury, but in Consequence of Appropriations made by Law; and a regular Statement and Account of the Receipts and Expenditures of all public Money shall be published from time to time.

8: No Title of Nobility shall be granted by the United States: And no Person holding any Office of Profit or Trust under them, shall, without the Consent of the Congress, accept of any present, Emolument, Office, or Title, of any kind whatever, from any King, Prince, or foreign State.

SECTION 10

1: No State shall enter into any Treaty, Alliance, or Confederation; grant Letters of Marque and Reprisal; coin Money; emit Bills of Credit; make any Thing but gold and silver Coin a Tender in Payment of Debts; pass any Bill of Attainder, ex post facto Law, or Law impairing the Obligation of Contracts, or grant any Title of Nobility.

2: No State shall, without the Consent of the Congress, lay any Imposts or Duties on Imports or Exports, except what may be absolutely necessary for executing it's inspection Laws: and the net Produce of all Duties and Imposts, laid by any State on Imports or Exports, shall be for the Use of the Treasury of the United States; and all such Laws shall be subject to the Revision and Controul of the Congress.

3: No State shall, without the Consent of Congress, lay any Duty of Tonnage, keep Troops, or Ships of War in time of Peace, enter into any Agreement or Compact with another State, or with a foreign Power, or engage in War, unless actually invaded, or in such imminent Danger as will not admit of delay.

ARTICLE II

SECTION 1

1: The executive Power shall be vested in a President of the United States of America. He shall hold his Office during the Term of four Years, and, together with the Vice President, chosen for the same Term, be elected, as follows

2: Each State shall appoint, in such Manner as the Legislature thereof may direct, a Number of Electors, equal to the whole Number of Senators and Representatives to which the State may be entitled in the Congress: but no Senator or Representative, or Person holding an Office of Trust or Profit under the United States, shall be appointed an Elector.

3: The Electors shall meet in their respective States, and vote by Ballot for two Persons, of whom one at least shall not be an Inhabitant of the same State with themselves. And they shall make a List of all the Persons voted for, and of the Number of Votes for each; which List they shall sign and certify, and transmit sealed to the Seat of the Government of the United States, directed to the President of the Senate. The President of the Senate shall, in the Presence of the Senate and House of Representatives, open all the Certificates, and the Votes shall then be counted. The Person having the greatest Number of Votes shall be the President, if such Number be a Majority of the whole Number of Electors appointed; and if there be more than one who have such Majority, and have an equal Number of Votes, then the House of Representatives shall immediately chuse by Ballot one of them for President; and if no Person have a Majority, then from the five highest on the List the said House shall in like Manner chuse the President. But in chusing the President, the Votes shall be taken by States, the Representation from each State having one Vote; A quorum for this Purpose shall consist of a Member or Members from two thirds of the States, and a Majority of all the States shall be necessary to a Choice. In every Case, after the Choice of the President, the Person having the greatest Number of Votes of the Electors shall be the Vice President. But if there should remain two or more who have equal Votes, the Senate shall chuse from them by Ballot the Vice President.

4: The Congress may determine the Time of chusing the Electors, and the Day on which they shall give their Votes; which Day shall be the same throughout the United States.

5: No Person except a natural born Citizen, or a Citizen of the United States, at the time of the Adoption of this Constitution, shall be eligible to the Office of President; neither shall any Person be eligible to that Office who shall not have attained to the Age of thirty five Years, and been fourteen Years a Resident within the United States.

6: In Case of the Removal of the President from Office, or of his Death, Resignation, or Inability to discharge the Powers and Duties of the said Office, the Same shall devolve on the VicePresident, and the Congress may by Law provide for the Case of Removal, Death, Resignation or Inability, both of the President and Vice President, declaring what Officer shall then act as President, and such Officer shall act accordingly, until the Disability be removed, or a President shall be elected.

7: The President shall, at stated Times, receive for his Services, a Compensation, which shall neither be encreased nor diminished during the Period for which he shall have been elected, and he shall not receive within that Period any other Emolument from the United States, or any of them.

8: Before he enter on the Execution of his Office, he shall take the following Oath or Affirmation:—"I do solemnly swear (or affirm) that I will faithfully execute the Office of President of the United States, and will to the best of my Ability, preserve, protect and defend the Constitution of the United States."

SECTION 2

1: The President shall be Commander in Chief of the Army and Navy of the United States, and of the Militia of the several States, when called into the actual Service of the United States; he may require the Opinion, in writing, of the principal Officer in each of the executive Departments, upon any Subject relating to the Duties of their respective Offices, and he shall have Power to grant Reprieves and Pardons for Offences against the United States, except in Cases of Impeachment.

2: He shall have Power, by and with the Advice and Consent of the Senate, to make Treaties, provided two thirds of the Senators present concur; and he shall nominate, and by and with the Advice and Consent of the Senate, shall appoint Ambassadors, other public Ministers and Consuls, Judges of the supreme Court, and all other Officers of the United States, whose Appointments are not herein otherwise provided for, and which shall be established by Law: but the Congress may by Law vest the Appointment of such inferior Officers, as they think proper, in the President alone, in the Courts of Law, or in the Heads of Departments.

3: The President shall have Power to fill up all Vacancies that may happen during the Recess of the Senate, by granting Commissions which shall expire at the End of their next Session.

SECTION 3

He shall from time to time give to the Congress Information of the State of the Union, and recommend to their Consideration such Measures as he shall judge necessary and expedient; he may, on extraordinary Occasions, convene both Houses, or either of them, and in Case of Disagreement between them, with Respect to the Time of Adjournment, he may adjourn them to such Time as he shall think proper; he shall receive Ambassadors and other public Ministers; he shall take Care that the Laws be faithfully executed, and shall Commission all the Officers of the United States.

SECTION 4

The President, Vice President and all civil Officers of the United States, shall be removed from Office on Impeachment for, and Conviction of, Treason, Bribery, or other high Crimes and Misdemeanors.

ARTICLE III

SECTION 1

The judicial Power of the United States, shall be vested in one supreme Court, and in such inferior Courts as the Congress may from time to time ordain and establish. The Judges, both of the supreme and inferior Courts, shall hold their Offices during good Behaviour, and shall, at stated Times, receive for their Services, a Compensation, which shall not be diminished during their Continuance in Office.

SECTION 2

1: The judicial Power shall extend to all Cases, in Law and Equity, arising under this Constitution, the Laws of the United States, and Treaties made, or which shall be made, under their Authority;—to all Cases affecting Ambassadors, other public Ministers and Consuls;—to all Cases of admiralty and maritime Jurisdiction;—to Controversies to which the United States shall be a Party;—to Controversies between two or more States;—between a State and Citizens of another State;—between Citizens of different States,—between Citizens of the same State claiming Lands under Grants of different States, and between a State, or the Citizens thereof, and foreign States, Citizens or Subjects.

2: In all Cases affecting Ambassadors, other public Ministers and Consuls, and those in which a State shall be Party, the supreme Court shall have original Jurisdiction. In all the other Cases before mentioned, the supreme Court shall have appellate Jurisdiction, both as to Law and Fact, with such Exceptions, and under such Regulations as the Congress shall make.

3: The Trial of all Crimes, except in Cases of Impeachment, shall be by Jury; and such Trial shall be held in the State where the said Crimes shall have been committed; but when not committed within any State, the Trial shall be at such Place or Places as the Congress may by Law have directed.

SECTION 3

1: Treason against the United States, shall consist only in levying War against them, or in adhering to their Enemies, giving them Aid and Comfort. No Person shall be convicted of Treason unless on the Testimony of two Witnesses to the same overt Act, or on Confession in open Court.

2: The Congress shall have Power to declare the Punishment of Treason, but no Attainder of Treason shall work Corruption of Blood, or Forfeiture except during the Life of the Person attainted.

ARTICLE IV

SECTION 1

Full Faith and Credit shall be given in each State to the public Acts, Records, and judicial Proceedings of every other State. And the Congress may by general Laws prescribe the Manner in which such Acts, Records and Proceedings shall be proved, and the Effect thereof.

SECTION 2

1: The Citizens of each State shall be entitled to all Privileges and Immunities of Citizens in the several States.

2: A Person charged in any State with Treason, Felony, or other Crime, who shall flee from Justice, and be found in another State, shall on Demand of the executive Authority of the State from which he fled, be delivered up, to be removed to the State having Jurisdiction of the Crime.

3: No Person held to Service or Labour in one State, under the Laws thereof, escaping into another, shall, in Consequence of any Law or Regulation therein, be discharged from such Service or Labour, but shall be delivered up on Claim of the Party to whom such Service or Labour may be due.

SECTION 3

1: New States may be admitted by the Congress into this Union; but no new State shall be formed or erected within the Jurisdiction of any other State; nor any State be formed by the Junction of two or more States, or Parts of States, without the Consent of the Legislatures of the States concerned as well as of the Congress.

2: The Congress shall have Power to dispose of and make all needful Rules and Regulations respecting the Territory or other Property belonging to the United States; and nothing in this Constitution shall be so construed as to Prejudice any Claims of the United States, or of any particular State.

SECTION 4

The United States shall guarantee to every State in this Union a Republican Form of Government, and shall protect each of them against Invasion; and on Application of the Legislature, or of the Executive (when the Legislature cannot be convened) against domestic Violence.

ARTICLE V

The Congress, whenever two thirds of both Houses shall deem it necessary, shall propose Amendments to this Constitution, or, on the Application of the Legislatures of two thirds of the several States, shall call a Convention for proposing Amendments, which, in either Case, shall be valid to all Intents and Purposes, as Part of this Constitution, when ratified by the Legislatures of three fourths of the several States, or by Conventions in three fourths thereof, as the one or the other Mode of Ratification may be proposed by the Congress; Provided that no Amendment which may be made prior to the Year One thousand eight hundred and eight shall in any Manner affect the first and fourth Clauses in the Ninth Section of the first Article; and that no State, without its Consent, shall be deprived of its equal Suffrage in the Senate.

ARTICLE VI

1: All Debts contracted and Engagements entered into, before the Adoption of this Constitution, shall be as valid against the United States under this Constitution, as under the Confederation.

2: This Constitution, and the Laws of the United States which shall be made in Pursuance thereof; and all Treaties made, or which shall be made, under the

Authority of the United States, shall be the supreme Law of the Land; and the Judges in every State shall be bound thereby, any Thing in the Constitution or Laws of any State to the Contrary notwithstanding.
3: The Senators and Representatives before mentioned, and the Members of the several State Legislatures, and all executive and judicial Officers, both of the United States and of the several States, shall be bound by Oath or Affirmation, to support this Constitution; but no religious Test shall ever be required as a Qualification to any Office or public Trust under the United States.

ARTICLE VII

The Ratification of the Conventions of nine States, shall be sufficient for the Establishment of this Constitution between the States so ratifying the Same.

The Word "the", being interlined between the seventh and eight Lines of the first Page, The Word "Thirty" being partly written on an Erazure in the fifteenth Line of the first Page. The Words "is tried" being interlined between the thirty second and thirty third Lines of the first Page and the Word "the" being interlined between the forty third and forty fourth Lines of the second Page.

done in Convention by the Unanimous Consent of the States present the Seventeenth Day of September in the Year of our Lord one thousand seven hundred and Eighty seven and of the Independence of the United States of America the Twelfth In witness whereof We have hereunto subscribed our Names,

Attest William Jackson Secretary Go: Washington -Presidt. and deputy from Virginia

Delaware
Geo: Read
Gunning Bedford jun
John Dickinson
Richard Bassett
Jaco: Broom

Maryland
James McHenry
Dan of St Thos. Jenifer
Danl Carroll.

Virginia
John Blair—
James Madison Jr.

North Carolina
Wm Blount
Richd. Dobbs Spaight.
Hu Williamson

South Carolina
J. Rutledge
Charles Cotesworth Pinckney
Charles Pinckney
Pierce Butler.

Georgia
William Few
Abr Baldwin

New Hampshire
John Langdon
Nicholas Gilman

Massachusetts
Nathaniel Gorham
Rufus King

Connecticut
Wm. Saml. Johnson
Roger Sherman

New York
Alexander Hamilton

New Jersey
Wil. Livingston
David Brearley.
Wm. Paterson.
Jona: Dayton

Pennsylvania
B Franklin
Thomas Mifflin
Robt Morris
Geo. Clymer
Thos. FitzSimons
Jared Ingersoll
James Wilson.
Gouv Morris

In Convention. Monday September 17th 1787.

Present

The States of

New Hampshire, Massachusetts, Connecticut, Mr. Hamilton from New York, New Jersey, Pennsylvania, Delaware, Maryland, Virginia, North Carolina, South Carolina and Georgia.

Resolved, That the preceeding Constitution be laid before the United States in Congress assembled, and that it is the Opinion of this Convention, that it should afterwards be submitted to a Convention of Delegates, chosen in each State by the People thereof, under the Recommendation of its Legislature, for their Assent and Ratification; and that each Convention assenting to, and ratifying the Same, should give Notice thereof to the United States in Congress assembled. Resolved, That it is the Opinion of this Convention, that as soon as the Conventions of nine States shall have ratified this Constitution, the United States in Congress assembled should fix a Day on which Electors should be appointed by the States which shall have ratified the same, and a Day on which the Electors should assemble to vote for the President, and the Time and Place for commencing Proceedings under this Constitution.

That after such Publication the Electors should be appointed, and the Senators and Representatives elected: That the Electors should meet on the Day fixed for the Election of the President, and should transmit their Votes certified, signed, sealed and directed, as the Constitution requires, to the Secretary of the United States in Congress assembled, that the Senators and Representatives should convene at the Time and Place assigned; that the Senators should appoint a President of the Senate, for the sole Purpose of receiving, opening and counting the Votes for President; and, that after he shall be chosen, the Congress, together with the President, should, without Delay, proceed to execute this Constitution.

By the unanimous Order of the Convention

W. Jackson Secretary.
Go: Washington -Presidt.

In Convention. Monday September 17th 1787.

SIR:

We have now the honor to submit to the consideration of the United States in Congress assembled, that Constitution which has appeared to us the most advisable.

The friends of our country have long seen and desired that the power of making war, peace, and treaties, that of levying money, and regulating commerce, and the correspondent executive and judicial authorities, should be fully and effectually vested in the General Government of the Union; but the impropriety of delegating such extensive trust to one body of men is evident: hence results the necessity of a different organization.

It is obviously impracticable in the Federal Government of these States to secure all rights of independent sovereignty to each, and yet provide for the interest and safety of all. Individuals entering into society must give up a share of liberty to preserve the rest. The magnitude of the sacrifice must depend as well on situation and circumstance, as on the object to be obtained. It is at all times difficult to draw with precision the line between those rights which must be surrendered, and those which may be preserved; and, on the present occasion, this difficulty was increased by a difference among the several States as to their situation, extent, habits, and particular interests.

In all our deliberations on this subject, we kept steadily in our view that which appears to us the greatest interest of every true American, the consolidation of our Union, in which is involved our prosperity, felicity, safety—perhaps our national existence. This important consideration, seriously and deeply impressed on our minds, led each State in the Convention to be less rigid on points of inferior magnitude than might have been otherwise expected; and thus, the Constitution which we now present is the result of a spirit of amity, and of that mutual deference and concession, which the peculiarity of our political situation rendered indispensable.

That it will meet the full and entire approbation of every State is not, perhaps, to be expected; but each will, doubtless, consider, that had her interest alone been consulted, the consequences might have been particularly disagreeable or injurious to others; that it is liable to as few exceptions as could reasonably have been expected, we hope and believe; that it may promote the lasting welfare of that Country so dear to us all, and secure her freedom and happiness, is our most ardent wish.

With great respect,

we have the honor to be,

SIR,

your excellency's most obedient and humble servants:

GEORGE WASHINGTON, President.

By the unanimous order of the convention.

His Excellency
the President of Congress.

Amendments to the Constitution

(The procedure for changing the United States Constitution is Article V—Mode of Amendment.)

(The Preamble to The Bill of Rights)

Congress OF THE United States

begun and held at the City of New-York, on Wednesday the fourth of March, one thousand seven hundred and eighty nine.

THE Conventions of a number of the States, having at the time of their adopting the Constitution, expressed a desire, in order to prevent misconstruction or abuse of its powers, that further declaratory and restrictive clauses should be added: And as extending the ground of public confidence in the Government, will best ensure the beneficent ends of its institution.

RESOLVED by the Senate and House of Representatives of the United States of America, in Congress assembled, two thirds of both Houses concurring, that the following Articles be proposed to the Legislatures of the several States, as amendments to the Constitution of the United States, all, or any of which Articles, when ratified by three fourths of the said Legislatures, to be valid to all intents and purposes, as part of the said Constitution; viz.

ARTICLES in addition to, and Amendment of the Constitution of the United States of America, proposed by Congress, and ratified by the Legislatures of the several States, pursuant to the fifth Article of the original Constitution.

Article the first. . . . After the first enumeration required by the first Article of the Constitution, there shall be one Representative for every thirty thousand, until the number shall amount to one hundred, after which, the proportion shall be so regulated by Congress, that there shall be not less than one hundred Representatives, nor less than one Representative for every forty thousand persons, until the number of Representatives shall amount to two hundred, after which the proportion shall be so regulated by Congress, that there shall not be less than two hundred Representatives, nor more than one Representative for every fifty thousand persons.

Article the second. . . . No law, varying the compensation for the services of the Senators and Representatives, shall take effect, until an election of Representatives shall have intervened. see Amendment XXVII

AMENDMENT I

Congress shall make no law respecting an establishment of religion, or prohibiting the free exercise thereof; or abridging the freedom of speech, or of the press; or the right of the people peaceably to assemble, and to petition the Government for a redress of grievances.

AMENDMENT II

A well regulated Militia, being necessary to the security of a free State, the right of the people to keep and bear Arms, shall not be infringed.

AMENDMENT III

No Soldier shall, in time of peace be quartered in any house, without the consent of the Owner, nor in time of war, but in a manner to be prescribed by law.

AMENDMENT IV

The right of the people to be secure in their persons, houses, papers, and effects, against unreasonable searches and seizures, shall not be violated, and no Warrants shall issue, but upon probable cause, supported by Oath or affirmation, and particularly describing the place to be searched, and the persons or things to be seized.

AMENDMENT V

No person shall be held to answer for a capital, or otherwise infamous crime, unless on a presentment or indictment of a Grand Jury, except in cases arising in the land or naval forces, or in the Militia, when in actual service in time of War or public danger; nor shall any person be subject for the same offence to be twice put in jeopardy of life or limb; nor shall be compelled in any criminal case to be a witness against himself, nor be deprived of life, liberty, or property, without due process of law; nor shall private property be taken for public use, without just compensation.

AMENDMENT VI

In all criminal prosecutions, the accused shall enjoy the right to a speedy and public trial, by an impartial jury of the State and district wherein the crime shall have been committed, which district shall have been previously ascertained by law, and to be informed of the nature and cause of the accusation; to be confronted with the witnesses against him; to have compulsory process for obtaining witnesses in his favor, and to have the Assistance of Counsel for his defence.

AMENDMENT VII

In Suits at common law, where the value in controversy shall exceed twenty dollars, the right of trial by jury shall be preserved, and no fact tried by a jury, shall be otherwise re-examined in any Court of the United States, than according to the rules of the common law.

AMENDMENT VIII

Excessive bail shall not be required, nor excessive fines imposed, nor cruel and unusual punishments inflicted.

AMENDMENT IX

The enumeration in the Constitution, of certain rights, shall not be construed to deny or disparage others retained by the people.

AMENDMENT X

The powers not delegated to the United States by the Constitution, nor prohibited by it to the States, are reserved to the States respectively, or to the people.

Attest,

John Beckley, Clerk of the House of Representatives.

Sam. A. Otis Secretary of the Senate.

Frederick Augustus Muhlenberg Speaker of the House of Representatives.
John Adams, Vice-President of the United States, and President of the Senate.

AMENDMENT XI

The Judicial power of the United States shall not be construed to extend to any suit in law or equity, commenced or prosecuted against one of the United States by Citizens of another State, or by Citizens or Subjects of any Foreign State.

AMENDMENT XII

The Electors shall meet in their respective states, and vote by ballot for President and Vice-President, one of whom, at least, shall not be an inhabitant of the same state with themselves; they shall name in their ballots the person voted for as President, and in distinct ballots the person voted for as Vice-President, and they shall make distinct lists of all persons voted for as President, and of all persons voted for as Vice-President, and of the number of votes for each, which lists they shall sign and certify, and transmit sealed to the seat of the government of the United States, directed to the President of the Senate;—The President of the Senate shall, in the presence of the Senate and House of Representatives, open all the certificates and the votes shall then be counted;—The person having the greatest number of votes for President, shall be the President, if such number be a majority of the whole number of Electors appointed; and if no person have such majority, then from the persons having the highest numbers not exceeding three on the list of those voted for as President, the House of Representatives shall choose immediately, by ballot, the President. But in choosing the President, the votes shall be taken by states, the representation from each state having one vote; a quorum for this purpose shall consist of a member or members from two-thirds of the states, and a majority of all the states shall be necessary to a choice. And if the House of Representatives shall not choose a President whenever the right of choice shall devolve upon them, before the fourth day of March next following, then the Vice-President shall act as President, as in the case of the death or other constitutional disability of the President.—The person having the greatest number of votes as Vice-President, shall be the Vice-President, if such number be a majority of the whole number of Electors appointed, and if no person have a majority, then from the two highest numbers on the list, the Senate shall choose the Vice-President; a quorum for the purpose shall consist of two-thirds of the whole number of Senators, and a majority of the whole number shall be necessary to a choice. But no person constitutionally ineligible to the office of President shall be eligible to that of Vice-President of the United States.

AMENDMENT XIII

Neither slavery nor involuntary servitude, except as a punishment for crime whereof the party shall have been duly convicted, shall exist within the United States, or any place subject to their jurisdiction.
Congress shall have power to enforce this article by appropriate legislation.

AMENDMENT XIV

1: All persons born or naturalized in the United States, and subject to the jurisdiction thereof, are citizens of the United States and of the State wherein they reside. No State shall make or enforce any law which shall abridge the privileges or immunities of citizens of the United States; nor shall any State deprive any person of life, liberty, or property, without due process of law; nor deny to any person within its jurisdiction the equal protection of the laws.

2: Representatives shall be apportioned among the several States according to their respective numbers, counting the whole number of persons in each State, excluding Indians not taxed. But when the right to vote at any election for the choice of electors for President and Vice President of the United States, Representatives in Congress, the Executive and Judicial officers of a State, or the members of the Legislature thereof, is denied to any of the male inhabitants of such State, being twenty-one years of age, and citizens of the United States, or in any way abridged, except for participation in rebellion, or other crime, the basis of representation therein shall be reduced in the proportion which the number of such male citizens shall bear to the whole number of male citizens twenty-one years of age in such State.

3: No person shall be a Senator or Representative in Congress, or elector of President and Vice President, or hold any office, civil or military, under the United

States, or under any State, who, having previously taken an oath, as a member of Congress, or as an officer of the United States, or as a member of any State legislature, or as an executive or judicial officer of any State, to support the Constitution of the United States, shall have engaged in insurrection or rebellion against the same, or given aid or comfort to the enemies thereof. But Congress may by a vote of two-thirds of each House, remove such disability.

4: The validity of the public debt of the United States, authorized by law, including debts incurred for payment of pensions and bounties for services in suppressing insurrection or rebellion, shall not be questioned. But neither the United States nor any State shall assume or pay any debt or obligation incurred in aid of insurrection or rebellion against the United States, or any claim for the loss or emancipation of any slave; but all such debts, obligations and claims shall be held illegal and void.

5: The Congress shall have power to enforce, by appropriate legislation, the provisions of this article.

AMENDMENT XV

The right of citizens of the United States to vote shall not be denied or abridged by the United States or by any State on account of race, color, or previous condition of servitude.
The Congress shall have power to enforce this article by appropriate legislation.

AMENDMENT XVI

The Congress shall have power to lay and collect taxes on incomes, from whatever source derived, without apportionment among the several States, and without regard to any census or enumeration.

AMENDMENT XVII

1: The Senate of the United States shall be composed of two Senators from each State, elected by the people thereof, for six years; and each Senator shall have one vote. The electors in each State shall have the qualifications requisite for electors of the most numerous branch of the State legislatures.

2: When vacancies happen in the representation of any State in the Senate, the executive authority of such State shall issue writs of election to fill such vacancies: Provided, That the legislature of any State may empower the executive thereof to make temporary appointments until the people fill the vacancies by election as the legislature may direct.

3: This amendment shall not be so construed as to affect the election or term of any Senator chosen before it becomes valid as part of the Constitution.

AMENDMENT XVIII

1: After one year from the ratification of this article the manufacture, sale, or transportation of intoxicating liquors within, the importation thereof into, or the exportation thereof from the United States and all territory subject to the jurisdiction thereof for beverage purposes is hereby prohibited.

2: The Congress and the several States shall have concurrent power to enforce this article by appropriate legislation.

3: This article shall be inoperative unless it shall have been ratified as an amendment to the Constitution by the legislatures of the several States, as provided in the Constitution, within seven years from the date of the submission hereof to the States by the Congress.

AMENDMENT XIX

The right of citizens of the United States to vote shall not be denied or abridged by the United States or by any State on account of sex.
Congress shall have power to enforce this article by appropriate legislation.

AMENDMENT XX

1: The terms of the President and Vice President shall end at noon on the 20th day of January, and the terms of Senators and Representatives at noon on the 3d day of January, of the years in which such terms would have ended if this article had not been ratified; and the terms of their successors shall then begin.

2: The Congress shall assemble at least once in every year, and such meeting shall begin at noon on the 3d day of January, unless they shall by law appoint a different day.

3: If, at the time fixed for the beginning of the term of the President, the President elect shall have died, the Vice President elect shall become President. If a President shall not have been chosen before the time fixed for the beginning of his term, or if the President elect shall have failed to qualify, then the Vice President elect shall act as President until a President shall have qualified; and the Congress may by law provide for the case wherein neither a President elect nor a Vice President elect shall have qualified, declaring who shall then act as President, or the manner in which one who is to act shall be selected, and such person shall act accordingly until a President or Vice President shall have qualified.

4: The Congress may by law provide for the case of the death of any of the persons from whom the House of Representatives may choose a President whenever the right of choice shall have devolved upon them, and for the case of the death of any of the persons from whom the Senate may choose a Vice President whenever the right of choice shall have devolved upon them.

5: Sections 1 and 2 shall take effect on the 15th day of October following the ratification of this article.

6: This article shall be inoperative unless it shall have been ratified as an amendment to the Constitution by the legislatures of three-fourths of the several States within seven years from the date of its submission.

AMENDMENT XXI

1: The eighteenth article of amendment to the Constitution of the United States is hereby repealed.

2: The transportation or importation into any State, Territory, or possession of the United States for delivery or use therein of intoxicating liquors, in violation of the laws thereof, is hereby prohibited.

3: This article shall be inoperative unless it shall have been ratified as an amendment to the Constitution by conventions in the several States, as provided in the Constitution, within seven years from the date of the submission hereof to the States by the Congress.

AMENDMENT XXII

1: No person shall be elected to the office of the President more than twice, and no person who has held the office of President, or acted as President, for more than two years of a term to which some other person was elected President shall be elected to the office of the President more than once. But this article shall not apply to any person holding the office of President when this article was proposed by the Congress, and shall not prevent any person who may be holding the office of President, or acting as President, during the term within which this article becomes operative from holding the office of President or acting as President during the remainder of such term.

2: This article shall be inoperative unless it shall have been ratified as an amendment to the Constitution by the legislatures of three-fourths of the several states within seven years from the date of its submission to the states by the Congress.

AMENDMENT XXIII

1: The District constituting the seat of government of the United States shall appoint in such manner as the Congress may direct: A number of electors of President and Vice President equal to the whole number of Senators and Representatives in Congress to which the District would be entitled if it were a state, but in no event more than the least populous state; they shall be in addition to those appointed by the states, but they shall be considered, for the purposes of the election of President and Vice President, to be electors appointed by a state;

and they shall meet in the District and perform such duties as provided by the twelfth article of amendment.

2: The Congress shall have power to enforce this article by appropriate legislation.

AMENDMENT XXIV

1. The right of citizens of the United States to vote in any primary or other election for President or Vice President, for electors for President or Vice President, or for Senator or Representative in Congress, shall not be denied or abridged by the United States or any state by reason of failure to pay any poll tax or other tax.

2. The Congress shall have power to enforce this article by appropriate legislation.

AMENDMENT XXV

1: In case of the removal of the President from office or of his death or resignation, the Vice President shall become President.

2: Whenever there is a vacancy in the office of the Vice President, the President shall nominate a Vice President who shall take office upon confirmation by a majority vote of both Houses of Congress.

3: Whenever the President transmits to the President pro tempore of the Senate and the Speaker of the House of Representatives his written declaration that he is unable to discharge the powers and duties of his office, and until he transmits to them a written declaration to the contrary, such powers and duties shall be discharged by the Vice President as Acting President.

4: Whenever the Vice President and a majority of either the principal officers of the executive departments or of such other body as Congress may by law provide, transmit to the President pro tempore of the Senate and the Speaker of the House of Representatives their written declaration that the President is unable to discharge the powers and duties of his office, the Vice President shall immediately assume the powers and duties of the office as Acting President.

Thereafter, when the President transmits to the President pro tempore of the Senate and the Speaker of the House of Representatives his written declaration that no inability exists, he shall resume the powers and duties of his office unless the Vice President and a majority of either the principal officers of the executive department or of such other body as Congress may by law provide, transmit within four days to the President pro tempore of the Senate and the Speaker of the House of Representatives their written declaration that the President is unable to discharge the powers and duties of his office. Thereupon Congress shall decide the issue, assembling within forty-eight hours for that purpose if not in session. If the Congress, within twenty-one days after receipt of the latter written declaration, or, if Congress is not in session, within twenty-one days after Congress is required to assemble, determines by two-thirds vote of both Houses that the President is unable to discharge the powers and duties of his office, the Vice President shall continue to discharge the same as Acting President; otherwise, the President shall resume the powers and duties of his office.

AMENDMENT XXVI

1: The right of citizens of the United States, who are 18 years of age or older, to vote, shall not be denied or abridged by the United States or any state on account of age.

2: The Congress shall have the power to enforce this article by appropriate legislation.

AMENDMENT XXVII

No law varying the compensation for the services of the Senators and Representatives shall take effect until an election of Representatives shall have intervened.

Glossary

Accusation A charging document that charges a defendant with a misdemeanor—used only on the state level, not the federal level.

Actus reus Guilty act.

Adjudication Similar to a trial in adult court, in an adjudication the juvenile court judge decides the culpability of the juvenile and then makes a decision about appropriate treatment or rehabilitation.

Admissible Proper to be used in reaching a decision; describes evidence that should be "let in" or introduced in court, or evidence that the jury may use.

Admission of evidence A decision by a judge to allow evidence to be used by the jury (or, in a trial with no jury, by the judge).

Affirm A decision by an appellate court that the lower court's finding or verdict was legally valid and not tainted by prejudice or other legal impediment.

Affirmative defense A defense that is something more than a mere denial and requires that the defense present evidence and/or testimony to establish. An affirmative defense may offer mitigation or a legal excuse for the defendant's actions

***Alford* plea** A plea that allows a defendant to enter a guilty plea, but basing the plea on the amount and quantity of evidence against him instead of the defendant's belief in his actual guilt.

Answer The defendant's written response to the complaint, usually containing denials of the defendant's responsibility for the plaintiff's injuries.

Appeal A request for an appellate court to review the actions and ruling of a lower court in order to correct mistakes and remedy an injustice.

Appellant The party bringing the current appeal from an adverse ruling in a lower court.

Appellee The party who won in the lower court.

Arraignment A court hearing at which the defendant is informed of the charge against him and given the opportunity to enter a plea of guilty or not guilty.

Arrest Restraint of a person by the police such that the person is not free to leave.

Attorney-client privilege A legal protection governing the communications, both oral and written, between an attorney and her client that prevents any legal process from forcing the attorney to reveal those communications.

Bail/bond Terms that are used interchangeably to refer to an amount posted by a defendant (or posted on the defendant's behalf) to ensure that the defendant will return for future court hearings.

Bar A physical barrier that separates the trial area from the public gallery.

Battered woman's syndrome An affirmative defense that asks the jury to excuse a woman's attack on her alleged long-time abuser or asks the judge to mitigate her sentence in reflection of the fact that she was responding to a long period of abuse at the hands of the "victim."

Bench trial A trial where the judge decides both questions of law and the final verdict in the case; no jury is present.

Bench warrant A court order directing law enforcement to arrest a specific individual and to hold him until a specific court date.

Beyond a reasonable doubt The burden of proof in a criminal case; when one has a reasonable doubt, it is not mere conjecture, but a doubt that would cause a prudent, rational person to hesitate before finding a defendant guilty of a crime.

Bifurcated trial Separate trials for different issues in the same prosecution; the most common use of a bifurcated jury trial is a first trial to decide whether the defendant is guilty of murder and then a second trial to determine the defendant's sentence: life, life without parole, or death.

Bill of particulars A motion filed by the defendant that requests additional information about the crime listed in a charging document.

***Brady* material** Information available to the prosecutor that is favorable to the defendant, because it mitigates either his guilt or his sentence. This material must be provided to the defense prior to trial.

Brief A written argument presented to an appellate court that argues a position based on the facts of the case and the applicable law; a brief urges the appellate judges to adopt the party's position.

Burden of persuasion The obligation on the party who has the burden of proof to not only establish facts but to convince the jury or judge that the facts are true and beyond dispute.

Burden of proof The amount of proof that a party must bring to sustain an action against another party. The burden of proof is different in civil and criminal cases.

Calendar/docket A list of pending cases before a particular court.

Case in chief The body of evidence and testimony offered by a party during its presentation of a jury trial.

Case law The written decisions by appellate courts explaining the outcome of a case on appeal.

Certiorari (cert) (Latin) To make sure. Cert is a court's authority to decide which cases it will hear on appeal and which it will not.

Chain of custody The chronological list of those in continuous possession of a specific physical object. A person who presents evidence (such as a gun used in a crime) at a trial must account for its possession from time of receipt to time of trial in order for evidence to be admitted by the judge.

Challenge for cause A formal objection to the qualifications or attitude of a prospective juror.

Charging decision The decision made by a prosecutor concerning the crimes that the defendant will be charged with.

Circumstantial evidence Facts that indirectly prove a main fact in question.

Citizen's arrest A legal doctrine that holds harmless a citizen who detains a person observed to have committed a crime. When a person makes a citizen's arrest, she is immune from civil suit for battery or false imprisonment of the person detained, provided the person detained actually committed a crime.

Clerk A court official who maintains records of dispositions in both civil and criminal cases.

Closing argument An summation of the case, during which each attorney seeks to convince the jury to return a verdict favorable to his side.

Coaching Telling a witness how she should answer specific questions without strict regard for the actual truth of the statement.

Code A collection of laws.

Common law 1. Either all case law or the case law that is made by judges in the absence of relevant statutes. 2. The legal system that originated in England and is composed of case law and statutes.

Commutation Changing a criminal punishment to one less severe.

Complaint The document filed by the plaintiff and served on the defendant that sets out the plaintiff's factual allegations that show the defendant is responsible for the plaintiff's injuries.

Complete defense A defense that would completely exonerate the defendant of the crime charged, assuming the defendant presents sufficient evidence to meet his burden of proof (usually preponderance of the evidence).

Concurrent prison sentences Sentences that permit a defendant to serve time on all of his pending charges at the same time.

Consecutive prison sentences Sentences that require a defendant to begin serving time for subsequent charges only after his first sentence is completed.

Contraband Items that are illegal to possess, import, export, or sell.

Cross-examination Asking questions of a witness to determine, bias, lack of knowledge, prejudice, or some other failing.

Damages A jury's assessment of the money that a liable party owes to the other party in a civil case.

Defendant The person charged with a crime.

Delinquency A criminal act committed by a minor.

Demonstrative evidence Charts, diagrams, or other displays designed to persuade the jury to a particular viewpoint.

Dependent A court finding that a child's living conditions pose a substantial risk to the child or that the child is being neglected in his current home setting.

Depose Give sworn testimony out of court.

Diminished capacity Inability of the defendant to understand the actions that he took and why his actions constituted a crime.

Direct evidence Proof of a fact without the need for other facts leading up to it. For example, direct evidence that dodos are not extinct would be a live dodo.

Direct examination The questions asked of a witness by the attorney who has called him to the stand.

Directed verdict A ruling by a judge that there is not sufficient evidence of the defendant's guilt to present to the jury.

Discovery The exchange of information between sides in both civil and criminal lawsuits.

DNA evidence Comparing body tissue samples (such as blood, skin, hair, or semen) to see if the genetic materials match. It is used to identify criminals by comparing their DNA with that found at a crime scene; it is also used to identify a child's parents.

Document Something with a message on it—for example, a contract, a map, a photograph, or a message on wood, etc.

Documentary evidence Evidence supported by writings and all other documents.

Element A necessary and component part of the crime.

Evidence All types of information (observations, recollections, documents, concrete objects, etc.) presented at trial or other hearing. Statement made by judges and lawyers, however, are not considered evidence.

Exclusionary rule A rule imposed by the U.S. Supreme Court that prohibits evidence seized illegally from being used in the prosecution of the defendant.

Exculpatory Refers to evidence that tends to provide an excuse or a justification for the defendant's actions or that shows that the defendant did not commit the crime charged.

Exigent circumstance An emergency situation that calls for swift action to avoid danger to people or property and allows law enforcement to bypass some constitutional rules.

Expectation of privacy A two-part test created in *Katz v. U.S.*, where the Court created a standard by which searches could be evaluated to see if they are in violation of the Fourth Amendment. The test is both subjective and objective. The party who is searched must have a subjective expectation of privacy in the area to be searched, and an objective, hypothetical third party must also believe that the area to be searched has a high degree of expectation of privacy.

Felony A crime punishable by more than one year in prison.

Fiduciary A relationship in which one person is obliged to act in a trustworthy and honest relationship to another person. The fiduciary has the responsibility to act in the best interests of the other.

Foundation questions Particular questions that are asked to establish the relevancy of particular types of evidence.

Fresh pursuit doctrine A court-created doctrine that allows police officers to arrest suspects without warrants and to cross territorial boundaries while they are still pursuing the suspect.

Fruit of the poisonous tree doctrine The rule that evidence gathered as a result of evidence gained in an illegal search or questioning cannot be used against the person searched or questioned even if the later evidence was gathered lawfully.

Guilty The verdict in a criminal case in which the jurors have determined that the defendant has committed a crime.

Habeas corpus (Latin) You have the body. A judicial order to a prison system ordering that the incarcerated person be brought to court for a hearing; a constitutional mechanism that allows convicts to challenge their sentences.

Hung jury A jury that cannot reach a unanimous verdict.

Immunity A grant to an individual that exempts him from being prosecuted based on the testimony that he gives.

In absentia (Latin) Refers to a trial conducted when the defendant is not present.

In camera (Latin) In chambers; refers to a review of a file by a judge carried out in his private office.

Indictment A charging document that charges a defendant with a felony.

Inference A fact that is probably true or a fact that a jury can reasonably believe is true.

Information A charging document that charges a defendant with a misdemeanor.

Initial appearance A court hearing held shortly after a defendant's arrest, during which the judge advises the defendant of her constitutional rights and appoints an attorney to represent the attorney if the defendant is unable to afford one.

Intake A juvenile court proceeding in which a judge determines whether the juvenile should be processed by the court or released.

Join issue To officially submit the case to a jury for a determination and verdict.

Jurisdiction The persons about whom and the subject matters about which a court has the right and power to make decisions that are legally binding.

Jurors Those people who have been selected to sit on a jury; they will consider the evidence and reach a verdict in the case.

Jury instructions A judge's directions to the jury about the law that pertains to the issues in the trial and the jury's function once they retire to the jury room.

Jury tampering/embracery The crime of attempting to influence a juror or jurors in their deliberations on a case.

Liable A finding that a party has a duty or obligation to the other party to pay damages or to carry out some other action.

Limited jurisdiction The authority of a court to hear and consider only specifically enumerated matters.

Lineup A group of persons, placed side by side in a line, shown to a witness of a crime to see if the witness will identify the person suspected of a committing the crime. A lineup should not be staged so that it is suggestive of one person.

Mens rea Guilty intent; the requirement that the defendant is aware of and conscious of his actions before a crime can be charged.

Misdemeanor A crime punishable by a maximum sentence of one year in prison.

Mistrial An order that a trial is terminated because of a hung jury or for some other action that occurred during the trial. A mistrial is the legal equivalent of a nullity, and all parties must behave as though the trial did not occur.

Modify To alter the lower court's decision without necessarily reversing or affirming it.

Motion A request that a judge make a ruling or take some other action.

Motion for continuance A request by one party to postpone a trial or other hearing for a future date.

Motion for a new trial A defendant's request that the trial judge set aside the jury's verdict and order a new trial; the request is based on alleged improper, unfair, and prejudicial rulings.

Motion in limine (Latin) Motion at the beginning; a motion by one party that requests specific judicial rulings at the outset of the trial.

Motion to join A prosecution motion that requests two or more codefendants to be tried at the same time.

Motion to suppress A motion that requests that a court not allow the jury to hear specific information, such as the defendant's confession or other statements, based on improprieties in obtaining the information.

No bill A grand jury's determination that there is insufficient probable cause to continue the prosecution against the accused.

Nolle prosequi (Latin) Will not prosecute. An entry into the official record of the prosecutor's intention to dismiss a case and refuse to carry through with the prosecution of a particular individual in a pending case

Nolo contendere (Latin) I do not contest. A plea offered in a criminal case in which the defendant does not contest his guilt and asks for the court's mercy.

Notice of appeal The document giving official notice that a party intends to appeal; it is filed with the appellate court and served on the opposing party.

Officer of the court A person, such as a prosecutor, judge, bailiff, defense attorney, or clerk, who has an ethical and legal obligation to promote justice, to tell the truth, and to help avoid perpetrating any fraud upon the court.

Ordinance A law passed by a local government, such as a town council or city government.

Panel/venire A group of people who have been called for jury duty; the final jury will be selected from this group.

Pardon A president's or governor's release of a person from punishment for a crime.

Parens patriae (Latin) The country as parent; the philosophy that when parents or guardians fail a child, the government fills the gap by providing basic necessities, protection, education, and counseling, as needed.

Parole The supervised portion of a convict's sentence that he serves once he has been released from prison.

Peremptory challenge A strike of a juror for any reason, except one based on race or sex.

Plaintiff The name for the party who brings a civil suit.

Plea bargain A prosecutor's recommendation for a somewhat lighter sentence than a defendant might normally receive in exchange for the defendant's plea of guilty to the offense charged.

Preliminary hearing A court proceeding that determines whether there is probable cause to believe that the defendant committed the crime with which he is charged.

Preponderance of the evidence A showing by one side in a civil suit that its version of the facts is more likely to be true than not.

Presumption A conclusion of fact that is based on the existence of another fact. Example: The defendant is charged with a crime; the jury must presume that he is innocent.

Prima facie (Latin) At first sight; a presumption that the facts as presented are true and establish a fact.

Privilege A right to refuse to answer questions and to prevent disclosure of information communicated within a legally recognized confidential relationship.

Pro se (Latin) By oneself, a person who chooses to represent himself in a legal proceeding.

Probable cause The reasonable belief that a crime has occurred or is about to occur

Probation Allowing a person convicted of a criminal offense to avoid serving a jail sentence, so long as she abides by certain conditions (usually including being supervised by a probation officer).

Quash Do away with, annul, overthrow, cease.

Rebuttal Evidence offered by a party that directly refutes evidence or pleading by the opposing party.

Recognizance bail The person accused simply gives his word that he will return for a specific court date.

Record The official file containing the evidence, pleadings, motions, and the transcript of the trial, as well as any other documents regarding the case

Relevant Describes evidence that tends to prove or disprove some point in contention in the case.

Remand Send back. For example, a higher court may remand a case to a lower court, directing the lower court to take some action.

Reverse To set aside. When an appellate court reverses a lower court, it issues a decision that the lower court's ruling was incorrect; if the lower court's finding was that the defendant was guilty, then the conviction is reversed and set aside.

Sentence The punishment, such as a prison sentence and/or fine, that is imposed on a convicted defendant by a judge.

Sequester To cut off from contact, to prevent jurors in a case from reading, watching, or listening to any media accounts of the trial and from returning home until the trial is over.

Sever Separate or cut off into constituent parts.

Show-up A pretrial identification procedure in which only one suspect and a witness are brought together.

Similar transactions A motion filed by the prosecution that shows a defendant's state of mind or criminal intent by giving the jury in the current case evidence of a defendant's similar crime in a previous case.

Simple defense A defense that is automatically triggered when a defendant is charged with a crime. A defendant is not required to submit any evidence or testimony to raise a simple defense.

Standing A recognized legal right to bring suit or to challenge a legal decision.

Status offense An action that is prohibited for a child but is not necessarily a crime.

Statute A law that is voted on by the legislature branch of government and enacted by the executive branch.

Style The title or heading listing the parties to a case.

Subpoena A court order demanding that a person or item be produced to the court at a specific date and time.

Summons A court order for a person to appear at a specific time and place.

Supremacy Clause The provision in Article VI of the U.S. Constitution that the U.S. Constitution, laws, and treaties take precedence over conflicting state constitutions or laws.

Suspect A person who police believe may have committed a crime.

Term of court The period of time slated for court hearings; it can be as short as a week or as long as a year.

Testimony Evidence given by a witness under oath. Testimonial evidence is different from demonstrative evidence.

True bill A grand jury's determination that there is sufficient probable cause to continue the prosecution against the accused.

Venue The geographic area, often based on a county's boundaries, where a court may hear an action. In criminal cases, venue refers to the location where the crime occurred.

Verdict The jury's finding in a trial.

Victim impact statement A procedure that allows the victim of a crime to address the court and the defendant and explain the trauma that the defendant's actions have caused.

Voir dire (French) "To look, to speak. The process of questioning jurors about their potential biases in the case.

Work product The prosecuting attorney's mental notes and strategy ideas about the case.

Index